"The last chapter alone titled 'Summary, Recommendations, and Conclusions, ...valuable for educators, counselors, pastors, youth workers, and the secular public who want to understand LGB+ emerging adults who deeply value and live out their faith. This book gives a framework to understand that Christian LGB+ men and women are navigating their sexual identity and lives differently than the prevailing cultural narrative, and Christian leaders and mentors should want to know how that is going for them. This book allows us to listen in to the actual voices and stories of students on Christian college campuses. We find out how much they value their faith. We find out that having people to walk with them who are willing to listen, understand, and guide is invaluable. Good guides find out about the people they shepherd. And this book is an essential guidebook for the men and women who guide and mentor students."

Shirley Hoogstra, president, Council for Christian Colleges & Universities

"This groundbreaking book is a must-read for all who care about faith-based schools and the LGBTQ students who are a part of these communities."

Pat Griffin, professor emerita, University of Massachusetts Amherst, and member of the NCAA Seeking Common Ground Leadership Team

"The research and insight found in *Listening to Sexual Minorities: A Study of Faith and Sexual Identity on Christian College Campuses* is profoundly timely and relevant—not just for Christian educators, but for all of us who are committed to loving and sharing life with the many sexual minority individuals in our families, churches, and communities. One of the greatest hindrances to this end is that although many strong opinions abound, there are few opportunities to listen and bear witness to the actual stories, experiences, and complexities of our sexual minority friends and colleagues—especially those who are professing Christians. Yarhouse, Dean, Stratton, and Lastoria have assembled a scholarly, comprehensive, readable, and human introduction to the stories of such individuals; I highly recommend it because the world needs to hear what they have to say."

David C. Wang, associate professor of psychology, Rosemead School of Psychology, and editor of *Journal of Psychology and Theology*

"Just as a plane requires both wings to fly, so too the gospel cannot soar in a culture without the two wings of truth and grace. No other issue confronting the twenty-first-century church in America requires the need for both wings than the intersection of human sexuality and genuine Christian faith. Without sacrificing the wing of truth, *Listening to Sexual Minorities* helps lift the wing of grace. Where the church has excelled at telling, this book excels at listening. Thankfully, *Listening to Sexual Minorities* is not a theological or political treatise telling believers what they should believe or do. Gratefully, it is an archive of conversations, thoughts, and feelings, gleaned from individuals within our churches and institutions."

Jon S. Kulaga, president, Ohio Christian University

"Professor Mark Yarhouse and his collaborators continue their remarkable efforts to produce informative, original, and even-handed empirical research into the life experiences of Christians experiencing same-sex and other non-normative sexual attractions. This book reports on the results of a study of remarkable breadth and comprehensiveness. It offers understandable syntheses of the complex findings and wise, biblical suggestions based on the findings for implementation by Christian educational institutions and churches. It is a unique and valuable contribution deserving the attention of thoughtful Christian leaders everywhere."

Stanton L. Jones, professor of psychology, Wheaton College, and coauthor of *God's Design for Sex*

"Loving our neighbors should always involve listening to them. This carefully researched study does us all an immense service by giving us the opportunity to listen in to the varied experiences of people we often haven't been listening to carefully enough."

Ed Shaw, author of *Same-Sex Attraction and the Church*

"For more than forty years I've worked with college students. The complexities of the issues they deal with personally are exciting, challenging and (at times) overwhelming. Some of the most difficult issues they face are found at the intersection of faith and sexuality. Within the Christian university context those intersecting issues take on an additional dimension for LGB+ students because of the cultural tensions surrounding these issues. *Listening to Sexual Minorities* is a gold mine of research, wisdom, and practical application in understanding more accurately the journeys of sexual minority students. The student stories embedded in each chapter range from encouraging to heart wrenching. For campuses seeking to take both faith and sexuality seriously, working through *Listening to Sexual Minorities* will be time well spent."

Jay Barnes, president, Bethel University

"Issues of sexuality are at the forefront of American culture. Navigating this conversation can be difficult for those who aren't equipped to understand the complexities of human sexuality. *Listening to Sexual Minorities* provides a much-needed framework for having these important discussions. While grounded in academic research, this book also provides much-needed, practical insight for those navigating these conversations. This book is a must-read for anyone serious about honest dialogue related to sexual minorities on our Christian college campuses."

Brian L. Powell, district superintendent, Kentucky District Church of the Nazarene, Louisville

"This is exactly the kind of book to serve as a catalyst for discussion in the Christian community, especially on college campuses. Its power comes in large part from its concreteness and its foundation in empirical experience, and it brings to life a category that many in the Christian community (and perhaps even in the LGB+ community) are not fully aware of: individuals who fully own their identity as Christians and their identity as sexual minorities. The students' own stories draw attention to ways in which our policies and our theology—as currently articulated—are not rich enough to encompass reality. So, by beginning with lived experience rather than theology or policy, the book humanizes the issues and requires something of us that an abstract discussion does not. It is also a book that focuses on ministering to the needs of these students. By seriously reckoning with the pastoral dimension of these issues, readers may take greater courage to move beyond and enter into other dimensions of the situation. Finally, this book is an implicit call for more work to be done. From those who believe there is something of deep importance in the traditional Christian understanding of sexual ethics, more work needs to be done to explain that importance in terms that make sense within a broader conversation. I believe we owe this to those who are the subject of this book—and who are currently left alone to work out the painful tension they feel between two identities they truly own. I believe we owe this to those in the LGB+ community who want to understand why many conservative Christians seem willing to risk relationships and community for what appears to be an abstract doctrine. I believe we owe this as a matter of faithful witness to the gospel—in a culture that increasingly sees religious freedom as simply code or cover for bigotry."

Shirley Mullen, president, Houghton College

LISTENING TO SEXUAL MINORITIES

A STUDY OF FAITH AND SEXUAL IDENTITY

ON CHRISTIAN COLLEGE CAMPUSES

MARK A. YARHOUSE,
JANET B. DEAN, STEPHEN P. STRATTON
& MICHAEL LASTORIA

IVP Academic

An imprint of InterVarsity Press
Downers Grove, Illinois

InterVarsity Press
P.O. Box 1400, Downers Grove, IL 60515-1426
ivpress.com
email@ivpress.com

InterVarsity Press® is the book-publishing division of InterVarsity Christian Fellowship/USA®, a movement of students and faculty active on campus at hundreds of universities, colleges, and schools of nursing in the United States of America, and a member movement of the International Fellowship of Evangelical Students. For information about local and regional activities, visit intervarsity.org.

While any stories in this book are true, some names and identifying information may have been changed to protect the privacy of individuals.

Cover design: Cindy Kiple
Interior design: Jeanna Wiggins
Images: © nata789 / iStock / Getty Images

ISBN 978-0-8308-2862-3 (print)
ISBN 978-0-8308-8657-9 (digital)

Printed in the United States of America ⊗

Library of Congress Cataloging-in-Publication Data
A catalog record for this book is available from the Library of Congress.

P	23	22	21	20	19	18	17	16	15	14	13	12	11	10	9	8	7	6	5	4	3	2	1
Y	37	36	35	34	33	32	31	30	29	28	27	26	25	24	23	22	21	20	19	18			

To the Christian college and

university students who shared

their life stories with us.

CONTENTS

Preface   1

1 The Tension: Faith and Sexuality   7

2 A Closer Look: Understanding the Population   25

3 Milestones and Identity   61

4 Identity Development   87

5 Faith and Sexuality   137

6 How Sexual-Minority Students Fit
into Their College Campuses   187

7 How They Move from College to Postcollege   235

8 Summary, Recommendations, and Conclusions   271

Author Index   313

Subject Index   317

PREFACE

IT WOULD HAVE BEEN DIFFICULT TO IMAGINE over twelve years ago that the work we were doing on the experiences of sexual minorities at Christian colleges would culminate in a book-length manuscript. What we knew at the time was that there were many students at Christian colleges and universities around the United States who experienced same-sex attraction and were navigating questions about their sexual identity and their faith. Many people were speaking for them, and some voices were at times conflicting. We suspected it could be potentially helpful to hear directly from them about their experiences. But before we say a bit more about that, let us take a moment to introduce ourselves. It will be helpful background to lead into how this project came to be.

For the past twenty years, Mark Yarhouse has been conducting research and providing clinical services to Christians who experience a conflict between their sexual identity and their religious identity. He is executive director of the Institute for the Study of Sexual Identity at Regent University. He codirects the institute with Dr. Olya Zaporozhets, who works alongside him in the School of Psychology and Counseling. Mark works in the doctoral program in clinical psychology alongside a number of terrific colleagues, who have encouraged him in these discussion of faith and sexuality, including William Hathaway, James Sells, Jennifer Ripley, Cassandra Page, Carissa Dwiwardani, Judy Johnson, Linda Baum, Andy Rowan, Erynne Shatto, and Glen Moriarty. He also has a deep and abiding interest in the mission of Christian colleges and universities. Mark completed his undergraduate degrees in philosophy and art with a minor in psychology at Calvin College and his graduate studies in theology and clinical psychology at Wheaton College. Earlier in his career he collaborated with his mentor, Stan Jones, on a study of whether people could change their sexual orientation through involvement in Christian ministries. His experience studying whether people could change orientation influenced him to explore the conflict Christians often experience from a different angle. In other words, he wanted to study sexual-identity development and the experiences of Christians navigating sexual- and religious-identity conflicts over time. This led to several lines of research, including the one culminating in this book project.

Janet Dean entered Asbury Theological Seminary as a relatively new Christian with a bachelor's degree in psychology from the University of Akron. There, as she completed a master's in counseling and a master's of divinity, her interest in the integration of faith and psychology, particularly how this con-tributes to mental health and well-being, took root. At the same time, several of her seminary friends were involved with ex-gay ministries in the area, and she was privileged to walk with them through that part of their journey, lis-tening and supporting as they worked toward making sense of their sexual identity in light of their faith. Her graduate education then continued with doctoral studies in clinical psychology at the Ohio State University, where there was seemingly less room for faith to be considered as anything but det-rimental to mental health, especially in areas related to sexuality. Even so, her experiences there brought new perspectives on sexual identity and a greater awareness of how harmful religion had been for many sexual minorities. In the early 2000s, Janet joined the student counseling center at Asbury Uni-versity as a staff psychologist, working under the direction of Steve Stratton. There she counseled many students, including many sexual minorities, who were working through the integration of their faith into the rest of their lives. This work continued as she moved into a faculty position, where she now teaches, researches, mentors, and counsels in this area and greatly appreciates the Christian liberal arts environment, which has tremendous potential to foster psychological, sexual, and spiritual development.

Steve Stratton deeply appreciates his undergraduate degree in psychology with minors in Bible and sociology from Asbury University, a Christian liberal arts institution in Kentucky. He found a rigorous and relational academic environment where he could formally integrate his growing passions for psy-chology and his faith. During those formative years, he roomed with another student, who became a lifelong contact and friend. This friend came out after graduating and after his opposite-sex marriage ended. Surprised, Steve recog-nized that he had not been and still was not a very effective listener for this dear brother. Steve began listening more formally to sexual minorities while a counseling psychology doctoral student at Auburn University's student counseling center in the mid-1980s. Still learning to listen, he had the chance to hear from sexual minorities at student counseling centers at Texas A&M University and then, coming full circle, at Asbury University, where he eventually served as director of student counseling services for sixteen years. As he added more teaching and research at Asbury Theological Seminary to his clinical work, Steve realized that his interest in the intersection of religious and spiritual development and sexual development had a common theme— serving marginalized persons. Christian colleges, such as the ones where he worked, endeavored to prepare students to enter a vocational world where authentic and orthodox faith was often misunderstood and even rejected. Regretfully, Steve saw that Christian sexual minorities frequently faced similar misunderstanding from the very same educational communities that could have empathized with that experience. Steve continues to hope that listening to diverse stories of marginalization at the intersection of sexuality and faith will chart a path into the future for Christian colleges and universities and provide clues for navigating this complicated cultural discussion.

Michael Lastoria recently ended his thirty-five-year tenure as director of counseling services at Houghton College, a Christian liberal arts college in the Wesleyan tradition located in western New York. In this capacity "listening to" was a way of life for him as a Christian therapist. Although he had always believed in God, Mike's Christian experience did not begin in earnest until his early twenties, after college. The start of his faith journey coincided with the beginning of his work as a therapist, and these two disciplines, psychology and theology, have remained present in his internal dialogue to this day. Mike completed his graduate work in counseling at the University of Nebraska (Omaha), his doctoral training in counselor education at Loyola University (Chicago), and training in marriage and family therapy at the University of Rochester.

During the '80s and '90s Mike's listening to students with same-sex attraction was with understanding but always focused on "change." Early in his work, change was always possible with faith, and therapy was designed to repair. As others influenced his thinking, such as the late Lewis Smedes (*Sex for Christians*) and Mark Yarhouse (*Ex-Gays?*), the terrain became less clear as causation and cure became hotly contested. This gradually allowed for a deeper connection with students as the counseling focus became not solely on changing the direction of one's sexual attractions but on students' holistic growth, including their spiritual experience, and how they made sense of their Christian faith and same-sex attraction. Mike heard the stories of deeply committed young men and women who were desirous of becoming "washed and waiting" (Wesley Hill) and also the stories of equally committed gay students wanting to follow Christ while remaining open to a same-sex relationship (à la Justin Lee/Gay Christian Network). His counseling became more focused on how to encourage a student's walk with God and to understand the narrative that was the foundation for this walk. As such he has been able to come alongside students and support their convictions to remain celibate with same-sex attractions while also serving as a faculty mentor to the informal LGBT group on campus. This perspective has allowed him to envision a Christian campus that remains faithful to a sexual ethic while providing students with the challenge and support so essential to their formation as mature adults.

Mark met Steve and Janet at Asbury University in 2005, and they began working together on the first of three national studies. The development of the first study took place with the support of the Council for Christian Colleges and Universities (CCCU), and we often refer to that as the "2009 study" because of the date of publication. At that time there were also outside (of the university) voices claiming to represent the concerns of sexual minorities on Christian college campuses. Some of these voices protested the policies that were viewed by them as discriminatory against sexual minorities. Our thought at that time was that it would be beneficial for Christian colleges and universities to undertake their own study of the experiences of sexual minorities on Christian college campuses, rather than risk being overreactive to activists, which could become polarizing in a broader culture-war atmosphere.

We knew Mike Lastoria and were delighted when he contacted us about a study he was a part of that looked at sexual attitudes and behavior among students who attend Christian colleges. The researchers were working with the Association for Christians in Student Development (ACSD). We were invited to add items for students who experienced same-sex attraction, and this became our second national study. We often refer to this as the "2013 study" (again to reference the publication date).

The third study will be featured throughout this book, although we will reference all three studies and make comparisons among samples where it is helpful to the reader. The third study was also with the support of the ACSD, but it is different from the two previous studies because it is the only one that is a longitudinal study. In this book we will refer to it as "the longitudinal study" or "the current study." By longitudinal we mean that we invited the same students at Christian colleges to share their experiences *over time*. So anytime we are writing about students and what they shared with us at time 1 and time 2, we are referencing the longitudinal study. Students are simply providing us with information at a point in time (time 1) and then roughly a year later (time 2).

We also want to thank the project coordinators from the Institute for the Study of Sexual Identity at Regent University. Emma Bucher (for times 1 and 2 data collection) and Julia Sadusky (for time 3 data collection) were responsible for managing contact with participants, coordinating communication, scheduling interviews, and much more. We are grateful to them and to the many interviewers and transcribers who acted with integrity and displayed great professionalism and committed themselves to this project. In addition, we want to express appreciation to the consensual qualitative research (CQR) team, who dedicated significant hours to the task of coding, analyzing, and "storying" the transcribed interviews for times 1 and 2. Jeffrey Reed, Greg Koprowski, Christina Dillon, Jessica Foreman, Sarah Halford, Taylor Zimmerman, and Paulk Parrish provided dedicated service as volunteer research partners.

We learn more each time we conduct a study. It would be difficult to count how many times we said, "Why didn't we think to ask that?" in reference to a topic that today seems obvious. Perhaps we are getting better at it.

In any case, this book is titled *Listening to Sexual Minorities* because we wanted to take a posture of respect for students who are navigating sexual and religious identities. This book represents what we know at present about sexual minorities at Christian colleges. It represents what they are telling us about their faith, their sexuality, their attitudes and behaviors, and their experience of the campus climate. We hope that by sharing this information we will all be better off, that there will be a greater sense of empathy and compassion for emerging adults who are navigating important questions about their faith and their sexual identity. There is an opportunity here, too, for the Christian community to think about how it discusses what it believes (doctrine) and reflects on how it functions (policies) and how it relates (relationships). In that sense, a study of Christian colleges is a microcosm of a larger cultural discussion for Christian institutions. Not everything will transfer over to a different setting, but some ideas will. We hope that the discussions that take place on the other side of this kind of research will be deeper and more meaningful discussions that are informed by what sexual minorities say about their experience.

What are we after? What do we hope you will take away from this book? We hope that readers will *listen* to the range of voices and experiences of these students. They are not all saying one thing, and so we have to listen carefully. We hope that Christians will also be more *intentional* as they engage the people represented in this project. We hope that Christian institutions will support a comprehensive and more nuanced view of personhood, including our sexuality and sexual identity, and that our hopes to build one another up will be reflected in the quality of our programming and in our interpersonal relationships.

THE TENSION
FAITH AND SEXUALITY

[My sexuality] was just something I kind of ignored. So college, which is where discovery came, because I started out with the mindset—I'm at a Christian college, so I'm obviously a straight Christian because I'm a Christian. I know that! One of my friends actually confronted me. He asked me, "Are you gay?" And I was like, "No!" And he was like, "I'm pretty sure you are." And I was like, "What? You can't say that!" [laughs] But I ended up telling him things that I never had really expressed before. . . . Gradually, it was like discovering and realizing these are legitimate feelings that are not going away, no matter how hard I try to push them away, and not dealing with them is not healthy. I think that was some discovery, like "Okay, this is something I need to address and handle and work with," which has turned into a lot of learning and research and scouring the Bible. What does it say, and reading what people have said about it, and talking to friends about it, and talking to pastors and teachers about it. There's been a lot of learning . . . but it's also confusing. So I've been leaning on God—what are you saying to me? What are you wanting from my life? And [I have been] learning the person, too. . . . As a gay Christian, how do I reconcile these things? [I've encountered] a lot of growth from one [leaning on God] to the other [learning about myself—"the person"].

—*Justin, a junior, identifies as gay, time 2*

▼▲▼

PERHAPS NO TOPIC HAS BEEN as potentially divisive in religious circles in the last quarter-century as that of same-sex sexual identity and behavior. Or, in the common vernacular, what it means to be *gay*. What it means for a

Christian. In the midst of the sexual revolution of the 1970s and following, we have witnessed the emergence of a lesbian, gay, bisexual, transgender, queer (LGB+) community as a culture to be celebrated.[1] For simplicity we will refer to the above as simply the "gay community." Today, the gay community is celebrated in pride parades, while its culture is prominent on television and in other entertainment and social media.

We can acknowledge the shift in culture without either joining in the celebration or being overly reactionary. Another posture, that of being intentional, is what we are looking for.[2] For the purposes of this book, we want to unpack the tensions that exist for Christians who are navigating sexual-identity questions in their own lives and who are part of faith-based institutions, whether a Christian college or a church or a ministry. Multiple tensions exist for both the particular Christian and for the institution. These tensions exist in a cultural context of increased acceptance and celebration, which leaves many Christian institutions wondering how to position themselves in the broader culture.

One way to think about the tension that exists is, in part, with reference to competing frameworks for understanding sexuality and sexual identities. These frameworks function as lenses through which people see same-sex sexuality and sexual identities. Although by no means exhaustive, at least three lenses exist today to account for some of the tensions between faith and sexuality. These three lenses are integrity, disability, and diversity.[3]

The *integrity* lens reflects a widely agreed-on understanding of sex and gender that is held by many adherents of several major world religions, including many followers of Christianity. As one theologian put it, the reference

---

[1]When referencing the gay community, we will be broader and inclusive when appropriate, using the word *gay* to encompass what we think of as the mainstream LGB+ community. The LGB+ community, of course, includes persons who identify as transgender and queer, but neither was a focus of the three studies we conducted. For readers interested in the discussion of gender identity and transgender persons, see Yarhouse (2015). Still other times we will use LGBT or LGBTQ as used in another researcher's report/quote of his or her research, or a quote of one of our participants on how they designate the community.

[2]The term *intentional* will be developed throughout this book to describe a strategic method of engagement for members of the Christian higher-education community who are in reciprocating relationship with students who are sexual minorities.

[3]The three lenses of integrity, disability, and diversity are discussed in greater detail in Yarhouse (2015). Those interested in the idea of different lenses through which people see matters of sexuality may find it helpful to read Caroline J. Simon's *Bringing Sex into Focus* (2012), where she discusses six sexual lenses through which sexuality has been understood: covenantal, procreative, expressive, plain sex, romantic, and power.

point is "the sacred integrity of maleness or femaleness stamped on one's body" (Gagnon, 2007). This is primarily a religious and theological argument. Same-sex sexual behavior is a concern to those who adhere to this framework in large part because such behaviors are thought to threaten the integrity of male/female distinctions. Conventionally religious persons of the Abrahamic faiths, that is, Christians, Jews, and Muslims, cite passages from their sacred texts that they view as supporting this sacred integrity, including references to the importance of complementary male/female differences from the creation narrative.

A second way people in contemporary society think about matters of same-sex sexuality has been referred to as a *disability* framework (Yarhouse, 2015). Adherents often use what is referred to as person-first language (see Dunn & Andrews, 2015, who discuss person-first language with reference to disability rather than LGB+ issues). For example, rather than referring to people as "gay," those who adopt this framework may refer to themselves as "a person who is navigating sexual-identity questions" and "a person who experiences gender identity concerns or who experiences gender incongruence" (see Yarhouse & Tan, 2004; Yarhouse, 2013; 2015).

Someone from a religious faith tradition might view their same-sex sexuality as a "disability," likely due to a normative view of sexuality and sexual functioning in which attraction to the opposite sex is viewed as intended from creation; variations would be departures from that norm and would be the result of "fallenness" (of the creation order; see Yarhouse & Nowacki, 2007).

A third framework for discussing LGB+ issues in the broader society is a *diversity* framework that conceptualizes *gay* (as an umbrella term) as an identity and LGB+ persons as part of an LGB+ community—a unique culture to be recognized, celebrated, and honored. The sociocultural context in which we live in the West has been rapidly moving toward the direction of celebrating diversity in areas of sexuality and gender identity. Thus we refer to this as a diversity framework because it highlights LGB+ issues as reflecting an identity and a people group to be celebrated as a culture.

We will come back to these lenses at different points throughout the book, but when we consider the tensions between faith and sexuality, they are most acute between representatives of the integrity framework and representatives of the diversity framework. Those are the two primary voices in the broader cultural wars about norms surrounding sex and gender, as well as public policies that reflect those norms and so on.

Recent events highlight these different frameworks that are present among individuals and institutions.[4] Robert Oscar Lopez, a tenured professor at California State Northridge University, has been criticized by the Human Rights Campaign (HRC) and now his university for more conservative views on family and the rights of children (Siggins, 2015). Lopez, a bisexual man, suspects that he has been targeted for believing that children have a right to a mother and father and disagreeing with redefining marriage. He was not raised by biological parents, and he, along with others raised by same-sex couples, filed a brief with the Supreme Court surrounding these beliefs. Lopez sees these issues through a disability lens, while those at his school utilize a diversity lens. The HRC and California State Northridge, both reflecting a diversity lens, do not appear to believe that Dr. Lopez's beliefs are compatible with what they would deem acceptable for his current position.

In an article about faith and sexuality, Peter Smith (2015) writes about Wesley Hill, an associate professor and author who identifies as a celibate gay Christian. Hill believes that gay Christians should be committed to celibacy while also affirming their sexual orientation. Smith states that this "stance runs counter to the growing American majority that supports legalized same-sex marriage among Americans, including religious progressives" (2015, p. 1). Additionally, it runs counter to many Christian conservatives who do not affirm being gay as an identity. Hill's stance, through a disability lens, is seen by those in the diversity framework as not fully embracing who he is and by those in the integrity lens as his covering up or avoiding a problem he may have. It's easy to see how misunderstandings based on different lenses can cause many difficulties in this discussion.

These same tensions exist at Christian colleges and universities throughout the United States. David Wheeler, in an *Atlantic* article called "The LGBT Politics of Christian Colleges" (2016), cites one example of a student reportedly being expelled from a Christian college for being in an intimate sexual relationship with another student of the same gender and suggests that that fear is real among sexual minorities at Christian colleges and universities.

We discuss this more in chapter six, but for now a couple of examples will suffice. In our interviews Kris, a nineteen-year-old lesbian freshman student, offered this response when asked about specific campus resources: "At this university, from what I have understood, the institution looks down on same-sex attraction and behaviors. This has made me hesitant to try counseling on

---

[4]Adapted from Yarhouse, Sides, & Page (in press).

campus since I fear that if I reveal my sexual identity I could get expelled." Another student, Justin, a freshman, shared, "I've heard stories of them expelling students who went for help from the school."

An additional source of tension has been the interpretation of Title IX, which is one of several education amendments codified in 1972. Title IX was written to protect students from discrimination based on sex in education programs and activities that receive federal funds. Title IX's interpretation has been expanded to include protection from sexual harassment, and in 2014, under the Obama administration, the interpretation was expanded further to include protection for sexual minorities and gender-nonconforming students and employees (Mitchell, 2016). These guidelines for interpreting Title IX were not continued under the Trump administration.

In response to the initial expanded interpretation, some Christian colleges, expressing concern for religious liberty, requested an exemption that would allow them to continue to receive federal funding while operating and developing policies that reflected their religious doctrinal commitments regarding norms for sex and gender. Other conservative Christian colleges sought no such exemption and instead have asserted that the right to function as a faith-based institution is directly protected by the Constitution. In any case, these developments have brought into sharp focus some of the tensions that exist surrounding Christian institutions and LGB+ persons and advocates.

A WORD ON LANGUAGE

We use the phrase "sexual minorities" to recognize that people who experience same-sex attractions are in the numeric minority when we contrast them to those who experience attraction to the opposite sex. In doing so we are following a standard approach among those who conduct research in this area. A sexual minority is a person who experiences same-sex attraction independent of identity label (such as, say, "gay" or "lesbian" or "queer") or sexual behavior. This is similar to the approach taken in mainstream LGB+ research. For example, Diamond (2007, p. 142) defines sexual minorities as "individuals with same-sex attractions or behavior, regardless of self-identification." This is especially important when discussing Christian college students, many of whom may choose not to publicly adopt a sexual-identity label and some of whom do not adopt a private sexual-identity label. Many, too, decide not to engage in same-sex sexual behavior.

Is the desire to pursue an exemption born out of a desire to discriminate against LGB+ students and employees? That is certainly the belief of those whose primary lens is that of diversity. This has led to a listing of all institutions that requested a Title IX exemption on the U.S. Education Department's website. Recall that the diversity lens sees the LGB+ community as a culture to be celebrated. Gay marriage is viewed as highly symbolic of a cultural endorsement of LGB+ personhood.

In contrast, the question can be asked: Is what is referred to as discrimination a reflection of longstanding religious liberties, the kind of liberties that allow for the very real differences in worldview to coexist in a diverse and pluralistic society? That tends to be the view of those whose lens is that of integrity. The integrity lens primarily concerns the male/female distinctions and norms that lay a theological foundation for ethics and morality.

Also, apart from the very real challenge of different lenses contributing to what stakeholders see in these policies and exemptions, another question may also be worth asking: Is it also possible to intend one thing but have multiple results and unintended consequences? Could a Christian college have policies that reflect Christian doctrine but have procedures or (perhaps more likely) the implementation of procedures in actual practices that have been unevenly applied at times and in ways that have been difficult or confusing for students navigating sexual identity concerns?

Joel Wentz and Roger Wessel (2011) offered a "small sample" reflection on the intersection of sexual identity and religious identity as a Christian on Christian college campuses.[5] They discuss two layers of an identity conflict. The first layer is the "prevailing historical, cultural sentiment among Christianity regarding the issues of homosexuality" (p. 2). They cite a document from the Council for Christian Colleges and Universities (CCCU) that reflects "a historical consensus regarding the issues of same-sex sexual behavior within the church, which is grounded in biblical interpretation" (p. 2). That view is that "homosexual behavior represents a distortion of the creational intent of God in providing sexual intercourse as a means for creating a one flesh union, of uniting husband and wife (CCCU, 2001, p. 4)" (Wentz & Wessel, 2011, p. 2).

---

[5]Wentz and Wessel (2011) draw their conclusions about faith-based institutions from an apparently small qualitative research sample. We use their discussion of issues related to Christian higher education because the research literature pertaining to this population of students is currently so small. Such qualitative studies are helpful and appreciated as new areas of research are initially explored (Creswell, 2014).

This conclusion reflects, then, one layer of an identity conflict:

Because this belief is identified as one that has been consistently affirmed in the church throughout the previous two millennia, CCCU-affiliated universities find themselves operating within the broader culture of the Christian church, which maintains that homosexual behavior is a violation of God's intent for human sexuality, while also serving as an institution of higher education that is available for any young adult to attend, including gay and lesbian individuals. (Wentz & Wessel, 2011, p. 2)

This brings us to the second layer of an identity conflict, according to Wentz and Wessel. "The second layer of this identity conflict lies within American higher education's commitment to holistic growth and development" (p. 2). This is essentially an identity-development model that focuses on "congruence between [students'] internal values and external behavior patterns" (p. 2). This identity development is far reaching and may include moral development, cognitive development, and sexual-identity development (Wentz & Wessel, 2011). These two layers are each powerful, and powerfully felt by leaders and constituents on college campuses, and their overlap is what makes the tension intrinsic to institutions.

The three lenses through which people understand or see these topics may be helpful here. What Wentz and Wessel identify as the first layer of the identity conflict reflects what we refer to as the integrity lens. The integrity lens provides a theological foundation for normative assertions regarding sexuality and gender. Insofar as Christian institutions reflect the integrity lens in their doctrinal positions, we will see that lens inform policy and student development.

The second layer of an identity conflict depends greatly on how American higher education views holistic growth and development, but the views today are clearly reflecting a diversity lens as discussed above.

In his article for *The Atlantic*, David Wheeler offers this observation about Christian universities:

In the past, many conservative Christian colleges condemned both same-sex attraction and same-sex intimacy. But now that gay marriage is legalized, and as the country undergoes broad cultural shifts, that's changing. Some of these same schools are attempting to separate sexual identity from sexual behavior in their policies and campus customs.

However awkwardly, they're trying to welcome gay students while preserving rules against same-sex "behavior."

What Wheeler observes are the different lenses represented by Christian colleges and the changing cultural landscape. The coexistence of different lenses through which people see these concerns will need to be better understood if there is interest in fostering environments of intentional engagement and mutual understanding.

THE CURRENT PROJECT

This book is about the experiences of sexual-minority students at Christian colleges and universities in the United States. Little research has been conducted to date on the experiences of sexual minorities on Christian college campuses. Wolff and his colleagues (2016), for instance, reported on the experiences of sexual-minority students at a range of faith-based institutions, including evangelical Christian colleges, but also Catholic, Mormon, and mainline Protestant contexts. Evangelical students reported more difficulty navigating sexual and religious identity conflicts than students from many of the other settings, especially Catholic and mainline institutions.

In our study the Christian colleges and universities often represent and reflect the integrity framework in their doctrinal statements and policies. Wolff and his colleagues refer to this position as "nonaffirming," which is language and a reference point that makes sense from a diversity lens in which being "affirming" or "nonaffirming" of LGB+ is the salient distinction (and in which an "affirming" position is defined with reference to viewing same-sex behavior as morally permissible). There are other ways to orient the reader toward these institutions, as reflecting the integrity or disability frameworks. A more neutral label would be "religious."[6] The people who operate such institutions or work there often refer to them as "faith-based" or "religiously affiliated" or "Christian" to distinguish them from, say, a state university. In any case, the colleges themselves operate in a broader cultural context in which many elements of the culture have rapidly embraced a diversity framework—within really just a generation or two. Christian students who experience same-sex attraction and who are navigating sexual-identity questions represent a range of beliefs and values regarding their sexuality and behavior.

---

[6]Shelley Craig and her research group refer to such institutions as "religious colleges and universities" or "RCUs." See Craig, Austin, Rashidi, & Adams (2017).

While this book is about the experiences of these Christian sexual minorities, it has broader applications to how Christians and Christian institutions interact with those broader cultural changes and the people they interact with or serve in the context of their work or ministry.

OUR THREE STUDIES

The three main studies we worked on together are referenced throughout this book.

The 2009 study: Our first study of sexual minorities who attend Christian colleges and universities, with support from the CCCU.

The 2013 study: Our second national study of sexual minorities who attend Christian colleges and universities, with support from the ACSD.

The current study: Our longitudinal study that is the primary focus of this book. There is survey data at both time 1 and a year later, time 2, as well as interviews that we discuss throughout the book.

We began working as a team many years ago. As we mentioned in the preface, we have all worked in Christian colleges or universities, and we have worked with sexual-minority students in various capacities. In knowing and walking with many sexual-minority students, we are well aware of some of the challenges they face. To try to gain a deeper understanding of the experiences of sexual-minority students, we have conducted a line of research reflected in several studies (e.g., Dean, Stratton, Yarhouse, & Lastoria, 2011; Stratton, Dean, Yarhouse, & Lastoria, 2013; Yarhouse, Doolin, Watson, & Campbell, 2015; Yarhouse, Dean, Stratton, & Lastoria, 2017; Yarhouse, Stratton, Dean, & Brooke, 2009) of the experiences of sexual minorities at Christian colleges and universities. These studies have been presented at professional conferences, such as the American Psychological Association and the Christian Association for Psychological Studies, and published in peer-reviewed journals. What we wanted to do in this book is bring these findings together along with our first longitudinal study and see whether we can draw some implications from this work that may be a resource to Christians and to Christian institutions.

STUDY DESIGN

We have in the past worked with organizations such as the Council for Christian Colleges and Universities (CCCU) to conduct research at Christian colleges (the 2009 study). As we mentioned in the preface, our 2013 study was with support from the Association for Christians in Student Development (ACSD). In our most recent study, we again approached and received support from the ACSD to conduct a study of the experiences of sexual minorities at Christian colleges and universities.[7]

We then approached student development officers affiliated with the ACSD about functioning as gatekeepers to the study. Over forty schools initially showed some interest in participating in the study, and of these fifteen schools (representing ten states) elected to participate.[8] There was broad geographic representation, with two participating schools in the Northeast, six in the Midwest, two in the South, three in the central region, and two in the West. Likewise, participants live broadly across the United States, with thirty from the East (18.8%), forty-three from the Midwest (26.9%), thirty-six from the central region (22.5%), thirty-two from the South (20.0%), and sixteen from the West (10.0%), with one from outside the United States and two unknown.

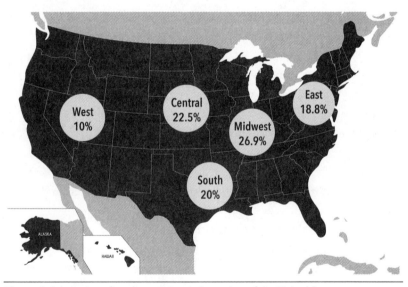

Figure 1.1. Location of study participants by region of the United States

---

[7]Some of our findings from time 1 were published first in a peer-reviewed journal. See Yarhouse, Stratton, Dean, Lastoria, & Bucher (2017).

[8]Fifteen schools elected to participate, but only fourteen followed through with this agreement and shared the study with their students.

A common consideration in conducting research of this nature has to do with access to students. How will students hear about the study? That can present a challenge because how students hear about a study can speak to whether they believe that that source has their best interest in mind, which may determine willingness to participate.[9]

Participating schools first announced the study to their students in their chapel services by a brief verbal announcement and/or a short video presentation. Following this announcement, invitations to participate, along with confirmation that the study had been approved by their institution and a link to the online survey, were emailed to all students. Participation in the study required online interaction with a survey that was developed and hosted at SurveyMonkey with encryption; no contact with any campus personnel was required. This was important because we did not want a student to have to be "out" to campus personnel to participate.

However, due to the longitudinal design of the study, participants provided their names and contact information for follow-up. This is one of the most significant departures from our previous research (e.g., Stratton et al., 2013; Yarhouse et al., 2009), in which students could be completely anonymous. Of course, the tradeoff in the earlier studies was that we only collected information on their experiences at that one point in time. This is called cross-sectional research. What we have with a longitudinal study is an opportunity to see how students' experiences, attitudes, and behaviors change over time. In this book we will draw on all of these studies as we share what we are finding about the lived reality of Christian sexual minorities in faith-based institutions of higher education.

The sample for the longitudinal study was 160 participants. These represent 19.8% of initial responders and are those participants who completed the entire

---

[9]The question of how potential participants will hear about a study is a concern to any researcher who studies the experiences of sexual minorities at religiously affiliated institutions. The use of convenience sampling is common in this line of research. For example, Shelley Craig and her colleagues (2017) recruited their sample through a notice on the HeartStrong, Inc., website. HeartStrong describes its work as follows: "HeartStrong offers help and hope to GLBT students of religiously-based educational institutions which do not permit GLBT students to fully express themselves socially, emotionally, romantically and spiritually." The placement of an announcement may limit the kinds of students or alumni who will learn about the study or participate. While, on the one hand, we can appreciate that some sexual minorities may choose not to participate in a study such as ours in which the administration of their institution approves, we appear to be reporting on a sample with a wider range of beliefs, values, and experiences. See Craig, Austin, Rashidi, & Adams (2017).

survey, which was thirty-five pages in length, electronic format.[10] The final sample looked similar to the typical population across Christian colleges and universities, except with regard to gender, where females tend to be the majority. However, males do have a higher prevalence estimate than females in studies that ask about sexual orientation and identity, often at a two-to-one ratio. For example, in Edward Lauman's sexuality study, 2% of adult males identified having a homosexual orientation compared to about 1% of adult females (with an additional 0.8% of males and 0.5% of females identifying as bisexual).

The gender distribution included 45% female respondents ($n = 72$), 51% male respondents ($n = 81$), and 4% respondents indicating "other" ($n = 7$). Their average reported age was 21.4 years ($SD = 4.58$). Respondents tended to identify as single, never married (94%). Among the four school classifications, junior and seniors were overrepresented (freshmen 16%, sophomores 20%, juniors 22%, seniors 33%, fifth-year seniors 2%, and graduate students 6%). The ethnic/racial makeup of the sample was primarily Caucasian/White (81%), with 7% identifying as African American, 4% as Hispanic/Latin, and 3% Asian/Pacific Islander.

All participants identified as Christian were included in the study. When asked about how spiritual and religious they are, participants rated themselves as more spiritual than religious (see fig. 1.2).[11] What this often means is that people have a personal, private faith but may not always care to affiliate with an institution or a structure. In this case, we do not see a lack of religious affiliation (after all, these are students who attend a Christian college or university), and they rate on average as religious, and on other measures we will examine as highly religious, but here they may be showing us their personal, private faith commitments. We will look into religion and spirituality throughout the book, as the faith of our students is a particularly salient aspect of who they are.

---

[10] An initial combined sample of 807 students from these institutions responded to campus-wide requests for students who experience same-sex attraction to complete the online survey. Of the initial 807 respondents, 24.7% ($n = 199$) refused to participate in the study by directly indicating their refusal, closing out of the survey before providing their names, or not answering any of the qualifying questions. Another 49.9% ($n = 403$) were disqualified from participating because they indicated that they did not experience same-sex attraction ($n = 374$), they did not identify as a Christian ($n = 13$), they did not attend a Christian college or university ($n = 6$), or they gave nonsensical identifying information ($n = 10$). Of those who participated to some degree, 3.1% ($n = 25$) gave their contact information but did not respond to any other item on the survey, and 2.3% ($n = 20$) stopped answering at various points of the survey, completing on average a quarter of the items.

[11] The differences in ratings as more spiritual ($M = 8.46$, $SD = 1.94$) than religious ($M = 6.74$, $SD = 2.22$) was statistically significant [$t (158) = 10.33$, $p < 0.001$].

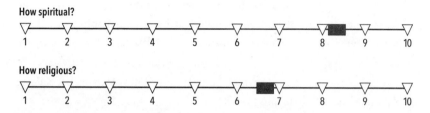

Figure 1.2. Rating scale on spirituality and religiosity

When we look at the demographic information of participants in this study as compared to our previous studies, we see that this sample tended to be older, with juniors and seniors being overrepresented. What might that mean for the findings? When we get to specific topics, such as milestone events in the formation of sexual identity, we can see that older students will have simply had more time to reach various milestones. In our previous studies, with a younger sample and more equal distribution across years in college, students may not have had as many opportunities to experience as many different milestones. In any case, we will discuss differences across the studies where appropriate and where a discussion of differences may be helpful to the reader as we think together about what the findings mean for Christians navigating sexual identity, as well as for Christian institutions.

We also interviewed by phone a subset of students who completed surveys. This was an option each year as students completed the questionnaire. We draw on the interviews throughout the book to illustrate key points and help put a personal experience on a finding. We have changed the names of all interviewees and created names for the purposes of the book—rather than refer to "Participant 005." The interview samples at time 1 (n = 39) and time 2 (n = 45) looked similar to our larger survey sample.[12]

This chapter provided a bit of an overview of the felt tension between faith and sexuality. The three lenses of integrity, disability, and diversity through

---

[12]The gender distribution of the interview sample included 41% female respondents ($n = 16$) and 59% male respondents ($n = 23$). They were significantly older, with their average reported age at 22.8 years ($SD = 7.53$). Respondents tended to identify as single, never married (93.2%). Among the four school classifications, seniors were overrepresented (freshmen 10%, sophomores 10%, juniors 18%, seniors 51%), with a few graduate students, 10%, included. The ethnic/racial makeup of the sample was primarily Caucasian/White (81%) with African American 8%, Asian/Pacific Islander 5%, and other 5%. All participants identified as Christian. When asked about how spiritual and religious they were at the time of the survey, participants rated themselves as more spiritual ($M = 8.46$, $SD = 1.95$) than religious ($M = 7.21$, $SD = 2.08$), t (38) = -4.68, $p < 0.001$.

which different people and institutions view sexuality—and sometimes the very same people and institutions at different times—inevitably create dissonance as they come into contact. This tension sets the stage for the study we conducted of sexual minorities at Christian colleges and universities around the United States. We then provided an overview of how we approached the study and a little glimpse into the sample.

We turn our attention now to who these students are and what matters to them. We will later take a more in-depth look at both their faith and their experience of same-sex sexuality, as well as what they say they believe about sexuality and sexual behavior. We will also learn more about what it is like for them to engage with others in an explicitly Christian setting.

CHAPTER 1 TAKEAWAYS

1. A tension exists for many people who are navigating their same-sex sexuality, sexual-identity questions, and religious faith identity as Christians.

2. It may be helpful to identify three lenses through which different people and institutions view sexuality and sexual-identity concerns: integrity, disability, and diversity.

3. The integrity lens emphasizes male/female differences intended by God from creation. These differences lay the foundation for what is considered morally permissible sexual behavior in the context of the covenant of marriage.

4. The disability lens emphasizes how differences are the result of variations that occur in nature and may reflect a nonmoral reality that can be addressed with compassion. The variation may be the result of living in a fallen world.

5. The diversity lens views "gay" as an identity and the LGB+ community as a culture to be celebrated.

6. This book is primarily about a longitudinal study that we refer to as "the current study." We will also discuss the "2009 study," which was done with the support of the CCCU, and the "2013 study," which was conducted with support from affiliates associated with the ACSD.

7. The "current study" is of 160 students from fourteen Christian colleges and universities.

REFERENCES

Center for Collegiate Mental Health. (2012). *CCAPS 2012 Technical Manual.* University Park, PA.

Craig, S. L., Austin, A., Rashidi, M., & Adams, M. (2017). Fighting for survival: The experiences of lesbian, gay, bisexual, transgender, and questioning students in religious colleges and universities. *Journal of Gay & Lesbian Social Services, 29*(1), 1-24.

Creswell, J. W. (2014). *Research design: Qualitative, quantitative, and mixed method approaches.* Thousand Oaks, CA: Sage.

Dean, J. B., Stratton, S. P., Yarhouse, M. A., & Lastoria, M. (2011). Same sex attraction. In M. Lastoria (Ed.), *ACSD research series: Sexuality, religiosity, behaviors, attitudes: A look at religiosity, sexual attitudes, and sexual behavior of Christian college students* (pp. 56-70). Houghton, NY: Association for Christians in Student Development.

Diamond, L. M. (2007). A dynamical systems approach to the development and expression of female same-sex sexuality. *Perspectives on Psychological Science, 2*(2), 142-57.

Doolin, H., High, K., Holt, R., Atkinson, A., & Yarhouse, M. A. (2011, April). Comparing visual analogue and ordinal scales measuring sexual attraction in mixed-orientation couples. Poster presented at the Virginia Psychological Association Conference.

Dunn, D., & Andrews, E. (2015). Person-first and identity-first language developing psychologists' cultural competence using disability language. *American Psychologist, 70*(3). http://dx.doi.org/10.1037/a0038636

Gagnon, R. A. J. (2007, August). Transsexuality and ordination. Retrieved from www.robgagnon.net/articles/TranssexualityOrdination.pdf

HeartStrong. (n.d.). Who HeartStrong reaches. HeartStrong (Website). Retrieved from www.heartstrong.org/whoheartstrongreaches

Jones, S. L., & Yarhouse, M. A. (2007). *Ex-gays? A longitudinal study of religiously mediated change in sexual orientation.* Downers Grove, IL: IVP Academic.

Koenig, H. G., Meador, K. G., & Parkerson, G. (1997). Religion index for psychiatric research. *American Journal of Psychiatry, 154,* 885-86.

Lauman, E. O., Gagnon, J. H., Michael, R. T., & Michaels, S. (1994). *The social organization of sexuality.* Chicago: University of Chicago Press.

Locke, B. D., McAleavey, A. A., Zhao, Y., Lei, P.-W., Hayes, J. A., Castonguay, L. G., Li, H., Tate, R., & Lin, Y.-C. (2012). Development and initial validation of the Counseling Center Assessment of Psychological Symptoms-34 (CCAPS-34). *Measurement and Evaluation in Counseling and Development, 45,* 151-69.

Mitchell, M. (2016, February). How Christian universities are becoming a battleground for LGBT rights. *Newsweek*, February 3, 2016. Retrieved from www.newsweek.com/how-christian-universities-are-becoming-battleground-lgbt-rights-422354

Riley, J. L. (2015, November 10). Christian belief cost Kelvin Cochran his job. *The Wall Street Journal*. Retrieved from www.wsj.com/article_email/christian-belief-cost-kelvin-cochran-his-job-1447200885-lMyQjAxMTE1NDExMTcxMjE3Wj

Ryff, C. D. (1989). Happiness is everything, or is it? Explorations on the meaning of psychological well-being. *Journal of Personality and Social Psychology, 57*(6), 1069-81.

Ryff, C. D., & Keyes, C. (1995). The structure of psychological well-being revisited. *Journal of Personality and Social Psychology, 69,* 719-27.

Siggins, D. (2015, November 14). Public university joins LGBT radicals in targeting professor who thinks kids should have mom, dad. *The Daily Signal*. Retrieved from http://dailysignal.com/2015/11/14/public-university-joins-lgbt-radicals-in-targeting-professor-who-thinks-kids-should-have-mom-dad/

Simon, C. J. (2012). *Bringing sex into focus.* Downers Grove, IL: IVP Academic.

Smith, P. (2015, May 10). Gay and celibate: Some Christians affirming their homosexuality but pledging to forgo sex. *Pittsburgh Post-Gazette*. Retrieved from www.post-gazette.com/news/nation/2015/05/10/Gay-and-celibate-Some-Christians-affirming-their-homosexuality-but-pledging-to-forgo-sex/stories/201505100014

Stratton, S. P., Dean, J. B., Yarhouse, M. A., & Lastoria, M. (2013). Sexual minorities in faith-based education: A national survey of attitudes, milestones, identity, and religiosity. *Journal of Psychology and Theology, 41*(1), 3-23.

Wentz, J. M., & Wessel, R. D. (2011). The intersection of gay and Christian identities on Christian college campuses. *Journal of College and Character, 12*(2). http://dx.doi.org/10.2202/1940-1639.1789

Wheeler, David R. (2016, March 14). The LGBT politics of Christian colleges. *The Atlantic*. Retrieved from www.theatlantic.com/education/archive/2016/03/the-lgbt-politics-of-christian-colleges/473373/

Wolff, J. R., Himes, H. L., Soares, S. D., & Kwon, E. M. (2016). Sexual minority students in non-affirming religious higher education: Mental health, outness, and identity. *Psychology of Sexual Orientation and Gender Diversity, 3*(2), 201-12.

Yarhouse, M. A. (2013). *Understanding sexual identity: A resource for youth ministry.* Grand Rapids, MI: Zondervan.

Yarhouse, M. A. (2015). *Understanding gender dysphoria: Navigating transgender issues in a changing culture.* Downers Grove, IL: IVP Academic.

Yarhouse, M. A., Dean, J. B., Stratton, S. P., & Lastoria, M. (2017). A survey of sexual minorities who attend faith-based institutions of higher education. *Growth Journal, 16,* 20-38.

Yarhouse, M. A., Doolin, H., Watson, K., & Campbell, M. C. (2015). Experiences of students and alumni navigating sexual identity in faith-based higher education: A qualitative study. *Growth Journal, 14,* 16-27.

Yarhouse, M. A., & Nowacki, S. K. (2007). The many meanings of marriage: Divergent perspectives seeking common ground. *The Family Journal: Counseling and Therapy for Couples and Families, 15*(1), 36-45.

Yarhouse, M. A., Sides, J., & Page, C. (In press). The complexities of multicultural competence with LGBT+ populations. In C. Frisby and W. O'Donohue (Eds.), *Cultural competence in applied psychology: Theory, science, practice, and evaluation.* New York: Springer.

Yarhouse, M. A., Stratton, S. P., Dean, J. B., & Brooke, H. L. (2009). Listening to sexual minorities on Christian college campuses. *Journal of Psychology and Theology, 37*(2), 96-113.

Yarhouse, M. A., Stratton, S., Dean, J., Lastoria, M., & Bucher, E. K. (2017). A survey of sexual minorities who attend faith-based institutions of higher education. *Growth Journal, 16*, 20-38.

Yarhouse, M. A., & Tan, E. S. N. (2004). *Sexual identity synthesis: Attributions, meaning-making, and the search for congruence.* Lanham, MD: University Press of America.

▼

APPENDIX

Here is information about the various quantitative measures we used and will be discussing throughout the book.

Duke University Religiosity Index (DUREL; Koenig, Meador, & Parkerson, 1997). This modified seven-item scale measures frequency of church attendance (one item; organizational religiosity, OR), frequency of three personal religious practices (one item; nonorganizational religiosity, NOR), and personally motivated spirituality (three items; intrinsic religiosity, IR). Participants indicate the frequency of their religious practices on the first two items using a six-point Likert scale, ranging from zero = *never* to five = *more than once a week*. Participants also rated their agreement with three attitudinal statements on a five-point Likert scale, ranging from one = *definitely not true of me* to five = *definitely true of me*. The intrinsic religiosity (IR) score was created by averaging ratings across these three items: "In my life, I experience the presence of the Divine (i.e., God)," "My religious beliefs are what really lie behind my whole approach to life," and "I try hard to carry my religion over into all other dealings in life."

Counseling Center Assessment of Psychological Symptoms (CCAPS-34; Locke, McAleavey, Zhao, Lei, Hayes, Castonguay, Li, Tate, & Lin, 2012). This abbreviated form of the original CCAPS has thirty-four items that measure psychological symptoms or distress in college students. Participants indicate the degree to which each item describes them on a five-point Likert scale, ranging from zero = *not at all like me* to four = *extremely like me*. In addition to a distress index, its seven subscales include: (1) depression, (2) generalized anxiety, (3) social anxiety, (4) academic distress, (5) eating concerns, (6) alcohol use, and (7) hostility. The subscales of the CCAPS-34 are highly correlated with the full CCAPS-62 (Locke et al., 2012), with correlation coefficients ranging from 0.92 to 0.98 (Center for Collegiate Mental Health, 2012). In addition, initial validation research found the CCAPS-34 to have strong convergent validity, good discrimination power, and fair test-retest stability over one-week and two-week intervals (Locke et al., 2012).

Ryff scales of psychological well-being (Ryff-54; Ryff, 1989; Ryff & Keyes, 1995). The Ryff-54 assesses six theory-guided dimensions of psychological well-being by having participants rate their agreement with each of its fifty-four items on a six-point Likert scale, ranging from one = *strongly disagree* to six = *strongly agree*. Only three subscales were utilized in the current study: (1) personal growth, (2) purpose in life, and (3) self-acceptance.

Yarhouse sexual orientation thermometers (Jones & Yarhouse, 2007; Doolin, High, Holt, Atkinson, & Yarhouse, 2011). These two items asked participants to independently rate the degree of other-sex attraction (OSA) and same-sex attraction (SSA) they experience. Using a ten-point Likert scale, the ratings of OSA vary from one = *strong OSA* to ten = *no OSA*. The scale for same-sex attraction was reversed, with one = *no SSA* and ten = *strong SSA*.

Attitudes about same-sex attraction (Yarhouse et al., 2009). These nine attitudinal statements were created to measure attitudes about theological, biological, and sociological belief statements regarding SSA, based on perceived controversial discussions on Christian college and university campuses. Approximately half of the items were written to reflect a perspective intended to be consistent with the worldview of conservative Christian colleges and universities. The remaining items were crafted to reflect a perspective to some degree at variance with that worldview. Participants indicate their degree of agreement with each attitudinal statement on a five-point Likert scale, where one = *strongly disagree* and five = *strongly agree*.

A CLOSER LOOK

UNDERSTANDING THE POPULATION

For a long time, [my sexuality felt] like this awkward person that I carried around that I didn't know what to do with. But for me it was like a door for me to explore my faith. Because all of a sudden, it's like, "Here's something that I know to be true about myself, but I also know that I'm a child of God . . . so how do I start reconciling the two?" I think that's really moved me to go deeper in my faith and a lot broader, which is really why I'm here at this college. . . . Even though it's been burdening at times, it's really been an eye opener and also a catalyst of sorts to draw me closer in my faith and my relationship with God. I think sadly that's kind of rare for people with same-sex attraction who are in Christian contexts.

—*Liam, a junior, identifies as gay, time 2*

▼▲▼

JOCELYN SAT IN THE CHAIR across from her counselor, shifting nervously and hesitating to make eye contact. She had initially asked to see this particular counselor because she believed this counselor was one of the few people on campus who both could really understand what she was experiencing and had a solid theological perspective. She shared how she had decided on a college because of her faith, her desire to work with horses, and a real sense that God opened the doors for her to come here to study. Jocelyn shared how, now, while here, she was happy, connected to others, and making good friends, but that was part of the problem. Her closeness to one friend, in particular, had led to physical attraction and even some physical arousal, and she was trying to make sense of that. What did that mean about their friendship? What did that mean about her sexuality?

Thomas met with his campus counselor to discuss his declining grades and poor class attendance, but Thomas and his counselor both knew that these were merely symptoms of his growing depression. He had known from a very early age that he was "different" from the other boys, and that difference became more obvious when he began to experience attraction to his male friends. After years of wrestling with this attraction, Thomas had claimed his identity as gay but still wanted to attend a conservative Christian college because such a school fit with his faith. As he lived and studied in this environment, and matured in his faith and sexuality, he struggled even more with this sexual identity and felt a great deal of shame. At that time, neither he nor his counselor knew that he would find some good friends in this community who would support him to "come out"—at least, as much as was possible with the behavioral constraints of the college. His senior year would bring some healing, and his coursework would be full of research papers and presentations actively investigating LGBT issues—issues that would stretch the faculty and students of this conservative religious community.

Eric came to his Christian college community with an awareness of his same-sex attractions and an understanding that he was likely gay. He was not drawn to the college for its religious stance but rather for the strong program it offered in social work. The tension between his understanding of his sexual identity and the religious stance on sexuality of this institution became too much for him. He grew more and more outspoken about its seemingly discriminatory policies until he graduated. After his graduation, his anger at the school and its community grew even more intense as he wrote multiple letters, blog posts, and newspaper articles to raise awareness about the school.

Jacob struggled with his same-sex attraction and begged his counselor to pray with him that God would take it away. Over many hours of conversation and tears, Jacob realized that this was a part of him and would be always. Over the years, his faith grew, as did his comfort with his own self. Even so, he never chose to identify as being gay, as he never understood himself in that way. Years later, as a psychologist himself, he married a kind, intelligent woman and had two lovely children, and Jacob feels fulfilled and happy with his life. "I cannot believe how much God has blessed me," he recently posted on Facebook. This same joy is evident in my personal and professional interactions with him.

Taryn quietly reflected on what it means to live a life of celibacy as a lesbian. In her college community, she found acceptance, friendship, and support from both men and women, both straight and gay students, and both staff and faculty. Over the years here, figuring out relationship boundaries with other women has been the one of her more challenging tasks. She's shared many stories where the pull of sexual attraction worked sometimes toward friendship and sometimes away from it, always in search of fulfilling that aching need for intimacy and connectedness. In one of her last meetings with her counselor, she discussed what Wesley Hill's book *Spiritual Friendship* meant to her. She simply said, "Being celibate allows me to be friends with other women—really intimate friends—in a way that might not be possible otherwise. It is hard, but God is making something beautiful out of all of this."

These students represent so many men and women on our Christian campuses who are navigating the relationship, and the seeming tension, between their faith and their sexual identity. They are searching and learning—step by step, hurt by hurt, victory by victory—how to hold both essential pieces of their identity together at the very same time.

In this chapter we want to help you as a reader understand sexual minorities who attend Christian colleges in the United States. We will discuss why students attend Christian colleges and then provide an overview of what we know about the students from our sample.

WHY GO TO A CHRISTIAN COLLEGE?

In the previous chapter we referred to Wentz and Wessel's 2013 work in understanding why sexual-minority students might go to faith-based colleges. Let's revisit that study here, as it is one of only a handful that looks at this distinct population. Wentz and Wessel interviewed eight college students who identified as gay and attended one of four various faith-based institutions across the country. Two of these students indicated they had sought out a Christian college or university with restrictive behavioral standards, thinking this would help them to manage their sexual attraction, even keeping them from becoming gay. One student described his decision this way, "So when looking at my university, I saw what their policies were, and for me I felt that it would be best if I was trying to change something, which at the time I felt like being gay was something that needed to change. . . . It provided the restrictions that I felt would be needed for that change to occur."

These students, and others like them in our faith-based institutions, seem to understand their sexual attraction through a disability lens. Their same-sex attraction was something "wrong" with them, and that attraction needed to be controlled and changed. A Christian campus, then, with more restrictive policies about sexuality, would help them to put boundaries around their sexual behavior, and in essence help them better manage their perceived disability.

The other six students in Wentz and Wessel's study, however, did not seem to be motivated to attend a Christian college or university by a need to manage their same-sex attraction. They instead saw their attractions as something they experienced but also as something that likely would go away over time. Even if the attraction didn't go away, many of these students believed they would never engage in the associated sexual behavior. One student commented, "At the time I was very religious. . . . I didn't really ever expect to be 'out' or comfortable with being a lesbian." The perspective of these students fits better within the integrity lens. Holding to a more orthodox view of sexuality, these students likely saw their attractions as something other than who they are and not something they would ever act on. Engaging in a Christian community, even one with more restrictive sexual standards, would not seem threatening or problematic.

In contrast, Wentz and Wessel described the perspective of these students as identity denial, asserting that these students were not being true to who they really are. Given that these particular students did come to identify as gay or lesbian, perhaps this denial is true for them, and even for many other students, but not for all. In this "identity denial" interpretation, the implied message is that these students should embrace their attractions and engage freely in same-sex sexual behavior. Here, the diversity lens serves as the arbiter of healthy development, without recognizing the importance of faith in how these students make sense of both their attractions and who they are.

Yet faith commitments may be the most distinguishing characteristic of the students in our sample and consequently the many sexual minorities they represent who are enrolled in numerous faith-based institutions of higher education. These students are living in a space within a campus climate that, at least regarding matters of sexuality, identity, and religion, is often open for discussion and values the integration of faith and sexuality (or other important concerns), but also where conflict with the broader culture is present. It's there, amid the conflict, in the middle of multiple lenses being used to understand sexuality, that these students are forging their identity.

WHO ARE THESE STUDENTS?

Sexual-minority students on our faith-based college and university campuses are distinct not only in their task of juggling sexuality, identity, and religion in a multicontextual framework; they themselves are different. Of course, they are different from many of their college peers because of their same-sex attraction. What might not be so obvious, however, is how different they are from many sexual minorities at more secular institutions.

They are relatively young. One of the faith-based universities in our study is located about sixteen miles southeast of a major public university. While both attract traditional undergraduates, the age differences in their two student bodies are significant. Undergraduates at the smaller Christian school have an average age of twenty, and only 2% of them are twenty-five or older. In contrast, at the state school up the street, undergraduates have an average age of twenty-one, but 7% are twenty-five or older. That is not the only age difference, either. Because the state school has a much larger population of graduate students, nearly a third of its student body lives in an environment that represents an even older average age.

As mentioned in chapter one, our sample of students for this study contained more upper-class students (57%) and graduate students (6%) than lower-class students (36%). Including more of these slightly older students raised the average age to 21.4 years ($SD = 4.6$). The students in this sample are young.

The average ages of participants in our previous studies were 20.3 ($SD = 2.0$; Yarhouse et al., 2009) and 20.1 ($SD = 2.03$; Stratton et al., 2013). Again, our students are young.

In terms of developmental stages, they are undergraduates who are in the stage of what is often referred to as emerging adulthood (Arnett, 2000). This is a time in between late adolescence and early adulthood where individuals are becoming independent, exploring possibilities, and figuring out who they are. Our students are right in the middle of this dynamic, critical, and, lately, much-debated, stage of development.

They are quite religious. In 2014 the Pew Research Center concluded from their Religious Landscape Study that millennials were less religious than older Americans (Masci & Hout, 2016). That is, they were less likely to engage in religious practices, such as prayer, attending services, volunteering time/ giving money, or fasting. In fact, only 41% of the young adults in the Pew study claimed that religion was important to them at all. In all other age groups, more than half of the people, and sometimes a lot more than half, held religion as important in their lives—at least to some degree. Contrast that to the same-aged students in our sample, surveyed the same year. While we didn't ask them the exact same question, we did simply ask, "On a scale from 1 to 10, with 10 being *very religious* and 1 being *not religious at all*, rate how religious you are." A notable 20% described themselves as very religious, rating themselves a nine or a ten. But, even more surprising, a full 60% suggested they were more religious than not by rating themselves anywhere from six to ten. Only two students out of the whole group of 160 denied being religious at all.

Seeing oneself as religious, particularly when attending a Christian college or university, is expected. How does this really translate to the daily lives of these students? The Pew report would suggest that this generation is not typically engaged in religious activities. Just over a quarter of the millennials in the national study said that they attended church services at least once per week. Michael Hout, a sociology professor at New York University, suggests that today's young adults do not trust organized religion and have turned to more personalized religious activities, if they remain engaged at all. In an interview with a representative from the Pew Research Center, he commented,

> Many Millennials have parents who are Baby Boomers and Boomers expressed to their children that it's important to think for themselves—that they find their own moral compass. Also, they rejected the idea that a good kid is an obedient kid. That's at odds with organizations, like churches, that have a long tradition of official teaching and obedience. And more than any other group, Millennials have been and are still being formed in this cultural context. As a result, they are more likely to have a "do-it-yourself" attitude toward religion. (Masci & Hout, 2016)

Our sample of students, though, differs greatly from other millennials in their religious behaviors. For a generation that has pulled away from the institution of the church, a surprisingly large majority of the students in this study—a full 70%—attend worship services at least once a week, and that's in addition to any mandatory campus chapel events they may be required to attend.

Their religious practices don't stop with church attendance, either. About 76% of them spend time in private religious activities, such as prayer, Bible study, or meditation, at least two times per week. Nearly half are engaged in these private practices daily or even multiple times per day. Contrast this frequent personal religious activity to that of their same-aged peers across the nation, of whom only about 42% are praying daily and only 17% are reading Scripture at least once per week. Compared to most undergraduates, this is a highly religious group of students.

They are very spiritual. While religiosity includes the behavioral compo-nents of faith, spirituality tends to include our thoughts about our relationship with God, our sense of purpose, and the ways in which we make sense of our existence. The 2014 Pew report found that millennials were pretty similar to older generations in their degree of spirituality. While fewer of them (only 52%) expressed a certain belief in the existence of God, they were more similar in their senses of wonder and of gratitude (again just over 50%). They also were just about as likely to think about the meaning of life (55%). Millennials, however, are more anxious and less likely to experience spiritual peace and well-being, with only 51% reporting such peace compared to 60% to 70% of the older generations.

Similarly, spirituality is very central in the lives of the students in our sample. In fact, very few of them see themselves as not very spiritual. Only 10% of these students claimed having less spirituality than more, rating them-selves on the low end of the scale between one = *not spiritual at all* and five = *moderately spiritual.* That means that 90% saw themselves as moderately to very spiritual, with a full 62% rating themselves as a nine or ten on a ten-point scale of spirituality. These students understand themselves as being very spir-itual, even to the degree that they use spirituality to make sense of their lives. As such, just over 80% claimed that they experience the presence of God in their daily lives, with their religious and spiritual beliefs guiding their whole approach to life.

So, not only is this a highly religious group of students, but this is also a highly spiritual group of students. They stand out compared to other college students—and to other sexual minorities. While many sexual minorities identify a religious background or hold a high regard for personal spirituality (Ritter & Terndrup, 2002), they become less likely to report a current religious affiliation as they move from adolescence to young adulthood (Rostosky, Danner, & Riggle, 2008). Our sample of students, then, is truly exceptional in the degree to which they hold religion and faith as important in their lives.

They are sexual minorities. These students all report some experience of same-sex sexual attraction or behavior. In fact, that was a criterion for par-ticipating in this study. Even so, while some of these students have taken on the identity of a sexual minority, others haven't. And while some will engage in same-sex sexual behavior, others will not. As mentioned earlier, it is not uncommon to understand these students as being sexual minorities—par-ticularly in light of their same-sex sexuality—regardless of how they label themselves or what behaviors they choose (Diamond, 2007, p. 142). They are sexual minorities by virtue of their same-sex attraction, and that adds a layer of complexity that other students do not face in quite the same way.

In our first project with sexual-minority students at faith-based institutions, the 2009 study, 49% of the students indicated that they had a heterosexual orientation, with 13% not being sure (Yarhouse et al., 2009). Only 17% claimed a homosexual orientation, and the rest suggested more mixed attractions by choosing the terms *bisexual* or *transsexual* to describe their sexual orientation. Contrast this to our current study. This time only 9% of the students said they had a heterosexual orientation, and 46% reported a homosexual one. The numbers are almost reversed! More of them are also now reporting having a bisexual (28%) or uncertain (18%) orientation.

This greater acknowledgment of their sexual attractions is seen in how the students in this study label themselves. We simply asked them to "describe [their] sexual identity (this is a sociocultural label that helps people communicate to others something about their sexual preferences)." Only 15% used the term *straight*. Students chose terms that clearly reveal their same-sex attractions, terms such as *lesbian/gay* (43%) or *bisexual* (24%). Almost one out of five of these college students seemed to be somewhere in the middle, describing themselves as questioning, or having no label, or just something other than straight, gay, or bisexual.

Another way to understand where these students are in their sexual-identity process is to ask them about their private and public sexual identities separately. Only 5.6% privately identified as heterosexual, but 50% did so publicly. The majority of the sample—63.1%—did not have congruence between these two identities.[1] That means that most of these students did not publicly identify in the same way they privately thought of themselves. Of those students with matched private and public identities, 54% were gay/lesbian, 18.6% were bisexual, and 13.6% were heterosexual.

They are fairly moderate. Higher education tends to contribute to an increased appreciation of minority groups (Decoo, 2014; Keleher & Smith, 2012).

---

[1]A chi-square analysis revealed a significant difference between private and public sexual identities, $\chi^2 (9) = 70.17$, $p < 0.001$. More congruence than expected was found for heterosexuals ($ADJR = 2.4$), bisexuals ($ADJR = 4.6$), and lesbians/gays ($ADJR = 6.7$), whereas private-public incongruencies were less than expected for bisexual-gay/lesbians (respectively, $ADJR = -4.0$), lesbian/gay-heterosexuals ($ADJR = -4.6$), and lesbian/gay-bisexuals ($ADJR = -3.0$). Those privately questioning their sexual identity were more likely than expected to identify as heterosexual ($ADJR = 2.4$).

COMMON TERMS AND PHRASES

It is our belief, from listening to the students who spoke to us, that some level of disclosing sexual identity or same-sex attraction is essential for the psychological and spiritual well-being of sexual-minority students. Navigating this important life task was never intended to be done in isolation. Critical to students electing to disclose, however, is their perception of the climate in which they live. Are the surrounding voices perceived as shaming? Welcoming? Ambivalent? And central to this is language; the words we use to talk about sexual identity and orientation are important, as their meanings have changed in recent past. Below we offer some suggestions about language use.

Suggested terminology when referencing LGB+ people:

Gay: predominant sexual and emotional attraction toward the same sex among males (or used generically for any gay or lesbian person).

Lesbian: predominant sexual and emotional attraction toward the same sex among females.

Bisexual or *bi:* Sexual and emotional attraction toward both the same and opposite sex.

Use "gay," "lesbian," and "bisexual" as an adjective, not a noun. So, "a gay person" or "gay couple." Avoid "she is a lesbian" or "he is a gay." Avoid the term *homosexual*, as it tends to stigmatize sexual minorities by reducing their lives to the nature of their sexual attractions. *Homosexual* was first coined at the turn of the twentieth century as a medical category defining solely one's sexual preferences/attractions.

Avoid "lesbianism," as well as "that's so gay"; the former is considered pejorative, the latter a hurtful slur. Also, "gay or lesbian lifestyle" implies that there is one lifestyle that all gay, lesbian, and bisexual persons live. It also raises questions about what is volitional. You may be thinking about behavior, but they may hear you discussing attraction or identity, as though they chose to experience their same-sex sexuality.

Use "lesbian, gay, and bisexual" on first usage, then LGB+, simply for audiences who may not be familiar with the terms.

Queer are nonheterosexual sexual orientations.

Pansexual is a term to describe an individual whose primary drive for connection and attractions is dependent on the nature of the relationship and not the gender or sex of the other.

Asexual is a term to describe a person who does not appear to have interest in either males or females as a potential sexual partner. This is a lack of sexual but not emotional attraction.

In general, if you are unsure of what term to use, ask your LGB+ friend how they would like to be addressed. And don't worry about making mistakes, since a sincere apology is always a remedy.

Additional phrases and terms used when talking about LGB+ and faith:

Side A, Side B, Side C, and Side X: These terms originated with Bridges Across the Divide Project and have been used by the Gay Christian Network. Simply stated, Side A refers to gay Christians who believe that same-sex sexual relationships can be morally permissible, whereas Side B refers to gay Christians who view same-sex sexual relationships as morally impermissible. Side C has referred to those who are either undecided or in tension around these conclusions. Side X refers to those who believe Christians should disidentify with gay identity and pursue heterosexuality.

Love the sinner, hate the sin: We recommend you avoid this phrase. You may be simply trying to separate out behavior from personhood, but many sexual minorities tell us that they have not often felt loved by Christians or that because they experience their behavioral expression as an extension of identity that it is not a simple separation that makes sense to them.

Even back in 2002, Donald Hinrichs and Pamela Rosenberg of Gettysburg College found that heterosexual students at small liberal arts colleges were fairly accepting of gay, lesbian, and bisexual persons. Faith, though, tends to be associated with greater sexual conservatism (Lefkowitz, Gillen, Shearer, & Boone, 2004). Because Christian sexual minorities live with an awareness of both their own same-sex attraction and their faith, we might wonder how these experiences shape their attitudes about same-sex attraction in general.

To better understand this, we asked students to read a number of statements that are often heard about same-sex attraction and then to rate their degree of agreement on a five-point scale. These statements reflected some controversial ideas that are much debated in today's discussion about sexuality (for details, see table A1.1 in the appendix to this chapter). For example, how would you respond to this idea, "Persons who experience same-sex attraction can change this aspect of their attractions to the opposite sex," or this one, "Monogamous sexual relationships between members of the same gender can be blessed [or receive God's grace and love]"? The nine questions fell into two categories: questions about the causation or biological nature of same-sex attraction and questions about the moral acceptability of same-sex sexual behavior.

Our participants sometimes answered as you might expect given that they value Christianity, and other times they responded as you might anticipate given that they are sexual minorities. But rarely did they respond as strongly as you probably suspected that they would. They somewhat don't believe that people have a choice in their sexual attractions or that people can later change these attractions; they tend to believe that people might be born this way. In other words, they somewhat disagree that we have free will (or any "say") in our sexual attraction. Because of that, being attracted to members of the same sex can be morally acceptable, they hold; even so, sexual minorities probably can be celibate. Notice the tentativeness in these positions. Our students tend to agree with each of these—but only moderately.

Interestingly, even though participants were somewhat confident that people could not choose their sexual attractions, they were less certain about the role that environment and learning experiences play in our attractions. When asked whether environment and experiences play a greater role in sexual attraction than does biology, the average response was right in the middle of our scale—"I agree and disagree"—but a fraction more toward the "disagree" side. So, what are the causes of our attraction, according to our students? Biology—likely yes; experience—probably no.

Accepting that biology has a pretty significant role in sexual attractions and that people probably cannot change these attractions fits into a more naturalistic perspective on sexual orientation. More and more people have come to believe this very thing, such that even most people with varying views on sexuality will hold to biological causation. And many have argued that if we hold this understanding of the causation of sexual orientation, that people are just born this way, we are more likely to be more accepting of sexual behavior.

Patrick Grzanka of the University of Tennessee, Knoxville and his colleagues (2015), however, caution us that our beliefs about sexual orientation may not be simply based on our understanding of causation. Instead, we have other beliefs about sexual minorities that shape how we see them and how we understand their behavior. These include beliefs about how discrete or distinct different kinds of sexual orientations are, how universal different kinds of sexual orientation are (is a homosexual orientation found throughout history and across cultures?), whether sexual orientations are immutable (unchanging) aspects of a person, whether there is "group-ness" associated with people based on sexual orientations (p. 69), and so on. There is likely a complex interplay among different sets of beliefs that are associated with attitudes toward sexual minorities, sexual behavior, and so on.

So, when it comes to sexual behavior, our students are still in the process of making up their minds on a number of issues. Can same-sex sexual relationships be blessed? Are these relationships morally acceptable? Is same-sex experimentation among teens okay? Maybe, say our participants. Yes and no. "We're not sure." Possibly. There was a hint of more agreement than disagreement in their average responses, but not much. The means were just over three on a five-point scale, where three means "agree and disagree." When it comes to same-sex sexual behavior, we perhaps see a bit more influence of traditional Christian beliefs on their judgment of what is right and wrong, as we did in their understanding of its causes.

Overall, with all items scored in such a way that high scores meant agreement was more in line with less traditional attitudes and low scores meant agreement was similar to more traditional sexual values, our students' average response was a 3.4. That 3.4 suggests very slight agreement with the more gay-affirming values, but they still are very much in the middle of both perspectives. And much of this slight agreement is due to their understanding of the causes of same-sex attraction, not so much their acceptance of the behavior.

In our 2013 study (Stratton, Dean, Yarhouse, & Lastoria, 2013), students also were in the middle of both perspectives, but a bit farther on the other side. Their average level of agreement was a 2.6, suggesting they slightly agreed with more orthodox sexual values around same-sex attraction.

In any case, as we look at sexual-minority students from several years ago and the ones in this study, we see that while both groups seem to be moderate in their perspectives, there was a significant change in students' attitudes over the five or so years between these two studies. Students with same-sex attraction at faith-based institutions seem to be becoming more accepting of less traditional attitudes, although, on average, they are still very moderate compared to what secular samples might believe about these issues.

Of course, we have been talking about the average sexual attitudes of these students. That doesn't give much insight into how they vary within our group. We know that some of them are less traditional, while others are more traditional in their understanding. Because our earlier work showed that this varied by their sexual attractions, we wanted to look at that more closely.

We measured attraction to the same sex and attraction to the opposite sex on two separate scales. Students were then divided into low and high same-sex attraction based on their ratings on the scale from one to ten.

"IT'S COMPLICATED!"

We are just beginning to identify the many layers of complexity for our students. This is a theme we will come back to time and again throughout this book. It's an important one to understand. Our students are not going to speak with one voice. There are many individual differences in their experiences, their understanding of their faith, and their understanding of their sexuality. What you will read about is how they are navigating their sexual identity and their faith as a Christian. We also know that they will be navigating this terrain for many years to come. What makes it so complex? They are at an age when they are figuring out what they believe about how they were raised and what they were taught to believe. This includes beliefs about God and sexuality and how their faith and sexuality are to be related to each other. They are navigating this terrain toward the end of a stage of development that is concerned with identity formation ("Who am I?") that will lead to a stage of development concerned with intimacy ("How will my needs for intimacy be met?"). They are sorting this out in the context of a community of faith with its own position on these highly charged topics. They are wrestling with this in a larger societal context in which LGB+ discussions have become more central (think lightning rod) and in which norms regarding sexuality are changing.

So we might ask the question, is there a theory that explains how and why "it's complicated"? It's a difficult question to answer. There are so many ways in which the individual differences among our students, as well as the unique stage of life and context in which they navigate these concerns, make it difficult to land on one coherent theory for explaining the complexity. The sheer breadth of attitudes, beliefs, and experiences, all still under construction, mitigate against one overarching theory or narrative that will encapsulate every student that we encountered, even when we are looking at one setting—private liberal arts Christian colleges and universities. The nature of the interaction of sexuality and faith in the context of Christian community requires almost an idiographic approach. We will likely need to acknowledge from chapter to chapter that as much as we have come to know about these students, they are even more diverse and multifaceted. They frankly don't agree with each other on every topic. The bottom line is that we have to admit that these issues are not simple, because these students are unique persons navigating complicated circumstances. The complexities should lead us away from easy answers ("It's right versus wrong, so just do this . . .") and toward more nuanced reflection on sexuality, human development, and flourishing.

We then looked at the relationship between strength of attractions and attitudes and values. What we found was that students' level of same-sex attraction was much more connected to their attitudes than was their level of opposite-sex attraction, which was only related to responses on a couple of items (see fig. 2.1). Put simply, students who have more same-sex attraction were less traditional, both in terms of understanding causation and moral acceptability. That is, students with greater same-sex attraction more strongly believed that sexual attractions were biologically determined, and they felt more comfortable with various forms of same-sex sexual behavior. But, remember, even these students only showed moderate acceptance, with ratings between "slightly agree" and "agree." (See table A2.2 in the appendix to this chapter.)

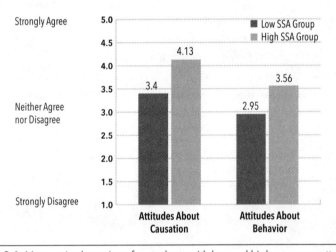

Figure 2.1. Mean attitudes ratings for students with low and high same-sex attraction

Students with low same-sex attraction were also about at this middle point of the responses when asked about the causes and biological nature of same-sex attraction. But when asked about the moral acceptability of same-sex sexual behaviors, these students clearly showed a bit more disagreement. Many of them were not okay with these behaviors. While this may not influence how they identify in terms of their own sexuality, it may shape how they choose to live out their sexuality.[2]

---

[2]In contrast, students' levels of opposite-sex attraction were largely unrelated to their attitudes about same-sex sexual attraction and behavior. See table A2.3 in the appendix.

If the degree of same-sex attraction is related to these differences in attitudes, how would the sexual minorities in our sample compare to a heterosexual peer group at Christian colleges? We looked back at the data of another study, our 2010 study, which was a large study of mostly heterosexual students at Christian colleges (Lastoria, Bish, & Symons, 2011), to explore this very question, and we recalculated data from that previous study of Christian college students and compared attitudes of those *who experienced* same-sex attraction to those who *did not experience* same-sex attraction (omitting students who said "I don't know" to attitudinal items). This sample comprised students at nineteen Christian colleges across fourteen states. The majority answered "no" to the question "Have you ever experienced SSA?" and they were compared to those in the same study who had answered "yes," as well as to our current sample.[3] We found that heterosexual students were even more traditional in their attitudes about sexual behavior than our sexual-minority students—both back then and in comparison with our current sample of students. (See figs. 2.2 and 2.3; for greater details, see A2.4 in the appendix to this chapter.)

If we look at these figures closely, we'll notice that the means for the nine attitudinal items are quite different in the older study than they are in our

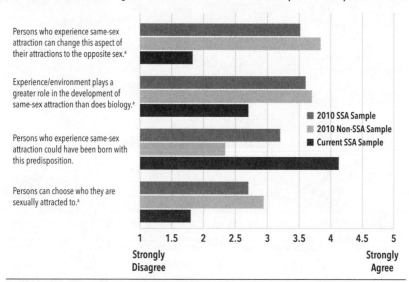

Figure 2.2. Attitudes about same-sex sexual attraction across samples
[a]These items indicate a more traditional Christian view that sexual attractions are mutable. The remaining item was reverse scored when computing average scores for attitudes about causation.

[3]The 2011 sample size is stable around 1,780 to 1,790 for the nine attitudinal items; however, the number of "I don't know" responses omitted varied by item and was in some cases rather high (250 to 300).

current one. We considered two factors to account for these differences. Given cultural shifts toward more permissive sexual mores in the past several years, it appears that a movement toward less traditional attitudes is occurring, especially in the younger population. Perhaps you recall the book *UnChristian* (Kinnaman, Lyons, & Barna, 2007). In that work, the authors reported the attitudes of "Mosaics, Busters, Boomers, and Elders," representing population cohorts from younger to older. They asked "churchgoers" ("regular participants" in a Christian church) whether a "homosexual lifestyle" was perceived to be a major problem facing America. In response, 29% of the Mosaic and Buster (ages 18-41) churchgoers responded in the affirmative, compared to 46% of the Boomers (ages 42-60) and 58% of the Elders (ages 61+; Kinnaman et al., 2007, p. 102).

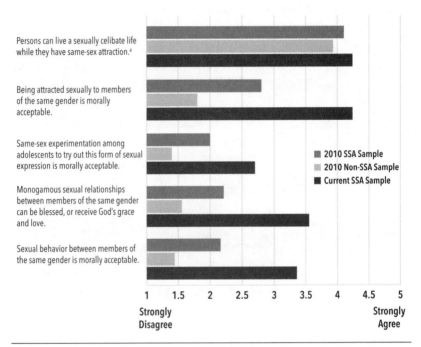

Figure 2.3. Attitudes about same-sex sexual behavior across samples

ªThis item indicates a more traditional Christian view regarding same-sex sexual behavior. It was reverse scored in computing average scores for attitudes about the morality of same-sex sexual behavior.

This shift in attitudes is also representative of the inherent tension present in young Christian adults attempting to reconcile the integrity and diversity lenses that were mentioned earlier—feeling loyal to friends who come out as gay while attempting to remain loyal theologically. David Kinnaman relates his experience with Katie, a young journalist and Christian responding to this dilemma:

"You're telling my story," Katie said. "My best friend for the last eight years just told me he is gay. I was shocked and really pretty upset about it. I know what the Bible says, but I also know what I feel about this guy. I have a hard time looking down on him for being gay. But I don't know what to think. I have not told my parents because they would just be too . . . I don't know . . . I have no idea of what they would do." (Kinnaman et al., 2007, p. 102)

Second, the current sample may represent students further along in developmental milestones and gay identity formation. Our earlier sample in the 2010 study was with the general Christian college population, and we asked anonymously whether participants had "ever experienced" same-sex attraction. Respondents may have had wide variation in same-sex sexual attraction, with some being more transient. Our current sample by contrast was limited to sexual minorities who agreed to allow us to reinterview them over time for this longitudinal study. Hence their data was confidential but not anonymous. We believe this smaller group represents young Christians more settled in identity and moving along a path to accepting themselves as gay with more affirming attitudes.

They are doing better than expected. About ten years ago, Ritch Savin-Williams (2006a), in his book *The New Gay Teenager* and in related publications, challenged the pervasive narrative that "homosexuality is inherently pathological" or that society's reaction to same-sex sexuality drives young gays and lesbians to attempt suicide. Rather, it may be that early sexual behavior among some of these sexual minorities is the more important contributor to psychological distress, just as it is among heterosexual young people (Savin-Williams & Diamond, 2004; Meier, 2007; Hallfors, Waller, Ford, Halpern, Brodish, & Iritani, 2004; Spriggs & Halpern, 2008; Madkour, Farhat, Halpern, Godeau, & Gabhainn, 2010).

We wanted to understand how our sample of students was doing psychologically. Did they fit the larger cultural narrative of struggling, particularly given that they are sexual minorities on faith-based campuses that hold to a more traditional sexual ethic? Or did they look more like the gay teenager in Savin-Williams's book, typically healthy and doing well? In addition to many other scales included in our survey, students completed a measure widely used by college campuses and college counseling centers to assess psychological functioning. Because it's used so widely, we do know what the broader college population looks like in their responses, and we can compare our sample of students to college students in general (but not specifically to heterosexual students on our campuses). We are able to see level of distress—low, moderate, and marked elevations.

As might be expected, our students, on average, are reporting three moderate-level psychological symptom clusters when compared to the wider college population (see tables A2.5 and A2.6 in the chapter appendix). Depression, generalized anxiety, and social anxiety are all moderately higher in our current sample than in a normative sample for a college mental health measure developed by researchers at Penn State University (Center for the Study of Collegiate Mental Health, 2010). In addition, our students say they are having more academic problems than typical college students, even though they have fewer alcohol problems than their college-aged peers.

This point—that they have fewer alcohol problems—stands in contrast to other research on sexual-minority college students (and college students in general, for that matter). In 2015 Dianne Kerr of Kent State University and her colleagues specifically looked at the substance-use patterns of lesbian and bisexual college women, who tended to use more alcohol, tobacco, marijuana, sedatives, hallucinogens, nonprescribed prescription drugs, and other illegal drugs than did heterosexual women. This substance use and abuse may occur in response to victimization, as undergraduates use substances to manage their emotions in the wake of being bullied and mistreated. Using substances to self-medicate after such victimization may even increase the likelihood that sexual minorities attempt or commit suicide, as Ethan Mereish (2014) of Boston College and his colleagues have proposed. In fact, the use of substances as a coping mechanism in managing discrimination may actually increase the likelihood of suicidal ideation and behaviors.

However, unlike as seen in the previous literature, the sexual minorities in our sample did not have more alcohol problems than the broader population of their same-aged peers. The most plausible explanation for this difference is their environment. Most of the Christian campuses that our students attend have strict prohibitions against alcohol use—either on campus or at all—suggesting that the campuses may offer a particular kind of support in deterring the development of alcohol issues for these students.

In addition to less alcohol use, our students also reported lower levels of hostility than other college-aged students from samples collected at state universities. This is contrary to what one might anticipate given the larger cultural narrative and studies such as the one done by Christopher Yuan, a Christian who experiences same-sex attraction and is an author, speaker, and instructor at Moody Bible Institute. Through his qualitative work with same-sex-attracted students at Christian colleges and universities, Yuan (2016) concluded that these students typically felt angry and frustrated—regardless of their degree of agreement with their schools' policies and beliefs. He described their feelings like this: "At times, the venting of anger and frustration turned into rants, which may be typical of this age group. Some respondents used all capital letters and others expressed their anger through expletives." If this anger is present in the students of our sample, it does not seem to appear as hostility. And our students, on average, did not respond with much agreement at all to statements such as "I have difficulty controlling my temper," "I get angry easily," and "I frequently get into arguments." By their own report, their anger and hostility were low.

Of course, not all is good. While they aren't drinking enough to have a lot of alcohol-related problems, nor do they report some of the other behavioral concerns, such as hostility and eating issues, the sexual-minority students in our sample still are reporting more anxiety and depression than what students from state universities report.

Does this mean that Christian sexual minorities are worse off than their same-age peers? Maybe, but probably not. The nonclinical sample referred to above may not be the best comparison group for us to use. To establish that normative sample, the Center for Collegiate Mental Health (CCMH, 2010) and the NASPA Student Affairs Research Consortium surveyed over twenty-one thousand students across forty-six colleges and universities, and then they removed all students who had ever sought treatment for psychological reasons. What this means is that we are comparing a sample of only healthy college students to our sample of healthy and struggling students. We therefore would expect to see some higher scores in our sample because we haven't excluded the strugglers.

To better understand how our students are doing, we also compared them to a sample of students seeking mental health services at their colleges and universities (CCMH, 2015; see table A2.6 in the appendix). In comparison to this group, our students, as a whole, were doing pretty well. We might even say really well. Even with everyone included in our sample, both strugglers and nonstrugglers, our students as a whole group showed no markedly elevated mean scores in any category of symptoms. While their symptoms of depression, generalized anxiety, and social anxiety were elevated, these were fairly typical elevations for students seeking counseling. Remember, though, these were average scores. While most of our students were doing well, there surely were some who were really struggling.

But how many are really struggling? We know, as we've heard from these students above, that many of them experience anxiety and depression. It's hard to tease out what degree of this distress is due to their sexual attractions, or due to the tension between their sexual attractions and their faith, or due to just being in this particular stage of life, or some combination of the above. Even so, by looking at their overall scores on our psychological measure, we can get a sense of the severity of their distress. In light of what they've told us in interviews, about half of them (50%) surprisingly fall in the "low distress" range, suggesting they have few if any psychological symptoms beyond what we would see in a generally healthy college population (see fig. 2.4). Another 41% experience some moderate distress, but not enough to cause alarm. Only 9%, somewhat less than one out of ten sexual-minority students, report psychological issues severe enough to put them in the clinically elevated range, indicating they were experiencing marked distress; they are the ones who are really struggling.

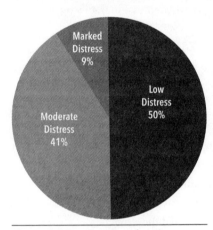

Figure 2.4. Percentages of students experiencing psychological distress, year 1

This is where they were during the first year of our study. For some of these students, things got worse over that next year. While a few students (6%) moved into the low-distress category for time 2, a higher percentage (10%) saw an increase in their symptoms that moved them from moderate distress to marked distress (see fig. 2.5). Why? The easiest explanation to offer might be to attribute this increase in distress to the campus climate, with its tension between faith and sexuality, particularly for sexual minorities. That explanation is likely true to some degree, but this "singular cause" statement overlooks the myriad of other changes occurring in these students' lives as they progress through college. They must engage increased difficulty in courses, increased financial pressures, impending graduation for some, the postcollege job hunt for others, important family transitions, relationship issues, and so on. Any adequate explanation needs to consider the multicausal issues that students are facing, not just their sexuality and faith. We as a research team are interested in the experiences of those students who reduce their distress in their college experiences as much as those who increase their distress. To cultivate a realistic and adequately complex view, we want to learn from students who seem to improve and those who seem to worsen in the campus climate of faith-based institutions.

Toward this goal, let's take a look at psychological health from the perspective of what's going well rather than what's not. In other words, well-being includes what strengths are present, not merely what symptoms are absent. Carol Ryff, a psychologist at the University of Wisconsin–Madison and the director of its Institute on Aging, has proposed that psychological well-being is an indication of how well we function and the degree to which we have qualities that promote health (Ryff & Singer, 1998). In this way, psy-

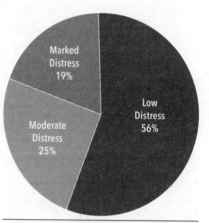

Figure 2.5. Percentages of students experiencing psychological distress, year 2

chological well-being is so much more than how happy we feel or how free from illness we are. Psychological well-being may be a buffer for sexual minorities as they encounter discrimination and marginalization by others.

Using Ryff's measure to capture three aspects of psychological well-being, our sexual-minority students completed three of its subscales—personal growth, purpose in life, and self-acceptance. For each item, students rated the degree to which it described them on a six-point Likert scale. Scores closer to six indicate higher levels of well-being. Our students rated these items, on average, as being more like them than not, with scores falling between a four and a five on a six-point scale.

Among our sexual-minority students, their level of personal growth was significantly higher than the other two characteristics, purpose in life and self-acceptance.[4] According to Ryff, the personal growth subscale represents continued growth in the individual, marked by openness to new experiences,

---

[4]Using a paired-samples t-test, sexual-minority students in our sample reported higher personal growth scores ($M = 4.94$, $SD = 0.67$) than scores of purpose in life ($M = 4.55$, $SD = 0.66$), t (159) = 6.29, $p < .001$, and scores of self-acceptance ($M = 4.10$, $SD = 1.00$), t (159) = 11.75, $p < 0.001$.

an engagement with life, a sense of having realized one's own potential, increasing self-knowledge and effectiveness, with improvement in the self and in one's behavior (Ryff & Keyes, 1995).

In contrast, participants' self-acceptance scores were lower than scores for the other two subtests.[5] The mean was still positive, even though it was lower than scores for the other two subscales. This suggests our students have a somewhat positive attitude toward the self, with some acceptance of their many aspects of the self and a comfortableness with their lives up to this point.

Our students' ratings of purpose in life fell in between those for the other two scales, in the moderately positive range. Ryff held that a positive purpose in life indicated having goals and a sense of directedness. People with positive ratings on this subscale typically have found meaning in life through their beliefs, whether more philosophical or more theological (Ryff & Keyes, 1995).

A general overview of our students' ratings would suggest a moderate level of psychological well-being, but we really wanted to know how they compared to other groups. Maybe our students experience moderate well-being, while everyone else is doing much better—or much worse. Finding these comparison groups was more difficult than expected. We are using two samples for comparison, but neither is a really good fit. The university sample was composed of 1,072 students between eighteen and forty-eight years old who were attending school in northern Spain, a sample collected by Freire and colleagues (2016). Geographically and age-wise, this sample was quite a bit different from our sample. Thus we also included one of Ryff's early validation samples that she used to first develop her measure. Its full sample of 1,108 adults were also older than our students. For comparison, we are using one of its subsamples—133 adults between twenty-five and twenty-nine years of age (see fig. 2.6).

Scores for purpose in life are essentially the same across all three groups. Our Christian sexual-minority students seem to have the same degree of meaning and direction in their lives as do these Spanish undergrads and these slightly older American young adults. Our students do report lower levels of self-acceptance than the Spanish students, but not in comparison to the validation sample.[6] Interestingly, our students indicated they had

---

[5]Using a paired-samples t-test, sexual-minority students in our sample reported lower self-acceptance scores ($M = 4.10$, $SD = 1.00$) than scores of purpose in life ($M = 4.55$, $SD = 0.66$), t (159) = 6.37, $p < 0.001$, and scores of personal growth ($M = 4.94$, $SD = 0.67$), t (159) = 11.75, $p < 0.001$.

[6]Using an independent-samples t-test, sexual-minority students in our sample ($M = 4.10$, $SD = 1.00$) reported lower levels of self-acceptance than did the Spanish undergraduates ($M = 4.64$, $SD = 0.85$), t (1230) = 7.30, $p < 0.001$, Cohen's $d = 0.58$ (large effect size).

much higher personal growth than did the slightly older young adults, but they looked very similar to their Spanish peers.[7] (See tables A2.7 and A2.8 in the chapter appendix.)

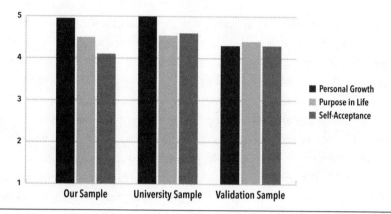

Figure 2.6. Average ratings for Ryff scales of psychological well-being (*n* = 160)

A few years ago, in 2014, Gregg Henriques, a psychologist at James Madison University, shared in a blog post at *Psychology Today* how he uses the Ryff scales of well-being with the undergrads at JMU. As a means of teaching his students about optimal psychological functioning, he describes each of the six components of well-being within Ryff's theory and then asks students to rate how well they are doing on each of these. Note that he does not use the actual measure developed by Ryff, and he also told students what was being measured before they assessed themselves, which often allows for some self-protective bias in responding (Ransom, Kast, & Shelly, 2015). Across over five hundred students, average scores for each component of psychological well-being varied between 5 and 5.5 on a six-point scale. His sample of students, like ours, showed moderate to high levels of well-being, but his students reported slightly higher than what we saw in our students, who had average scores between four and five. However, the differences in assessment procedure, along with any tendency toward self-enhancement or protection, could account for this difference in scores, suggesting the scores are probably more similar than different.

Even so, some of our sexual-minority students are truly struggling. Researchers from the University of Michigan posited that the difficulties experienced by their

---

[7]Using an independent-samples *t*-test, sexual-minority students in our sample ($M = 4.94$, $SD = 0.67$) reported higher levels of personal growth than did the slightly older young-adult sample ($M = 4.34$, $SD = 1.41$), $t (291) = 4.62$, $p < 0.001$, Cohen's $d = 0.54$ (large effect size).

sexual minority sample are largely due to heterosexism, or beliefs and corresponding behaviors that suggest heterosexuality is the only normal form of sexuality (Woodford, Kulick, Sinco, & Hong, 2014). This is not a simple relationship, though; self-acceptance mediates this relationship. The more self-acceptance students have, the less they will be bothered by the heterosexism they encounter. In our sample, the fifty-one students with a negative self-acceptance had much higher psychological distress than the 109 students who held a positive view of the self, even if this was only slightly positive.[8]

Overall, our Christian sexual-minority students on average look pretty healthy psychologically. Their symptoms are largely minimal, looking very similar to their straight peers even though they have some symptoms of depression and anxiety. Not only that, but our Christian sexual-minority students have similar levels of key psychological strengths—a sense of personal growth and meaning in life—as do their peers. They may struggle some with self-acceptance relative to their peers, but they typically are still reporting a positive degree of being comfortable with themselves.

Interviewees look like their peers. As we mentioned in chapter one, we also interviewed a subset of students from among those who completed the online survey, and we will hear from them throughout the book. The option of being interviewed was made available to all participants each time they completed the survey. We draw on this subset of students to illustrate key findings and to help put numbers and themes into perspective by drawing on their personal experiences. (Names have been created to protect the identity of interviewees.)

It's important to ask whether those students who agreed to be interviewed are different from their peers from the sample in any way. Other than being a little bit older (i.e., more likely to be upperclassmen), the answer is simply no, they were not different in any significant way. The interviewed students looked like the larger sample in key characteristics. They were just as religious and as spiritual; they were just as likely to identify as a sexual minority; they were just as moderate in their attitudes about same-sex sexuality; they were doing just as well psychologically; they were not different to any significant degree. Because of these similarities, we can be more confident that our interviewed students were good representatives of our larger survey sample.

---

[8]Using an independent-samples t-test, sexual-minority students with negative self-acceptance (n = 51; M = 1.74, SD = 0.59) reported significantly higher psychological distress than did students with more positive self-acceptance (n = 109, M = 1.08, SD = 0.57), t (158) = 6.75, p < 0.001, Cohen's d = 0.58 (large effect size).

WHO ARE THESE INSTITUTIONS?

We want to close this chapter by also introducing you to the institutions that students attend. All of the students in our sample attended one of the fourteen colleges and universities that agreed to participate in our research study. A general overview of these institutions will give us a better understanding of the context that these students are living in, a context that by its very nature pushes our students to consider their faith and their sexual identity simultaneously—and often in light of each other.

As mentioned in chapter one, the chief student affairs officers of our fourteen participating schools are all members of the Association for Christians in Student Development (ACSD). The mission of ACSD is to equip and challenge members to infuse their Christian faith into student development practice and scholarship. To belong to the ACSD, individual members must agree with its doctrinal statement, which really is a statement of orthodox Christian faith. Its tenets fall in line with the core doctrinal beliefs in most Christian denominations and organizations (ACSD, 2015). Here they are:

1. We believe there is one God, eternally existing in three persons: Father, Son, and Holy Spirit.

2. We believe the Bible to be inspired, the only infallible, authoritative Word of God.

3. We believe in the deity of our Lord Jesus Christ, in His virgin birth, in His sinless life, in His miracles, in His vicarious death and atonement through His shed blood, in His bodily resurrection and ascension to the right hand of the Father, and in His personal, visible return in power and glory.

4. We believe man and woman created in the image of God, were tempted by Satan and fell, and that, because of the exceeding sinfulness of human nature, regeneration by the Holy Spirit is absolutely necessary for salvation.

5. We believe in the present ministry of the Holy Spirit by whose indwelling the Christian is enabled to live a godly life, and by whom the church is empowered to carry out Christ's great commission.

6. We believe in the bodily resurrection of both the saved and the lost; those who are saved unto the resurrection of life, and those who are lost unto the resurrection of damnation.

Again, these tenets are broad and in keeping with historic Christian doctrines related to the nature of a trinitarian God, the Scriptures as the revealed Word of God, the Lordship of Christ, the nature of humankind as made in the image of God, the nature of salvation through Jesus Christ alone (predicated on Jesus' birth, death, and resurrection), and the work of the Holy Spirit in the lives of believers.

The importance of faith in identity formation was a salient theme in Donna Freitas's work *Sex and the Soul* (2008). Freitas interviewed students on college campuses across the country and sampled from three types of campus environments, which she labeled evangelical, Catholic, and spiritual. As the study progressed, Freitas eventually collapsed the latter two categories into one, the spiritual, to be contrasted to the evangelical campuses. The spiritual campuses were characterized by a clear boundary separating religion from discussions in the public square, a general distrust of institutional religion, and an unsupervised approach to making sense of the relationship with the divine or forming a purpose in life (pp. 40-41). Evangelical campuses were marked by the creation of shared communities of faith where mentoring relationships and integrative conversations were the norm. Freitas comments,

> Most students at evangelical schools go to college in part to learn how to live a good Christian life in the presence of not only of peers but also of mentors who can serve as role models for integrating the life of faith, the life of the mind, and the real world. Evangelicals are rightly renowned for integrating religion and culture ... but evangelicals are also adept at integrating religion and learning, values and education. Overall at the spiritual colleges I visited, no one seemed to have any idea how to integrate ultimate concerns with the proximate concerns of education. (p. 68)

There are no real surprises when you read these broad tenets of Christian faith. There are not real surprises, either, when you consider that teachings on sexuality and sexual behavior are in keeping with a traditional biblical sexual ethic. Such an ethic references Scripture, creational intent, and proscriptions about specific behaviors considered sinful. Such an ethic locates acceptable genital sexual activity as between a husband and wife in a covenantal view of marriage. As such, behaviors that occur outside that context are considered morally impermissible. So this is the context in which our students are navigating both their faith as Christians and their same-sex sexuality.

We mentioned in chapter one that evangelical institutions have been referred to as nonaffirming by those who approach the topic through a diversity lens (Wolff et al., 2016). While we understand this point of reference, insofar as we wish to understand these institutions from the institution's perspective (or reference point), it may be helpful to recognize the different lenses that may be part of the discussion, as these lenses color how we see data, the institutions, the students who attend, and so on. These institutions reflect doctrinal positions that are in keeping with Christian theological positions in the area of ethics that have been held by the vast majority of Christians historically and even today if we consider global Christianity (extending the discussion beyond the US). In any case, these Christian institutions function from an integrity, and sometimes a disability, lens when it comes to sexuality (integrity of sexual differences) and the impact of the fall on sexuality and sexual expression (disability).

We have a better sense of who the students are and of the Christian setting in which they live and study. We will look next at their experience of same-sex sexuality. A common way to do this is to consider how a person's sexual identity develops over time. That is, what are the milestone events in the formation of a gay or lesbian identity? Are the milestones events any different for Christians? Are they different for heterosexual students? Are there points of tension for the students in this sample? We will look at these questions in the next chapter.

CHAPTER 2 TAKEAWAYS

1. Sexual minorities at faith-based educational institutions are their own unique subpopulation, different in many ways from both their Christian university peers and their peers in the broader LGB+ community.

2. While many of these students do not identify publicly as sexual minorities, the large majority understand themselves to be such privately.

3. These sexual-minority students are quite religious and spiritual, and most are attempting to hold their faith and their sexual identity together in meaningful and helpful ways.

4. Mental health among these sexual minorities tends to be better than might be expected but not as good as might be hoped.

5. While these students tend to hold more biologically based beliefs about the causation and nature of same-sex attraction, their attitudes about

the moral acceptability of same-sex sexual behavior tend to be more moderate, not rejecting of the behavior but not accepting of it, either.

6. Their faith-based institutions tend to hold to a more orthodox Christian view of sexuality, which largely counters the view of sexuality found in the broader culture. This creates a unique context, with both strengths and weaknesses, for sexual-minority students to mutually engage faith and sexual-identity development.

7. There is a significant amount of diversity even within this subpopulation of Christian sexual minorities. They vary in their levels of attraction, their perceptions of their campuses, their attitudes regarding same-sex sexuality, their degree of religiosity and spirituality, their mental health, their shared sexual identities, and the lenses they use to understand their attractions, as well as in other areas.

▼

REFERENCES

Arnett, J. J. (2000). Emerging adulthood: A theory of development from the late teens through the twenties. *American Psychologist, 55*(5), 469-80. http://dx.doi.org/10.1037/0003-066X.55.5.469

Association for Christians in Student Development. (2015). *Constitution of the ACSD.* Retrieved from www.acsd.org/discover/mission-statement/purpose/

Center for Collegiate Mental Health [CCMH]. (2015a). 2014 annual report. University Park, PA: Author.

Center for Collegiate Mental Health [CCMH]. (2015b). CCAPS user manual. University Park, PA: Author.

Center for Collegiate Mental Health [CCMH]. (2016). CCAPS 2015 user manual. University Park, PA: Author.

Center for the Study of Collegiate Mental Health. (2010, March). 2010 annual report (Publication no. STA 11-000). Retrieved from http://ccmh.psu.edu/wp-content/uploads/sites/3058/2014/07/2010_CCMH_Report.pdf

Dean, J. B., Stratton, S. P., Yarhouse, M. A., & Lastoria, M. (2011). Same sex attraction. In M. Lastoria (Ed.), *ACSD Research Series: Sexuality, religiosity, behaviors, attitudes: A look at religiosity, sexual attitudes, and sexual behavior of Christian college students* (pp. 56-70). Houghton, NY: Association for Christians in Student Development.

Decco, E. (2014). Changing attitudes toward homosexuality in the United States from 1977 to 2012. *All Theses and Dissertations.* Paper 4091. Retrieved from http://scholarsarchive.byu.edu/cgi/viewcontent.cgi?article=5090&context=etd

Diamond, L. M. (2007). *Natural fluidity.* Cambridge, MA: Harvard University Press.

Freire, C., María Del Mar Ferradás, M., Valle, A., Núñez, J. C., & Vallejo, G. (2016). Profiles of psychological well-being and coping strategies among university students. *Frontiers in Psychology, 7,* 1554. http://dx.doi.org/10.3389/fpsyg.2016.01554

Freitas, D. (2008). *Sex and the soul: Juggling sexuality, spirituality, romance, and religion on America's college campuses.* Oxford: Oxford University Press.

Grzanka, P. R., Zeiders, K. H., & Miles, J. R. (2015). Beyond "born this way"? Reconsidering sexual orientation beliefs and attitudes. *Journal of Counseling Psychology, 63*(1), 67-75. http://dx.doi.org/10.1037/cou0000124

Hallfors, D. D., Waller, M. W., Ford, C. A., Halpern, C. T., Brodish, P. H., & Iritani, B. (2004). Adolescent depression and suicide risk: Association with sex and drug behavior. *American Journal of Preventive Medicine, 27*(3), 224-31. http://dx.doi.org/10.1016/j.amepre.2004.06.001

Haslam, N., & Levy, S. R. (2006). Essentialist beliefs about homosexuality: Structure and implications for prejudice. *Personality and Social Psychology Bulletin, 32,* 471-85. http://dx.doi.org/10.1177/0146167205276516

Henriques, G. (2014, May 15). Six domains of psychological well-being. *Psychology Today* [Blog]. Retrieved from www.psychologytoday.com/blog/theory-knowledge/201405/six-domains-psychological-well-being

Hinrichs, D. W., & Rosenberg, P. J. (2002). Attitudes toward gay, lesbian, and bisexual persons among heterosexual liberal arts college students. *Journal of Homosexuality, 43*(1), 61-84.

Hubbard, K., & de Visser, R. O. (2014). Not just bi the bi: The relationship between essentialist beliefs and attitudes about bisexuality. *Psychology and Sexuality, 6*(3), 258-74. http://dx.doi.org/10.1080/19419899.2014.987682

Keleher, A., & Smith, E. R. A. N. (2012). Growing support for gay and lesbian equality since 1990. *Journal of Homosexuality, 58*(9), 1307-26.

Kerr, D., Ding, K., Burke, A., & Ott-Walter, K. (2015). An alcohol, tobacco, and other drug use comparison of lesbian, bisexual, and heterosexual undergraduate women. *Substance Use & Misuse, 50,* 340-49. http://dx.doi.org/10.3109/10826084.2014.980954

Kinnaman, D., Lyons, G., & Barna, G. (2007). *unChristian: What a new generation really thinks about Christianity . . . and why it matters.* Grand Rapids, MI: Baker Books.

Lastoria, M. D., Bish, G. T., & Symons, C. S. (2011). Sexual behaviors. In M. Lastoria (Ed.), *ACSD research series: Sexuality, religiosity, behaviors, attitudes: A look at religiosity, sexual attitudes, and sexual behavior of Christian college students* (pp. 30-35). Houghton, NY: Association for Christians in Student Development.

Lefkowitz, E. S., Gillen, M. M., Shearer, C. L., & Boone, T. L. (2004). Religiosity, sexual behaviors, and sexual attitudes during emerging adulthood. *The Journal of Sex Research, 41*(2), 150-59. http://dx.doi.org/10.1080/00224490409552223

Madkour, A. S., Farhat, T., Halpern, C. T., Godeau, E., & Gabhainn, S. N. (2010). Early adolescent sexual initiation and physical/psychological symptoms: A comparative analysis of five nations. *Journal of Youth and Adolescence, 39*(10), 1211-25. http://doi.org/10.1007/s10964-010-9521-x

Masci, D. (Interviewer), & Hout, M. (Interviewee). (2016, January 8). *Q&A: Why millennials are less religious than older Americans* [Interview transcript]. Retrieved from www.pewresearch.org/fact-tank/2016/01/08/qa-why-millennials-are-less-religious-than-older-americans/

Meier, A. M. (2007). Adolescent first sex and subsequent mental health. *American Journal of Sociology, 112*(6), 1811-47.

Mereish, E. H., O'Cleirighb, C., & Bradford, J. (2014). Interrelationships between LGBT-based victimization, suicide, and substance use problems in a diverse sample of sexual and gender minorities. *Psychology, Health & Medicine, 19*(1), 1-13. http://dx.doi.org/10.1080/13548506.2013.780129

Pew Research Center. (2014). *Religious Landscape Study.* Retrieved from www.pewforum.org/religious-landscape-study/

Ransom, M. R., Kast, C., & Shelly, R. K. (2015). Self-enhancement, self-protection and ingroup bias. *Current Research in Social Psychology* [Electronic journal]. Retrieved from https://uiowa.edu/crisp/sites/uiowa.edu.crisp/files/crisp_23_7.pdf

Ritter, K. Y., & Terndrup, A. I. (2002). *Handbook of affirmative psychotherapy with lesbians and gay men.* New York: Guilford.

Rostosky, S. S., Danner, F., & Riggle, E. D. B. (2008). Religiosity and alcohol use in sexual minorities and heterosexual youth and young adults. *Journal of Youth and Adolescence, 37,* 552-63.

Ryff, C. D., & Keyes, C. L. M. (1995). The structure of psychological well-being revisited. *Journal of Personality and Social Psychology, 69,* 719-27.

Ryff, C. D., & Singer, B. (1998). The contours of positive human health. *Psychological Inquiry, 9,* 1-28.

Savin-Williams, R. C. (2006a). *The new gay teenager.* Cambridge, MA: Harvard University Press.

Savin-Williams, R. C. (2006b). Who's gay? Does it matter? *Current Directions in Psychological Science, 15*(1), 40-44.

Savin-Williams, R. C., & Diamond, L. M. (2004). Sex. In R. M. Lerner & L. Steinberg (Eds.), *Handbook of adolescent psychology* (2nd ed., pp. 189-231). New York: John Wiley & Sons.

Savin-Williams, R. C., & Ream, G. L. (2003). Suicide attempts among sexual-minority male youth. *Journal of Clinical Child and Adolescent Psychology, 32,* 509-22.

Spriggs, A. L., & Halpern, C. T. (2008). Sexual debut timing and depressive symptoms in emerging adulthood. *Journal of Youth and Adolescence, 37*(9), 1085-96.

Stratton, S. P., Dean, J. B., Yarhouse, M. A., & Lastoria, M. (2013). Sexual minorities in faith-based education: A national survey of attitudes, milestones, identity, and religiosity. *Journal of Psychology and Theology, 41*(1), 3-23.

Wagnera, G. J., Aunona, F. M., Kaplan, R. L., Karama, R., Khouric, D., Tohmec, J., & Mokhbatc, J. (2013). Sexual stigma, psychological well-being and social engagement among men who have sex with men in Beirut, Lebanon. *Culture, Health & Sexuality, 15*(5), 570-82. http://dx.doi.org/10.1080/13691058.2013.775345

Wentz, J. M., & Wessel, R. D. (2013, May 5). Experiences of gay and lesbian students attending faith- based colleges: Considerations for improving practice. *ACSD Ideas.* Retrieved from www.acsd.org/article/experiences-of-gay-and-lesbian-students -attending-faith-based-colleges-considerations-for-improving-practice/

Wolff, J. R., Himes, H. L., Soares, S. D., & Kwon, E. M. (2016). Sexual minority students in non-affirming religious higher education: Mental health, outness, and identity. *Psychology of Sexual Orientation and Gender Diversity, 3*(2), 201-12.

Woodford, M. R., Kulick, A., Sinco, B. R., & Hong, J. S. (2014). Contemporary heterosexism on campus and psychological distress among LGBQ students: The mediating role of self-acceptance. *American Journal of Orthopsychiatry, 84*(5), 519-29. http://dx.doi.org/10.1037/ort0000015

Yarhouse, M. A. (2015). *Understanding gender dysphoria: Navigating transgender issues in a changing culture.* Downers Grove, IL: IVP Academic.

Yarhouse, M. A., Stratton, S. P., Dean, J. B., & Brooke, H. L. (2009). Listening to sexual minorities on Christian college campuses. *Journal of Psychology and Theology, 37*(2), 96-113.

Yuan, C. (2016). *Giving a voice to the voiceless: A qualitative study of reducing marginalization of lesbian, gay, bisexual, and same-sex attracted students at Christian colleges and universities.* Eugene, OR: Wipf & Stock.

APPENDIX

Table A2.1. Mean attitudes and standard deviations about same-sex sexuality (*n* = 160)

	M (SD)
Attitudes About Causation	
Persons can choose who they are sexually attracted to.	1.82 (1.06)
Persons who experience same-sex attraction could have been born with this predisposition.	4.11 (1.16)
Experience/environment plays a greater role in the development of same-sex attraction than does biology.	2.75 (1.14)
Persons who experience same-sex attraction can change this aspect of their attractions to the opposite sex.	1.87 (1.07)

Attitudes About Behavior	
Being attracted sexually to members of the same gender is morally acceptable.	4.16 (1.05)
Sexual behavior between members of the same gender is morally acceptable.	3.30 (1.50)
Monogamous sexual relationships between members of the same gender can be blessed, or receive God's grace and love.	3.53 (1.49)
Same-sex experimentation among adolescents to try out this form of sexual expression is morally acceptable.	2.68 (1.32)
Persons can live a sexually celibate life while they have same-sex attraction.	4.23 (0.99)

Table A2.2. Mean attitudes and standard deviations about same-sex sexuality by level of same-sex attraction (SSA) (*n* = 160)

Attitudes by SSA Groups	Low SSA (*n* = 34) *M (SD)*	High SSA (*n* = 126) *M (SD)*	*t* (df)
Attitudes About Causation			
Persons can choose who they are sexually attracted to.	2.46 (1.23)	1.65 (0.94)	4.18 (158)***
Persons who experience same-sex attraction could have been born with this predisposition.	3.66 (1.34)	4.23 (1.08)	-2.59 (158)*
Experience/environment plays a greater role in the development of same-sex attraction than does biology.	3.24 (1.28)	2.61 (1.06)	2.89 (157)**
Persons who experience same-sex attraction can change this aspect of their attractions to the opposite sex.	2.63 (1.22)	1.66 (0.92)	5.07 (157)***
Attitudes About Behavior			
Sexual behavior between members of the same gender is morally acceptable.	2.51 (1.53)	3.52 (1.41)	-3.64 (157)***
Being attracted sexually to members of the same gender is morally acceptable.	3.69 (1.17)	4.28 (0.98)	-2.99 (158)**
Monogamous sexual relationships between members of the same gender can be blessed, or receive God's grace and love.	2.77 (1.56)	3.72 (1.41)	-3.36 (157)***
Same-sex experimentation among adolescents to try out this form of sexual expression is morally acceptable.	2.13 (1.09)	2.83 (1.34)	-2.79 (158)**
Persons can live a sexually celibate life while they have same-sex attraction.	4.39 (0.79)	4.19 (1.03)	1.07 (155)

* $p \leq 0.05$
** $p \leq 0.01$
*** $p \leq 0.001$

Table A2.3. Average attitudes about same-sex sexuality by level of opposite-sex sexual attraction (n = 160)

Attitudes by OSA Groups	Low OSA (n = 108) M (SD)	High OSA (n = 52) M (SD)	t (df)
Attitudes About Same-Sex Attraction			
Persons can choose who they are sexually attracted to.	1.72 (1.21)	2.44 (1.45)	-3.30 (158)***
Persons who experience same-sex attraction could have been born with this predisposition.	5.09 (1.31)	4.65 (1.74)	1.78 (158)
Experience/environment plays a greater role in the development of same-sex attraction than does biology.	3.07 (1.48)	3.29 (1.60)	-0.87 (157)
Persons who experience same-sex attraction can change this aspect of their attractions to the opposite sex.	1.79 (1.20)	2.58 (1.51)	-3.58 (157)***
Attitudes About Same-Sex Sexual Behavior			
Being attracted sexually to members of the same gender is morally acceptable.	5.06 (1.35)	4.87 (1.30)	0.84 (158)
Sexual behavior between members of the same gender is morally acceptable.	3.97 (1.90)	3.79 (1.95)	0.57 (157)
Monogamous sexual relationships between members of the same gender can be blessed, or receive God's grace and love.	4.24 (1.85)	4.04 (2.03)	0.63 (157)
Same-sex experimentation among adolescents to try out this form of sexual expression is morally acceptable.	3.11 (1.76)	3.06 (1.67)	0.18 (158)
Persons can live a sexually celibate life while they have same-sex attraction.	5.05 (1.35)	5.23 (0.96)	-0.87 (155)
Religiosity and Spirituality			
How religious do you consider yourself to be?	6.74 (2.18)	6.73 (2.34)	0.02 (157)
How spiritual do you consider yourself to be?	8.50 (2.00)	8.38 (1.80)	0.35 (158)

* $p \le 0.05$
** $p \le 0.01$
*** $p \le 0.001$

Table A2.4. Mean attitudes and standard deviations about same-sex sexuality across samples

	Current Sample M (SD)	2011 Heterosexual Sample M(SD)	2011 SSA Sample M(SD)
Attitudes About Causation			
Persons can choose who they are sexually attracted to.	1.82 (1.06)	2.97 (1.30) $n = 1607$	2.67 (1.38) $n = 228$
Persons who experience same-sex attraction could have been born with this predisposition.	4.11 (1.16)	2.33 (1.33) $n = 1534$	3.13 (1.43) $n = 212$
Experience/environment plays a greater role in the development of same-sex attraction than does biology.	2.75 (1.14)	3.63 (1.18) $n = 1479$	3.54 (1.21) $n = 200$
Persons who experience same-sex attraction can change this aspect of their attractions to the opposite sex.	1.87 (1.07)	3.86 (1.10) $n = 1534$	3.51 (1.30) $n = 221$
Attitudes About Behavior			
Being attracted sexually to members of the same gender is morally acceptable.	4.16 (1.05)	1.83 (1.11) $n = 1716$	2.85 (1.42) $n = 227$
Sexual behavior between members of the same gender is morally acceptable.	3.30 (1.50)	1.46 (0.90) $n = 1739$	2.12 (1.36) $n = 228$
Monogamous sexual relationships between members of the same gender can be blessed, or receive God's grace and love.	3.53 (1.49)	1.55 (0.95) $n = 1656$	2.21 (1.44) $n = 220$
Same-sex experimentation among adolescents to try out this form of sexual expression is morally acceptable.	2.68 (1.32)	1.42 (0.77) $n = 1737$	1.99 (1.13) $n = 229$
Persons can live a sexually celibate life while they have same-sex attraction.	4.23 (0.99)	3.94 (1.09) $n = 1534$	4.09 (1.03) $n = 229$

Table A2.5. Mean distress index scores and standard deviations for psychological symptoms across two samples—SSA sample and nonclinical sample

Psychological Symptoms	Our Sample ($n = 160$) M (SD)	Nonclinical Sample ($n = 14869$) M (SD)	t (df)	p	Cohen's d
Depression	1.33 (1.02)	0.82 (0.74)	8.63	0.059	0.57**
Generalized Anxiety	1.56 (1.03)	1.00 (0.74)	9.47	<0.001	0.62**
Social Anxiety	1.82 (0.98)	1.52 (0.84)	4.48	<0.001	0.33*
Academic Distress	1.37 (1.08)	1.23 (0.84)	2.09	0.037	0.15*
Eating Concerns	0.95 (1.17)	0.99 (0.79)	2.22	0.060	0.04
Hostility	0.72 (0.86)	0.66 (0.69)	1.09	0.280	0.08
Alcohol Use	0.51 (0.94)	0.70 (0.83)	2.88	0.004	0.21*

* Small effect size
** Moderate effect size

Table A2.6. Mean distress index scores and standard deviations for psychological symptoms (*n* = 160)

Psychological Symptoms	M (SD)	Distress Level
Depression	1.33 (1.02)	Moderate Distress (Scores from 1.00 to 1.75)
Generalized Anxiety	1.56 (1.03)	Moderate Distress (Scores from 1.30 to 2.10)
Social Anxiety	1.82 (0.98)	Moderate Distress (Scores from 1.65 to 2.50)
Academic Distress	1.37 (1.08)	Low Distress (Scores up to 1.45)
Eating Concerns	0.95 (1.17)	Low Distress (Scores up to 1.07)
Hostility	0.72 (0.86)	Low Distress (Scores up to 0.74)
Alcohol Use	0.51 (0.94)	Low Distress (Scores up to 0.64)
Distress Index	1.29 (1.65)	Moderate Distress (Scores from 1.21 to 2.15)

Table A2.7. Mean psychological well-being scores and standard deviations across two samples–SSA sample and Spanish university sample

	Our Sample (*n* = 160) M (SD)	Spanish University Sample (*n* = 1072) M (SD)	t (df)	p	Cohen's d
Personal Growth	4.94 (0.67)	5.00 (0.70)	1.09 (1230)	0.276	
Purpose in Life	4.55 (0.66)	4.58 (0.80)	0.51 (1230)	0.610	
Self-Acceptance	4.10 (1.00)	4.64 (0.85)	7.30 (1230)	0.0001	0.58

Table A2.8. Mean psychological well-being scores and standard deviations across two samples–SSA sample and validation sample

	Our Sample (*n* = 160) M (SD)	Validation Sample (*n* = 133) M (SD)	t (df)	p	Cohen's d
Personal Growth	4.94 (0.67)	4.34 (1.41)	4.62 (291)	0.0001	0.54
Purpose in Life	4.55 (0.66)	4.51 (1.47)	0.31 (291)	0.76	
Self-Acceptance	4.10 (1.00)	4.34 (1.47)	1.66 (291)	0.10	

MILESTONES AND IDENTITY

I first realized that I was gay here at [school]. . . . It's like trying to figure out what does God think about this, how should I act, what's okay and what's not. I think I have struggled with it a few times, like "Why do I have to be gay?" That's something I say, but for the most part it has been a blessing for my relationship with him. It just pulls me closer to him, like "God, I need you and I don't know what I am doing; I don't know what the future holds. I am going to trust you and work through this with you."

—*Justin, twenty-two-year-old male junior, identifies as gay, time 1*

▼▲▼

SEXUAL IDENTITY IS COMMONLY thought of as the labels by which people think about themselves and/or share with others something about their sexual preferences. Common sexual-identity labels include gay, straight, and bi. In this chapter we begin with a brief sketch of the history of psychological models of sexual-identity formation—that is, how people come to make self-defining attributions, for example, "I am gay." We then turn to findings from our longitudinal study to identify important milestone events in the formation of sexual identity.

Sexual identity is, according to Althof (2000, p. 247), a "substructure of sexual functioning" that includes "gender identity, object choice and intention."[1] A person's *gender identity* is his or her sense of being either male or female. *Object choice* refers to "the multiple sources of one's personal attraction—who or what a person finds sexually arousing" (p. 248). We are discussing in this book same-gender object choice or both same- and opposite-sex object choice,

---

[1]Adapted from Yarhouse (2001).

as in the case of students who adopt a bisexual identity. *Intention* is "what one wishes to do with a sexual impulse" (p. 249). For many Christian sexual minorities, this includes whether one chooses to act on sexual impulses and in what ways doing so facilitates the experience of those impulses as central to one's core sense of self or identity.

One of the earliest and most widely recognized models of sexual-identity development that was applied to both male and female experience was Cass's (1979) six-stage model. According to Cass, gay and lesbian identity develops as follows: (1) *identity confusion* (questioning what one's identity is in light of experiences of same-sex attraction), (2) *identity comparison* (reaching the conclusion that one is different based on experiences of same-sex attraction), (3) *identity tolerance* (assuming that experiences of same-sex attraction mean that one is probably gay), (4) *identity acceptance* (identifying same-sex attraction as signaling that one is gay), (5) *identity pride* (taking pride in one's gay identity to the exclusion of what might be seen as good among heterosexuals), and (6) *identity synthesis* (reaching the conclusion that one's self-identification as "gay" is one part of who one is and achieving a kind of balance in that).

Other general models of sexual-identity development would follow and include one by Troiden (1979; 1989) and another by Coleman (1982). It has been common to see a developmental trajectory in which people would become aware of their same-sex sexuality and explore a possible sexual identity, often in relationships, and reach an endpoint of some kind of sexual-identity synthesis or achieved identity.

Models of sexual-identity development would then evolve by distinguishing gay male and lesbian experiences. Several models of gay male identity formation were proposed. McDonald (1982), for example, reported on 199 self-identifying gay men and identified psychological awareness of attractions, behaviors, and relationships, as well as self-defining attributions as one identified oneself as gay and ultimately adopted a positive gay identity.

Early models of lesbian identity development challenged the notion that there was a stable "gay" identity as reported by gay males. Some models recognized greater "fluidity of sexual orientation" and a "process of self-definition" (Reynolds & Hanjorgiris, 2000, p. 40). For example, Sophie (1986) noted sexual fluidity among female sexual minorities and concluded: "We are mistaken if we interpret the notion of stability to mean that individuals who have become lesbian cannot subsequently change" (p. 49). Chapman and Brannock (1987) noted early experiences among female sexual minorities of "feeling connected to other girls/women" that eventually led to "incongruence," the awareness that such a connection is in contrast to what heterosexual females around them experienced. According to the model, the women then questioned and explored their feelings and later identified as lesbian.

Other models of sexual-identity development were then proposed. These included models of bisexual-identity development. Some theorists have argued that bisexuality can be part of a stage in coming out as lesbian or gay; others argue that bisexuality as an identity occurs after coming out as either lesbian or gay (Fox, 1995). In any case, the developmental process includes first attractions, behavior, and relationships with the opposite sex, then the same sex (a little later), and then even later self-identification and disclosure of a bisexual identity (Fox, 1995).

Ethnicity and race as salient considerations were then considered in models of sexual-identity development. There has been discussion of a "dual development" of identification with racial and ethnic minority communities and sexual-minority communities (McCarn & Fassinger, 1996). The tensions that often exist for racial and sexual minorities are felt in choosing between a cultural community that rejects their sexual identity and a gay or lesbian community that may or may not be racially prejudiced (Chan, 1989).

We have also been a part of proposing ways in which religious identity and personal values may influence sexual-identity development (Yarhouse, 2001). From this perspective, it was noted that most models of sexual-identity development, even those accounting for gender, bisexuality, and ethnicity and race, still have as their main assumption a common developmental trajectory toward a singular outcome.

> The typical developmental sequence proceeds from a point of departure (first homosexual attractions) through a set of intermediate experiences (seeking out similar others, initiating same-gender sexual experiences and relationships, identifying oneself as gay or lesbian, and disclosing one's sexual orientation to others) to an endpoint (exclusively homosexual relationships and an integrated lesbian or gay identity). (Fox, 1995, p. 52)

There is what we might call a trajectory associated with the existing models. The trajectory is toward same-sex identity synthesis as LGB+. In other words, though there may be a few exceptions to the norm, the models hold that normal same-sex identity development moves the person toward an integrated LGB+ identity, which has come to mean celebrating one's identity as reflecting standing within a culture that is celebrated (to return to the lenses or frameworks introduced in chapter one).

Most of these models also held common assumptions that might be referred to as a strong form of essentialism (Yarhouse & Jones, 1997). Essentialists hold that sexual orientation is universal across cultures and time. Some essentialists also hold that orientation is a real thing or essence. A strong form of essentialism holds that same-sex attraction is a part of who one is as a person and that acting on those inclinations is a necessary part of self-identification and identity development and synthesis. Other forms of essentialism might agree that sexual orientation is a real thing or essence but may resist making a claim that people should or would need to act on their inclinations to actualize their sexual identity, and neither would they see acting on sexual impulses as requisite for identity formation.

Few models of sexual-minority identity development even consider the possibility of an alternative sexual identity to an integrated or synthesized LGB+ identity. The theoretical models are especially prone to this oversight (e.g., Cass, 1979). The empirical studies, such as that by Chapman and Brannock (1987), cannot overlook the empirical evidence that supports an alternative identity synthesis, but these other outcomes are essentially not well regarded. Reports of chastity or celibacy are often treated as denial or worse: "Women and men who *capitulate* avoid homosexual activity because they have internalized a stigmatizing view of homosexuality. The persistence of homosexual feelings in the absence of homosexual activity, however, may lead them to experience self-hatred and despair" (Troiden, 1989, p. 61).

We recognize that this raises an important question: Does having same-sex feelings but not acting on them lead to "self-hatred and despair"? We want to be careful in exploring various trajectories here, but we encourage those who are dismissive of alternative life trajectories from letting a potential bias overshadow the role of careful analysis of the question.

In a fascinating review of both sexual-identity and racial-identity literature, McCarn and Fassinger (1996) drew on models of racial identity development to clarify misconceptions in gay and lesbian identity development. They challenged linear models that presume all people pass through fixed stages in a predictable fashion. They noted that existing models view "alternative outcomes" as "developmental arrest" for the gay or lesbian person (p. 520). Presumably this would hold true for a range of alternative life trajectories, not just heterosexuality. Although the authors fail to develop the implications of what they proposed, they have paved the way for a more nuanced discussion of sexual-identity development that accounts for the experiences of those who make different decisions about sexual identity and behavior. Of those who may explore an alternative life trajectory, some may do so on personal and religious grounds.

Raising the question of the impact of religion and sexual-identity formation is complicated, since how one "holds religion" varies considerably. For some, religion is a cultural and social expression (one might say nominally religious) that is seen as secondary to a "core" sexual identity. These individuals are more likely to consider their experiences of same-sex attraction as something that defines them more centrally than a religion with which one is identified. They may identify as gay, lesbian, or bisexual Christians. Others identify the same way but do so not out of a nominally held religious belief. They are seriously committed and sincere in their Christian beliefs but have concluded through their more traditional theological and historical position of the church as opposed to same-sex unions and therefore are drawn to pursue the alternative outcomes to sexual identity mentioned earlier. These individuals will challenge the default position of integrating same-sex attraction automatically into a gay, lesbian, or bisexual identity or at least to celebrating a gay identity in keeping with a diversity lens. We will return to this theme from time to time in the book.

MILESTONE EVENTS

We have seen that early models of sexual-identity development (e.g., Cass, 1979) posited a linear approach to identity formation in which each sexual minority went through predictable stages toward a final synthesis, that is, as LGB+. Subsequent models did not challenge assumptions of linearity and final identity outcome, but they did begin to recognize differences among sexual minorities based on gender (e.g., Sophie, 1986), ethnicity (e.g., Chan, 1989), and religion (e.g., Yarhouse, 2001).

Although recent research has called into question several assumptions about linearity and fixed identity outcomes for sexual-minority females (e.g., Diamond, 2007) and males (e.g., Rosario, Schrimshaw, Hunter, & Braun, 2006), many today find it helpful to identify the key milestone events in sexual-identity formation. In other words, a shift has occurred away from theoretical models—none of which has really emerged as a complete or comprehensive model of sexual-identity development—toward more empirical study of identifiable milestone events.

Milestone events include first awareness of same-sex attraction, first same-sex behavior to orgasm, first ongoing same-sex relationship, and so on. Savin-Williams and Cohen (2004) reported great diversity among sexual minorities, but they stated, "Most homoerotic youth recall same-sex attractions, fantasies, and arousal several years—on average—before questioning the meaning of these feelings" (p. 540). For example, in their study of White, Black, Asian, and Latino male adolescents, Dube and Savin-Williams (1999) reported a range of awareness of same-sex attraction (eight to eleven years old), first same-sex behavior (twelve to fifteen years), labeling of oneself (fifteen to eighteen years), disclosure of identity to others (seventeen to nineteen years), and first same-sex relationship (eighteen to twenty years). The commitment to an identity label may be falling off among sexual-minority youth, however, as many youth prefer not to label themselves or may be open to a number of identity-label options over time (Diamond, 2007; Savin-Williams, 2005).

Similarly, Savin-Williams and Diamond (2000) reported common milestone events about gay young adults. These included a remarkable early awareness of same-sex attractions (between ages seven and nine, which the researchers noted is likely an artifact of the way they worded the question and not typical for recalling first awareness of attractions), first behavior to orgasm (between ages fourteen and seventeen), first labeling of oneself as gay or lesbian (at about ages sixteen to eighteen), and first disclosure of one's sexual identity as gay or lesbian to others (at about age seventeen or eighteen).

Milestones may be tied directly to sexual behavior and experiences, such as romantic kissing, fondling, and first same-sex relationship. Milestones can also include psychological processes involved in identity formation as a gay person, such as attributions and meaning making (that is, attributing experiences of attraction to a sense of identity). This is somewhat of an artificial distinction. Behavior is a reflection of both psychological experiences and processes, and behavior also reinforces ways of thinking about oneself and one's identity.

In their study comparing Christian sexual minorities who identified as gay with those who disidentified with a gay identity, which referred to choosing not to identify with the broader gay community or to adhering to a personal gay identity, Yarhouse and Tan (2004) reported that Christians who disidentified with a gay identity were less likely than those who currently identified as gay to attribute their same-sex attractions to a gay identity. Sorting out their sexual identity was complicated for both groups and not resolved until an average age of twenty-six for those who identified as gay and an average age of thirty-four for those who disidentified with a gay identity.

We saw something similar to this in our 2009 and 2013 studies of sexual minorities at Christian colleges and universities (Stratton, Dean, Yarhouse, & Lastoria, 2013; Yarhouse, Stratton, Dean, & Brooke, 2009). For example, in our first study, published in 2009, we reported that fewer than a third of sexual minorities (30%) attributed their attractions to a possible gay identity, and only 14% labeled themselves gay (Yarhouse et al., 2009).

In the 2013 study, published a few years later (Stratton et al., 2013), only 18% of sexual minorities attributed their attractions to a gay identity, and only 11% labeled themselves gay.

We are not taking a position for or against a gay identity or labeling oneself as gay, but we note a shift in the percentage of students who are adopting *gay* as a label, which may be a function of *gay* being the common vernacular for describing one's sexual orientation today. In other words, a generation ago, it was common for people to describe sexual orientations as homosexual or heterosexual (or bisexual). Today it is more common to use the words *gay* or *straight* (or *bi*). This change in what is the common vernacular may also be reflected in a higher percentage of sexual-minority students adopting *gay* as an identity and as an adjective (which we see in our most recent findings below).

We also want to consider whether the use of the word *gay* means something different for different students. For example, in Michelle Wolkomir's (2006) ethnographic study of gay Christians who embraced a gay identity and the persons and institutions that supported that identity compared to Christians who were participating in faith-based ministries to change or experience healing, she described two different trajectories and corresponding narratives for a sense of personhood and associated values. For gay Christians who were more affirming and walking a road that supported a gay identity and relationships, Wolkomir described a path of resolution that was characterized by valuing inclusive love. This required a hermeneutical strategy for meaning and community. In contrast, those Christians who disidentified with a gay identity and community used a different hermeneutical strategy that emphasized personal righteousness (Wolkomir). We don't see these as the only two options. Rather, we simply want to note that there is more than one option, opening the door to more nuance and more careful reflection when we walk alongside sexual minorities who are navigating sexual and religious identity.

IDENTITY LABELS AND IDENTITY DEVELOPMENT

We asked our participants about sexual-identity labels. Sexual-identity labels, such as lesbian, gay, bi, or queer, are increasingly common and often public ways of communicating identity and/or sexual preferences to others. In terms of percentages, 43% of sexual minorities in our study identified as lesbian or gay, 24% as bisexual, 15% as straight, 5% as questioning, 4% as queer, 5% as no label, 4% as "other," and 1% did not respond.

We later came at the question of labeling from another angle. That is, we asked students about various milestones in the formation of their sexual identity. Students were asked their age when they reached a series of sexual milestones (see table 3.1). We can see that not all students experienced all of the milestones. Some, of course, are behavioral and may represent a set of values that a student sees as precluding them from engaging in that behavior. Others may simply reflect lack of opportunity.

Table 3.1. Milestones in sexual-identity development

Milestone	Age at Same-Sex Sexual Milestones		
	n	%	*M (SD)*
Awareness of same-sex feelings	159	99.4	12.92 (3.91)
Initial attribution that I am same-sex attracted	158	98.7	13.08 (4.39)
Confusion about same-sex feelings	152	95.0	13.26 (3.54)
Been fondled (breasts or genitals) by someone (without orgasm)	97	60.6	16.18 (4.55)
Fondled (breasts or genitals) someone (without orgasm)	93	58.1	16.22 (4.37)
Intimately/romantically kissed by someone	94	58.8	16.79 (3.99)
First disclosure of same-sex attraction	130	81.3	17.20 (2.83)
Initial attribution that "I am gay/lesbian/bisexual"	135	84.4	17.34 (2.35)
Adopted the label of "gay" for myself privately	118	73.8	17.89 (2.40)
Sexual behavior (to orgasm)	68	42.5	18.09 (3.31)
First same-sex relationship	64	40.0	18.22 (2.68)
Adopted the label of "gay" for myself publicly	64	40.0	19.47 (1.89)

Our sample of Christian sexual minorities is similar in many ways to other sexual minorities on several milestones. For example, our sample became aware of their same-sex sexuality at about the time they went through puberty, which we would expect, and then recognized their feelings as sexual attractions. To many students (95%) it was confusing to experience same-sex attractions. We are not here suggesting that people experience same-sex sexual "confusion" or explaining this as a condition; rather, we are saying that finding oneself experiencing same-sex attractions can be confusing when so many of their peers report attraction to the opposite sex. Imagine being age thirteen, and all the other guys in the locker room are talking about the new girl who transferred to the school. They might go on about her looks, and if you do not experience attraction to the opposite sex, you can wonder what's going on and what the big deal is. It can be confusing. For example, Kevin, a twenty-two-year-old junior, shared:

> I remember as a first grader feeling very different, and I didn't know quite what it was. I felt different from other boys somehow. I had a much easier time around girls, and that's something that was confusing for me, even as a little child before I was attracted to anyone. I think I first realized I was attracted to same sex in sixth grade. I didn't really know what to do with it. I don't think the word, gay, popped into my mind until seventh grade.

Similarly, Mia, a freshman, shared:

> If I'm being honest, I didn't really know what [first experiences with same-sex attraction] meant. It's just kind of been a thing that I didn't really think about much. It didn't just all of a sudden start happening when I was older or anything. It's just kind of been a thing since I was little. And I didn't really know what it was, and I didn't really think it was a problem or anything because I didn't really know how to respond to any of it.

Other experiences could contribute to feelings of confusion. We asked about experiences with kissing and fondling behaviors. We do not have specifics here, but we know from past discussions with sexual minorities that some of this can be exploratory play with a same-sex peer, while other experiences can be unwanted experiences with an older teenager or adult. Both kinds of experiences can complicate sexual-identity development, of course, but experiences of childhood sexual abuse, in particular, can be difficult to navigate.[2]

---

[2]If for some students there was unwanted sexual experience, what might that mean? It is hard to say how unwanted sexual experience may influence later sexual-identity development. Interestingly, in a thirty-year longitudinal study of sexually abused, physically abused, and neglected children, physical abuse and neglect was not associated with same-sex behavior or relationships in adulthood, but there was a relationship between childhood sexual abuse and later same-sex experiences in adulthood (for a discussion of this research, see Suarez & Yarhouse, 2011).

Whether the reports here of same-sex kissing and behavior are essentially part of a developmental process among those who experience same-sex attraction or whether some of these instances reflect unwanted sexual experiences, we can see that later sexual-identity development entails finding meaning in one's same-sex sexuality.

Part of exploring meaning is to ask about attributions, which is another way of saying, "How did you make sense of this?" We asked specifically about initial attributions of a gay (or lesbian or bi) identity. Most of our sample (84%) initially attributed their same-sex sexuality to a gay identity.

These percentages are higher than what we saw in our previous two studies of sexual minorities on Christian college campuses. We previously reported that 30% of our 2009 sample (Yarhouse et al., 2009) and only 18% of our 2013 sample (Stratton et al., 2013) reported initially attributing their same-sex attractions to a gay identity.

Meaning making is an important aspect of identity formation that is frequently overlooked in the sexual-identity development literature. What a person attributes his or her attractions to tends to start them down a pathway of meaning and purpose. We sometimes refer to this as the person being on an "attributional search for sexual identity" (Yarhouse & Beckstead, 2011, p. 108).

Attributions and meaning making may well contribute to adopting labels that make sense. In this study nearly three-fourths of the sample adopted the label gay for themselves privately, and 40% of our sample adopted the label gay for themselves publicly.

How do these findings line up with our previous research? In our first two studies we found that those samples were much less likely to adopt a gay identity, only 14% in our 2009 study (Yarhouse et al., 2009) and 11% in the 2013 study (Stratton et al., 2013). We did not in those previous studies distinguish private and public identity, but the smaller percentages suggest participants were likely thinking of a public gay identity, as that is the smaller percentage when we did break out the two kinds of identity labels in this study. So we are seeing a higher percentage of sexual-minority students adopting a public gay identity.

Disclosure or coming out is also an important developmental milestone. In our sample this occurred at an average age of seventeen, which is a couple of years later than what we have seen in community samples from mainstream LGB+ researchers.

Ron Belgau, a celibate gay Christian who launched (with Wesley Hill) the blog *Spiritual Friendship,* has shared some of what coming out means for a Christian who identifies as gay:

Adolescence is, of course, a very difficult time for everyone; everyone has secrets, fears, and insecurities. Social life, dating, and romance can be very frustrating for heterosexuals as well. However wide the gap is between their real self with all its insecurities and fears and their carefully packaged public face, however, there are significant connections. Even if the girl they are interested in thinks they are a pimple-faced geek, they can at least talk about her unattainable beauty with their other pimple-faced geek friends. Even if society has labeled them a nerd, they can band together with other nerds and plot to take over the world. Students mocked for their race can go home to a family which understands racism and can be supportive and sympathetic. Girls frustrated with boys' sexual harassment can go to their mothers, who likely dealt with the same issues growing up. But when I realized that I was attracted to other guys, the last thing I wanted to do was to tell anyone. Which meant that navigating the continual conversations about dating and romance was like navigating a minefield, with the constant threat that a wrong turn would destroy everything. (Belgau, 2016)

We can begin to appreciate that coming out or disclosure is not merely an act in a string of acts that are part of solidifying identity, but that coming out is weighty and significant in the life of a sexual minority. *Who do I trust with what I've been going through?* This is an important perspective for those who are not sexual minorities to appreciate. In other words, if someone were to share with you about his or her same-sex sexuality, it is likely the result of you having created a kind of climate that allows for greater mutual transparency.

Climate issues are often cited as a reason for students to avoid or delay milestone events related to same-sex and opposite-sex intimacies. Christian college and university campuses were often perceived by students to be structured by policy or covenant to limit any sexual behaviors outside marriage. But the prohibitions for same-sex behaviors were viewed as more sweeping. Opposite-sex affection, such as handholding or hugging, did not seem to prompt the same responses as same-sex expressions of affections. Not surprisingly with the faith-based campus culture, same-sex behaviors that communicated romantic or intimate attachments were identified as

COMING OUT OR DISCLOSURE TO PARENTS

Recent research on the experiences of Christian parents whose children come out to them as LGB suggests that parents face a dual task of trying to find help for themselves to gain a better understanding of sexual identity while also trying to maintain a relationship with their loved one (Maslowe & Yarhouse, 2015). They may want to understand what happened that brought the child to this place (at times questioning their own parenting), while often moving toward a problem-solving mode with their child. Christian parents report a range of emotions; they often say that they love their child but that they are also confused. Accompanying the confusion may be shock, anger, frustration, and so on. Christian parents most often explore ways to connect with their loved one, and they report needing to be intentional in doing so.

Coming out, children may also be somewhat veiled and confrontational. Parents may be last to know, being preceded by revelations to closest friends, a broader peer group, siblings, and perhaps trusted mentors. Parents may find text messages or other social media that suggests an LGB identity or relationship, which leads them to confront their teen- or college-age son or daughter. Such exchanges can escalate quickly.

For sexual minorities, the experience of the coming-out process can range considerably. A person may be sharing in early adolescence in a context in which they receive little or no empathy or support. Some may find themselves at risk of verbal or physical abuse. Others may share with their parents and receive remarkable support and understanding. These more positive exchanges may look similar to telling their parents about an important aspect of what they experience and/or who they are as a person. Still others announce an identity in a way that is almost a declaration of independence—an identity that may function as an act of resilience in relation to what they believe their parents believe and value and how they think their parents will respond. These different and far-ranging experiences suggest that coming out or disclosure is best thought of as an experience that has to be individualized to the person and that person's context.

more complicated than opposite-sex behaviors. There appeared to be more shame and fear associated with public relationality that might suggest a same-sex relationship. For better or worse, this complicated the way this milestone was engaged. At time 1, we interviewed thirty-nine students, and as part of the structured inquiry, we asked about their current relational status.[3] We asked them whether they were currently involved romantically or intimately with persons of the same sex or the opposite sex. We found that for the most part our interviewed students were not currently involved romantically or intimately with partners of either sex. When it came to this relational milestone, 87% of our interviewees told us they were not in a same-sex relationship, and 79% told us they were not in an opposite-sex relationship. Although the interviewees were clearly not a representative sample (see footnote below), this number of students denying a current relationship with either the opposite or same sex seemed curiously high for a college group. The most commonly cited reasons for avoidance of relationships was campus climate and community rules related to public and private sexual behaviors.[4] We even heard from study participants who had been in opposite-sex relationships and who were aware of how certain displays of affection could be experienced by others. Owen, a self-identified straight male who experiences same-sex attraction, acknowledged that he was "probably not very comfortable [participating in public displays of affection] just because of our student code, and I know it would make most of my dorm mates uncomfortable."

In cultural conversations, we have found that some consider such constraining institutional structures to be damaging to a natural developmental process related to sexuality. We have also heard from others that such restraining institutional structures may actually support a healthy developmental process that affirms delays in certain milestones. In fact, our research team tends to see that both are possible depending on the context

---

[3]The gender distribution of the interview sample included 45% female respondents ($n = 72$), 51% male respondents ($n = 81$), and 4% respondents indicating "other" ($n = 7$). Their average reported age was 21.4 years ($SD = 4.58$). Respondents tended to identify as single, never married (94%). Among the four school classifications, junior and seniors were overrepresented (freshmen 16%, sophomores 20%, juniors 22%, seniors 33%, fifth-year seniors 2%, and graduate students 6%). The ethnic/racial makeup of the sample was primarily Caucasian/White (81%), with African American at 7%, Hispanic/Latin at 4%, and Asian/Pacific Islander at 3%. All participants identified as Christian to be included in the study. When asked about how spiritual and religious they were at the time of the survey, participants rated themselves as more spiritual ($M = 8.46$, $SD = 1.94$) than religious ($M = 6.74$, $SD = 2.22$), t (158) $= 10.33$, $p < 0.001$, although both religious and spiritual descriptors are accurate when we look at the high mean values on a ten-point scale.

[4]It is important to note that we asked only about current status—not past history. A small number (four students) volunteered without being asked that they had previously been in same-sex relationships but were no longer. Again, a small number (four), but not the same as those cited above, volunteered that they had previously been in opposite-sex relationships. The interesting point is the low number of students in the interview sample who were currently in a more intimate relationship.

and conditions. The purpose of this discussion is simply to point out that Christian colleges and universities may at times affect the developmental process in light of milestones—at least in the lives of our interviewees.

In their study comparing Christian sexual minorities who identified as gay with those who disidentified with a gay identity, Yarhouse and Tan (2004) reported that Christians who disidentified with a gay identity often chose not to engage in same-sex behavior. Among our thirty-nine interviewed students, only five students admitted that they were involved in current same-sex romantic relationships. Of those five, four were classified by their beliefs and their behaviors as gay identifying. They tended to hold their sexuality as more defining than their faith, even though both remained vital to these persons. For the most part, their relationships took place off campus because of the campus climate and the prohibitions related to same-sex behaviors. We also saw this off-campus method for opposite-sex behaviors as well. Eight students were currently in opposite-sex relationships, including one who was married to an opposite-sex partner. As might be expected, the majority of those interviewees were classified in their beliefs and behaviors as being more gay disidentifying. The strong majority of interviewed students, however, were currently in the "no relationship" category, and it did not matter whether they were more gay identifying or gay disidentifying. In future interviews it will be important to expand this area to include other intimate relationships with friends, family, or other relational connections. To get a fuller view of the relational landscape for these students, it will be important to consider nonromantic but intimate attachments.

OPPOSITE-SEX BEHAVIORS AND RELATIONSHIPS

Recall what we said earlier about how researchers have documented shifts in sexual behavior, sexual-identity labels, and other aspects of sexuality. This has been true for sexual-minority females (e.g., Diamond, 2007) and males (e.g., Rosario, Schrimshaw, Hunter, & Braun, 2006). It made sense, then, to ask participants about their experiences with the opposite sex in terms of attractions, behavior, and relationships. We are not suggesting that this is then a sample of bisexual persons. We realize that many sexual minorities may pursue experiences with the opposite sex for a variety of reasons. They may date to see whether they are or could become attracted to the opposite sex. Do they have the capacity for a meaningful and fulfilling relationship? That is a question they are exploring. Others date heterosexually to keep people from asking questions. They do not want friends suggesting they are gay. They do not want their parents to worry. So they go to prom.

We asked participants in our study, then, about experiences with the opposite sex (see table 3.2). Sixty-two percent reported that they had romantically kissed someone of the opposite sex at an average age of about sixteen. A little under half (46%) reported that they had been fondled by someone of the opposite sex, and 43% reported fondling someone of the opposite sex (at about age sixteen). About one-third (32%) reported sexual behavior with someone of the opposite sex that led to orgasm. This activity occurred at around age eighteen.

Table 3.2. Experiences with opposite-sex behaviors and relationships

Milestones	N	%	M (SD)
Intimately/romantically kissed by someone of the opposite sex	99	61.9	15.53 (3.18)
First relationship with someone of the opposite sex	106	66.3	15.74 (3.07)
Been fondled (breasts or genitals) by someone (without orgasm) of the opposite sex	74	46.3	15.77 (4.06)
Fondled (breasts or genitals) someone (without orgasm) of the opposite sex	69	43.1	15.97 (3.85)
Opposite-sex sexual behavior (to orgasm)	51	31.9	17.51 (3.09)

This discussion of opposite-sex behavior and experiences can lead to the questions, "What are heterosexual students' experiences with identity development? What milestones do they report on the path to identifying themselves as straight?" Although it was not a focus of our line of research, it is a good question, so let's take some time to discuss heterosexual-identity development.

HETEROSEXUAL-IDENTITY DEVELOPMENT

We are often asked how the various milestones in sexual-identity development among sexual minorities line up with the experiences of people who identify as straight. In other words, are there models of heterosexual-identity development?

We mentioned above that early sexual-identity development models (e.g., Cass, 1979; Coleman, 1982; Troiden, 1989) were based primarily on self-identification with a label of gay or lesbian. They were also more simplistic in that they focused on sexual attraction and movement toward the coming-out experience and membership within a like-minded community. Identifying this pathway to identity was an important focus for researchers. Heterosexual-identity development, by contrast, has not been associated with a coming-out experience, and models discussing heterosexual-identity development (Eliason, 1995; Sullivan 1998; Worthington, Savoy, Dillon, & Vernaglia, 2002) have tended to assume that heterosexual identities develop and synthesize without a great deal of critical examination—certainly not the type that is experienced in early accounts of sexual-identity development models among LGB persons and expressed in many of the student voices heard in our line of research.

More recent research, however, suggests that heterosexual-identity development is more complex than originally thought, and contemporary models include the multiple dimensions of sexual fantasies, emotional attractions, and behaviors. Although we have seen how some sexual minorities engage in opposite-sex behavior for various reasons (we presented the average ages in fig. 3.2), we are seeing studies that indicate a fairly high percentage of heterosexual college students have questioned their sexual identity. For example, Morgan and Thompson (2011) shared findings from an exclusively heterosexual group of college students and reported that 53% of the men and 67% of the women engaged in some form of sexual-identity questioning. In addition, in a related study (Morgan, 2012), 19% of the men and 28% of the women purposefully engaged in sexual-identity exploration. Apparently, for emerging heterosexual adults, heterosexual-identity development may not be as smooth as has been noted in the past.

But what about Christian college students who are straight? After all, we are looking in this book primarily at Christian college students who are navigating same-sex sexuality, so a better comparison might be straight students who also attend Christian colleges and universities. Michael Lastoria and his colleagues collected data from Christian college students and asked whether a particular behavior had been experienced and the age of the first experience (see table 3.3; Lastoria, Bish, & Symons, 2011).

While showing only behaviors, this table has a resemblance to table 3.1 and suggests that heterosexual students also follow a time-sequenced path toward heterosexual-identity development. Morgan (2015) elaborates:

> Because understanding heterosexual-identity development has not been subject to the same emphasis on milestones associated with "coming out," researchers do not typically examine these variables to understand heterosexual adolescent and emerging adult heterosexual-identity development. Nonetheless, we do know that the emergence of sexual

Table 3.3. Incidence of experience and average age of first experience (*n* = 1913)

Behavior	"Yes" % have experienced	Mean Age of First Experience
Kissing	70.4	14.3
French kissing	64.1	15.5
Breast fondling	51.4	16.3
Male fondling female genitals	42.8	16.8
Female fondling male genitals	41.6	16.7
Genital-genital contact without intercourse	28.5	17.0
Male oral contact with female genitals	28.5	17.4
Female oral contact with male genitals	30.4	17.2
Anal intercourse	6.4	17.9
Vaginal intercourse	21.3	17.5
Same-sex experimentation	4.5	13.9

feelings and other-sex attractions generally occurs in late childhood or early adolescence, followed by the onset of dating and partnered sexual activities in middle to late adolescence. (Morgan, 2015, p. 267)

Of particular interest here is the percentage (4.5%) of heterosexual students who included same-sex experimentation in the experience of navigating their path to heterosexual-identity development. On the one hand, this percentage is small in comparison to Morgan's more diverse sample of undergraduate students from state universities, who reported same-sex experiences at a higher rate. Perhaps norms regarding sexual behavior and associated ethical and moral teachings preclude many Christians from permission to explore sexuality in quite the same way as documented in some of the broader and more recent research on heterosexual-identity development. On the other hand, while certainly small, this percentage suggests that the road to hetero-sexual-identity development may be more diverse and multidimensional than first thought, at least among a small number of heterosexual Christians.

Let's return now to our line of research on the experiences of sexual minorities on Christian college campuses. We turn our attention now to what happens with milestones over time.

MILESTONES OVER TIME

One unique feature of our study is that for the first time we are tracking students' experiences over time. The details are in the appendix to this chapter. Over the course of the first year of our study, only a few students experienced any new sexual milestones. Eight (8.5%) had their first intimate kiss with a same-sex partner. More extensive physical contact happened for the first time for some of the students. Seven were fondled by their same-sex partner, while six actively fondled their partner. Many of these same students were among the seven who lost their virginity by reaching orgasm with a same-sex partner for the first time. Almost 10% of the students (nine of them) newly found themselves in a same-sex dating relationship.

Most of the change in same-sex sexual milestones over this one year can be seen in how students talk about their sexual attractions and behaviors. While very few, only four, made an initial attribution that they were attracted to members of their own sex, even fewer, only one student, took on the label of gay to describe him- or herself privately. Of course, most of these students had already made such an attribution about their attractions and had even come to see themselves as gay when we first surveyed them at the beginning of the study. More movement happened in terms of how they describe themselves to others. Almost 11% of students had decided over the past twelve months that they were ready to let others know that they were gay, but overall still less than half of the students had taken on this public identity.

With regard to opposite-sex sexual experiences, even fewer students hit these milestone events for the first time. About seven students had the new experience of kissing someone of the opposite sex since they were first surveyed. And just a few first engaged in fondling or reached orgasm with an opposite-sex partner over the year of the study.

When asked about their sexual orientation, 46% identified as homosexual and 28% as bisexual. Nine percent identified as heterosexual, 7% declined a label, 5% were unsure, and 6% indicated "other" to the question.

The reader will note that whether we ask about sexual identity or sexual orientation, we are asking students to locate themselves in a designation about themselves that suggests something about their sexual preferences or attractions. But what researchers are finding is that such designations do not always tell the whole story.

In other words, it's possible for someone who adopts an identity label as gay to also report attraction to the opposite sex. A female who identifies as lesbian can also report attraction to men. Ask Lisa Diamond. Lisa Diamond is a researcher at University of Utah who has reported on the experiences of sexual-minority women over several years. Nearly 60% of lesbian-identified women reported sexual contact with a man during the ten-year longitudinal study.

A twenty-nine-year-old woman who identified as lesbian in Diamond's study captures some of the complexity in all of this:

> I would say a large portion of choosing a lesbian identity relates more to the emotional connection. . . . I've had sexual interactions with both men and women, but I don't really feel that "bisexual" is accurate—well, it's an accurate behavioral label, but I don't feel like it's an accurate reflection of how I actually feel. I feel much more fulfilled and connected and intimate with women. So, I feel that "lesbian" is probably a better term for it. (Diamond, 2008, p. 113)

Certainly we can appreciate how complex identity formation and decisions about labeling can become for sexual minorities. Experience of same-sex attraction or what we sometimes think of as awareness of one's same-sex sexuality is certainly a milestone, and subsequent identity-shaping events are also milestones. But between the starting point (awareness) and endpoint (achievement), there is a time of development. As we have been noting, milestones include exploring same-sex sexual behavior, attributions about what attractions mean, disclosing the reality of one's same-sex attractions to others, adopting a private identity label, and adopting a public identity label.

Challenges sexual minorities face may also interact with attributions they make. Some who experience same-sex attraction attribute their experiences to an emerging gay or lesbian identity. In a culture or subculture that supports such an identity, such a person would presumably have less difficulty with confusion or crisis, but such attributions may also place them in some conflict with their religious identity.

We mentioned that milestones often (but not always) include behavior. In the broader literature on milestones, many people who later adopt a gay identity appear to go through a time of same-sex experimentation and exploration that many theorists believe is important to identity synthesis.

The most frequently achieved identity outcome today is in keeping with some of the earliest and most-often-cited models of gay identity development, that is, a gay identity. It often coincides with sexual exploration, disclosure, or expansion of cultural contacts as important milestones (e.g., McDonald, 1982; Spaulding, 1982; Sophie, 1986). Indeed, there are many studies of the experiences of gay, lesbian, and bisexual persons who have achieved identity synthesis.

There really are no models of identity development for those sexual minorities who do not adopt a gay identity or who use *gay* to describe their experiences but are not necessarily identifying with the gay community or holding to values often associated with the mainstream gay community.

Are there other possible identity outcomes? Sure. Some may use other identity labels, such as heterosexual, or distinguish a public identity as straight but hold a private identity as gay or bisexual. Still others may use *gay* as a descriptor of sexual orientation but not mean to convey what some in the broader culture assume about beliefs and values. For example, many celibate gay Christians use the word *gay* to designate sexual orientation but insert *celibate* to convey beliefs and values. Still others may eschew a sexual-identity label in favor of other ways of thinking of identity. For example, some sexual minorities adopt an identity "in Christ" as an alternative to a gay identity or an identity based on one's same-sex sexuality. Christopher Yuan has shared some of his experiences as a Christian who experiences same-sex attraction:

> My identity as a child of God must be in Jesus Christ alone. I read passages in Scripture, which told me, "Be holy, for I am holy." I had always thought that the opposite of homosexuality was heterosexuality, but I realized that the opposite of homosexuality is holiness. God was telling me, "Don't focus upon feelings. Don't focus upon your sexuality, but focus upon living a life of holiness and living a life of purity." (Yuan, n.d.)

CONCLUSION

It is common today to ask sexual minorities to look back on their lives for key milestone events that brought them to a sense of sexual identity and personhood. We discussed many common milestone events and to what extent these experiences shaped how our sample saw themselves.

Most of our sample admitted feeling confused by their experiences of same-sex attraction. Most initially attributed their same-sex feelings to a gay identity. Some milestones may consolidate an identity and trajectory, while other milestones may reflect exploration and possibilities. We looked in some detail at how people make meaning of their same-sex sexuality, including initial attributions and the decision to adopt *gay* as an identity label.

In the next chapter we pick up the topic of identity labels by exploring private and public labels further, and we also look at strength of attraction to the same and opposite sex.

CHAPTER 3 TAKEAWAYS

1. Most theories of sexual-identity development assume a common LGB+ identity outcome and look rather critically at alternative outcomes.

2. There has been a shift away from models of sexual-identity development toward discussions of milestone events in LGB+ identity formation.

3. Our sample of Christian sexual minorities is similar in many ways to other sexual minorities on several milestones, particularly those milestones that are not volitional (e.g., awareness of one's same-sex attractions).

4. Most of our students initially attributed their same-sex sexuality to a LGB+ identity, and this was much higher than in our two previous studies.

5. Nearly three-fourths of our students adopted a private gay identity, while only 40% adopted a public gay identity. These rates are higher than what we saw in our two previous studies.

6. Some of our students also had experience with opposite-sex behaviors. More common opposite-sex behaviors included romantic kissing and dating the opposite sex. Less common behaviors included fondling breasts or genitals (or being fondled) and sex.

▼

REFERENCES

Althof, S. E. (2000). Erectile dysfunction: Psychotherapy with men and couples. In S. R. Leiblum & R. C. Rosen (Eds.), *Principles and practices of sex therapy* (3rd ed., pp. 242-75). New York: Guilford.

Belgau, R. (2016, October 11). Coming out. *Spiritual Friendship: Musings on God, Sexuality, Relationships* [Blog]. Retrieved from https://spiritualfriendship.org/2016/10/11/coming-out/

Cass, V. C. (1979). Homosexual identity formation: A theoretical model. *Journal of Homosexuality, 4*, 215-35.

Chan, C. S. (1989). Issues of identity development among Asian-American lesbian and gay men. *Journal of Counseling and Development, 68*, 16-20.

Chapman, B. E., & Brannock, J. C. (1987). Proposed model of lesbian identity development: An empirical examination. *Journal of Homosexuality, 14*, 69-80.

Coleman, E. (1982). Developmental stages of the coming out process. In J. Gonsiorek (Ed.), *Homosexuality and psychotherapy: A practitioner's handbook of affirmative models* (pp. 31-44). New York: Haworth.

Diamond, L. M. (2007). A dynamical systems approach to the development and expression of female same-sex sexuality. *Perspectives on Psychological Science, 2*(2), 142-57.

Diamond, L. M. (2008). Female bisexuality from adolescence to adulthood: Results from a 10-year longitudinal study. *Developmental Psychology, 44,* 5-14.

Dube, E. M., & Savin-Williams, R. C. (1999). Sexual-identity development among ethnic sexual-minority male youths. *Developmental Psychology, 35,* 1389-99.

Eliason, M. J. (1995). Accounts of sexual identity formation in heterosexual students. *Sex Roles, 32,* 821-34.

Fox, R. (1995). Bisexual identities. In A. D'Augelli & C. Patterson (Eds.), *Lesbian, gay and bisexual identities over the lifespan: Psychological perspectives.* New York: Oxford University Press.

Fukuyama, M. A., & Ferguson, A. D. (2000). Lesbian, gay, and bisexual people of color: Understanding cultural complexity and managing multiple oppressions (pp. 81-105). In R. Perez, K. DeBord, & K. Bieschke (Eds.), *Handbook of counseling and psychotherapy with lesbian, gay, and bisexual clients.* Washington, DC: APA.

Lastoria, M. (Ed.). (2011). *Sexuality, religiosity, behaviors, attitudes: A look at religiosity, sexual attitudes and sexual behaviors of Christian college students.* Houghton, NY: Association for Christians in Student Development.

Lastoria, M. D., Bish, G. T., & Symons, C. S. (2011). Sexual behaviors. In M. Lastoria (Ed.), *ACSD research series: Sexuality, religiosity, behaviors, attitudes: A look at religiosity, sexual attitudes, and sexual behavior of Christian college students* (pp. 30-35). Houghton, NY: Association for Christians in Student Development.

Maslowe, K. E., & Yarhouse, M. A. (2015). Christian parental reactions when a LGB child comes out. *American Journal of Family Therapy, 43*(4), 352-63.

McCarn, S., & Fassinger, R. (1996). Revisioning sexual minority identity formation: A new model of lesbian identity and its implications for counseling and research. *The Counseling Psychologist, 24*(3), 508-34.

McDonald, G. J. (1982). Individual differences in the coming out process for gay men: Implications for theoretical models. *Journal of Homosexuality, 8,* 47-60.

Morgan, E. M. (2012). Not always straight path: College student narratives of heterosexual-identity development. *Sex Roles, 66,* 79-93.

Morgan, E. M. (2015). Sexual identity and orientation. In J. J. Arnett (Ed.), *Oxford handbook of emerging adulthood: The winding road from the late teens through the twenties* (p. 267). New York: Oxford University Press.

Morgan, E. M., & Thompson, E. M. (2011). Processes of sexual orientation questioning among heterosexual women. *Journal of Sex Research, 48,* 16-28.

Reynolds, A. L., & Hanjorgiris, W. F. (2000). Coming out: Lesbian, gay, and bisexual development. In R. M. Perez, K. A. DeBord, & K. J. Bieschke (Eds.), *Handbook of counseling and psychotherapy with lesbian, gay, and bisexual clients* (pp. 35-55). Washington, DC: American Psychological Association.

Rosario, M., Schrimshaw, E. W., Hunter, J., & Braun, L. (2006). Sexual-identity development among lesbian, gay and bisexual youths: Consistency and change over time. *The Journal of Sex Research, 43*(1), 46-58.

Savin-Williams, R. C. (2005). *The new gay teenager.* Cambridge, MA: Harvard University Press.

Savin-Williams, R. C., & Cohen, K. M. (2004). Homoerotic development during childhood and adolescence. *Child and Adolescent Psychiatric Clinics of North America, 13*, 524-49.

Savin-Williams, R. C., & Diamond, L. M. (2000). Sexual identity trajectories among sexual-minority youths: Gender comparisons. *Archives of Sexual Behavior, 29*, 419-40.

Sophie, J. (1986). A critical examination of stage theories of lesbian identity development. *Journal of Homosexuality, 12*, 39-51.

Spaulding, E. C. (1982). *The formation of lesbian identity during the "coming out" process* (Unpublished doctoral dissertation). Northampton, MA: Smith College School for Social Work.

Stratton, S. P., Dean, J. B., Yarhouse, M. A., & Lastoria, M. (2013). Sexual minorities in faith-based higher education: A national survey of attitudes, milestones, identity, and religiosity. *Journal of Psychology and Theology, 41*, 3-23.

Suarez, E. C., & Yarhouse, M. A. (2011). The impact of sexual abuse on adult sexual identity. In A. J. Schmutzer (Ed.), *The long journey home: Understanding and ministering to the sexually abused.* Eugene, OR: Wipf & Stock.

Sullivan, P. (1998). Sexual-identity development: The importance of target or dominant group membership. In R. L. Sanlo (Ed.), *Working with lesbian, gay, bisexual, and transgendered college students: A handbook for faculty and administrators* (pp. 3-12). Westport, CT: Greenwood.

Troidon, R. R. (1979). Becoming homosexual: A model of gay identity acquisition. *Psychiatry, 42*(4), 362-73.

Troiden, R. R. (1989). The formation of homosexual identities. *Journal of Homosexuality, 17*, 43-73.

Wolkomir, M. (2006). *Be not deceived: The sacred and sexual struggles of gay and ex-gay Christian men.* New Brunswick, NJ: Rutgers University Press.

Worthington, R. L., Savoy, H. B., Dillon, F. R., & Vernaglia, E. R. (2002). Heterosexual-identity development: A multidimensional model of individual and social identity. *The Counseling Psychologist, 30*, 496-531.

Yarhouse, M. A. (2001). Sexual identity development: The influence of valuative frameworks on identity synthesis. *Psychotherapy, 38*(3), 331-41.

Yarhouse, M. A., & Beckstead, A. L. (2011). Utilizing group therapy to navigate and resolve sexual orientation and religious conflicts. *Counseling and Values, 56*(1-2), 96-120.

Yarhouse, M. A., & Jones, S. L. (1997). A critique of materialist assumptions in interpretations of research on homosexuality. *Christian Scholar's Review, 26*(4), 478-95.

Yarhouse, M. A., Stratton, S. P., Dean, J. B., & Brooke, H. L. (2009). Listening to sexual minorities on Christian college campuses. *Journal of Psychology and Theology, 37*(2), 96-113.

Yarhouse, M. A., & Tan, E. S. N. (2004). *Sexual identity synthesis: Attributions, meaning-making, and the search for congruence.* Lanham, MD: University Press of America.

Yuan, C. *Leaving behind a double life* [Interview]. (n.d.). The Christian Broadcasting Network. Retrieved on from www1.cbn.com/700club/christopher-yuan-leaving-behind-double-life

APPENDIX

Table A3.1. Mean ages and standard deviations of same-sex sexual milestones across year 1 and year 2 (n = 160)

	Age at Same-Sex Sexual Milestones (*n* = 160)				Time 1 and Time 2 Combined (*n* = 94)			
	n	Min.	Max.	*M (SD)*	*n*	Min.	Max.	*M (SD)*
AGE: Initial attribution that I am same-sex attracted	158	1	22	13.08 (4.39)	158	1	22	13.08 (4.39)
AGE: Awareness of same-sex feelings	159	4	20	12.92 (3.91)	159	4	20	12.92 (3.91)
AGE: Confusion about same-sex feelings	152	4	20	13.26 (3.54)	152	4	20	13.26 (3.54)
AGE: Intimately/romantically kissed by someone	94	5	25	16.79 (3.99)	102	5	25	16.98 (4.13)
AGE: Been fondled (breasts or genitals) by someone (without orgasm)	97	4	30	16.18 (4.55)	104	4	30	16.45 (4.54)
AGE: Fondled (breasts or genitals) someone (without orgasm)	93	4	24	16.22 (4.37)	99	4	24	16.47 (0.37)
AGE: Sexual behavior (to orgasm)	68	5	30	18.09 (3.31)	75	5	30	18.35 (3.29)
AGE: Initial attribution that "I am gay/lesbian/bisexual"	135	12	24	17.34 (2.35)	139	12	36	17.50 (2.84)

AGE: Adopted the label of "gay" for myself privately	118	10	25	17.89 (2.40)	119	10	25	17.91 (2.40)
AGE: Adopted the label of "gay" for myself publicly	64	15	25	19.47 (1.89)	74	15	26	19.58 (1.93)
AGE: First relationship	64	11	25	18.22 (2.68)	73	11	25	18.56 (2.72)
AGE: First disclosure of same-sex attraction	130	8	24	17.20 (2.83)	133	6	24	17.21 (2.55)

Table A3.2. Mean ages and standard deviations of opposite-sex sexual milestones across year 1 and year 2 (*n* = 160)

	Age at Opposite-Sex Sexual Milestones (n = 160)				Time 1 and Time 2 Combined (n = 94)			
	n	Min.	Max.	*M (SD)*	*n*	Min.	Max.	*M (SD)*
AGE: Intimately/romantically kissed by someone	94	5	25	16.79 (3.99)	101	5	28	15.46 (3.33)
AGE: Been fondled (breasts or genitals) by someone (without orgasm)	74	3	28	15.77 (4.06)	77	3	28	15.94 (4.19)
AGE: Fondled (breasts or genitals) someone (without orgasm)	69	6	28	15.97 (3.85)	71	6	28	16.10 (3.94)
AGE: Sexual behavior (to orgasm)	51	9	30	17.51 (3.09)	54	9	30	17.70 (3.24)
AGE: First relationship	106	9	30	15.74 (3.07)	107	9	30	15.77 (3.07)

IDENTITY DEVELOPMENT

I guess when I approach my faith I feel like what I believe and what I know of God should not contradict what is clearly and obviously visible in the world. . . . I know so many people, including myself who are in stable, functional, healthy same-sex relationships. . . . So I don't understand why the Bible says what it says, and I don't understand why people believe such things about what the Bible says. It's very hard to reconcile, to be honest. I guess I do my best to proceed onward anyway—to take my belief in God, to trust that there is a Creator who cares about his creation. And yet, [I try] to accept that there's something that I don't understand and hopefully someday we'll understand. I don't know.

—Brent, a senior who identifies as gay, time 1

▼▲▼

A YOUNG MAN IN HIS MID-TWENTIES—let's call him Ted—sat across from his therapist and struggled to find the words for his identity. He said,

I don't know. I think of myself as gay. I've certainly been in several gay relationships and met other men at least for sex, even if we both knew there wasn't really a relationship. But I don't think of myself as gay other places. Or, at least, no one at work thinks of me as gay. I don't talk about myself that much. I don't give people a reason to think of myself any differently than the default, than straight. So, I think I'm essentially straight at work. Probably straight at church, too. But there's the rub: when I go to church I sometimes feel pretty miserable for doing things the day or a couple of days before, and I don't know how to think about myself.

Like many people who are navigating sexual identity and religious identity, Ted is trying to find a way to make sense of several things, including his behavior, his sexual attractions, his religious identity, and how he is known publicly as well as how he thinks of himself privately.

Other people are more like Brent, the senior in the opening quote, who is in a "stable, functional, healthy same-sex relationship" and who has serious and profound questions about why the Bible says what it says and why so many Christians interpret the texts as they do. In both cases (and many, many more cases), there is a person actively trying to make sense of so many layers of identity and meaning and personhood.

As we will find out in this chapter, sexual-minority students are somewhere in between being "out" to the campus and being completely closeted. In other words, most have a handful or more people they are open with. They are selective. They have to make decisions every day about who knows what about them.

ATTRACTIONS

We asked participants about their experiences of sexual attraction. This group of students, not unlike our previous sample from the 2013 study (Stratton et al., 2013), reported varying degrees of attraction to the same and opposite sex. This is consistent with what is represented in early literature stemming from Kinsey's (1948) original observation that there is a continuum of sexual attraction rather than a simple dichotomy in which everyone is either exclusively attracted to the same sex or the opposite sex. With Kinsey's scale, which is one measure with varying strength of attraction to the same or opposite sex, there is a linear aspect to it in which reporting less same-sex attraction is simultaneously reporting more opposite-sex attraction (and vice versa). It has been suggested that another way to address this is to offer two separate measures of attraction. One is for reporting attraction to the same sex; the other for reporting attraction to the opposite sex. This was the approach we took.

So, to what degree is our sample attracted to others—both those of the opposite sex and those of the same sex? We asked students to rate their sexual attractions on two ten-point scales, one for opposite-sex attraction and one for same-sex attraction. Very strong attraction would be given a score of ten, whereas no attraction would be given a score of one. Across all students, same-sex attraction tended to be stronger than did opposite sex attraction (see table 4.1). Students on average reported strong attraction to same-sex peers, with a score of 8.0 ($SD = 2.3$), but only moderate attraction to opposite-sex others, with a score of 4.9 (*SD* = 3.3). As with any statistical average, this only tells part of the story. While most students—a full 69.4% of them—experienced more same-sex attraction than opposite-sex attraction, a few look very different from this. A small group (8.1%) held equal attractions for men and women, and just over one out of five of them (22.5%) were more attracted to members of the opposite sex than to those of the same sex. Most of these students (84.4%) are currently experiencing attraction to both members of their same sex and members of the opposite sex. Sexual attraction is a much more complicated aspect of these students' sexuality than one might expect.

Table 4.1. Sexual attraction among sexual-minority Christian college students

	Current attraction to the opposite sex n (Percent)	Current attraction to the same sex n (Percent)
1–No attraction	26 (16.3)	2 (1.3)
2	37 (23.1)	1 (0.6)
3	17 (10.6)	3 (1.9)
4	12 (7.5)	11 (6.9)
5	9 (5.6)	9 (5.6)
6	7 (4.4)	8 (5.0)
7	7 (4.4)	14 (8.8)
8	15 (9.4)	25 (15.6)
9	6 (3.8)	23 (14.4)
10–Strong attraction	24 (15.0)	64 (40.0)

You can begin to realize that not all students are going to have the same experiences by virtue of the strength of their attractions to the same or opposite sex. It is particularly interesting to consider how strength of attractions is related to beliefs and values, as well as religiosity, which we discuss further in chapter five.

CHANGES OVER TIME

Sexual attractions did not change much over the first year of the study. While some of the participants experienced new sexual milestones, and some changed their understandings of their own sexuality, their degrees of attraction as a whole group on average were quite stable. The second-year mean rating of same-sex attraction was 8.1 (*SD* = 2.5), and the corresponding score for other-sex attraction was 4.7 (*SD* = 3.3). The large majority of students reported no change in their level of same-sex attraction (76.6%) or in their level of other-sex attraction (70.2%). Only nine students (9.6%) had more than a three-point change in any of their attraction scores.

Even though degree of attraction remained relatively stable over the two years of this study, most students experienced some attraction to both opposite-sex and same-sex peers. This may add to the questions some of these students have about their own sexual identity, and it seems to be reflected in their labeling of their own sexual orientation and sexual identity. The American Psychological Association (2008) stated that "sexual orientation refers to an enduring pattern of emotional, romantic, and/or sexual attractions to men, women, or both sexes." When asked what their sexual identity was, just over half of these students saw themselves as being attracted to a single sex. Only fifteen students (9.4%) reported having a heterosexual orientation; in contrast, 46.9% claimed to have a homosexual orientation. This means that nearly 45% reflected this dual attraction in their description of their own orientation. Most of these students, 28.1% of the larger sample, used the term *bisexual* to capture this. The other students used terms such as *pansexual, asexual, no label, not sure*, and *other* to express their patterns of attraction. After the first year of the study, these labels changed only slightly, with the most noticeable change in the decreased number of students seeing themselves as heterosexual in orientation (5.3%). This, however, does not seem to be because students' orientations, or their understanding of their orientations, changed; rather, students who initially espoused a heterosexual orientation were more likely to drop out of the study after the first year. These findings appear to contrast with recent research suggesting a natural fluidity among some sexual minorities, particularly women (Diamond, 2007). Indeed, there were no differences in changes in same-sex attraction and opposite-sex attraction from time 1 to time 2 between men and women.

If sexual orientation can be understood as a person's pattern of attractions, then sexual identity is how that person makes sense of the self in light of those attractions (Reiter, 1989) and the label they use to communicate that to others. For the students in this study, sexual identity paralleled sexual orientation to a large extent, but not perfectly. For example, more students (15.6%) claimed a straight identity, even though only 9.4% said they had a heterosexual orientation. On the one hand, only 23.8% affirmed a bisexual identity, while almost 5% more had used the same term to describe their orientation. Those seeing themselves as gay or lesbian (43.8%) most likely also professed a homosexual orientation. There were few changes in identity over the two years of the study; most people held to the same labels.

Interestingly, when we asked students to tell us about their private sexual identity, that is, how they think of themselves, and their public sexual identity, how they present themselves to others, they gave us somewhat different labels than what we've seen above. We will return to public and private sexual identity later in this chapter, as that is an important distinction in many Christian settings.

HETEROSEXUAL PEERS

We previously discussed the strength of attraction for a group identifying as sexual minority, that is, students who experience same-sex attraction (review table 4.1). The reader may wonder about strength of attraction for a group identifying as heterosexual. By way of comparison we looked at a sample of heterosexually identified Christian college students (Dean, Stratton, Yarhouse, & Lastoria, 2011) who reported some level of same-sex attraction (SSA). The number, 245 (11.9%, $n = 2051$), was then filtered for students who privately identified as heterosexual or questioning, omitting students who identified as LGB. Table 4.2 shows the breakdown for this group by strength of attraction.

Table 4.2. Sexual attraction among heterosexual Christian college students

Participants ($n = 202, 9.8\%, n = 2051$) related their strength of current attraction to the opposite sex and to the same sex on a 1 (no attraction) to 10 (strong attraction) scale.

	Current attraction to the opposite sex n (Percent)	Current attraction to the same sex n (Percent)
1–No attraction	0 (0)	40 (19.8)
2	1 (0.5)	61 (30.2)
3	8 (4.0)	49 (24.6)
4	1 (0.5)	16 (7.9)
5	1 (0.5)	11 (5.5)
6	6 (3.0)	6 (3.0)
7	13 (6.4)	6 (3.0)
8	23 (11.9)	4 (2.0)
9	33 (16.3)	3 (1.5)
10–Strong attraction	116 (57.4)	6 (3.0)

Although representing only a small percentage (9.8%) of the total sample, this group identifying privately as heterosexual suggests that the pathway to achieving a sexual identity is not always and solely based on whether one's attractions are either toward the same or opposite sex. For example, in this heterosexually identifying group, thirty-six (18.0%) students reported a same-sex attraction from five (moderate) to ten (strong), while an even smaller number, eleven (5.5%), reported opposite-sex attraction in the lower half (from one to five).

Elizabeth Morgan (2012) noted that while models of same-sex sexuality have been given increased visibility (e.g., Savin-Williams, 2005), "sexual identity typically only becomes a visible aspect of development once an individual begins diverging from the heterosexual norm" (Morgan, 2012, p. 79). In other words, talking about "developing" a sexual identity has not been a salient aspect of *heterosexual*-identity development; it was assigned the default status. Other researchers suggested that heterosexual individuals do not as a rule think a great deal about their sexual identity (Diamond, 2008; Konik & Stewart, 2004; Wilkinson & Kitzinger, 1993).

Morgan (2012) found only two other studies examining variations in heterosexual sexual-identity development among a sample of young adults: one in the United States (Eliason, 1995) and one in Turkey (Bolak-Boratov, 2006). In an effort to alleviate this dearth, she examined the narratives of 1,051 undergraduate students who identified as "exclusively straight/heterosexual" and classified them according to one of five delineated statuses in Worthington and others' (2002) model. Her sample was not random and used lower-division psychology students at two public universities in California and Idaho. The five statuses were (1) diffusion, (2) unexplored commitment, (3) active exploration, (4) passive deepening and commitment, and (5) active deepening and commitment. These statuses roughly correlated to Marcia's (1966) four ego-identity statuses of diffusion, foreclosure, moratorium, and achieved.

Morgan found that while the majority of her sample (71% of the males, 60% of the females) were characterized as passive deepening and commitment (stable commitment to a heterosexual identity without a great deal of active or purposeful exploration), there was a small subsample that engaged in active exploration (2.8% of the males, 6.6% of the females). The second-most prevalent status was active deepening and commitment (19% of the males, 28% of the females). This group was characterized by young adults who were committed to defining themselves as heterosexual but also engaged in active exploration that was at times with members of the same sex. The scope of this work does not permit a detailed analysis of this topic. It is mentioned presently to make an important point. Traditional notions of sexual identity as exclusively binary, that one is either heterosexual or homosexual, are not supported by current research among both heterosexual and sexual-minority populations.

Of course, Morgan's sample is far more religiously diverse and not limited to Christian students, but there were narratives clearly representative of Christian sexual mores as students listed religious reasons for not being sexually active while embracing a stable heterosexual identity. These young adults were most likely classified as unexplored commitment. One participant explained, "I am a Christian and my religious background dictates that that is the way that it should be. Males should like females and females should like males. That is how I have always grown up and I will always believe that" (Morgan, 2012, p. 87).

Nevertheless, as we will see in the next section, sexual identity is a complex construct for men and women and includes a variety of factors in addition to sexual attraction. Gender, biological sex, behavior, intentions, and beliefs and values all contribute to the construct of identity.

THE IMPORTANCE OF ASPECTS OF IDENTITY

Let's continue, then, with exploring identity. What do students say are the most important considerations in identity? We tried to get at this two ways. The first way was to simply ask about the importance of terms such as *gay* and *Christian* and even terms such as *celibate*, which might designate a more conservative sexual ethic. Second, we asked about the relative weight of a number of variables, such as behavior, attractions, and values in the formation of a gay identity.

On this first question about the importance of key terms, our students were asked how important it was to identify themselves in particular ways. We asked about their identity as a Christian. We asked about a gay identity. We asked about a gay Christian identity, and we asked about a celibate gay Christian identity.

Participants indicated it was more important to identify themselves as a Christian than any of these additional labels. This was truly the most important identity for this group of students. Less important was to identify as gay or to identify as a gay Christian. Much less important (the least important, on average) was to identify themselves as a celibate gay Christian.[1]

The relative lack of importance or regard for a celibate gay Christian identity may on the one hand reflect a less conservative sample in which the primary concern isn't with an underlying and traditional Christian sexual ethic. On

---

[1] $F (3, 474) = 118.87, p < 0.001$.

the other hand, celibacy may be viewed not as abstaining for the time being or for this season of life but as a lifelong commitment, which is a typical understanding of celibacy as experienced vocationally, and this is a rather young group to commit themselves to a life of celibacy even in cases in which some students may report a more conservative sexual ethic.

We think it is important to come back to the primary and most salient identity as Christian. The salience of this label and identity does not preclude a person from also adopting a gay or gay Christian identity, of course, but it is worth noting that Christian students sorting out sexual identity and faith are Christians, at least in terms of their own sense of what matters to their sense of self and personhood. We stress this finding as it is not always a starting point for heterosexual Christians who may make the opposite assumption about matters of faith and salvation. That is, we often run into the assumption that if a person is gay then they are not Christian. The two identity labels cannot coexist.[2] Part of this may be a cohort effect of older Christians assuming that to be gay is to hold to a sexual ethic that contrasts with a biblical understanding of sexual behavior that precludes same-sex intimacy. Younger Christians not only use *gay* differently (to explain sexual orientation using the common vernacular) but also may be challenging the traditional Christian sexual ethic or the idea that same-sex sexual intimacy is precluded by a biblical sexual ethic.

---

[2]Roger E. Olson's (2002) typology may be helpful here. Olson presented three categories of *beliefs*: *dogma,* which are essential creedal statements of the faith (e.g., the Nicene Creed); *doctrine,* a second category of teachings that may vary across traditions but can be very significant; and *opinion* (adiaphora), matters of a speculative nature about which there is no consensus in the church. While Olson's categories were presented to examine beliefs and not ethics, a parallel with ethics might be drawn. For many Christians, same-sex sexual behavior may not reflect dogma, but questions about ethics and same-sex behavior are tied to theological matters closely related to dogma and ongoing patterns of sexual behavior (ethics) that characterize a person over time and suggest a concerning trajectory with potential spiritual consequences. For a discussion about whether this is a primary or secondary issue, see Sprinkle (2017, July 28; 2017, July 31).

Other Christians would not be as concerned about sexual identification (e.g., "I am gay") but would be primarily concerned with behavior, and the concerns about behavior would be for similar reasons noted above. A person could be both gay and Christian in terms of describing one's sexual preferences while refraining from same-sex sexual behavior. Still other Christians, particularly in more liberal mainline denominations, view same-sex behavior (let alone sexual-identity labels) as not rising to the level of dogma or a category of teaching closely related to dogma, or have reached a different conclusion regarding traditional scriptural prohibitions, or are otherwise moving toward affirming same-sex relationships and identity as both gay and Christian.

THE WEIGHT OF ASPECTS OF IDENTITY

The second way we explored the question of importance and weight of identity was to ask about aspects that a person might consider and the relative weight the person gives to those aspects. In giving consideration to one's sexual identity (whether to identify as gay, straight, bi, lesbian, etc.), it has been helpful to some people to reflect on factors that might contribute to one label over another. There may be many facets that contribute to a person's sexual identity. It was in the spirit of understanding the relative weight of these factors that we asked students to think about their own sexual identity (whether to identify as gay, straight, bi, lesbian, etc.) and to assign weights to the following factors:

- biological sex (as male or female)
- gender identity (as a man or woman, including how masculine or feminine a person feels)
- intentions (how a person intends to act, the kind of person one intends to become)
- sexual behavior (what one does with the intentions and attractions one has)
- beliefs and values (about what is morally permissible or impermissible)
- persistence and direction of sexual attraction (toward the same or opposite sex or both)

We asked participants to provide a percentage for each so that the whole added up to 100%. They could also share other factors that were important but not listed. Several other factors were mentioned and included things such as social pressure, sexual trauma, genetics, and family dynamics.

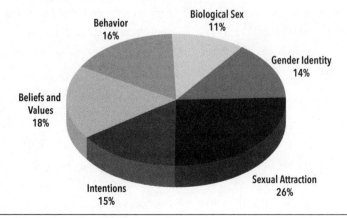

Figure 4.1. Average weighted aspects of identity

Over the course of a year, there was not much change in the importance of each of these aspects of identity for our participants. Perhaps the most notable difference was that their values and beliefs regarding sexuality, on average, became more equally weighted with their sexual attraction. This, though, was an average ranking, suggesting that some students moved in this direction while others gave more weight to their attractions and still others to their values (see fig. 4.2).

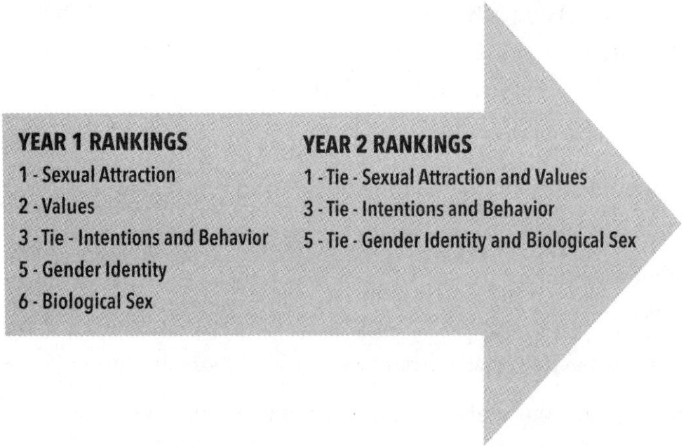

YEAR 1 RANKINGS
1 - Sexual Attraction
2 - Values
3 - Tie - Intentions and Behavior
5 - Gender Identity
6 - Biological Sex

YEAR 2 RANKINGS
1 - Tie - Sexual Attraction and Values
3 - Tie - Intentions and Behavior
5 - Tie - Gender Identity and Biological Sex

Figure 4.2. Average weighted aspects of identity time 1 to time 2

We wanted to know whether the weight given to various aspects of identity varied based on the strength of attraction and based on religiosity. Neither the strength of same-sex attraction nor opposite-sex attraction was related to the relative weight. When it came to religiosity, only strength of intrinsic religiosity was related to the weight given to these various aspects of identity.

We wanted to take a closer look at religious faith and especially how faith informs sexual identity. Our previous experience has been that religious faith often informs how people choose to behave and charts a course of how a person lives his or her life.

FAITH AND SEXUAL IDENTITY

Part of our students' stories is how they make sense of their sexual identity in light of their faith. We will go into more detail in chapter five, but we do offer a preliminary look at faith and sexual identity here. We looked at faith by measuring what is referred to as *intrinsic religiosity*, which has to do with how religious faith informs what one does and what one believes in all aspects of one's life. Scoring high on intrinsic religiosity suggests that one's faith is integrated into every aspect of one's life. Intrinsic religiosity does not seem to be related to students' actual degree of sexual attraction, either to the same sex or to the opposite sex. Even so, those with more religiosity are more likely to claim a heterosexual orientation; those who are less religious are more likely to say they have a homosexual orientation. This, however, doesn't seem to translate into sexual-identity labels. The labels students privately put on themselves and the labels they use to describe themselves to others look pretty similar in students who are less religious compared to those who are more so. Religious beliefs may not be as important as social pressures in using these labels, especially given the large discrepancy between private and public identity. Slightly more than three out of four of our students privately identify as a sexual minority, but only two out of four claim to be that sexual minority with others.

This has changed somewhat over the past ten years of our research. In our 2013 sample (Stratton, Dean, Yarhouse, & Lastoria, 2013), which was collected in 2010, we saw significantly lower levels of same-sex attraction in all students, and those with higher levels of intrinsic religiosity reported even lower levels of same-sex attraction than did any of the other students. Somehow there was a relationship between their attractions and their faith, perhaps with religiosity dampening their attractions—or at least the reporting of these attractions. Even so, students' understanding of their own sexual identity did not differ by their faith. Just as many of those with high intrinsic religiosity were likely to take on a gay identity as those who had low intrinsic religiosity. We will get into more detail in the next chapter, but we should note here that even our low intrinsic religiosity group is probably better understood as being moderately religious because we had so few students who denied that faith played a role in how they live their lives. This narrow distribution when reporting intrinsic religiosity may affect our ability to really see how the use of sexual-identity labels differs based on religiosity.

Several years earlier than our work, Yarhouse and Tan (2004) reported on a sample of gay Christians and Christians who experienced same-sex attraction but did not identify as gay. Both groups scored high on religious commitment and on intrinsic religiosity, suggesting a ceiling effect when asking religious samples about commitment and motivation. (A ceiling effect is a large concentration of scores among participants on the high end of a scale. This is what we see in our sample too.) In their study, those who did not identify as gay scored higher as a group on religious commitment and intrinsic religiosity (the impact of their faith on a day-to-day basis) and were more alike in how they responded to various items on these measures than those who did identify as gay. Yarhouse and Tan, reflecting on the items in Hodge's measure of intrinsic religiosity, considered that there may be a tendency among those who disidentify with a gay identity to respond "more readily with the concepts proposed by Hodge, which tends to reflect a more traditional religious perspective than what may be endorsed by" those who identify as gay (Yarhouse & Tan, 2004, p. 125). This seems to fit with our present sample's differences on attitudes and how attitudes correlate with amount of attraction and religiosity, as we have discussed above. In any case, it should be noted that Yarhouse and Tan did not report on degree of same-sex attraction and how that correlated with religiosity—rather, they reported on the difference between identifying as gay or disidentifying with a gay identity.

One way to conceptualize the relationship between religious identity and sexual identity is an identity-development continuum with sexual core values anchoring one side and religious/spiritual core values on the other side. In the middle would be an area of the continuum that represented a compromise or integration instead of the primacy of either extreme over the other. Some of our prior research considered this kind of conceptualization. An alternative and more nuanced understanding of religious identity and sexual identity and the interaction of these aspects might not be one continuum but two—one for high and low sexual valuing, and one for high and low religious/spiritual valuing. Sexual-identity development may not hinder or promote religious/spiritual identity development. Neither can we say that religious/spiritual development will increase or decrease sexual-identity development. These may in fact be complex but apparently separate constructs whose intersecting relationship needs greater exploration.

In the previous section we looked at the weight our participants gave to particular aspects of the self that might be related to how they understand their sexual identity. During the first year of our study, our students on average considered their sexual attractions to be the most important factor. By the second year, they equally weighted their attractions and their values. It's here that we see some of the interaction between sexual identity and religiosity/spirituality.

If intrinsic religiosity indicates the degree to which we allow our faith to influence the way we live, then students' religious beliefs should be an important factor in how they understand their own sexuality, and indeed it is. Students who are less likely to use their religious beliefs as a guide for their lives tend to see their sexual attractions as the single most important factor in their sexuality. Those with higher intrinsic religiosity are more balanced, holding their sexual attractions and their values as equally important. This difference stayed the same from year one to year two of our study. This balancing of attractions and values lends more support to our understanding of sexual identity and religiosity/spirituality as separate but related constructs in identity formation, for if they lay on the same continuum, more religious students should rely on values more than attractions, just the opposite of what less intrinsically religious students do.

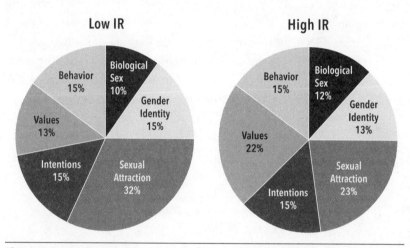

Figure 4.3. Weighted aspects of identity by low and high intrinsic religiosity

So what does this really mean for students as they try to make sense of their sexual identity? It doesn't mean that their religiosity lessens their need to identify as gay, lesbian, or bisexual. It doesn't mean that it's more important to label themselves as gay, lesbian, or bisexual Christians. (Neither of these are particularly strong needs, by the way. Students rated these labels between a five and a six on a ten-point importance scale.)

This dual consideration of sexual attraction and values in sexual-identity development does mean that those reporting more intrinsic religiosity hold the label of Christian as much more important than those with less intrinsic religiosity. The latter group still thinks it's important, giving it about a seven on that ten-point scale of importance; their more religious counterparts, though, are closer to a perfect ten. It also means that those with more intrinsic religiosity hold the label of celibate gay/lesbian/bisexual Christian in higher regard than do their less religious peers. Neither group is sold on this label, however, with both being at the less important side of that ten-point scale. The more religious students are at four; the less religious students are just under two in their ratings.

Looking at these average responses, we might conclude that these students are pretty similar in how they view sexual-identity labels, with much more variation in their religious identity. This is probably true to some extent because we purposely are looking at high and low religiosity groups. Yet, the actual variability in their responses differs more than we might anticipate, suggesting that students have found multiple ways of holding together these two identities.

To better understand this, let's revisit these four questions that address importance by looking at the patterns of responses. First, here is the distribution of the responses to the question "How important is it for you to identify as a Christian?" There was a huge three-point difference in the mean ratings

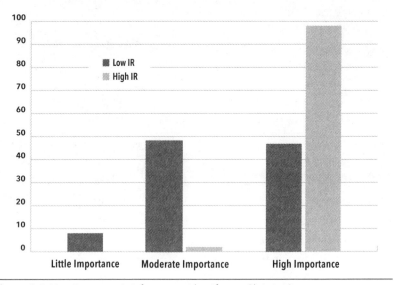

Figure 4.4. How important is it for you to identify as a Christian?

between our two religious groups, but here we can see that most students value that label to at least a moderate extent, with a bit more variability in the low intrinsic religiosity group (see fig. 4.4). Of course, this fits with what we know about that group. "Low intrinsic religiosity" in our sample really means "moderate intrinsic religiosity," with just a few students with truly low religiosity. There are still significant group differences. A full 97% of the highly religious students rated this label as being greatly important to them, and none of them rated it as being unimportant to them. In fact, only three of them gave it a rating of moderate importance. The students with low religiosity were quite a bit more scattered in their ratings, with just under a half rating it as moderately important and nearly another half rating it as highly important. Calling oneself a Christian is somewhat to greatly important for nearly all of the sexual minorities in our sample.

A different picture emerges when we move to the second question dealing with importance: "How important is it for you to identify as a gay, lesbian, or bisexual?" There was no mean difference here between the two religious groups, but clearly students were not of one mind (see fig. 4.5). The students with less intrinsic religiosity tended to give this higher ratings, with almost half saying it was highly important. But not all of them do; a good 50% said this label was only moderately or less important. The students with more intrinsic religiosity tended to assign lower importance to this label, with just under 40% saying this label is not important at all, yet a good number—about a third—said this was very important to them. While our discussion above about mean responses led us to believe that students were more varied in their religious identity than in their sexual identity, the patterns of responses here show quite the opposite. Our students are more alike in their identity as Christians than they are in their identity as sexual minorities.

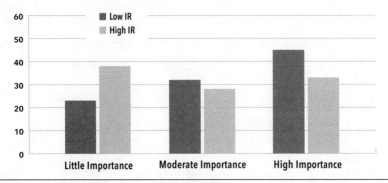

Figure 4.5. How important is it for you to identify as a gay, lesbian, or bisexual?

The third question we asked students was this: "How important is it for you to identify as a gay, lesbian, or bisexual Christian?" The average responses were right in the middle of the ten-point scale for both religious groups (see fig. 4.6). Intrinsic religiosity didn't seem to matter in the choice of this label, and students seemed somewhat moderate in their perspective. The distribution of responses, though, tells a very different story. There are fewer students in the middle of the scale seeing this as moderately important. Those in the high religiosity group tend to be a bit more extreme in their opinions, with the majority of them assigning little or much importance to this label. Those low in the intrinsic religiosity group, however, showed more of a linear pattern, with most tending toward the high end of the scale. That is, 41% say it's very important to identify as a gay Christian, and only 27% say it's not important to do so, with a third in between. Given students' general commitment to identify as Christian, the variations we see here may be due to how they hold their sexuality and faith together, particularly what they do with their sexuality. While some seem to value holding both labels together, others may clearly prefer one label over the other.

The highly intrinsically religious students much more strongly held to their identity as Christians, as we saw above, yet they showed remarkable variability here. Nearly a third of them said it was not important to them to identify as a gay, lesbian, or bisexual Christian, and another 44% of these students said it was extremely important to them. The somewhat dichotomous distribution of responses seems connected to how they value that sexual-minority label and how they feel about using these two labels together. Some students absolutely want to be known as a sexual-minority Christian; other students absolutely want to be known as a Christian—with no modifiers. Owen, a self-identified "straight" freshman with same-sex attraction, chose the latter of those two options. He reported, "I feel that sexual attraction can happen or not. I choose to be okay with that and not identify with that. So I can live with that."

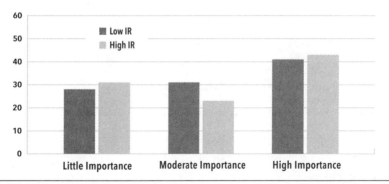

Figure 4.6. How important is it for you to identify as a gay, lesbian, or bisexual Christian?

This bifurcated response to the label of "gay, lesbian, or bisexual Christian" among those with high levels of intrinsic religiosity has been the topic of great conversation online. Matt Moore (2014), who describes himself as a Christian and who was formally sexually active with same-sex partners, refuses to call himself a gay Christian even though he openly discloses his same-sex attraction.[3] His rationale is threefold: he sees his desires as coming from his sinful nature, he doesn't believe that this is God's plan for sexuality, and he doesn't believe that this label helps him to communicate the possibility, in Christ, of transformation in his identity. He writes: "If I were to continue to call myself gay, whether I'd want to admit it or not I would be uniting myself to a worldly, godless identity. And that wouldn't help in the slightest in reaching the gay community with the gospel. Rather, it would communicate a cheap gospel that really doesn't do all that much in changing one's identity" (Moore, 2014).

James, a self-identified "straight" graduate student with same-sex attraction, appeared to agree with Moore. When it comes to labeling, he did not want to be identified in a way that did not fit his faith-based identity. He said, "I definitely don't identify myself as a sexual minority. I identify myself as a human being and a Christian." Adriana, a bisexual senior, likewise affirmed her dedication to her Christian identity, but she took a different approach to the matter. She said,

> I do consider myself gay, and I identify myself as bisexual. I would say the majority of people in dialogue with me were comfortable with that being an aspect of my identity. However, moving forward to the behavior aspect, if I had begun engaging in a relationship with another woman, I think the reaction would not have been positive, and I think my experience would probably not have been as positive [at school] as it was.

Joshua Gonnerman (2012) would likely confirm what Adriana reported in her social situation. He believes that identifying as a gay Christian is important, as it more fully represent who he is. He writes:

> The central locus of my identity, which shapes all other aspects of it, is Christ. But no one, upon honest self-reflection, can realistically claim that this entirely does away with all other aspects of one's identity. Christ

---

[3]In this section we will look at some of what our participants say and also what is being said on the web and on relevant blogs. There is a lot of current writing in these venues, and in our experience many Christian college students navigating sexual identity and faith would be familiar with the different voices that chime in on language, identity, and sexuality.

is the foundation which shows how other aspects of my identity can and cannot be expressed, but other aspects of who I am do say something significant about me.

This label, he holds, represents gay Christians' "call to otherness" and allows them to connect with one another—and with the gay community and with the church community—in a way that might bring healing between the two.

Both Moore and Gonnerman have chosen celibacy in light of their religious convictions, yet they hold different opinions about using the gay Christian label. Some prefer this label because they understand themselves as both Christian and gay, often immersed in the LGB+ community. Kevin Garcia (2015), for example, actively dates men and holds firmly to his faith. He has written about his coming out as a gay Christian. In seeming desperation, he got to a point in his own process of figuring out faith and sexuality that he wanted God to give him clear direction: "Either He needed to speak clearly and tell me to begin my commitment to celibacy, or He was gonna have to do something new." That something new was taking him to a large training conference helping people engage churches and move them to being more gay affirming. He explains,

Walking in the space and worshiping alongside 300ish other LGBT Christians was incredible. I've read articles and blogs by straight people who say that it was transformative for them because they never expected the Holy Spirit to show up and then Holy Spirit DOES?! I was in the same boat. I never expected it. But the Holy Spirit was there, and present and moving and I felt loved in a way I had never felt loved before.

My entire Christian journey, I felt like I was a second class son. I felt welcomed, but only so much. I could participate, but only to a degree. But in that moment, I finally felt welcomed into the family of God. I was affirmed in my sonship in its entirety. I never felt more free of shame, more set free from the expectation and approval of man. Jesus met me in the realest way possible.

It wasn't a person, a teaching, or my emotions which convinced me it was possible to be gay and [a Christian]. It was Holy Spirit, present, living, breathing, speaking. And today, I'm walking in the fullness of God. I am unashamed, unrestrained, and fully in love with Jesus. More in love with Him than I've ever been. And this is just the beginning of my story. (Garcia, 2015)

For these highly religious people, both of these decisions—to use the label of gay Christian or not to use the label—tend to hold a great deal of theological importance for their self-identity and for their ability to communicate with others. In this sense, one label is not necessarily more or less Christian, or more or less correct, than the other. Rather, the label chosen and the reason for which it was chosen tell us something about how the person holds faith and sexuality together. Ethan, a gay senior, noted how claiming the label "gay" was a useful description for where he has settled in his faith and sexual identity.

> Over the last couple of years, I usually try to come out to people like pretty early on if we are friends, because I just think it is important to know. . . . Like I've had some female friends that I have made and didn't come out to them right away, but then they found and it was kind of weird because they were like, "Oh." Or like, it's not weird, but then they're like kind of surprised. . . . It's easier to tell them early on because it makes the relationship formation much more authentic and genuine.

Some sexual minorities add the word *celibate* to their identity as a gay Christian, so we asked the students in our sample about how they value being known as a celibate gay, lesbian, or bisexual Christian (see fig. 4.7). As we saw above, both groups were on the lower end of the scale on this issue, with those in the high intrinsic religiosity group being more moderate than those in the low intrinsic

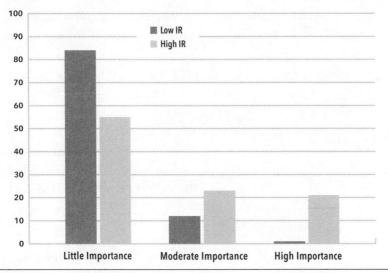

Figure 4.7. How important is it for you to identify as a celibate gay, lesbian, or bisexual Christian?

religiosity group. Again, look at this distribution. Nearly 85% of the low-religiosity students said this is not very important, as did 55% of the high-religiosity students.

The reasons for not valuing the label of celibate gay Christian are quite varied. For some, the term evokes emotional reactions related to homophobia and the sense that celibacy is too often forced on sexual minorities. Carter, a single gay junior at time 2, volunteered his take on the complications of celibacy. "*Washed and Waiting*, it's encouraging and it's a depressing book in a lot of ways, too.[4] I feel like any conversations that I've had about celibacy have not been uplifting. It's almost like, 'Oh, you have to do this. It's really sad.' Or, people that I'm close to are like, 'Gosh, I could never do that. Or, I don't know how you'll do that.'" Carter described the view of celibacy in his peer circle as one of simply loss and very little gain.

Kimberly Knight (2015), who describes herself as a progressive Christian trained in liberation, feminist, and queer theology, strongly rejects this label and the idea of celibacy as faulty traditional ideas stemming from reading the Bible literally when it shouldn't be read that way. As a result, she holds, that Christianity has harmed sexual minorities. She concludes her response to a *Washington Post* article on celibate gay Christians like this:

> When gay and lesbian Christians accept the abusive lie that the right path to God's heart is either celibacy or heterosexual sex within the confines of marriage we are internalizing and identifying with our abusers, perpetuating their abuse and setting the stage for others to fall prey to the same. We are suffering from Stockholm Syndrome.
>
> This lesbian, this follower of Jesus, this middle-age mamma living and learning to love in the south will not now or ever validate the self-destructive delusion that lesbian, gay, bisexual and transgender people are called to a life of celibacy (or false marriage) to be in right relationship with God or community.
>
> This is nothing more than rejecting our sacred worth and therefore rejecting the justification that has already occurred, is occurring and will occur continuously in Christ. To do so is a rejection of God. And that is the sin that leads to death.
>
> I choose freedom in Christ. I choose life.

---

[4]*Washed and Waiting: Reflections on Christian Faithfulness and Homosexuality* is a "theological memoir" by Wesley Hill on celibacy as an option in the cultural debate on life as a sexual minority. His follow-up, *Spiritual Friendship: Finding Love in the Church as a Celibate Gay Christian*, continues this conversation.

A rejection of the label of celibate gay Christian is not all this distribution tells us. While the low-religiosity participants were almost single-minded in not valuing this term, among their more religious peers almost one out of five said adding the word *celibate* to this label was very important. The *Washington Post* article that Knight addressed in her blog ran in 2014 with this headline: "Gay Christians choosing celibacy emerge from the shadows." At that time, choosing to identify as Christian and gay and celibate—at the same time—was a relatively new construction, and there was a great deal of ambivalence from both the gay and the Christian communities.

In explaining why an emphasis on celibacy is important in understanding the experience of some sexual-minority Christians, Chris Damian offers the following:

> When I hear men and women approaching the idea of celibacy, the approach is most often framed by fear. Fear-driven questions ground the approach and force conclusions. How can I possibly do this? Will I be forever lonely? Is it possible to be faithful to this? And for those consumed by these questions, the failure to fulfill a promise of celibacy becomes almost inevitable, transforming eventually into the gradual self-justification of unfaithfulness, self-justification based on a fearful focus on the difficulty of the choice. (Damian, 2014)

A blogger known only as Lindsey (2015), who is in a committed celibate LGBT Christian relationship with Sarah, told her story of choosing celibacy and how she struggled to figure out what that meant for her life. She writes:

> Simply put, I call myself celibate because I see celibacy as integral to how I experience my sense of self, my life in Christ, and my life in the world. My celibate vocation influences so many of my decisions that it's impossible for me to envision my life any other way.
>
> I haven't always been committed to celibacy. I hadn't even encountered *celibacy* as a word until I was 24 years old. It's incredibly difficult to live into a vocation if you don't even know what to call it. . . .
>
> Almost immediately, I had a sense of deep and abiding peace wash over me when I realized that I *could* forgo marriage. Yet, I found myself in a place that some would describe as "overwhelming with creative *potential*" in much the same way real estate agents speak of

the *potential* of a home requiring significant repairs. I felt like I had entered No-Man's Land. There was no roadmap, but I thought I might be able to find a way forward. . . .

The *problem* I faced was that I didn't have a clear set of next steps. I couldn't go to my church and say, "I'd like to make a public profession that I intend on fully embracing celibacy." Even though I had been trying to spend time with any celibate person I could find, everyone I found lived in a monastery as a monk or nun. I had university debt to pay off, and my story didn't seem to mesh with any of the monastics I talked to. It bothered me that almost every church I could think of was prepared to help my brother marry, but I couldn't think of any church that was prepared to help me embrace celibacy. I thought back to everything I had learned from the monastics that I had already met. I couldn't help but remember people who had entered monasteries later in life. All of them had started living out celibate vocations long before they committed to a particular monastic community. I heard a chorus of voices telling me, "I entrusted myself to God's care."

So I did the next thing I could think of: I stood in the privacy of my own prayer corner to ask for God's help in cultivating a celibate vocation that would bring me life. I knew that I had no idea what I was doing, but I knew equally that the time had come for me to tell God about my earnest intentions. The time had come to trust Christ that he would guide me as the good shepherd. The time had come for me to start to say, "I'm celibate." (Lindsey, 2015)

For Lindsey, taking on the label of celibate was powerful in understanding herself and in claiming her trust in God to help her live this out. Other authors have shared that claiming celibacy as part of one's identity helps them to shape how they will live out their faith and their lives—not just as abstinence, as a "saying 'no'" (Tushnet, 2012).

ON-CAMPUS IDENTITY AS A SEXUAL MINORITY

We turn our attention now to on-campus identity as a sexual minority. In the broader literature, this is sometimes referred to as "outness," or one's decision to be out as a sexual minority in specific settings. In their study of 213 sexual minorities at various faith-based institutions, Wolff and others (2016) reported no differences in students' outness by type of faith-based institution (evangelical, mainline Protestant, Catholic, Mormon). This was a somewhat surprising finding that the researchers acknowledged may have been due to a mediating factor, that is, whether a sexual minority had a handful of friends to whom they could be more forthcoming about their sexual identity: "We question whether an individual's perception of openness may be mediated by the presence of having a few individuals they could talk to openly about their orientation regardless of the actual campus environment" (p. 209). In that same study, more than half of the sample of sexual minorities at faith-based institutions reported having "talked to a faculty member or classmate about their sexual orientation, [while] more than two thirds have talked to a roommate" (Wolff et al., 2016, p. 209).

In our study we then asked about on-campus experiences with sexual identity. Students were asked how they would describe their on-campus identity as a sexual-minority member. The highest percentage (about 60%) of students agreed with the statement "I am known only to a few close friends as a sexual minority (someone who experiences same-sex attraction)." This is the most common experience—to share about one's same-sex sexuality or sexual identity with a small number of close friends.

The next-highest percentage (24%) of students agreed with the statement "I am not known to anyone as a sexual minority." So about one in four sexual-minority students are completely in the closet, if you will, and not known by anyone to have experiences of same-sex attraction or to be navigating questions about their sexual identity.

About 17% of sexual-minority students in our study agreed with this statement: "I am known to many individuals on campus as a sexual minority (someone who experiences same-sex attraction)." This is the most "out" group of students and the smallest percentage in our sample. This may reflect some of the challenges in campus climate that may make it difficult to be forthcoming about experiences of same-sex sexuality. We discuss campus climate further in chapter six.

Along these lines of being known by others on campus as a sexual minority, students were asked to indicate their public and private sexual identities. A public sexuality identity is how one is known by others. This can be voluntary and shared with others by coming out or disclosure of one's sexual identity as gay, lesbian, or bisexual, or public sexual identity. Public sexual identity can also be involuntary when a group that labels a person as gay and can reflect a kind of harassment or bullying if such public labeling is unwanted.

A private sexual identity is how one thinks about oneself. We can think about it as the way people see themselves when they look at themselves in the mirror at night. Many people may think of themselves one way while presenting to others another way. Or, because of the normative expectation that all people are straight unless they give you a reason to think otherwise, a person may allow you to draw the conclusion that they are straight (a public identity) while maintaining a private sexual identity as gay.

In our sample, half of those reporting on this distinction said that they publicly identify as heterosexual, while about 28% identify as gay, lesbian, or bisexual. These findings seem consistent with our previous question about people knowing about their sexual identity. We will find more details in chapter six related to the influence of the campus climate on decisions about public and private identity. At this point we can say that the question for students about whether to be more public or more private can be influenced by the unique environment that exists in Christian colleges and universities.

Pertinent to this issue of a unique environment in faith-based institutions, interviews with thirty-nine sexual-minority students depicted their colleges and universities as places that could be welcoming and supporting, accepting and tolerant, struggling and ambivalent, disengaged and resistant, or even hostile.[5] That's a broad range. Even when students from the same school were trying to describe their own campus experiences, they did not all agree. The most common classification of the "general campus attitude" among the interview sample was "disengaged and resistant," meaning that other students were perceived as being avoidant of engaging sexual-minority issues (disengaged) and possibly averse to discussing the topic if confronted (resistant). Nineteen students who participated in interviews described their campuses predominantly in these terms. However, this characterization did not represent all the institutions, nor did it represent the view of all sexual-minority students from the same institution. In fact, fourteen interviewees chose more inviting categories. Nine institutions were classified as being more "accepting and tolerant" in their description. Five campuses were seen by interviewees as "welcoming and supportive" from their experiences. Only two were classified as "hostile," or actively engaging sexual minorities in a negative way.

---

[5]Recall that in this study we invited students to participate in an interview if they wished to share in greater detail about their experiences at Christian colleges. Thirty-nine students shared their thoughts on campus climate and how this affected public and private identity.

The diversity represented across and within Christian colleges and universities suggested a complex environment for interviewees to negotiate. Rachelle, an eighteen-year-old freshmen, described the situation in the following way:

> One of [my school's] statements is "You are loved." Even when that's being thrown out, I still feel like it's like, "You are wrong, but you are still loved, and yada yada." That's not coming from everybody. It just makes me feel that I am always wrong even if I am still loved. . . . It's still frowned upon by students, not the community as a whole, but some students, and they wouldn't invalidate me as a person or anything, but they would put me in a box as someone who still needs to be—I don't know—evangelized or something.

Loved and judged. Accepted by some but not others. Not invalidated but boxed up. All college and university students have precarious elements to manage during these formative years. Trying to negotiate this kind of complexity can often result in decisions by students about how to manage the resulting insecurity. Questions about being public and private in this prime identity-development era were usually handled cautiously by interviewees.

Most of our interviewed students did find a relational context at their colleges and universities in which they could disclose their more private thoughts and questions. In fact, most of the interviewees chose to disclose for the first time during their undergraduate years in a selective way. Even in environments that could be a mixture of welcoming, supportive, ambivalent, disengaged, or even to a lesser degree hostile, most of our interviewed students found peers to whom they could disclose their identity-based thoughts and feelings. Others disclosed during these years to family members, faculty, and counselors, but most found places to selectively "go public" among their friends or social peers. As mentioned above, our survey results affirmed the same thing. Yet, there were a few interviewees who said that they have never risked going public and didn't intend to do so. Adriana, a senior who identifies as bisexual, considered retrospectively her decision to stay private in her sexual identity. She now says, "I've spent the majority of the past five years intentionally choosing to behave and act as if I'm straight. And I have only recently begun to consider that this is not healthy for me."

To the extent that the interviewees represented a broader constituency, the public-and-private discussion suggested that experiences of sexual minorities on Christian college campuses are a mixture of private identity labels (for themselves) and being more public about their identity labels. There were a few students who were "out" to the whole campus, as well as a few students who were completely "in." Students who were out to everyone or out to no one appeared to be less common, while most of the interviewees were somewhere on the continuum in between those extremes. They were to some degree public to selected friends, family, and school representatives, but they were also to some degree private to the broader institutional constituency. That decision tended to be strongly influenced by issues such as campus climate, campus resources, and access to accepting, often older, peers. But disclosure also seemed to be affected by a student's personal values and faith-based commitments. This interaction of person and context during these prime identity-development years appeared to be significant in navigating a complicated course of integrating sexuality and faith in a Christian community.

What do these findings mean? We find it encouraging that most sexual-minority students have been able to confide their experiences, their journey, with close friends. Having even one confidant appeared to make a significant difference for the interviewees. At the same time, we recognize that some sexual-minority students are not confiding with anyone on campus. It is unclear in all cases why that is, but we have to think about how they experience the campus and what makes it difficult for them to share their experiences. We share the concern of Adriana, who is now reflecting on whether not disclosing to anyone was in fact unhealthy over time. In other words, while there may be wisdom in selecting when and with whom to be more transparent, there may be a point over time at which the decision to "pass" as straight or to keep one's sexuality to oneself may not be as healthy, particularly if what is internalized are negative or shaming messages.

Some of what we are discussing is related to what in the literature is sometimes referred to as identity synthesis or identity achievement, which we discussed in chapter three. Recent research also refers to this as identity integration. For example, Rosario, Schrimshaw, and Hunter (2011) looked at psychological adjustment among LGBT youth with varying degrees of integration in their identity development. They reported on the benefits of achieving and maintaining identity integration and noted that there may be psychological consequences in not achieving and maintaining identity integration, such as low self-esteem and anxiety. One finding related to what we have been discussing in this chapter has to do with social relationships. That is, Rosario and colleagues found that "supportive relationships were related to better psychological adjustment and that negative social relationships were related to poorer adjustment" (p. 12).

Integration may be more nuanced and complex than suggested by Rosario and colleagues' study. When we add in religious identity and related beliefs and values, questions about identity integration may take on another meaning and another layer of complexity when it comes to development. The interaction between one's sexual identity and one's religious/spiritual identity is not simply an either-or or a both/and process; rather, students seem to be developing both identities simultaneously, with reciprocal influence and maybe even some interdependency between the two.

MANAGING TWO FULL BOXES

When we try to understand the challenges that Christian college students who experience same-sex attraction face, we might consider this image: our interviewees are standing, metaphorically, in the middle of their college community, endeavoring to maintain their grasp on two very large and heavy boxes. There are other boxes that also have to be carried as they move into college, but for this image we'll talk about just the two in question.[a] The boxes represent sexual development and religious/spiritual development. It's an awkward and depleting task for these students to manage these cumbersome containers as they move on campus, but the boxes feel important and, for some at least, significant. So they work responsibly to position their load in their arms in ways that allow for an effective sense of balance as they walk through their college experience. They hope to maintain a grasp that will minimize the threat of dropping one or the other, spilling the contents for others to see. That could be embarrassing! They inevitably negotiate a functional way to hold these two very full boxes—at least for a period of time. That hold always involves positioning one box relative to the other. To achieve that unique and dynamic in-arm balance, one box may be held closer than the other for awhile. It could be said in that moment that one box is more central for balance at that moment. Of course, the boxes might also shift along the way to gain a better or more effective hold. Maybe at some point the contents of these boxes might be contained in one box, but for now most of our interviewees are negotiating college life with two.

[a] The authors acknowledge that both sexual and religious/spiritual "boxes" are essential for healthy development. We do not believe that there is an either-or option for human personhood. We also realize that these are only two among other developmental boxes that a student carries to college. All are important for consideration in higher education, even though we are focused on sexuality and religion/spirituality.

HOLDING SEXUAL IDENTITY AND RELIGIOUS/SPIRITUAL IDENTITY

In the second year of our longitudinal study, we decided to ask students directly about their hold on their sexuality and their faith. Forty-six interviewees in year two responded to specific questions about how they intentionally negotiated the intersection of these vital developmental areas.[6] The actual questions were the following: "How do you see your sexual development and your religious/spiritual development influencing one another in your development as a person? Is one more important than the other for you right now? Please explain." As we considered their responses, it became apparent that there were three broad ways to manage the boxes (see "Managing Two Full Boxes" above) represented in their answers to the questions.

One way was to negotiate the boxes by dropping one and retaining the other. We called this option *rejection*, meaning that students became so frustrated by the developmental process that they tended to either abandon faith or deny their sexuality as significant at all. We only found two interviews in which rejection seemed to be present, but the consensual qualitative research team had long debates about whether one of the student transcripts was indeed accurately classified.[7] Carol, a bisexual junior, described her experience as "a war

---

[6]The reader will note that we actually had more interviewees at time 2 than time 1. This is because we invited those we interviewed at time 1 to be interviewed again; we also invited other participants who had not been interviewed at time 1 to be interviewed at time 2.

[7]Consensual qualitative research (CQR; Hill, Knox, Thompson, Williams, & Hess, 2005; Hill, Thompson, & Williams, 1997) was used to analyze the interview content and build consensus systematically about themes. The data analysis team consisted of master's- and doctoral-level students and a research team member who served as an independent coder and auditor. The graduate students received CQR training from one faculty member before coding commenced. Training consisted of readings in the professional literature and prior experiential sessions with other interview data. Supervision of the coding process was provided by the same training professor throughout the analysis process.

Following the CQR methodology (Hill, Thompson, & Williams, 1997), all verbatim transcriptions were divided into domains related to the interview topics. Each independent coder was assigned a certain number of interviews and given responsibility for creating an abstract of the content. Abstracting is a process by which "the coder tries to capture the essence of what the interviewee has said about the domain in fewer words and with more clarity" (Hill, Thompson, & Williams, 1997, p. 546). Coding at this point in the analysis makes few inferences about the meaning of the interview data, remaining as close as possible to the explicit perspective of the interviewee. The goal is to "skinny down" the content for a more efficient and systematized approach to the data analysis. The interviews were assigned so that the content was always viewed by at least two coders who worked independently to craft an abstract. Once the abstracts were completed without collaboration, the two coders were brought together in the context of the whole team to work toward consensus. Discrepancies were discussed and reviewed by the whole team of coders. At times, transcripts were reviewed

every day," but the war was completely cast as a spiritual battle between "flesh" and "spirit," not sexuality and faith. In fact, language noting sexuality was almost completely absent in her answer to the questions. In the end, the team decided on the basis of the information at hand that *rejection* was probably the best classification that could be given to this student's description of her conflicted life at college. In the case of Brent, a recently graduated gay student, it was more typical for those who reject one or the other. He reported, "I currently don't identify as Christian anymore, or as strongly as I used to. I suppose in a sense I would not consider myself a religious person, though I have definitely been shaped by my religious upbringing. But I would say currently religion doesn't impact my life, if that makes sense. At least it doesn't impact my life as I choose to live it."

We have certainly heard in broader cultural discussions how rejection appeared to be the only way to manage the conflict between sexuality identity and religious/spiritual identity, but we did not find it in the development process of our Christian college sample, except for these two students. And in Carol's case, she did not seem to find relief from her struggle. She might still be holding onto her religious/spiritual box, but we might say that she knew what was on the ground at her feet. She said it was a "fight every day against [her] urges and temptations." Brent, on the other hand, noted more resolution for his conflict, citing how the experience had resulted in becoming a "more compassionate person." For the rest of the forty-five interviewees, rejection seemed noticeable by its absence. We thought it might be more apparent as a conflict-reducing option among our interviewees, but then again, we probably should not have been surprised that this highly religious and spiritual group of students might work tenaciously to hold onto both of these valued aspects of personhood.

The second option, also not frequent but more present than rejection, was called *split*. It seemed in these cases that students compartmentalized their sexual identity and their religious/spiritual identity. They appeared to be walled off from

---

again to determine exact meanings. The auditor oversaw the consensus-building process and had the chance for conference with the coders.

Once the consensual abstracts were completed, the team began to analyze across interview areas to discover thematic similarities and dissimilarities. Again, coders worked independently on thematic identification and analysis before joining a fellow coder who assessed the same abstracted items. The cross-checking and consensus-building process was used again in the context of the whole group of coders and auditor. There was significant consistency in the identification of themes by the coders. Final themes were ultimately discussed in the group and reviewed by auditors.

each other in the narrative of these students. Those in this smaller category did not articulate any real integration of these areas of development. Both boxes were clearly present, but they appeared to be claiming that one box did not affect the other—at least not in a way that we could identify from their answers. For example, Kevin, a gay senior, put it in the following way: "[I am] starting to turn back to spiritual development. I am comfortable with my sexuality. I am just kind of comfortable with it and done thinking about it. And so, I've noticed that I've become very cynical and I'm very tired of being cynical and hardened so I've started to look back towards . . . to focus on my religious identity." Amber, a bisexual sophomore, said, "I guess at this point my sexual development is more at the forefront. . . . That's mostly because I've spent a lot of time thinking about my religious development, but until recently I had thought I was on the asexual spectrum, but now I realize that I'm not. . . . They [still] don't interact." Laura, a bisexual junior, also noted her split status and attributed the current wall between sexuality and faith to her reaction to traumatic experiences of childhood and youth. She said, "Right now my sexual development needs to be caught up with my age, and my spiritual development will be ongoing. My spiritual development is a rollercoaster [because of the trauma]." Again, we saw two nonintegrated aspects of identity development. She is working in both areas of life, but no influence could be discerned between them by her response.

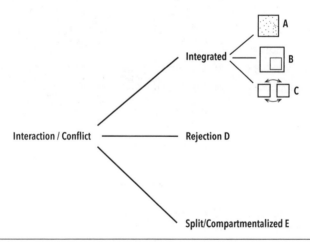

Figure 4.8. "Holding" sexual identity and religious/spiritual identity

The final option was called *integrated*, and those who described this option often used phrases such as "intertwined" or "hand-in-hand." This broader integration theme was by far the most frequent among our interviewees.

Grounded in their description were three discernable ways to hold sexuality and faith. The first way of holding the boxes appeared to describe a form of integration that we called a one-box approach, depicted in illustration A in figure 4.8 above. These students' descriptions seemed to suggest that their sexual identity and their religious/spiritual identities were hardly separable in ways they could easily explain. They had a hard time differentiating one without speaking of the other. Metaphorically it appeared that the contents of two boxes had been combined into one. Oliver, a gay senior, described his hold on the one box in this way.

> I don't really see them as separate categories. I don't really perceive them in different categories because they are so intimately intertwined. Because it's out of my sexual development and my sexual understanding that I pursue intimacy with God. But it's also out of intimacy with God that I learn to better understand and integrate my sexuality. So it's hard for me to see one above the other or in a hierarchy, because they're just so . . . I don't know how to explain it. If that makes sense, they're both important because they're both ones that are important to me.

The second way of holding the boxes we called the "box within a box" approach, depicted in illustration B in figure 4.8 above. Among the integrated models, this one was the most frequent. Students in this form of integration appeared to be holding two boxes, but they appeared to feel more stable by placing the smaller box inside the other larger and more "transcendent" box. At times students saw sexuality as the larger box that seemed to contain a still important but smaller religion/spirituality box. One student saw things from this perspective among our interviewees. We might say that sexuality assumed a more privileged perspective that defined integration for these students. On the other hand, we also found students who saw religion and/or spirituality as the transcendent box. For them their faith box contained the still important but smaller sexuality box.

The one interviewed student who placed the spiritual/religious box within the larger sexual box found it almost too close to call. Olivia, a queer junior, explained, "I understand that . . . my relationship with God is more important than my interaction with my sexuality, and I believe that. But, in terms of how the action are . . . how I personally interact with that, and how I am actually acting, and what I am actually thinking about, I think that my sexuality is more important right now. So both (laughing)."

Terry, a gay male student, described the larger religious/spiritual box and smaller sexual box this way:

> The way I see it is just in my view as a Christian the most important thing is centering your life on Christ and his Word and his ways and his action and what he did. So, being a Christian is a fundamental part of who I am, and I am also gay. I think they go hand in hand, and the spiritual element is just that much more important to me, so it kind of trumps out over the sexual identity. They are both important, but I guess sexual development won't necessarily lead to my spiritual development, but spiritual development will guide my sexual-identity development.

He went on to say, "They work together overall to make me a more thoughtful, empathic, and compassionate person. . . . I stopped and looked around at other groups who felt like outcasts, and I knew how it felt and how awful it is, so kind of just trying to feel empathy for anyone you [might] initially look down upon, if that makes sense. The Bible has those themes as well."

Michelle, a female graduate, told this story about the way she currently holds her sexual box within a larger religious/spiritual box. She explained,

> Currently, it's still good that I went to a Christian college. I got my life on the right track. [I went] from [a Christian college], a very tiny, religious based school to a secular college. . . . At [the former] you didn't talk about it, but at [the latter], they are like, "Everything is fine. Show your sexual identity. Everything is okay." If I went there, I wouldn't have had God finding me, me getting my life back. I would've fallen off track and gone into sexual identity completely. I'm okay now. I'm accepting of who I am, but I am also very cautious about not getting too far into letting my sexual identity define me. My first identity is a follower of Christ. Sexual identity doesn't define me.

Finally, the third way of holding the boxes was characterized as the two-box approach, depicted in illustration C in figure 4.8 above. Students described this form of integration by considering two separate boxes that interacted and dynamically influenced their hold. They were not as inseparable, as in the one-box approach, but they were not "split" apart, either. Jon, a gay graduate student, demonstrated how precarious holding onto two boxes can be. He spoke for a number of students when he explained, "Certainly they interact. . . . They are in conflict. They are fighting. There's no peace between them." Speaking less about conflict, Jonah, a gay senior, talked about the two influences as separate but equal. He explained, "I would definitely say that they influence each other, certainly. The fact that I'm gay kinda influences where I want to go to church. . . . And I think something like that, where you have a safe community, is important in that way because it influences my religious life." Chloe, a senior who identified herself as lesbian, described her interactive hold on sexuality and faith as "a dualism" with positive and negative influences.

SEXUAL IDENTITY AND FAITH IN STUDENT INTERVIEWS

There was another way we explored the relationship between sexual identity and faith. Thirty-nine students agreed to be interviewed in the first year of our longitudinal study. One section of the interview asked them to elaborate on how they understood their religious/spiritual development and their sexual development in the undergraduate years. We wanted to determine the role that faith might play in their current subjective experience of sexual attraction and behavior. We asked each of them, "How do you make sense of your same-sex attraction in light of your faith?" As was common for our time 1 interviews with students across the country, we found diverse perspectives represented among this group of self-reported committed Christians, but we also found some common themes.

Twenty of the thirty-nine interviewees were students who described themselves as being more "settled" in their identity development regarding their sexuality and their faith. These interviewees reported that they had reached a place of decision at the intersection of their same-sex attraction and their religious and spiritual development, and they described their settled position. The other eighteen interviewees were classified as "not settled."[8] They clearly indicated that they were still uncertain or even confused about these aspects of their lives.

This almost fifty-fifty breakdown among the settled and not-settled students was curious and frankly surprising. We anticipated that the undergraduate years would be a time of ongoing search and discovery, but in our interview group half said they had found a home in their developmental journey. It seemed surprising to find so many undergrad students reportedly

---

[8]One interviewee did not answer this question in the interview, so for this section we are looking at thirty-eight interviewees.

at home in this complicated interaction. Was this a permanent home, or might it have been a temporary house for their undergraduate years? If the future is like the reported past for these interviewees, it is likely that there will be more settled and unsettled moments at the intersection of sexuality and faith for these undergrads. But for now, the interviews provided a chance to see how they held both essential aspects of human development and culture at this point in their lives.

As we reviewed the twenty "settled" and the eighteen "unsettled" interviewees, we found students in both classifications who balanced their sexual development and religious/spiritual development by holding one more centrally than the other. Those who seemed to put more weight on their sexual-identity development tended to interpret doctrine and experience in light of that part of themselves (their same-sex sexuality and experiences there) being more salient to their personhood. They also demonstrated in their surveys of identity weighting (fig. 4.1) significantly higher scores for the importance of sexual attraction in defining themselves. Those students were viewed as being similar to what has been termed "Side A" Christians.[9] One such student, Sara, a twenty-year-old senior, said, "I've basically come to the conclusion that same-sex attraction may not have been something that was planned before the fall, but it is something that is part of humanity, and it is redeemable. There is good to be found in that, much like divorce wasn't necessarily part of the plan. It's not what would happen in an ideal world, but we have to allow for that." Notice that Sara talked about aspects of both sexuality and faith, not the absence of one or the other. She had found a way to hold these significant aspects of personhood in this moment of her life.

Those who gave more weight to their religious/spiritual development tended to interpret doctrine and experience in light of this aspect of personhood. They also demonstrated on their identity weighting (fig. 4.1) significantly higher scores for biological sex as an important feature when defining themselves. These students were seen as being more like what are often called "Side B" Christians. One such student, Savannah, viewed the intersection in the following way. "I have a strong faith that Jesus talks a whole lot [more] about love, equality, and

---

[9]The language of "Side A" and "Side B" gay Christians comes from Bridges Across the Divide (n.d.). Side A refers to gay Christians who believe that same-sex sexual relationships can be morally permissible, whereas Side B refers to gay Christians who view same-sex sexual relationships as morally impermissible. Side C has referred to those who are either undecided or in tension around these conclusions.

mutual respect for others than he does about same-sex attraction being a sin. And although it is a sin to engage in sexual activity with the same sex . . . there is no other sin that is greater than another." Again, we saw the presence of both sexuality and faith in this position. The difference appeared to be the student's unique hold on the two in this moment of identity development.

Both those who gave more weight to their sexuality and those who gave more weight to their faith appeared to have settled (or be in the process of settling) on a way to hold these unavoidable "boxes" of human development (see above "Managing Two Full Boxes"). Unquestionably, both aspects of personhood appeared to be vital, and the embrace of a sex-central narrative or a faith-central narrative seemed to make a difference for understanding how students lived at this intersection. Mia, a freshman, reported, "There are some things in Scripture that will always contradict . . . [like] sexuality that is not straight sexuality. In the end, though, I really don't think that God really cares that much [about] who you love and you sleep with."[10] Jonah, a twenty-year-old junior, explained it this way:

> Being more liberal has given me a more liberal take on all of this for sure. So, even when I was first going through things I was always just like, "Okay, well this is what it is and I have to figure out the best way to deal with it and figure out how to go about my life." And I definitely relied on God a lot through that process, and it definitely strengthened my relation with God.

This student saw his sexual experience as more central to his current settled place, but a relationship with God was not jettisoned, and faith development was not absent. Earlier Jonah explained his move to this more settled place by decentralizing his traditional doctrinal beliefs for a more experiential approach. He said, "I just got the point where I realized that what's in the Bible can be taken [as] anti-same-sex attraction or pro-same-sex attraction, and there's so many different ways to take from that. I just needed to go to God and figure

---

[10]Mia's comment is reminiscent of many made by emerging adults in Christian Smith's work *Lost in Transition* (2011). In his study emerging adults' answers to questions were often a jumbled mix of moral individualism, situational relativism, and firm moral commitments blended into a mix of confusing statements. So, as Mia says, "some things in Scripture will always contradict" (relativism?), "sexuality is not straight sexuality" (individualism?), and "I really don't think that God really cares that much [about] who you love and you sleep with" (committed statement?). Add to this a rather drastic decline in biblical literacy among even the most spiritually committed young people, and it is not hard to understand the difficulty this group has articulating a theologically grounded position on matters of such complexity as sexual identity.

out what is best for me or what He wants for my life as opposed to some overall truth. Because I don't know if there is one." For these students, at least for this point in their developmental process, their human experience overshadowed a more traditional faith-based interpretation of human experience.

It was apparent in all the interviews that students strongly desired a position that held both their sexual development and their religious/spiritual development. They were typically not willing to jettison either one completely. Although students might conceivably turn from their faith or deny their sexuality when trying to reconcile what might feel irreconcilable, as was mentioned above, most tried to hold them in their own unique way. They wanted, it appeared, to avoid losing their grip on either one. Of the twenty "settled" interviewees, ten were classified as maintaining their hold by positioning their sexual expression more centrally than their traditional faith expression. The other ten "settled" interviewees maintained their hold by positioning their traditional faith expression with its doctrinal beliefs more centrally than their sexual-identity status. None of the interviewees was unclassifiable in this regard.[11] Once they had settled, they appeared to be relatively clear on how they balanced sexuality and faith—at least for now. Moreover, it seemed important that most of these settled students worked diligently to avoid the loss of either their sexual experience or their religious/spiritual experience, even when one was held more centrally than the other.

Of the eighteen "unsettled" interviewees, the picture was less clear when it came to identity development in terms of both sexuality and religiosity/spirituality.[12] Four of the eighteen interviewees were simply not classifiable when it came to differentiating their lived experience at this intersection of same-sex attraction and faith. Some of those students were ambivalent in their beliefs and behaviors—"going back and forth," as Justin, a twenty-year-old junior, explained. Logan, a twenty-two-year-old junior, described the experience as

---

[11]To corroborate our CQR classifications of "settled while giving more weight to sexual identity" and "settled while giving more weight to traditional religious/spiritual identity," we checked these qualitative ratings against the attitudinal scores in the survey with regard to acceptance or nonacceptance of same-sex behaviors. We saw that our "settled" ratings ratings were 95% accurate when compared with their attitudinal scores.

[12]To corroborate our CQR classifications of "unsettled while giving more weight to sexual identity" and "unsettled while giving more weight to traditional religious/spiritual identity," we again checked the qualitative ratings against attitudinal scores associated with acceptance or nonacceptance of same-sex behaviors. We saw that our "unsettled ratings" ratings dropped to 85% accurate when compared with their attitudinal scores. The "messier" qualitative process appeared to lower the accuracy by 10%.

"floating." He said, "I just sit here without answers and just . . . try to . . . focus on my school and just do that." In a more animated discussion, Wyatt stated, "So how do I make sense of [my sexuality] in the context of my faith? I make it up as I go. I trust that God is doing something with it. I feel like oftentimes God is a big pain in the ass, but surely there is something good that happens with faith and . . . I'm just not totally sure what that is yet."

For these four unclassified interviewees, we could not reliably confirm that students had found a way to hold their sexuality and their faith. They seemed to feel on hold. At least, they did not provide enough information for us to discern how they lived at this intersection. But being on hold was not all about tension or discomfort. Jackson, a senior, noted that although the "conflict" between personal faith and same-sex attraction was "probably not resolved," he saw his current life experience as "an incredible blessing." He said, "I see it just as part of who I am and who God made me at this point." He had found a place of respite, even though without resolution on how to hold his sexuality and his faith.

The remaining fourteen unsettled interviewees continued to illustrate their indecision but not inaction. They cited their confusion or their uncertainties and at the same time talked about behavioral choices that gave more weight to either sexuality or faith in their identity development. Liam, a sophomore, described how the major obstacle that left him unsettled was a practical issue—vocation. He reported,

> I think my conflict comes in the sense of finding a spouse, because to be honest, it'd just be easier for someone who's looking to do theological work or someone looking to be a minister at a church, it's just easier to either be someone who's single or straight, and I think that's where my conflict comes in. . . . I think the biggest emotional thing I've felt is why do I keep pressing for the fact that I want a spouse. To live a single life would just be easier because you wouldn't have to think about it that much and you don't have to wrestle theologically with it.

We heard the added complexity of another intersecting identity for this student. Besides sexual and religious/spiritual development, he wrestled to integrate vocational/occupational identity in the already-complicated mix.

Aiden, a gay senior, was "still trying to decide" but cited a hope instead of an obstacle. He asserted, "I also think I can have both, because not to ignore certain parts of the teaching, but at the same time, I think they are both really important to me. I shouldn't be expected to be someone I'm not." Olivia, a queer sophomore, cited indecision, waiting for more evidence. "I don't think homosexual acts are sinful. And I don't think the desire is a temptation, but I'm not sure about that. I'm still trying to keep an open mind, and looking at different sides in the argument." Finally, Aaliyah, a senior who identified as queer, was unsettled but more what sounded to be fearful than hopeful. She explained, "I am still in a space where I would rather not date just in case I could be doing something wrong." She went on to describe the ambivalence caused reportedly by the fact that she is still "coming to terms with it on [her] own right now."

Nine of the unsettled students appeared to live with their uncertainties in a way that gave great weight to their more traditional religious and spiritual beliefs and values as influencing or shaping decisions about their sexuality and behavior. For many this seemed the safer route to follow at this point in their development, but they noted being caught between these two aspects of human development. It is also possible to have a third side in this discussion, what has been referred to as Side C, reflecting the unsettledness of the ambivalent position. Carter, a twenty-one-year-old junior who identifies as gay, seemed to speak for many in this category when he was asked how he made sense of his same-sex attraction in light of his faith. "That's definitely something on a day-to-day basis that I'm figuring out," he explained:

> I've figured out that, okay, this is who I am, but in that I'm still one of God's children. God still loves me for who I am. So, from that, I'm starting to process more detailed questions, you know, about relationships and stuff. And I think for me right now, I'm still figuring [it] out. So, at the moment I've decided to remain celibate, not because necessarily I wholeheartedly believe in that, but because I don't want to make any decisions and be scared of those right now. I think I have a fear that if I make a decision, it's going to be the wrong one, and so it's like I don't know yet how I feel about it completely. . . . That's why I don't feel okay with where I am right now because it is out of fear, not out of Scripture or out of God's love.

Five of the unsettled students appeared to give greater weight to their sexuality as they tentatively lived at this intersection, but it appeared to feel risky. Like the other unsettled students, theirs was a cautious position, more conscious of being caught in between than settled and secure. Might these students also be called Side C? Again, like the previous group, their ambivalence appeared to be the characteristic quality of their position. Chloe, a lesbian senior, responded in the following way to questions about making sense of same-sex attraction in light of faith.

> I don't know honestly if I have settled in my mind what I think about it. I feel so good about the relationship that I'm in and so confident in its holiness, if you want to say that. . . . I feel like it, it can't, I don't know, it's hard because I almost rationalize it in my head. Like how could this be a bad thing, which I know that's not, it's not a great way to think about things spiritually. But like, I'm definitely in prayer about it a lot, and we pray about it together. . . . We even pray for conviction . . . like if we're doing something wrong please convict us. I have never felt conviction in my relationship with her. . . . And I still don't know, like I can't say. I definitely live as if it's not [a sin]. And I live as if I'm happy with who I am, which I am. I am really happy with who I am, and I love how God made me. But I don't know if he has made me this way, I don't know. It's a really weird place to be in.

We hear this heartfelt internal conflict—not knowing how to hold her sexuality and her faith. Obviously, they are two important aspects of her identity, but she had not found a secure way to embrace these aspects of her personhood.

Being settled or unsettled about sexuality and religion also affected how students assessed their Christian college campuses. The unsettled nature for these fourteen classifiable students seemed to be especially complicated in a Christian college or university where there was clearly a designated party line to follow. Intentionally, through policy and stated community standards, or unintentionally, through "heteronormative" (as Hannah, a bisexual senior, noted) expectations, the campus communities were viewed as having established a place for all to settle. The end goal appeared to be clear for most all interviewed students. They could feel attraction for the same sex, but they could not exhibit behaviors that promote a sexual response. Unfortunately, the community was also viewed as having a general and possibly simplistic approach about how to develop this end goal. Students for the most part only perceived one strident message, and it was not usually couched in any developmental language. It was a behavioral prohibition without any sense of how to grow into that injunction. That message was primarily "Don't act on sexual attractions!" Absent in the interviews was any real sense that Christian colleges and universities viewed sexual development as having significant overlap for those who experience some level of opposite-sex attraction and those who experience some level of same-sex attraction. Absent was the idea that all students—no matter their orientation—need to grow into whole sexual persons. In the eyes of students, the developmental process for sexual identity seemed to be more informally engaged at best, often lacking any formative plan that students could identify. Programs and events were mentioned and even appreciated, but they did not seem to be connected with any kind of educational plan for sexual development.

Especially lacking in light of the whole-person educational mission of most Christian liberal arts institutions was a perceivable systematic curricular or cocurricular initiative to support sexual-identity development and religious/ spiritual development. This deduction is not meant to suggest that Christian colleges and universities ignored this developmental intersection—particularly in the cocurricular areas of these institutions. There were indeed support services at all the institutions that could be used to address these aspects of personhood. (More discussion will occur in chapter six about cocurricular resources that were available on campus to assist students who wanted to engage discussion about sexuality and/or faith.) Besides the most frequently noted resource, the college or university counseling center, about 25% of students in interviews also noted all-student events, and about 50% identified sexual-minority-only gatherings that were to one degree or another helpful. The curricular area, however, appeared to be noteworthy by its absence, except for a few classroom lectures that came up in the interview discussions. At least in the minds of the interviewed students, there was little evidence of an intentional institutional plan to assist them in the developmental process of learning to hold sexuality and religion/spirituality.

This issue of whole-person liberal arts education may be more necessary for sexual-minority students who are unsettled than for their settled peers. For those unsettled students, an intentional institutional plan, contributing to a secure holding environment, may well be an essential foundation for student development. As we compared the experience of unsettled students to those who were more settled, we found that settling, even if only for a period of time, appeared to be advantageous for our interviewees. Scores for anxiety and overall distress on the Counseling Center Assessment of Psychological Symptoms (CCAPS) were significantly higher for unsettled students than for settled students. This group of unsettled students was not only qualitatively different from the settled student group; it was quantitatively different on this measure. Does that mean that their unsettled status caused more negative psychological symptoms related to anxiety and distress? It is possible, but we don't know at this time. It could just as easily mean that higher anxiety and distress made it harder to settle. So, although we are not confident about the cause, it remains interesting to note that being unsettled for the interviewees was associated with a more taxing experience during their college experience. Settled students were not facing the same stresses, at least those we studied. They described an experience in their interviews that appeared to suggest they felt more clear in their perspective and more secure in their life direction. We don't know whether their status represented an achieved identity status that will avoid significant reevaluation in the future. We can only say for now that they as a group did not seem to experience the same level of anxiety or distress in their interviews, and it showed in their current CCAPS scores.

Whether students were settled or unsettled, Christian colleges and universities remained a place, for better or worse, where the majority wanted to move forward in their developmental process. Liam, an unsettled nineteen-year-old sophomore, described it more positively in the following way.

It was a door for me to explore my faith. Because all of a sudden, it's like, here's something that I know is true about myself, but I also know that I'm a child of God and all these other things, so how do I start to reconcile the two? I think that's really moved me to go deeper in my faith and a lot broader, which is really why I'm here at this college.... So even though it's burdening at times, it's really been an eye opener and also a catalyst of sorts to draw me closer to my faith and my relationship with God. I think sadly that's kind of rare for people with same-sex attraction who are in Christian contexts.

Regretfully, not all students were quite so positive when they described the developmental process in the campus climate, which we will discuss in greater detail in chapter six. Students seemed to learn quickly that the Christian college and university experience for sexual minorities is a mixed bag, but most came and stayed for a reason. They wanted to consider faith in these prime identity-development years of life, and they were hoping for a relational community that could participate in that process. The interviewees in our study strongly affirmed the hope for relationships that might help them with their identity development.

Remember the metaphor of the two boxes that was mentioned earlier in this chapter (see above "Managing Two Full Boxes")? One box represented sexual development, and the other represented religious/spiritual development. The metaphor presented students as individuals who are autonomously having the two-box experience in the college community. That being the case, it's easy to envision that the way students hold their identity development boxes is based only on their own strength or effort. It's hard to debate that the negotiation of these in-arm boxes is connected to some degree with internal qualities of individual students—their level of sexual attraction, their values or beliefs, their intentions, or their gender identity or biological sex. More mature and grown-up students can probably carry a heavier load. They might manage these awkward and hard-to-carry boxes more efficiently. More clever students might find innovative ways to carry the objects. It's possible that these factors do contribute something to the way the boxes are handled, but this individualized image is only half of the reality of moving in the college years. The campus community is the other half—just as influential in the minds of our interviewees as their own individual strengths and weaknesses. The social support of the institutional environment seems to be equally implicated in the way these boxes are handled. Friends and even strangers can help support the load. Staff and faculty can play a role in how boxes are held. It appears most reasonable to assume that a mature sexual identity grows best when individuals and the community work together to carry and unpack the boxes. We might assume that these two boxes are more efficiently and effectively managed when students and other community members collaborate. Our interviewees appear to believe this to be true. When a load is shared, it can make quite a difference for the lived experience of students at Christian colleges and universities.

In the next chapter we want to explore further the question of faith and sexuality, including whether religiosity is related to views of causation, attitudes about sexual behavior, the timing of reaching various milestone events in sexual-identity formation, and psychological health and well-being.

CHAPTER 4 TAKEAWAYS

1. Sexual attractions did not change much for our students over time. Some students experienced new sexual milestones, and some changed their understandings of their own sexuality, but their attractions on average were rather stable.

2. Among the various aspects of identity that could inform sexual-identity labels, attraction to the same sex was on average given the most weight. However, level of intrinsic religiosity appeared to make a difference in the weight. Those with higher scores on intrinsic religiosity showed increases in weight to their values over time.

3. There was also not much change in the importance of various aspects of identity for our students over time, although their values and beliefs regarding sexuality, on average, became more equally weighted alongside their sexual attraction.

4. Students who scored higher on intrinsic religiosity (in which personal religious commitment and motivation in their faith impacts all aspects of their lives) in particular held the label of Christian as much more important than students who scored lower on intrinsic religiosity, but both groups of students valued the label of Christian.

5. More students privately identify as a sexual minority than are willing to share this identity with others. While slightly more than three out of four of our students privately identify as a sexual minority (private identity), only two out of four claim this identity publicly (public identity).

6. Students valued identifying as a Christian, identifying as a lesbian, gay, or bisexual person, and identifying as a lesbian, gay, or bisexual Christian much more than they did identifying as a celibate lesbian, gay, or bisexual Christian. The term *celibate* was of lesser importance in how they understood themselves.

7. We introduced the image of students moving into liberal arts colleges holding two boxes that represent their sexual development and their religious/spiritual development. This metaphor appeared particularly apt in describing the narratives of interviewed sexual-minority students who reported that they were working to find a method for holding both of these large and heavy identity-based boxes.

8. There were three broad ways to manage the boxes: rejection of one or the other box, split or compartmentalize one or the other, and integration of both. Most sexual-minority students were endeavoring to integrate their sexuality and their faith development instead of rejecting one or living with a split. Of the integrative options, most students described holding the sexuality box "inside" the larger religion/spirituality box.

9. We saw about a fifty-fifty split in students who reported feeling settled and students who felt unsettled in their identity development regarding their sexuality and their faith.

▼

REFERENCES

American Psychological Association. (2008). Sexual orientation and homosexuality. Washington, DC: Author. Retrieved from www.apa.org/topics/sorientation.pdf

Bolak-Boratov, H. (2006). Making sense of heterosexuality: An exploratory study of young heterosexual identities in Turkey. *Sex Roles: A Journal of Research, 54*, 213-25.

Boorstein, M. (2014, December 13). Gay Christians choosing celibacy emerge from the shadows. *The Washington Post.* Retrieved from www.washingtonpost.com/local/ gay-christians-choosing-celibacy-emerge-from-the-shadows/2014/12/13/51c73aea -6ab2-11e4-9fb4-a622dae742a2_story.html?utm_term=.7c9a0bda76d1

Bridges Across the Divide. (n.d.). The sides of the divide. Retrieved from http://web .archive.org/web/20100716091027/http://www.bridges-across.org/ba/sides.htm

Chan, C. S. (1989). Issues of identity development among Asian-American lesbian and gay men. *Journal of Counseling and Development, 68*, 16-20.

Damian, Chris. (2014, August 11). Fear and celibacy. *Spiritual Friendship: Musings on God, Sexuality, Relationships* [Blog]. Retrieved from https://spiritualfriendship.org/2014/ 08/11/fear-and-celibacy-2/

Dean, J. B., Stratton, S. P., Yarhouse, M. A., & Lastoria, M. D. (2011). Same-sex attraction. In M. D. Lastoria (Ed.), *Sexuality, religiosity, behaviors, attitudes: A look at religiosity, sexual attitudes and sexual behaviors of Christian college students* (pp. 56-69). Houghton, NY: Association for Christians in Student Development.

Diamond, L. M. (2007). A dynamical systems approach to the development and expression of female same-sex sexuality. *Perspectives on Psychological Science, 2*(2), 142-57.

Diamond, L. M. (2008). *Sexual fluidity: Understanding women's love and desire.* Cambridge, MA: Harvard University Press.

Dube, E. M., & Savin-Williams, R. C. (1999). Sexual identity development among ethnic sexual-minority male youths. *Developmental Psychology, 35*, 1389-99.

Eliason, M. J. (1995). Accounts of sexual identity formation in heterosexual students. *Sex Roles, 32*(11), 821-34. http://dx.doi.org/10.1007/bf01560191

Fukuyama, M. A., & Ferguson, A. D. (2000). Lesbian, gay, and bisexual people of color: Understanding cultural complexity and managing multiple oppressions (pp. 81-105). In R. Perez, K. DeBord, & K. Bieschke (Eds.), *Handbook of counseling and psychotherapy with lesbian, gay, and bisexual clients.* Washington, DC: APA.

Garcia, K. (2015, September 14). Yes, I'm a gay Christian. *Kevin Garcia* [Blog]. Retrieved from www.thekevingarcia.com/yes-im-a-gay-christian/

Gonnerman, J. (2012, May 23). Why I call myself a gay Christian. *First Things.* Retrieved from www.firstthings.com/web-exclusives/2012/05/why-i-call-myself-a-gay-christian

Hill, C. E., Knox, S., Thompson, B. J., Williams, E. N., & Hess, S. A. (2005). Consensual qualitative research: An update. *Journal of Counseling Psychology, 52,* 196-205.

Hill, C. E., Thompson, B. J., & Williams, E. N. (1997). A guide to conducting consensual qualitative research. *The Counseling Psychologist, 25,* 517-72.

Hill, W. (2010). *Washed and waiting: Reflections on Christian faithfulness and homosexuality.* New York: HarperCollins.

Hill, W. (2015). *Spiritual friendship: Finding love in the church as a celibate gay Christian.* Ada, MI: Brazos.

Kinsey, C., Pomeroy, W. B., & Martin, C. E. (1948). *Sexual behavior in the human male.* Philadelphia: W. B. Saunders.

Knight, K. (2015, January 5). Why this Christian will never celebrate gay celibacy. *Coming Out Christian* [Blog]. Retrieved from www.patheos.com/blogs/kimberlyknight/2015/01/why-this-christian-will-never-celebrate-gay-celibacy/

Konik, J., & Stewart, A. (2004). Sexual-identity development in the context of compulsory heterosexuality. *Journal of Personality, 72,* 815-44.

Lindsey. (2015, January 28). Why I call myself "celibate." *A Queer Calling* [Blog]. Retrieved from http://aqueercalling.com/2015/01/28/why-i-call-myself-celibate/

Marcia, J. E. (1966). Development and validation of ego-identity status. *Journal of Personality and Social Psychology, 3*(5), 551-58.

Moore, M. (2014, October 27). I love Jesus too much to call myself a "gay Christian." *The Christian Post.* Retrieved from www.christianpost.com/news/i-love-jesus-too-much-to-call-myself-a-gay-christian-128719/#dei0YYb13BISeoLp.99

Morgan, E. M. (2012). Not always straight path: College students' narratives of heterosexual-identity development. *Sex Roles, 66,* 79-93.

Olson, R. E. (2002). *The mosaic of Christian belief.* Downers Grove, IL: IVP Academic.

Reiter, L. (1989). Sexual orientation, sexual identity, and the question of choice. *Clinical Social Work Journal, 17,* 138-50.

Rosario, M., Schrimshaw, E. W., Hunter, J., & Braun, L. (2006). Sexual-identity development among lesbian, gay and bisexual youths: Consistency and change over time. *The Journal of Sex Research, 43*(1), 46-58.

Rosario, M., Schrimshaw, E. W., & Hunter, J. (2011). Different patterns of sexual-identity development over time: Implications for the psychological adjustment of lesbian, gay, and bisexual youths. *Journal of Sex Research, 48,* 3-15.

Savin-Williams, R. C. (2005). *The new gay teenager.* Cambridge, MA: Harvard University Press.

Savin-Williams, R. C., & Cohen, K. M. (2004). Homoerotic development during childhood and adolescence. *Child and Adolescent Psychiatric Clinics of North America, 13,* 524-49.

Smith, C. (2011). *Lost in transition: The dark side of emerging adulthood.* Oxford: Oxford University Press.

Sprinkle, P. (2017, July 28). Is the debate about same-sex marriage a primary or secondary theological issue? *The Center for Faith, Sexuality, and Gender.* Retrieved from www .centerforfaith.com/blog/is-the-debate-about-same-sex-marriage-a-primary -or-secondary-theological-issue

Sprinkle, P. (2017, July 31). The debate about same-sex marriage is not a secondary issue. *The Center for Faith, Sexuality, and Gender.* Retrieved from www.centerfor faith.com/blog/the-debate-about-same-sex-marriage-is-not-a-secondary-issue

Stratton, S. P., Dean, J. B., Yarhouse, M. A., & Lastoria, M. D. (2013). Sexual minorities in faith-based higher education: A national survey of attitudes, milestones, identity, and religiosity. *Journal of Psychology & Theology, 41*(1), 3-23.

Tushnet, E. (2012, May 30). The botany club: Gay kids in Catholic schools. *The American Conservative.* Retrieved from www.theamericanconservative.com/2012/ 05/30/the-botany-club-gay-kids-in-catholic-schools/

Wilkinson, S., & Kitzinger, C. (1993). *Heterosexuality: A feminism & psychology reader.* London: Sage.

Wolff, J. R., Himes, H. L., Soares, S. D., & Kwon, E. M. (2016). Sexual minority students in non-affirming religious higher education: Mental health, outness, and identity. *Psychology of Sexual Orientation and Gender Diversity, 3*(2), 201-12.

Worthington, R. L., Savoy, H. B., Dillon, F. R. & Vernaglia, E. R. (2002). Heterosexual-identity development: A multidimensional model of individual and social identity. *The Counseling Psychologist, 30,* 496-531.

Yarhouse, M. A. (2001). Sexual-identity development: The influence of valuative frameworks on identity synthesis. *Psychotherapy, 38*(3), 331-41.

Yarhouse, M. A., Morgan, T., Houp, D., & Sadusky, J. (2017). Celibate gay Christians: Sexual identity and religious beliefs and practices. *Journal of Pastoral Care & Counseling, 71*(1), 52-59.

Yarhouse, M. A., & Tan, E. S. N. (2004). *Sexual identity synthesis: Attributions, meaning-making, and the search for congruence.* Lanham, MD: University Press of America.

APPENDIX

Table A4.1. Frequencies of reported sexual orientation across year 1 and year 2 (*n* = 93)

		YEAR 2 REPORTED SEXUAL ORIENTATION				
		Heterosexual	Homosexual	Bisexual	Other	Total
Year 1 Reported Sexual Orientation	Heterosexual	3[a]	0[b]	5	2	10
	Homosexual	0	37[a]	1[b]	4	42
	Bisexual	1	1[b]	20	4	26
	Other	1	3	4[a]	7[a]	15
	Total	5	41	30	17	93

[a] Count is higher than expected.
[b] Count is lower than expected.
$\chi^2 (9) = 85.41, p < 0.001$, suggesting change over time is different than expected.

Table A4.2. Frequencies of reported sexual identity across Year 1 and Year 2 (*n* = 93)

		YEAR 2 REPORTED SEXUAL IDENTITY				
		Straight	Lesbian/Gay	Bisexual	Other	Total
Year 1 Reported Sexual Identity	Straight	11[a]	0[b]	0	3	14
	Lesbian/Gay	2	37[a]	0[b]	2[b]	41
	Bisexual	1	0[b]	14[a]	7	22
	Other	1	1[b]	6	8[a]	16
	Total	15	38	20	20	93

[a] Count is higher than expected.
[b] Count is lower than expected.
$\chi^2 (9) = 85.41, p < 0.001$, suggesting change over time is different than expected.

Table A4.3. Frequency of on-campus identity as a sexual minority (*n* = 160)

	Frequency	Percent
I am known only to a few close friends as a sexual minority (someone who experiences same-sex attraction).	95	59.4
I am known to many individuals on campus as a sexual minority (someone who experiences same-sex attraction).	27	16.9
I am not known to anyone as a sexual minority.	38	23.8

Table A4.4. Frequencies of public and private sexual identities (*n* = 160)

		PUBLIC SEXUAL IDENTITY					
		Bisexual	Gay/Lesbian	Heterosexual	Other	Questioning	Total
Private Sexual Identity	No Response	0	0	1	0	0	1
	Bisexual	11[b]	0[a]	28	5	2	46
	Gay/Lesbian	1[a]	32[b]	23[a]	16	3	75
	Heterosexual	0	0	7	1	0	8
	Other	1	0	10	6	0	17
	Questioning	0	0	11	1	1	13
	Total	13	32	80	29	6	160

[a] Fewer responses than expected.
[b] More responses than expected.

Note: Participants were asked to indicate their public and private sexual identities, and these were different from expected, $c^2 (20) = 76.55, p < 0.001$. In particular, 80 of 160 (50.0%) publicly identify as heterosexual, and 45 of 160 (28.1%) identify as LGB. More people reported matching public and private sexual identities of bisexual or gay/lesbian than expected given the distribution of identities.

Table A4.5. Frequencies of importance of aspects of identity (*n* = 160)

	M (SD)
How important to you is it to identify yourself as a Christian?	8.77 (1.91)
How important to you is it to identify yourself as gay, lesbian, or bisexual?	5.58 (3.27)
How important to you is it to identify yourself as a gay, lesbian, or bisexual Christian?	5.87 (3.42)
How important to you is it to identify yourself as a celibate gay, lesbian, or bisexual Christian?	3.33 (3.16)

Note: Participants (*n* = 159) were asked how important it was to identify themselves in particular ways. Participants indicated it was more important to identify themselves as a Christian than it was any of these additional labels, and they indicated that it was less important to identify themselves as a celibate gay, lesbian, or bisexual Christian than any of these additional labels, $F(3, 474) = 118.87, p < 0.001$.

Table A4.6. Average weights for aspects of sexual identity (*n* = 160)

	Minimum Percent	Maximum Percent	M (SD)
Percent biological sex (as male or female)	0	90	11.45 (13.16)
Percent gender identity (how masculine or feminine a person feels)	0	90	13.86 (13.16)
Percent persistence and direction of sexual attraction (toward the same or opposite sex or both)	0	100	27.11 (20.53)
Percent intentions (how a person intends to act, the kind of person one intends to become)	0	89	15.50 (11.83)
Percent values (one's beliefs and values about sexual behavior)	0	80	19.45 (13.45)
Percent behavior (what one does with the intentions and attractions one has)	0	70	15.82 (10.34)

Table A4.7. Other aspects of sexual identity and their weights as given by individual participants (*n* = 160)

Curiosity	100%
Environmental/cultural?	15%
Experience (with persons of each gender)	50%
Family dynamics	
Genetically born this way	100%
Knowledge (how much I know about different identities)	30% or Relatively Important
My religious beliefs about myself are of equal weight to my values	
Natural feelings of same-sex attraction	35%
Parental role	40%
Peer/family pressure (how others react to perceived identity/behavior)	10%
Political or societal oppression	10%
Sexual abuse at 13, 16, and 17; would overlap everything	
Sexual trauma	25%
Sharing an identity with others of similar experiences	25% probably
Social pressure	20%
Societal pressure	40%
The support system in place	25%
Theological anthropology	30% if this was included; the other percentages would be 60%, 5%, and 5% respectively
Desire for sex physically	75%
Developmental?	15%
Environment	20%
I mean ugh. The random numbers. I think also cultural influence on what gender and sexuality have a big influence too. Let's give it a 20%? That would make it 120%? I'm sorry, it's hard to give weight to these things.	
The attitudes of those around you/family/friends	25%
Being immature and naive	60%
Personality attraction is more important than aesthetic	20%
This is a choice	0%

Note: Four commented on the difficulty of assigning these percentages.

FAITH AND SEXUALITY

I was a very young Christian when I came to [school]. I had only been a Christian for a couple of years. So, it's been interesting because a lot of what I now consider my core beliefs really have been shaped by friends that I have had. And a lot of my pet peeves and resentments have also been shaped by friends that I have had. So, that's been interesting, like I am trying to understand the Christian subculture.

   —*Miranda, a senior, identifies as bisexual, time 1*

[Most faculty and staff are] most likely committed to conservative interpretations, but they also realize how hard it is for LGBT students here. They don't really know how to reconcile what seems to be a toxic climate for LGBT students with their theology. That's something they are caught between. They are very compassionate but they just feel stuck, I guess.

   —*Kevin, a junior, identifies as gay, time 1*

I think the overwhelming Christian presence at [school] is a two-edged sword. On the one hand, we've been taught from childhood to love and accept and forgive and uphold our brothers and sisters. I think that affects the climate positively because we are instructed to love. . . . But then there is also the overwhelming perceived antigay agenda in Scripture. And that is what negatively affects the climate because it makes students think it is impossible to be gay and Christian at the same time. And so what happens is a lot of confusion. Because they don't know . . . you know, how does the love of Jesus pertain in that situation? How does it play out in real life?

   —*Adriana, a senior, identifies as bisexual, time 1*

▼▲▼

A FEW YEARS AGO, after hearing a class lecture on sexuality, Michael came to his professor asking for help. He was in pain; he was struggling to make sense of his sexual attraction in light of his more conservative Christian beliefs and to make sense of these religious beliefs in light of his attraction. His growing shame, confusion, and even hopelessness were becoming suffocating, and his desperation led to an unreported suicide attempt just days before he sat in his professor's office.

Michael wanted to see his professor for counseling, he said, because he believed that she was both comfortable with his attractions and understanding of how important his faith was to him. Obviously, for his professor, this dual role was problematic; after some discussion, Michael recognized this conflict and cautiously agreed to see someone else. But he had clear requirements in making this transition to a therapist. First, the therapist could not work in the college counseling center. Not only was he concerned about the limits of confidentiality on this small Christian college campus, but also his previous college counselor had made some comments regarding his sexual attraction that Michael felt were very invalidating. He never went back. Second, the therapist had to be a person of faith. He didn't want someone who had "bought into a watered-down form of Christianity"; rather, he felt he needed someone who resonated with his theological beliefs.

Finding such a therapist proved more difficult than expected. The college is in a fairly religiously conservative community. Even so, most conservative Christian therapists in the area don't have much experience with these sorts of sexual-identity issues, particularly in walking in this tension between sexual identity and faith. Few would ever consider the old conversion-therapy interventions, but there is a tendency to overemphasize faith and psychological health, with a seeming hesitancy to help clients accept and integrate their sexual attraction.

The search turned to the other Christian therapists in the area, those who are less conservative in their religious beliefs. Many of these professionals have found a way to synthesize a "gay-affirming" approach with their theology. Would they be a better fit for Michael? After requesting referrals, one conversation stood out among the rest as a good representation of what the professor was hearing from these clinicians. A self-identified Christian therapist asked for clarification on this case. He said, "Am I understanding this correctly? His main issue that he is gay, but also that he has been raised in a conservative Christian home which considers that to be 'wrong' and therefore he is struggling with the various levels of coming out (to self, family, God). I would never try to 'convert' anyone to a gay identity, but I do think self-acceptance is the first most important step." To his credit, this therapist never said that Michael's religious beliefs would need to change or become less, but the implication in the tone of the conversation was that his faith was wrong and that was the source of his problem.

There was no way that Michael or his professor could have known the path he would take to hold his sexual identity and his faith in balance. What they did know, however, was that he needed someone who could understand how thoroughly his faith was interwoven with his beliefs about sexuality, his sexual behaviors, and his developing sexual identity.

Fortunately, with a bit more searching, they did find a therapist who could walk alongside Michael as he explored the intersection of his faith and sexuality. Michael is another good example of a young adult wanting help in carrying his "two boxes," as alluded to in chapter four. And, over the next several months, this young man became more and more comfortable with himself, with his faith, with his sexuality, and with his place within this college community and his church.

FAITH MATTERS

As we saw briefly in chapter two, these sexual-minority students are religious and spiritual, more so than their same-aged peers and the broader population. This was true for Michael, and any help he received in understanding his sexual attraction and identity had to engage his faith. Not doing so would be unfair to him and most likely would cause further issues for him in the years to come.

What we'll see in the following pages is how faith affects nearly every aspect of how these students make sense of same-sex attraction and behavior. Their reliance on faith stands in stark contrast to the perspective of most of their same-aged peers. In their book *The Millennials: Connecting to America's Largest Generation* (2011), Thom S. Rainer and Jess Rainer called these millennials "the least religious of any generation in modern American history" (p. 47). Fewer young adults pray, fewer attend church, fewer are committed to their faith, fewer think that faith is important to their lives, and fewer call themselves Christian than those of previous generations. In fact, most are not thinking about religious matters at all.

The Christian college students in our sample are very different. Only two of the 160 students said they were not religious, and 60% said they were moderately to very religious. In other studies of college students, only 13% to 40% have claimed the same thing. To better understand our students' approach to faith, let's take a look first at their religiosity and spirituality in more detail.

In chapter two we focused on their responses to two simple questions—"How religious are you?" and "How spiritual are you?" In addition to simply asking them to describe their degree of faith on a scale, we wanted to know more, so we gave them a small questionnaire created by researchers at Duke University called the Duke Religion Index (DUREL; Koenig, Meador, & Parkerson, 1997). It's widely used to measure three components of religiosity very quickly.

The first component, called organizational religiosity, is an index of how often people attend public religious services, such as morning worship, prayer meetings, or Bible study classes. Nearly a third of our students said that they attend such services more than once a week, with another 42% saying they go at least once per week. That's over 70% of students going to a church service at least once a week—in addition to any required chapel services they might have at their schools. This is much higher than what was found in samples of the broader population using the Duke index or in the samples of the broader millennial generation studied by other researchers. In fact, most millennials, regardless of their sexual identity, have been leaving the church in record numbers, with about half of them seeing no value in such activity and only a fourth of them regularly attending church. Our students value their faith and consequently are intentional about engaging in worship, prayer, and religious study with their faith communities.

Religion is practiced with others; it also is practiced privately. The second component of the Duke index, known as nonorganizational religiosity, asks about personal religious activities. Prayer, meditation, Bible study, and fasting would be typical activities that people might do to engage their faith during their quiet, alone times. Among our students, 11% did some private practice at least once a day, with another 34% engaging in these at least two times per week. Another 31% prayed, studied the Bible, or did something else once a week. Only 5% rarely or never practiced their religion privately. These private practices again show how much they value their faith. They are engaging in activities that are largely unknown by others. While they may do these things because they think "that's what good Christians do," most likely they would not continue these activities if they weren't finding some meaning or value in them.

What we do as part of our religion can be motivated by multiple forces— our desire to fit in, what we get out of it, our need to be a "good person," among many others. But if it's true that one in four millennials believe that what they do is more important than what they believe, as Barna found in 2001, then these Christian students in our sample are saying through their actions that their faith matters to them in very significant ways.

And if faith matters so significantly, it only makes sense that they would integrate their faith beliefs into their personal lives so that faith actively and significantly informs what they do and what they believe *in all aspects of their lives*. This third aspect, intrinsic religiosity (IR), was introduced briefly in chapter four, and it was measured in the Duke index by responding to three statements ("In my life, I experience the presence of the Divine, i.e., God"; "My religious beliefs are what really lie behind my whole approach to life"; and "I try hard to carry my religion over into all dealings in life"). In general, across these items, 61% of our students indicated moderate to strong agreement with these statements, suggesting that their faith matters in their daily lives.

RELIGIOSITY

Organizational religiosity: Concerned with how often people attend public religious services, such as morning worship, prayer meetings, or Bible study classes.

Nonorganizational religiosity: A reflection of personal religious activities, such as prayer, meditation, Bible study, and fasting.

Intrinsic religiosity: How religious faith informs what people do and believe in all aspects of their lives.

To better understand this, look at the individual items reflecting IR. First, 72% of these students said, yes, in their lives, they "experience the presence of the Divine (i.e., God)." Faith is not just some intellectual or behavioral exercise for them; it is experiential, and it is real. They know, at least to some degree and at least at some times, that God is present with them. Second, even more students—a full 81%—agree that their "religious/spiritual beliefs are what really lie behind [their] whole approach to life," and third, 72% indicated that they "try hard to carry my religion over into all other dealings in life." If these are true, then it only makes sense that their faith also would inform how they think about and experience their sexuality. And that is exactly what we see throughout the data that we collected.

The more we allow our faith to shape how we live each day, the more intrinsically religious we are. Kevin Masters (2013) of the University of Colorado says that intrinsic religiosity is the very framework for our lives. It seems likely, then, that the degree to which students use their faith to inform their lives shapes everything—their attitudes, their sexual identity, their behaviors, their psychological health, and their experiences. For the large majority of these students, faith cannot be fully separated from their sexuality. And, just as we might expect, the degree to which they hold to their faith shapes nearly everything about them. Let's look at how faith is related to what they've told us about themselves.

FAITH AND SEXUAL ATTITUDES

In 2015 the Pew Research Center explored attitudes regarding same-sex marriage across the general population. In their questioning, they found that 54% of the public sees no tension between their religious views and homosexuality; however, among those who tend to be the most conservative—white evangelical Protestants—seven out of ten believed there was conflict, with six of these seven asserting that there is "a lot" of conflict. The majority of Catholics and black Protestants agreed that there was tension, but the great majority of those in white mainline Protestant churches and those with no religious affiliation disagreed. Religious beliefs, and how tightly these are held, seem to influence how we understand same-sex attraction and sexual behavior.

This connection between faith and same-sex sexual attitudes was true for the college students in our sample (see fig. 5.1). Those students with higher levels of intrinsic religiosity[1] held more conservative views about both the causation and nature of same-sex sexual attraction and the morality of same-sex sexual behavior,[2] even though all students, regardless of how religious they were, tended to be fairly moderate in their beliefs. In other words, students, regardless of their level of religiosity, tended to fall just to the "agree" side of the middle on a five-point Likert scale, where one = *strongly disagree*, three =

---

[1]Students with high intrinsic religiosity averaged between a 4.0 and 5.0 across three items, and students with low intrinsic religiosity averaged between 1 and 3.99 across those same three items. Notice that only fifteen students averaged below a 3, suggesting that our low intrinsic religiosity group more aptly could be called our moderate intrinsic religiosity group.

[2]Students with higher levels of intrinsic religiosity ($M = 3.35$, $SD = 0.34$) tended to agree less with causal views of same-sex attraction than did students with lower intrinsic religiosity ($M = 3.50$, $SD = 0.35$), $t(158) = 2.55$, $p = 0.012$, Cohen's $d = 0.43$ (medium effect size). Also, students with higher levels of intrinsic religiosity ($M = 2.59$, $SD = 1.11$) tended to agree quite a lot less that same-sex behavior was morally acceptable than did students with lower intrinsic religiosity ($M = 3.36$, $SD = 0.78$), $t(158) = 4.47$, $p < 0.001$, Cohen's $d = 0.80$ (large effect size).

neither agree nor disagree, and five = *strongly agree*. Attitudes regarding the moral acceptability of the behavior were more greatly related to intrinsic religiosity than were understandings of causality, with the more religious students being less accepting of these behaviors.

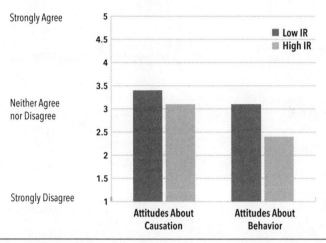

Figure 5.1. Attitudes about causation and behavior by low and high intrinsic religiosity

There has been significant cultural change in understanding how individuals experience same-sex attraction. Between 2013 and 2014, the percentage of the general population believing people were "born this way" increased six percentage points, from 41% to 46% (Pew Research Center, 2015). College graduates and millennials are even more likely to believe this. Among our student sample, who are nearly all religious to some degree, the percentage indicating some agreement that same-sex attraction is biologically caused and unable to change rose from 43.7% to 50% during the same time period.

To understand what students really believe, it's helpful to look at the four individual items about the causality and nature of same-sex attraction (see fig. 5.2). Students indicated their level of agreement on a five-point Likert scale, with one meaning that they strongly disagreed with the statement and five meaning they strongly agreed. Scores around three indicated that they weren't sure of where they stood, neither agreeing nor disagreeing; for some, this might have meant slight agreement or disagreement.[3]

---

[3]The original Likert scale used to indicate agreement was on a six-point scale, but this was converted to ease comparison with previous research, with ratings of three and four being collapsed into one category (slight agreement/disagreement). To compute the means, ratings of three were assigned a value of 2.75 on a one-to-five scale, and ratings of four were assigned a value of 3.25.

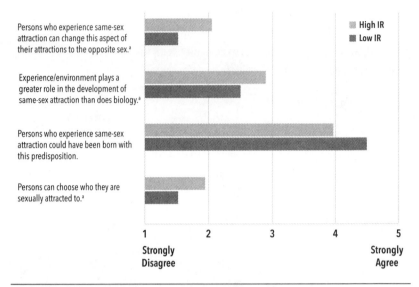

Figure 5.2. Attitudes about the causation of same-sex attraction by level of intrinsic religiosity

[a]These items indicate a more traditional Christian view that sexual attractions are mutable. The remaining item was reverse scored when computing average scores for attitudes about causation.

The strongest disagreement shown by both groups is in response to statements about people's ability to choose or change their attractions. Students also tended to disagree that environment and early learning were as important as biology in shaping this attraction. While those with low intrinsic religiosity are more likely to hold to a biologically based understanding of these attractions, both groups share this perspective to some degree. In other words, students, in general, tend to agree that same-sex attraction is not chosen, nor can it be changed.

What this actually looks like when we consider the distribution of responses is a bit more varied. Just about two-thirds of those with high intrinsic religiosity believed, to some extent, that "persons with same-sex attraction could have been born with this predisposition," whereas nine out of ten students low in intrinsic religiosity held the same belief. In asking about whether people have the choice in who they are attracted to, the gap is smaller. Just over eight out of ten highly religious students assert people have no choice, and nearly all (96.1%) of the less religious students feel the same.

The gap widens again when asked about the role of environment in sexual attraction. Just over one out of every two highly religious students felt the environment did not influence the development of same-sex attraction. Those with less intrinsic religiosity were more certain, with over 75% asserting environment did not matter.

Notice how both groups were more certain that biology did matter than they were that environment did not. This may reflect cultural perspectives that tend to highlight the importance of genetics when it comes to sexuality. Even though the research evidence for a genetic cause of same-sex attraction has been mixed over the years, the more popular news media has published multiple articles suggesting a much clearer connection. In 2014 alone, after the release of two research studies lending some support to this cause, many major news sources ran articles with headlines indicating more certainty than the findings warranted. The *Washington Post* ran "How our genes could make us gay or straight," by Jenny Graves, a distinguished professor of genetics at La Trobe University. *Nature World News* was just as definitive: "Homosexuality is genetic: Strongest evidence yet," with the subheading "Scientists have found even more evidence that sexual orientation is largely determined by genetics, not choice. That can undermine a major argument against the LGBT community that claims that these people are choosing to live 'unnaturally.'" The *Guardian* had a similar headline, "Male sexual orientation influenced by genes, study shows," but followed this with a less certain caveat, which may a bit closer to what we really know: "Genes examined in study are not sufficient or necessary to make men gay but do play some role in sexuality, say US researchers."

This sentiment is seen clearly in the students' agreement that people with same-sex attraction tend to be born this way. And, given their understanding that same-sex attraction is biologically based and immutable, both groups of students, regardless of their religiosity, tended to see the attraction as morally acceptable because "God makes no mistakes." Note that even though all students tend to agree, those with lower religiosity expressed more agreement with these ideas than did those with higher intrinsic religiosity. Only 6% of the less religious students failed to see same-sex attraction as being morally acceptable, but 33% of the more religious students took this stance.

The Pew Research Center (2015) found that beliefs about the changeability of same-sex attraction followed beliefs about causation; that is, people who saw these attractions as biologically based tended to see them as immutable also. Even in their research, the more conservative religious groups tended to agree that sexual attraction cannot be changed. This is in fact what we see in

WHAT CAUSES SEXUAL ORIENTATION?

"What causes sexual orientation?" remains a difficult question to answer. We continue to see studies published related to the biological hypothesis. These studies have examined direct genetic contributions, indirect genetic contributions, prenatal hormonal exposure, epigenetics, and other possible variables.

The American Psychological Association's (2017) online statement on causes captures our own understanding at present:

> There is no consensus among scientists about the exact reasons that an individual develops a heterosexual, bisexual, gay or lesbian orientation. Although much research has examined the possible genetic, hormonal, developmental, social and cultural influences on sexual orientation, no findings have emerged that permit scientists to conclude that sexual orientation is determined by any particular factor or factors. Many think that nature and nurture both play complex roles; most people experience little or no sense of choice about their sexual orientation.

Again, we agree that most people who experience same-sex attraction such that they would describe it as their sexual orientation "experience little or no sense of choice" in that matter. Whether the cause is nature or nurture or both is an open question. But attempts to remind us to avoid overconfidence in genetic causation tend to fall on deaf ears when the preponderance of the messages we hear confirms that our sexual attractions are fully genetically based. Even pop performing artist Lady Gaga contributed to ensuring this would be a culturally asserted fact with her 2011 award-winning song "Born This Way." Here is a short segment of the lyrics:

I'm beautiful in my way
'Cause God makes no mistakes
I'm on the right track, baby
I was born this way.

our students. About 96% of those with low intrinsic religiosity believed people could not change their own sexual attractions, while only 10% of their highly religious sexual-minority peers agreed with them that change is unlikely.

As we've seen so far, our students' opinions about the causes and permanency of same-sex attraction largely mirror what is happening in the general population, even if somewhat moderated by their religiosity. Where our students differ from the general population, and where we see religion play even a greater role, is in their views about same-sex sexual behavior (see fig. 5.3). Desires may be viewed as biologically caused and unchangeable, but behavior appears to still be considered within the realm of choice and is not justifiable to everyone. Those with higher intrinsic religiosity tended to see same-sex behavior as not permissible, while the less religious students were a little more lenient, leaning slightly to the acceptable side.[4] More specifically, 49% of those with high religiosity hold that same-sex sexual behavior is impermissible; only 13.7% of their less religious peers agree with that. Thus, for many of these students, same-sex sexual behavior is clearly understood as something different from its related attraction, especially among those who are more religious.

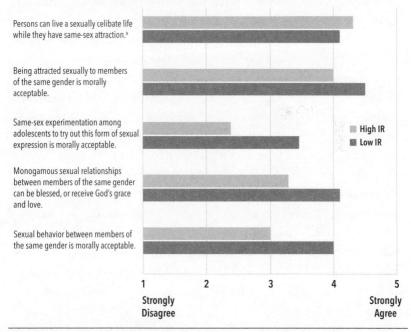

Figure 5.3. Attitudes about same-sex sexual behavior by level of intrinsic religiosity

[a]This item indicates a more traditional Christian view regarding same-sex sexual behavior. It was reverse scored in computing average scores for attitudes about the morality of same-sex sexual behavior.

[4]That high intrinsics tended to see same-sex sexual behavior as morally wrong should not lead one to the conclusion that respect or civility toward LGB+ persons might be reduced in those who make such judgments. Krull (2017) found evidence that higher levels of intrinsic religiosity were associated with persons who could make moral judgments about same-sex sexual behavior but still affirm the need for kindness toward LGB+ persons. He reported, "Indeed, high intrinsics seemed quite unlikely to display behaviors that would normally be associated with hatred (disrespectful comments and physical aggression)" (p. 105).

Of the behaviors presented to students, same-sex sexual experimentation among adolescents was the least accepted behavior of all of those asked about. About 71% of those with higher intrinsic religiosity disagreed that it was morally acceptable, but only 29.4% of their less religious peers felt the same. Another 39.2% were uncertain what they believed. This may contribute to the tendency for many sexual-minority youths to have little same-sex sexual experience in adolescence, even though their rates of heterosexual sexual activity match that of their same-sex heterosexual peers (Saewyc, Poon, Wang, Homma, & Smith, 2007; Tulloch & Kaufman, 2013; Saewyc, Bearinger, Blum, & Resnick, 1999). However, it's also quite possible that these Christian students would show fewer sexual behaviors across the board, compared to same-aged, non-Christian peers, especially given that they are quite likely to think that sexual experimentation of any sort is morally problematic.

When same-sex sexual behavior was removed from adolescent experimentation, students became a bit more accepting. Those with low intrinsic religiosity tended to agree that, in general, same-sex sexual behavior was morally acceptable, with only 13.7% disagreeing. Their more religious peers were unsure, with an average response right between agreeing and disagreeing; in fact, 51% agreed it was morally acceptable, and 49% disagreed. Here, as with the adolescent experimentation, it's unclear how much of its limited acceptance is due to the same-sex nature of the behavior or to its being outside a marriage relationship.

Interestingly, when this sexual behavior is considered in a monogamous relationship, it "fit" somewhat better for the students. Both religious groups of students agreed that sexual relationships, if monogamous, can be blessed with God's grace and love, and their agreement with this was just above that for all same-sex behavior.[5] Students with lower intrinsic religiosity expressed much higher agreement with this, but even the more religious students tended to agree to some small degree.[6]

Even though the level of agreement increased when this sexual activity was placed within the context of a monogamous relationship, the actual number of students expressing agreement did not. For the students with low intrinsic religiosity, 84.3% agreed that exclusive, committed same-sex relationships could be

---

[5]Using a dependent-samples *t*-test, students more strongly agreed that monogamous same-sex behavior was acceptable ($M = 3.53$, $SD = 1.50$) compared to all same-sex sexual behavior ($M = 3.31$, $SD = 1.48$), $t (157) = -3.09$, $p = 0.012$, Cohen's $d = 0.15$ (small effect size).

[6]Using an independent-samples *t*-test, students with higher levels of intrinsic religiosity ($M = 3.24$, $SD = 1.55$) tended to agree less with causal views of same-sex attraction than did students with lower intrinsic religiosity ($M = 4.13$, $SD = 1.17$), $t (157) = 3.63$, $p < 0.001$, Cohen's $d = 0.64$ (large effect size).

blessed, and 86.3% agreed that same-sex sexual behavior in general was acceptable. There is no real difference in those percentages. For the students with high intrinsic religiosity, there seemingly was a little more movement, but statistically it's not a real difference. While 56.5% agreed that monogamous same-sex relationships could be blessed, 50.9% thought any same-sex behavior was fine.[7] In other words, it's not that more students were more okay with sexual activity occurring within same-sex monogamous relationships; rather, it's just that the students who were okay with same-sex behavior in general were even more likely to hold that exclusive same-sex relationships could receive God's blessing, grace, and love.

Where we see no disagreement between the two religious groups of students is in their understanding of celibacy. The two groups equally agreed that celibacy was possible for people who experience same-sex attraction. In fact, nearly all students believed this to some degree, with 90.6% of the students with high intrinsic religiosity and 88.2% of the students with low intrinsic religiosity indicating they agreed that persons can live a sexually celibate life while they have same-sex attraction.

We didn't ask students whether they thought celibacy was the *preferred* way to manage same-sex sexual attraction in light of one's faith. If we had, the responses likely would have been more varied. The choice to pursue celibacy has often been viewed as an inauthentic, "less than" life for sexual minorities. We mentioned earlier that this path has been gaining momentum among Christian sexual minorities (recall that they are at times referred to as Side B; see Belgau, 2017).

Recall that Side A gay Christians believe that same-sex relationships can be morally permissible. In 2015, Julie Rodgers, a former chaplain at a private Christian college, resigned her position and eventually moved from Side B to Side A in her thinking. Explaining this perspective change, she wrote, "While I struggle to understand how to apply Scripture to the marriage debate today (just like we all struggle to know how to interpret Scripture on countless controversial topics), I've become increasingly troubled by the unintended consequences of messages that insist all LGBT people commit to lifelong celibacy." It was the perceived lack of choice for sexual minorities and corresponding risk of shame that seemed to most trouble her. She continued, "No matter how graciously it's framed, that message tends to contribute to feelings of shame and alienation for gay Christians."

---

[7]There is not a significant difference in the percentages of students with high intrinsic religiosity agreeing with these two statements, χ^2 (1) = 0.67, p = n.s.

While Wesley Hill (2015a) agreed with Rodgers that too often Christians have treated sexual minorities horribly—often due to their "straight up homophobia"—he disagreed that this is due to the traditional Christian understanding of sexuality and marriage itself. Scripture, he further explained in a response to Rodgers in the *Washington Post*, tells us that some will have to bear burdens for the kingdom that they do not choose, such as the eunuchs.

We are not surprised to learn that many of our students are largely unsure of where they stand on these topics. Popular and too-often-real narratives of how the church has harmed sexual minorities challenge what they hold about a biblical view of sexuality and marriage. When these students witness poor treatment of sexual minorities from the church, issues of justice may become more prominent and override considerations of what appears an esoteric theology of sexuality. For others, seeing this type of injustice may lead them further away from traditional religious beliefs. These young men and women, now less committed to allowing their faith to shape their lives, may follow popular culture that accepts same-sex sexual behavior as morally permissible and, when in a committed and monogamous relationship, even blessed. Finally, others, as noted earlier, do not necessarily see their faith as less salient in their daily living and are very sincere about their beliefs but have come to reject the traditional sexual ethic as error. An accurate understanding of the pathway young people take as they attempt to hold their "two boxes" is not possible without listening to the stories they tell.

It might be helpful at this point to look at data collected from an earlier sample of Christian college students (Dean et al., 2011). These results represent more than seventeen hundred students from nineteen Christian colleges. We filtered the responses to include only those students who reported "no same-sex attraction," since we wanted to see how their attitudes compared to those of the sexual-minority students we've looked at in our current study. In other words, does intrinsic religiosity influence beliefs about same-sex sexual attraction and behavior in straight students, as it does in sexual-minority students?

When we look at beliefs about the causation and nature of same-sex sexual attraction, intrinsic religiosity also affects the attitudes of students without same-sex attraction at Christian colleges (see fig. 5.4). Those students with high levels of intrinsic religiosity report greater agreement with idea that people can change their same-sex attraction. Along these same lines, they also show stronger endorsement of the statement that environment plays a greater role in the development of same-sex attraction than does biology. Notice, though, that both groups of students tend to agree with these statements, even though their religiosity is related to how strongly they agree.

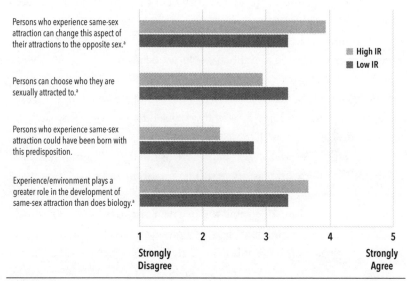

Figure 5.4. Attitudes about the causation of same-sex sexual attraction by level of intrinsic religiosity in non-sexual-minority students

[a]These items indicate a more traditional Christian view that sexual attractions are mutable. The remaining item was reverse scored when computing average scores for attitudes about causation.

Straight students with low intrinsic religiosity are more likely to endorse the other three attitudinal statements about the causation of same-sex attraction. Perhaps the better wording for this is that they tend to show less disagreement with these three statements. For example, while many students tend to see sexual attraction to members of the same gender as morally unacceptable, those with low intrinsic religiosity are more accepting. And even though both groups of students tend to oppose the idea that people can be born with same-sex attraction, those with low intrinsic religiosity are more neutral about this belief.

Contrary to what we might expect are the responses to the statement that people can choose whom they are sexually attracted to. The students with less intrinsic religiosity are slightly more likely to agree with this, with their average score barely in the agreement range. In contrast, those who are more religious are a little less likely to agree with this. In other words, both groups of students seem to respond to this particular statement in the opposite direction than we might expect given their responses to the other statements on the causation of same-sex attraction; however, because the scores of both groups hover so closely around that midpoint, a better interpretation is that, on average, both groups are unsure of where they stand on this issue of choice in one's attractions.

We see the same relationship of intrinsic religiosity to non-sexual-minority students in regard to the morality of same-sex behavior (see fig. 5.5). Notice that all students, regardless of their religiosity, tend to disagree that same-sex behavior is morally acceptable or can be blessed by God when occurring in a monogamous relationship. Those with greater intrinsic religiosity show the strongest disagreement with these statements.

In general, the attitudes of the low intrinsic religiosity group are more aligned with "progressive" views regarding causation and more "permissive" views regarding behavior as compared to their more religious peers.

The only item addressing same-sex behavior that both groups endorsed was the one suggesting that people with same-sex attraction can live celibate lives. Interestingly, this is the only item where there is no significant difference

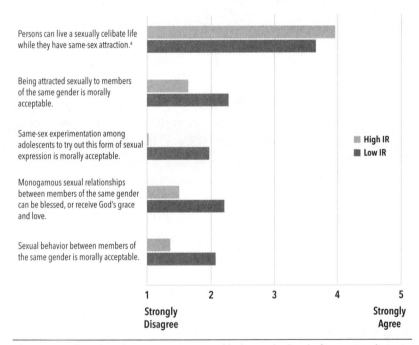

Figure 5.5. Attitudes about same-sex sexual behavior by level of intrinsic religiosity in non-sexual-minority students

[a]This item indicates a more traditional Christian view regarding same-sex sexual behavior. It was reverse scored in computing average scores for attitudes about the morality of same-sex sexual behavior.

between students with differing levels of religiosity, yet this is the item that many people would argue is the most religious. But, remember, nearly everyone in our samples—both the main sample of students without same-sex attraction and the smaller sample of students with same-sex attraction—is religious, moderately to strongly so. Celibacy may be the one option for people with same-sex attraction that most religious people agree is viable.

We've seen that intrinsic religiosity tends to correlate with Christian college students' attitudes about sexuality—in both sexual-minority students and in straight students. But how do sexual-minority and straight students compare? To look at this, the graphs from above have been combined into one (see fig. 5.6).

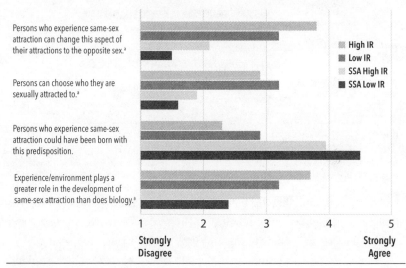

Figure 5.6. Attitudes about the causation of same-sex sexual attraction by level of intrinsic religiosity and sexual attraction

ªThese items indicate a more traditional Christian view that sexual attractions are mutable. The remaining item was reverse scored when computing average scores for attitudes about causation.

In regard to these five statements about the causation and nature of same-sex sexual attraction, it is clear that our sexual-minority students are responding differently from their straight peers. Yes, their intrinsic religiosity matters in their sexual attitudes, and, yes, their sexual attraction also matters in their attitudes. Sexual-minority students show greater endorsement of the biological causation, the immutability, and the moral acceptability of their sexual attractions.

Similarly, both intrinsic religiosity and sexual attraction are related to students' understanding of the morality of same-sex sexual behavior. Straight

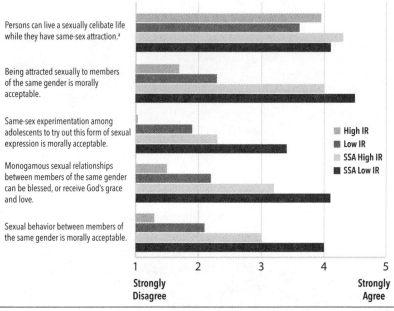

Figure 5.7. Attitudes about the morality of same-sex sexual behavior by level of intrinsic religiosity and sexual attraction

ªThis item indicates a more traditional Christian view regarding same-sex sexual behavior. It was reverse scored in computing average scores for attitudes about the morality of same-sex sexual behavior.

students tend to hold that this behavior is immoral, as do the sexual-minority students with high intrinsic religiosity. The most permissive attitudes were held by those sexual-minority students with lower intrinsic religiosity.

One somewhat surprising outcome is that the degree to which students believe it is possible to "live a sexually celibate life" is actually *higher* for our more current sample of exclusively sexual-minority students. Otherwise, our current sample expresses attitudes that are more permissive, not less, than our 2009 sample who experience no same-sex attraction. It appears that no matter how much our sexual-minority group's attitudes align with LGBT sympathies, even when religiosity is a bit less important to how they live their lives, they remain fairly moderate in their views, and they nevertheless believe it is indeed possible to live a celibate life.

FAITH AND SEXUAL MILESTONES

Among all teens and young adults, religiosity seems to delay sexual behavior. We've long known that people who are religious are much more likely to wait to have sexual intercourse (coitus). Sexual behavior, though, includes more

MULTIPLE PATHS FOR HOLDING
FAITH AND SEXUALITY TOGETHER

At a Pittsburgh-area seminary, a weekend conference focused on same-sex sexuality. Given that the theme was in support of a traditional Christian sexual ethic, the varieties of life choices were nevertheless creative to say the least. One keynote, Melinda Selmys, a married woman who identifies as queer, talked about the hours and hours of processing with her now-husband before they decided to get married. In what she termed a "mixed-orientation marriage," Selmys spoke of still being attracted to women and of being attracted to only one man, her husband, for which she had no easy explanation. Yet she is apparently happily married (she admits to a "good enough" marriage) after more than a decade of life together.

Another keynote, Wesley Hill, author of *Washed and Waiting* (2010), chooses a celibate life while acknowledging his gay identity and opening up to others in the church and seeking community from all those who claim identity in Christ. Hill's challenge is not solely to gay Christians to remain faithful in the midst of brokenness but also to the straight faithful to offer fellowship and belonging lived out in welcoming church families.

Another narrative was of two gay men living together but seeking the companionship that Wesley Hill writes about. Theirs is a nonsexual, covenant partnership in which both men are committed to celibacy. This arrangement, considered less common for men, is more common for lesbian and straight women, who often emphasize the emotional connection as central to their bond.

While the majority of Christian churches remain opposed to same-sex unions, other denominations (e.g., the Evangelical Lutheran Church in America), after many years of controversy and debate (some involving schism), have made the decision to bless same-sex monogamous unions.

Christians who seek to follow Christ and understand the meaning of their same-sex attractions will need support, compassion, and space from the church community as they navigate this journey that our research suggests is often done alone and with little understanding. It is our hope that our research and this book will aid churches and schools in making this path more traversable for our sexual-minority students, recognizing a range of potential resolutions.

than just sexual intercourse, and it wasn't until 1980 that researchers began exploring the relationship of faith and other sexual behaviors. Using this broader understanding of sexual behavior in his research, E. R. Mahoney, a sociologist at Western Washington University, concluded that "across a wide range of sexual behaviors and dimensions of sexuality, religiosity is found to be negatively related to sexual experience." That is, people with stronger religious beliefs are likely to wait longer before engaging in most sexual behaviors.

Multiple studies have since supported Mahoney's findings. In their 2003 work with a nationally representative sample of adolescents, Sharon Scales Rostosky, a psychologist at the University of Kentucky, working with Mark Regnerus and Margaret Comer Wright, showed that religiosity had both direct and indirect effects on sexual intercourse, both of which delay engagement in it (Regnerus, Rostosky, & Wright, 2003). Teens who are engaged in their faith tend to hold beliefs that engaging in sexual intercourse would bring about negative emotional consequences, and this, they argued, is one of the ways in which religiosity delays sexual behavior.

Is it just fear of the negative emotional consequences that allows religiosity to slow down sexual behavior? In a second study, Rostosky and her colleagues (2004) compiled data across multiple longitudinal studies, finding further support that religiosity has a protective effect on sexual intercourse, delaying it for most young adults. Faith and involvement in religious activities, asserted Rostosky, offered social control mechanisms, such as self-efficacy and normative pressure, which serve to delay sexual intercourse.

Some have argued that young adults who fear having sexual intercourse would instead engage in other sexual behaviors. So, yes, they delayed having sex, but they were still sexually active. Religious men, for example, may choose to engage in oral sex before sexual intercourse as a way to manage the prohibitions against the latter (Mahoney, 1980). While the order of sexual behaviors may or may not be reversed from what we might expect, it does seem that religiosity delays all sexual behavior, not just sexual intercourse. Shawnika Hull and colleagues (2011) found that religiosity not only changes one's beliefs about the potential negative consequences of having sex, but also changes one's intentions to have sex and one's beliefs about the potential positive consequences of having sex. And it seems just attending church occasionally can affect these beliefs.

Given that religiosity seems to delay sexual behavior, we wanted to see whether we saw the same patterns in our sexual-minority students. As mentioned earlier, we asked them to tell us whether they had engaged in each behavior and if so the age when they first did so. Here in table 5.1 below, we are just looking at the number of students who had reached several same-sex sexual milestones. Among those behaviors that likely occur with another person, students with high levels of intrinsic religiosity were less likely to have had their breasts or genitals fondled by someone of the same sex, and they were less likely to have been intimately or romantically kissed by someone of the same sex. There was no difference related to religiosity in the less frequently occurring behaviors.

The other striking finding is that, for the most part, our students with high intrinsic religiosity were just as likely to have experienced the typical cognitive and emotional milestones that occur with same-sex attraction as were those with less intrinsic religiosity. While some of the percentages in the table may look like there is a difference, the only response in which there was a true difference is the last one. Those students with higher levels of intrinsic religiosity are less likely to publicly adopt the label of gay for themselves than are their less religious peers. Notice also that nearly all students experienced awareness of same-sex feelings, an initial attribution that they are same-sex attracted, and confusion about their same-sex feelings. Most had disclosed their same-sex attraction to someone, and most had made the initial attribution that they are gay, lesbian, or bisexual, even adopting that label for themselves privately.

So maybe there isn't a difference in the number of students who have reached each milestone, especially given that they are already college students, but could it be that more religious students had hit these milestones later in their development than did their less religious peers? This also would show that religiosity delays behavior. Unexpectedly, this is not what we find among the students in our sample. There are no significant age differences for most of the same-sex sexual milestones among students with differing levels of religiosity (see table A5.3 in the appendix). In fact, there is only one true difference. Students with higher levels of intrinsic religiosity who had fondled the breasts or genitals of another person of the same sex did so about 2.5 years earlier than their less religious peers; on average, they were about fifteen years and four months old when they engaged in such behavior, but their peers were about seventeen years and nine months old when they did so.[8]

We should also note that the way the question is worded leaves the context open to interpretation: Is the participant thinking of sexual behavior with another person or self-stimulation? In other words, is it possible that some

---

[8]Using an independent-samples t-test, students with higher levels of intrinsic religiosity ($n = 58$; $M = 15.31$, $SD = 4.66$) were younger than students with lower intrinsic religiosity ($n = 35$; $M = 17.71$, $SD = 3.42$) when they first fondled the breasts or genitals of another person of the same sex, t (91) = 2.65, $p = 0.009$, Cohen's $d = 0.59$ (large effect size).

Table 5.1. Same-sex milestones in sexual-identity development by level of intrinsic religiosity

Milestones	PERCENTAGE REACHING SAME-SEX SEXUAL MILESTONES	
	Low IR (*n* = 51)	High IR (*n* = 109)
Same-Sex Sexual Behaviors		
Been fondled (breasts or genitals) by someone (without orgasm)	74.5	54.1[a] *
Fondled (breasts or genitals) someone (without orgasm)	68.6	53.2
Intimately/romantically kissed by someone	76.5	50.5[b] **
Sexual behavior (to orgasm)	49.0	39.4
First same-sex relationship	45.1	37.6
Understanding of Same-Sex Sexual Attraction and Behavior		
Awareness of same-sex feelings	98.0	100.0
Initial attribution that I am same-sex attracted	98.0	99.1
Confusion about same-sex feelings	92.2	96.3
First disclosure of same-sex attraction	88.2	78.0
Initial attribution that "I am gay/lesbian/bisexual"	90.2	81.7
Adopted the label of "gay" for myself privately	82.4	69.7
Adopted the label of "gay" for myself publicly	54.9	33.0[c] **

* $p \leq 0.05$
** $p \leq 0.01$
*** $p \leq 0.001$

[a] There is a significant difference in the percentages of students with high intrinsic religiosity and those with low intrinsic religiosity reaching this milestone, χ^2 (1) = 6.05, p = 0.014.

[b] There is a significant difference in the percentages of students with high intrinsic religiosity and those with low intrinsic religiosity reaching this milestone, χ^2 (1) = 9.70, p = 0.002.

[c] There is a significant difference in the percentages of students with high intrinsic religiosity and those with low intrinsic religiosity reaching this milestone, χ^2 (1) = 6.93, p = 0.008.

participants view masturbation as technically same-sex behavior, if they fantasized about the same sex and came to orgasm? Alternatively, is it possible that same-sex behavior happened to them rather than an act that they felt they freely engaged in, which might be more likely with sexual behaviors with the opposite sex?

Religiosity doesn't seem to have the same comprehensive protective effect in delaying same-sex sexual behavior in our sexual-minority students as research suggests it does with opposite-sex sexual behaviors. In fact, it seems to show very little delaying effect. Previous studies had been done with mostly heterosexual students and heterosexual behaviors, so perhaps religiosity just doesn't work the same way in sexual minorities with same-sex behavior. Is this because of the nature of the behavior or because the students are sexual minorities? Or perhaps the relative difficulty in finding a partner?

Table 5.2. Opposite-sex milestones in sexual-identity development by level of intrinsic religiosity

Milestones	PERCENTAGE REACHING OPPOSITE-SEX SEXUAL MILESTONES	
	Low IR ($n = 51$)	High IR ($n = 109$)
Intimately/romantically kissed by someone of the opposite sex	84.3	51.4[a] ***
First relationship with someone of the opposite sex	82.4	58.7[b] **
Been fondled (breasts or genitals) by someone (without orgasm) of the opposite sex	60.8	39.4[c] *
Fondled (breasts or genitals) someone (without orgasm) of the opposite sex	54.9	37.6[d] *
Opposite-sex sexual behavior (to orgasm)	49.0	23.9[e] ***

* $p \leq 0.05$
** $p \leq 0.01$
*** $p \leq 0.001$

[a] There is a significant difference in the percentages of students with high intrinsic religiosity and those with low intrinsic religiosity reaching this milestone, $\chi^2 (1) = 15.98, p < 0.001$.

[b] There is a significant difference in the percentages of students with high intrinsic religiosity and those with low intrinsic religiosity reaching this milestone, $\chi^2 (1) = 8.68, p < 0.001$.

[c] There is a significant difference in the percentages of students with high intrinsic religiosity and those with low intrinsic religiosity reaching this milestone, $\chi^2 (1) = 6.36, p = 0.012$.

[d] There is a significant difference in the percentages of students with high intrinsic religiosity and those with low intrinsic religiosity reaching this milestone, $\chi^2 (1) = 4.23, p = 0.039$.

[e] There is a significant difference in the percentages of students with high intrinsic religiosity and those with low intrinsic religiosity reaching this milestone, $\chi^2 (1) = 8.68, p = 0.003$.

To better understand this, we also looked for differences in the percentages of students hitting opposite-sex milestones based on their intrinsic religiosity. Here we found exactly what the previous research literature suggested that we would find. Students with higher levels of intrinsic religiosity were less likely to have hit every single opposite-sex sexual milestone than were their less religious peers. It's quite possible that their religiosity gives more attention—whether positive or negative—to opposite-sex sexual behavior than it does to same-sex behavior, resulting in a delaying effect in engaging in heterosexual sexual behavior. Interestingly, though, for those students who had engaged in those opposite-sex behaviors, there were no age differences between those with higher or lesser intrinsic religiosity, but as more students reach these milestones these age differences likely will begin to appear (see table A5.4 in appendix). That is, more students with high intrinsic religiosity will eventually "catch up" to their less religious peers in hitting these milestones, but they will be older when they do.

Another theme that emerges in the previous research literature on the relationship between sexuality and religiosity is about gender. The connection between religiosity and sexual behavior tends to be more consistent and more protective for women, whereas it is much more varied among men. Rostosky and her colleagues (2004) suggest this gender difference may be in the different messages that adolescent girls and boys receive regarding sexuality, particularly the double standard that girls should be the "responsible gatekeeper" and boys should be more sexually active.

To see if this same pattern occurs among our sexual-minority students, we looked at the men and women separately to see how their intrinsic religiosity was related to the percentages of students reaching each sexual milestone. The results were completely opposite of what we had predicted.

Surprisingly, there was a pretty consistent delaying factor of intrinsic religiosity on sexual behavior for our eighty-one men. For all of the sexual-behavioral milestones, except for their first same-sex relationship, male students high in intrinsic religiosity were much less likely to have reached these milestones than their less religious fellow students (see table A5.5 in appendix). Only about 50% of the more religious men had engaged in any of these behaviors, whereas 80% to 90% of the less religious men had done so. Interestingly, none of the emotional and cognitive responses to same-sex attraction varied by religion; all of the men, regardless of their faith, were just as likely to have experienced the various stages in processing their same-sex attraction. Most of them actually already had done so, except publicly identifying as gay or bisexual.

This delaying effect of intrinsic religiosity all but disappears for our seventy-two women. The more religious female students were just as likely to have reached one of the same-sex milestones as were their less religious peers (see table A5.5 in appendix). Also, religiosity does not seem to affect the likelihood the women would experience any of the cognitive and emotional responses to their same-sex attraction, except for one. The more religious female students were much less likely to publicly identify as lesbian or bisexual compared to their female counterparts with less religiosity.

Again, it's important to remember that we are not really comparing men and women in terms of who is religious and who isn't religious. Our low intrinsic religiosity group, compared to the broader population, is moderately religious. Thus, to reinterpret our findings, women may be getting a delaying effect from intrinsic religiosity across both groups, the low and the high religiosity groups, causing us to see no difference. This would explain why the percentages of women experiencing each milestone seem lower than those of the men, and this would fit the previous literature showing that even a little bit of religious engagement is beneficial to women in slowing down their engagement in sexual activity (Hull et al., 2011).

Men, on the other hand, have been shown to have a much more varied response to religiosity in terms of their sexual behaviors. For example, if adolescent boys internalize their parents' faith, then those boys will experience the same delaying effects on their sexual behavior as adolescent girls do. However, if the boys do not internalize this religion, they tend to respond negatively to it, becoming even more sexually active (Manlove, Logan, Moore, & Ikramullah, 2008). This may be the very dynamic that we are seeing in our male students. Those who have a very high level of intrinsic religiosity were less likely to have reached these behavioral milestones, even though they were just as likely to be aware of their same-sex attraction as their somewhat less intrinsically religious peers. Being less intrinsically religious, even moderately religious as they are here, may not be enough internalized faith to prevent experiencing these milestone behaviors. It may in fact reduce prohibitions, as a large majority of the men with low levels of religiosity have reached most of the same-sex sexual milestones.

FAITH AND PSYCHOLOGICAL HEALTH

How is mental health affected by religion and spirituality? In a 2013 interview the American Psychological Association spoke with Ken Pargament, a clinical psychologist on faculty at Bowling Green State University in Ohio and expert in the psychology of religion and spirituality, on this very topic. While he acknowledged that some forms of faith are potentially harmful to some people, most people benefit from their faith. In comparing secular and spiritual forms of meditation, forgiveness, hope, and numerous other more existential topics, he remarked,

> Some research has shown that mantra-based meditation to a spiritual phrase is more effective in reducing physical pain than meditation to a secular phrase. Similarly, other studies have shown that spiritual forms of support, meaning-making and coping predict health and well-being beyond the effects of secular support, meaning-making and coping. It appears that religion and spirituality cannot be fully reduced to or explained by other psychological and social processes. Belonging to a religious congregation is not equivalent to belonging to the Kiwanis or Rotary Club. What makes religion and spirituality special? Unlike any other dimension of life, religion and spirituality have a unique focus on

the domain of the sacred—transcendence, ultimate truth, finitude and deep connectedness. Any psychology that overlooks these parts of life remains incomplete.

A survey of the literature quickly reveals that religion generally has a positive effect on mental health (Rettner, 2015). For example, in his review of seventy-five articles exploring the connections between religion, spirituality, and health, Harold Koenig (2012), the director of the Center for Spirituality, Theology and Health at Duke University Medical Center, found ample support suggesting religion and spirituality positively affect our ability to handle adversity, our sense of well-being and happiness, our self-esteem, our sense of hope and optimism, and our sense of control and meaning and purpose in life. Not only that, but religion and spirituality also seem to be related to the development of positive character traits and social support. People with higher levels of religiosity and spirituality tend to have fewer issues with depression, substance use, crime and delinquency, anxiety, suicide, and marital instability.

In fact, just this year, Patrick Steffen and colleagues (2017) explored the mechanism between religiosity and its positive mental-health benefits, hoping to find the underlying mechanism for this relationship. The increased social support found in most churches was not the reason that most people did better in church. In fact, the strongest factor mediating the relationship between religious service attendance and depressive and anxiety symptoms was intrinsic religiosity. The extent to which people attempt to live out their faith in their daily lives has the greatest positive effect on their mental health, regardless of all of the other secondary benefits we get from going to church regularly.

There are some caveats to these findings. Ken Pargament, mentioned above, said, "If people have a loving, kind perception of God, . . . and feel God is supportive, they seem to experience benefits. . . . But we know that there's a darker side to spirituality. If you tend to see God as punitive, threatening or unreliable, then that's not very helpful" (Rettner, 2015).

Perhaps it's this negative view of God, embedded in the broader societal narrative, that creates such a tenuous relationship between religion and many sexual minorities. Some argue that there is a war between religion and the LGBT community, a war that, if won by the religious right, would be devastating to sexual minorities through widespread restrictions and prejudice that would ultimately cause harm to their well-being (Americans United for the Separation of Church and State, 2013). *Rolling Stone* tells the painful stories of

INTERNALIZED HOMOPHOBIA, ADHERENCE TO A TRADITIONAL CHRISTIAN SEXUAL ETHIC, OR BOTH?

Barnes and Meyer (2012) studied 355 lesbian, gay, and bisexual persons in New York City and were looking at participation in nonaffirming religious settings (by self-report of being a part of a nonaffirming religious setting and frequency of church attendance). They reported that participation in nonaffirming religious settings was associated with higher internalized homophobia. In other words, attending nonaffirming churches (and the authors reported that LGB Protestants are about 2.5 times as likely to attend a nonaffirming church compared to an affirming church) is associated with increased negative messages about homosexuality that are thought to be internalized by sexual-minority Christians. The researchers also thought that being a part of a nonaffirming faith community would be associated with poor mental health, but it wasn't.

One challenge with research like this is how to make sense of "internalized homophobia," which is a really tricky construct. It is measured by a scale with items that some might endorse simply because of how their faith community understands sexuality and sexual behavior or how they themselves have come to understand sexuality and sexual behavior (for example, "You have wished that you could develop more feelings toward the opposite sex"). So is the fact that a person holds a traditional Christian sexual ethic that may inform responses to items a sign in and of itself of internalized homophobia, or is it possible to be pathologized for conventional religious beliefs and values?

The other challenge is what to make of the finding that being part of a nonaffirming faith community was not associated with poorer mental health. We agree with the authors that their results may be explained, at least in part, by the "countervailing influences" (p. 513) of religion. In other words, participating in a faith community leads to various health-benefiting effects, such as social support and a broader meaning-making structure for making sense of the world, thus counterbalancing the potential negative effects (Barnes & Meyer, 2012).

It is not uncommon to hear people from the mainstream LGB community blame the church and related institutions for teaching doctrine that has a high view of chastity and heterosexual marriage and, by default, a critical view of same-sex sexuality and certainly same-sex behavior. In other words, to the mainstream of the LGB community, teachings that reflect the traditional Christian sexual ethic may lay the foundations for negative internalized messaging.

What is often overlooked is that some LGB people of faith choose to participate in traditional Christian settings for a range of reasons, including their own formed beliefs and values. There may be "a reiterative process" (Barnes & Meyer, 2012, p. 513) in which religious upbringing leads to a traditional Christian sexual ethic that encourages ongoing participation in a faith community that is more conservative. For some, this could be something akin to an internalized message that they might disagree with or later come to evaluate as wrong; for others, it is a reflection of sincerely held beliefs and values that reflect a kind of personal and institutional congruence, a part of a larger, coherent whole with an attending sense of meaning and purpose.

An interesting addendum to this discussion of choosing traditional church settings comes from Andrew Marin's (2016) book *Us Versus Us*—a national survey of religion and the LGB+ community.[a] He reported that the majority of respondents from 1,712 "usable" surveys were raised in a faith community (86%) but left after the age of eighteen (54%). Unexpectedly, Marin's findings go on to report that most who departed would be willing to return (76%) without "dramatic ecclesial overhauls" (p. 72). The majority of survey respondents would return to their faith community without theological or doctrinal changes if they found a "loving, patient, realistic, authentic, and supportive" collective. Much as we have found in our investigation of Christian college students, relational stability and security appears to be the most prominent hope, even in communities with very traditional religious and spiritual values. According to Marin (2016), relationality may be the key to learning to hold two seemingly incompatible worldviews.

---

[a] Marin's survey results have been legitimately criticized for its sample demographics, which limit generalization to less represented nonwhite and non-Protestant groups.

sexual-minority teens whose parents kicked them out of their homes, where they had suffered rejection and shame (Morris, 2014).

Once homeless, young sexual minorities are often thrown into a very dangerous situation, with drug use, risky sexual behavior, and survival crimes becoming significantly more likely for them. In fact, Caitlin Ryan, a clinical social worker, and her colleague Rafael Diaz (2009) investigated exactly what happened to these teens. The results are startling: "Those who are forcefully rejected by their families or caregivers are more than eight times as likely to attempt suicide, nearly six times as likely to report high levels of depression and more than 3 times as likely to use illegal drugs and be at high risk for HIV and STDs" (O'Neil, 2014).

This isn't just some political war fought in the abstract. Some sexual minorities experience very real negative psychological consequences on health and well-being (e.g., Bockting, Miner, Swinburne, Hamilton, & Coleman, 2013). Some of these challenges have been associated with faith communities and religious beliefs (e.g., Hatzenbuehler, Pachankis, & Wolff, 2012), although it can be a complex relationship, one than may increase minority stress but also have important "salutary" effects on religious sexual minorities (e.g., Barnes & Meyer, 2012, p. 513).

All this leaves us with a very mixed picture of how religiosity might affect our sexual-minority students. On the one hand, particularly given that so many of these Christian colleges and universities take a stand against same-sex sexual behavior, we might expect that students with greater levels of religiosity would show greater distress than would students with less religiosity. However, religiosity, when healthy, is a proven effective coping mechanism that fosters positive mental health outcomes (Pargament, Smith, Koenig, & Perez, 1998; Park, 2005; Koenig, McCullough, & Larson, 2001).

To get a sense of students' psychological well-being, we again turned to their scores on the Counseling Center Assessment of Psychological Symptoms (CCAPS; CCMH, 2015). This measure compared them to a sample of students seeking mental health services at their colleges and universities.

As might be expected, our results were mixed, with some areas of potential concern and others looking much better than might be expected. For students with greater levels of intrinsic religiosity, their degree of reported psychological symptoms—across all symptom categories—was lower than that of their less religious peers. In other words, on average, they were less likely to experience symptoms of depression, generalized anxiety, social anxiety, and hostility, and they were less likely to experience academic struggles or problematic alcohol use. Only with regard to eating concerns were there no differences related to students' degree of religiosity. So, yes, those with stronger intrinsic religiosity were doing significantly better than those with less religiosity, even though the latter were actually moderately religious.

How, though, do they compare to other students? We first compared them to the normative sample of students seeking counseling. Compared to this group, our sample of sexual-minority students, including both intrinsically religious groups, showed some slight elevation in their symptoms of depression and anxiety, indicating slight distress (see table A5.6 in appendix). The less religious sexual minorities actually showed marked symptoms of depression, significantly higher than both their more religious peers and their help-seeking peers. This less religious group of sexual minorities also showed slight distress in all of the other symptom areas; the more intrinsically religious group did not show any distress in these areas.

Our next comparisons looked at how our sexual-minority students fared compared to their non-help-seeking peers—a nonclinical sample (see table A5.8 in appendix). Because the researchers broke down their results by sexual-identity status, we are able to compare our sexual-minority students to their non-help-seeking heterosexual peers. Both intrinsically religious groups again showed some slight elevation in depression and anxiety. The less religious students also showed some small level of academic distress. Otherwise, both of our religious groups looked like this nonclinical population. In fact, both groups showed significantly fewer alcohol issues than did their peers.

To summarize all of these findings, a distress index was computed for each student. This index represents the overall level of psychological distress a given student is experiencing at the time they completed the survey. Sexual-minority students with lower levels of intrinsic religiosity reported a significantly higher average distress-index score than did their more religious peers.[9] In fact, students with less religiosity showed a slight elevation in these scores, indicating slight distress, whereas their more religious peers did not show any elevation.

While average distress scores tell us something about what the overall groups look like, these scores don't give us much insight into the levels of distress experienced by individual students. Therefore we also compared the percentages of students falling into each distress level and found that intrinsic religiosity was related to large differences in how likely it was that any given student would be psychologically distressed.[10]

For those sexual-minority students with high intrinsic religiosity, the majority of them, 60%, fell into the normal range of psychological functioning (see fig. 5.8). Very few, only 6%, fell in the marked-distress range. Compare these students to their less religious sexual-minority peers. Those with low intrinsic religiosity were about half as likely to have distress scores in the normal range (i.e., "low distress") and about two to three times more likely to be in the marked-distress range. Here intrinsic religiosity is shown to be important to students' mental health.

As we've mentioned earlier, intrinsic religiosity is the degree to which people experience God and incorporate their religious beliefs into their daily life

---

[9]An independent-samples t-test found that those sexual-minority students with low intrinsic religiosity had significantly higher distress index scores ($M = 1.58$, $SD = 0.61$) than did those with high intrinsic religiosity ($M = 1.16$, $SD = 0.62$), t (158) = 4.03, $p < 0.001$, Cohen's $d = 0.68$ (large effect size).

[10]There is a difference in distribution of scores. Those students with low intrinsic religiosity are less likely than expected to fall in the normal range, χ^2 (2) = 14.89, $p = 0.001$.

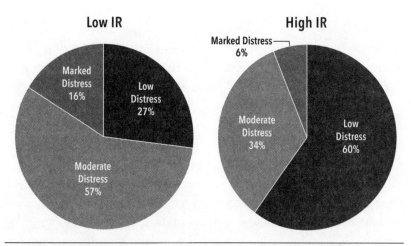

Figure 5.8. Degree of distress and low and high intrinsic religiosity, year 1

(Koenig & Büssing, 2010). This kind of "subjective religiosity" or experienced religiosity is very similar to how others might define spirituality. For example, Philip Tan (2005) argues that spiritual well-being includes both how one relates to God (religious well-being) and how one feels about life (existential well-being), which is essentially the same as intrinsic religiosity. Within the religious well-being subscale, more traditional forms of religiosity, such as going to church and identifying with a formal religious organization, were included. Using this definition of spiritual well-being, ninety-three gay and lesbian individuals were assessed to explore how their spirituality connected to their psychological health. Religious well-being was not found to be predictive of psychological health, but existential well-being was found to be a significant predictor. The conclusion Tan drew was that formal religion and theistic belief were not important for LGBT individuals; rather, what mattered was simply their beliefs about life.

In some ways Tan's research supports our findings here. If his understanding of spirituality does overlap our understanding of intrinsic religiosity, then we could say that spirituality or intrinsic religiosity—rather than the behaviors of religion—seems to be connected to psychological symptoms. Those with higher levels of spirituality or intrinsic religiosity are psychologically better off than those with lower levels.

Our findings, though, also challenge Tan's conclusions. The scale we used includes one question that specifically mentions God (Koenig & Büssing,

2010): "In my life, I experience the presence of the Divine (i.e., God)." This question is moderately correlated with the other questions on our intrinsic religiosity measure, meaning the more we experience God in our lives, the more likely it is that we also "try hard to carry [our] religion over into all other dealings in life" and that "[our] religious beliefs are what really lie behind [our] whole approach to life." In other words, an existential experiencing of religion in daily life is related to experiencing God in our daily life. Tan, however, tried to separate these things. In forcing this division, he found that only the former—the existential experiencing—mattered. But our results show that the two together are better predictors of psychological health than either separately. And the experience of the presence of the Divine in life alone predicts most of the psychological symptoms. At least for our students, living out faith and having a relationship with God—their intrinsic religiosity—make a difference in how well they are doing.

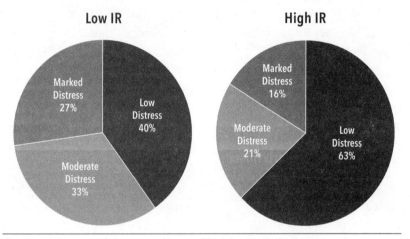

Figure 5.9. Degree of distress and low and high intrinsic religiosity, year 2

Would students' faith help them as they moved into the second year of the study? If you recall from chapter two, about half of the sample stayed in the normal- to low-distress category from the first time we tested them to the second time, but a small percentage of our students showed an increase in their level of distress. Intrinsic religiosity again plays an important role in mediating this change in distress (see fig. 5.9). While both religious groups had a number of students move into the marked-distress range, this was more true for those with low levels of religiosity than for those with high levels.[11] In other words, the more religious students were less likely to become more distressed over the first year of the study. Intrinsic religiosity seems to have a protective effect.

To summarize, students with higher levels of intrinsic religiosity showed significantly lower levels of psychological distress than did those with low to moderate religiosity. Most of our highly religious students showed no more distress than a typical healthy college student. However, most students with low to moderate intrinsic religiosity were significantly psychologically distressed, and they were more likely to see an increase in this distress.

CHURCH ATTENDANCE AND PSYCHOLOGICAL WELL-BEING

But what about attending church? Tan suggested that formal religious activities were associated with negative outcomes for LGB+ individuals, and she's not the only one to draw this conclusion. Steven Meanley and his colleagues (2016) assessed a group of LGB+ men in Detroit and found, like Tan, that greater spiritual coping was linked to better psychological well-being, including more positive life purpose and self-esteem, while religious participation seemed to be connected to poorer psychological functioning and more internalized homophobia.

Others have argued, directly or indirectly, that sexual minorities need to quit church in order to be psychologically healthy. As a case in point, consider the following study. Kelly Schuck and Becky Liddle (2001) found that two-thirds of their sample of LGB+ individuals experienced conflict between their sexuality and their faith, particularly denominational teachings, scriptural passages, and congregational prejudice, that resulted in poorer mental health. Participants used a variety of approaches to manage this cognitive dissonance, including reinterpreting Scripture and denominational teachings, "identifying as spiritual rather than religious," changing denominational affiliations, "remaining religious but not attending, and abandoning religion altogether" (p. 63).

In most of our analyses, we found that one's level of intrinsic religiosity seemed to be the influential factor in sexual-identity development, with organizational religiosity (i.e., how often one attends religious services) and nonorganizational religiosity (i.e., how often one engages in private religious practices) showing very

---

[11]While there was not a difference in distribution of scores, χ^2 (2) = 4.55, p = 0.10, those students with low intrinsic religiosity are less likely than expected to fall in the normal to low range, adj. r = -2.1, and those with high intrinsic religiosity were more likely than expected to fall in the normal to low range, adj. r = 2.1.

little direct contribution. Yet, given the number of studies that suggest that involvement in organizational religion was difficult for sexual minorities, we wanted to look more intentionally at this in our students.

Again, as mentioned in chapter two, we have a very religiously active sample. Only seventeen of our 160 students attend church less than a few times a month, not including any mandatory services on their campuses, so our low organizational religiosity group really has moderate organizational religiosity.[12] This matters here, as it does for intrinsic religiosity, because it shows just how much religiosity matters to these students.

Contrary to almost all of the research we have seen in less-religious samples, going to church matters for our students in a *positive* direction. In fact, in every symptom category, students who attended religious services once a week or more often were doing significantly better than students who attended these services less than once per week (see table A5.8 in appendix). On average, students who attended church less than once per week reported more symptoms of depression, generalized anxiety, anxiety, and hostility. These students also reported more academic distress, more eating concerns, and more problems with alcohol.

In fact, those with lower organizational religiosity show slight clinical elevation in *all* symptom categories as compared to a broader sample of college students seeking counseling. This slight elevation means these areas may be potentially problematic for students, with some mild distress, but further assessment is needed to understand what is going on. In contrast, our students who attended religious services more than once per week show this small elevation only in depression and anxiety. The good news is that neither group had average scores in the clinically elevated range, which would indicate marked distress.

Another way to think about the relationship of church involvement and mental health is to consider the overall distress index derived from the scores above. On average, students attending religious services less than once per week reported higher distress than did those going to church more often (see fig. 5.10).[13] As expected, then, students attending church less than once a week also were

---

[12]Students with high organizational religiosity attend religious services once a week or more, and students with low organizational religiosity attend less than once a week, outside mandatory religious services on their campuses.

[13]Using an independent-samples t-test, students with higher levels of organizational religiosity ($M = 1.16$, $SD = 0.56$) reported lower levels of distress than did students with lower organizational religiosity ($M = 1.61$, $SD = 0.74$), $t(158) = 4.20$, $p < 0.001$, Cohen's $d = 0.69$ (large effect size).

much more likely to have marked distress than students who more frequently attended services—about five and a half times more likely.[14] Only 4% of students with high organizational religiosity had scores in the marked-distress range, yet 23% of those attending religious services less than once per week showed this marked distress. Similarly, those who attended church more were almost two times as likely to fall within the normal range of psychological symptoms.

So what can we say about attending church? It matters. Sexual-minority students who attended church at least once per week showed much less psychological distress.

Students with Low OR   Students with High OR

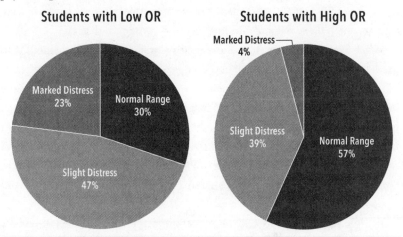

Figure 5.10. Degree of distress and low and high organizational religiosity

Looking at these relationships between religiosity and mental health clearly suggests that we must consider, and even engage, religiosity in our work with Christian sexual minorities. That religiosity includes their relationship with God, their integration of faith into their daily lives, and attending religious services. Students with higher levels of religiosity are doing better than even students with moderate levels of religiosity. But that doesn't necessarily mean that we should recommend more church involvement, more prayer, more religious belief, and the like to struggling students with same-sex attraction. Our results are correlational, not causal; therefore we know this is a relationship, but we don't know whether religiosity promotes psychological health, or whether psychological health promotes religiosity, or whether some other

---

[14]Students with high organizational religiosity are less likely than expected to fall in the marked distress range, and those with low organizational religiosity are more likely than expected to fall in this range, χ^2 (2) = 19.64, $p < 0.001$.

factor—such as being on a Christian campus, having Christian friends, or attending a particular kind of church—affects both.

In an attempt to better understand this, we ran a statistical test that allowed us to see which factors contribute to predicting a student's level of distress.[15] Into this analysis we added several factors: public sexual identity, private sexual identity, intrinsic religiosity, and level of same-sex attraction. We also included campus views of same-sex sexual behaviors and perceived support from family, college faculty and staff, church, heterosexual friends, and LGBT-identified friends.[16] And, of course, we added in the typical ones— age and gender. Each of these made sense as possible predictors, but we were unsure which ones really would matter to psychological distress.

What did we find? Of all of these factors, only two of them helped us to predict students' overall level of psychological distress: their level of intrinsic religiosity and their gender.[17] None of the other factors seemed to contribute in any meaningful way (see table A5.9 in appendix). Of these two factors, gender was the most significant predictor, with those choosing "other" for their gender experiencing the most distress. Perhaps given the current cultural salience of emerging and diverse gender identities, it may be important to come to a better understanding of students who might identify as "other" with respect to their gender.

Intrinsic religiosity was also an important factor. As we've seen in our discussion above, higher levels of intrinsic religiosity are associated with lower distress. What we do know is this—if we want to estimate how well sexual-minority students are doing psychologically, we could start with questions about their gender identity and their level of intrinsic religiosity. This will give us a very small start in making this prediction, but we still need to talk to the students to hear their stories.

William Summay, a celibate gay graduate from a Christian liberal arts university, reported much the same in a research symposium (*Sexual Minority Student Experiences in Faith-Based Higher Education*) of the 2017 American

---

[15]Linear multiple regression with the CCAPS distress index as the dependent variable. The linear regression model was significant, *adjusted* R^2 = 0.16, F (12, 137) = 3.36, p < 0.001.

[16]A few variables were left out because of their relationships with the other variables, creating collinearity issues. These variables included level of opposite-sex sexual attraction, perceived campus attitudes toward same-sex attracted people, and perceived campus attitudes toward same-sex sexual attraction.

[17]The model was a good fit, F (12, 140) = 3.76, p < 0.001, but explained only a small percentage of the variance, R = 0.489, *adjusted* R^2 = 0.174.

Psychological Association Convention about his own undergraduate experience. He explained:

> At various periods during my time at [Christian university], I certainly did experience some intense psychological distress due to my sexual minority status, but at many other times my mental health was no different than my peers, maybe even healthier due to my intentionality in the pursuit of intimate friendships and faith. . . . Research draws out two things that I know for a fact in my experience contributed to my being holistically healthy: faith and friends. It took having people who empathized well and were there for me to make me feel that I was not alone and was valued. Working on my faith was also vital to my well-being in that it grounded me and gave me hope. Both of these things were the pivotal game changers of my experience as a sexual minority, not only in a healthy integration of my sexuality and faith, but in my finding a space to be and grow into myself at [Christian university].

In this chapter we have considered the relationships of several aspects of religiosity/spirituality to sexual attitudes, developmental milestones, and psychological health/well-being. With this data in our rearview mirror, we turn to the experiences of our students on Christian college campuses, particularly their experience of campus climate. This combination of faith and relationship seemed central to the kind of experience that sexual minorities found vital for life at their colleges and universities.

CHAPTER 5 TAKEAWAYS

1. Sexual minorities on Christian college campuses tend to be highly religious—in terms of how often they attend church and engage in private religious activities and in the degree to which their faith affects all other aspects of their lives.

2. These students, like the general population, tend to hold that same-sex attraction is relatively biological and immutable. However, where our students differ from the general population, and where we see religion play an even greater role, is in their less-accepting views of same-sex sexual behavior.

3. Most of these Christian sexual-minority students believe that celibacy is one viable option for living out their sexuality in the context of their faith.

4. While intrinsic religiosity seems to have a small delaying effect on some same-sex sexual milestones, it has much larger delaying effect across opposite-sex sexual behaviors.

5. Students with higher levels of intrinsic religiosity showed significantly lower levels of psychological distress than did those with low to moderate religiosity. In fact, the majority of those sexual-minority students with high religiosity showed no more distress than a typical healthy college student. But the large majority of those with low to moderate intrinsic religiosity were significantly psychologically distressed.

6. Attending church matters. Sexual-minority students who attended church at least once per week showed much less psychological distress than those attending church less frequently.

7. For most of these students, faith cannot be separated from sexual-identity development. Approaches for helping these students must, ethically and practically, address both faith and sexual identity together.

▼

REFERENCES

American Psychological Association (2013, March 22). What role do religion and spirituality play in mental health? Retrieved from www.apa.org/news/press/releases/2013/03/religion-spirituality.aspx

American Psychological Association. (2017). Sexual orientation and homosexuality. Retrieved from www.apa.org/topics/lgbt/orientation.aspx

Americans United for the Separation of Church and State. (2013, February). The religious right's war on LGBT Americans: Church, state and your freedom at risk! Retrieved from www.au.org/resources/publications/the-religious-rights-war-on-lgbt-americans

Arnett, J. J., & Jensen, L. A. (2002). A congregation of one: Individualized religious beliefs among emerging adults. *Journal of Adolescent Research, 17*, 451-67. http://doi.org/10.1177/0743558402175002

Barna, G. (2001). *Real teens: A contemporary snapshot of youth culture.* Ventura, CA: Regal Books.

Barnes, D. M., & Meyer, I. H. (2012). Religious affiliation, internalized homophobia, and mental health in lesbians, gay men, and bisexuals. *American Journal of Orthopsychiatry, Mental Health, and Social Justice, 82*(4), 505-15.

Belgau, Ron (2017). The great debate. Retrieved from https://ronbelgau.com/great-debate.

Bockting, W. O., Miner, M. H., Swinburne, R., Hamilton, A., & Coleman, E. (2013). Stigma, mental health, and resilience in an online sample of the US transgender population. *American Journal of Public Health, 103*(5), 943-51.

Born This Way (song). (n.d.). In *Wikipedia*. Retrieved January 20, 2016, from https://en.wikipedia.org/wiki/Born_This_Way_(song)#Composition

Bryant, A. N., Choi, J. Y., & Yasuno, M. (2003). Understanding the religious and spiritual dimensions of students' lives in the first year of college. *Journal of College Student Development, 44*, 723-45. http://doi.org/10.1353/csd.2003.0063

Center for Collegiate Mental Health (2012). *CCAPS 2012 technical manual.* University Park, PA.

Center for Collegiate Mental Health. (2015). *CCAPS user manual.* University Park, PA: Author.

Center for Collegiate Mental Health. (2016). *CCAPS 2015 user manual.* University Park, PA.

Center for the Study of Collegiate Mental Health. (2010, March). 2010 Annual Report (Publication no. STA 11-000). Retrieved from http://ccmh.psu.edu/wp-content/uploads/sites/3058/2014/07/2010_CCMH_Report.pdf

Dean, J. B., Stratton, S. P., Yarhouse, M. A., & Lastoria, M. (2011). Same sex attraction. In M. Lastoria (Ed.), *ACSD research series: Sexuality, religiosity, behaviors, attitudes: A look at religiosity, sexual attitudes, and sexual behavior of Christian college students* (pp. 56-70). Houghton, NY: Association for Christians in Student Development.

Dean, J. B., Stratton, S. P., Yarhouse, M. A., Summay, W., Wolff, J., Hathaway, W., Cunningham, J., Lastoria, M., Bucher, E., & Sadusky, J. (2017, August). *Sexual minority student experiences in faith-based higher education.* Presentation at the 2017 Annual Convention of the American Psychological Association, Washington, DC.

Entwistle, D. N., & Jackson, E. A. (2015). *Perspectives on Christianity and psychology: Viewpoints of CCCU undergraduate psychology majors.* Paper presented at the annual conference of the Christian Association for Psychological Studies, Denver, CO.

Graves, J. (2014, June 4). How our genes could make us gay or straight. *The Washington Post.* Retrieved from www.washingtonpost.com/posteverything/wp/2014/06/04/the-science-of-sexuality-how-our-genes-make-us-gay-or-straight/?utm_term=.c25ee0c106f8

Hall, M. E. L., Ripley, J. S., Garzon, F. L., & Mangis, M. W. (2009). The other side of the podium: Student perspectives on learning integration. *Journal of Psychology and Theology, 37*, 15-27.

Hatzenbuehler, M. L., Pachankis, J. E., & Wolff, J. (2012). Religious climate and health risk behaviors in sexual minority youths: A population-based study. *American Journal of Public Health, 102*(4), 657-63. http://doi.org/10.2105/ajph.2011.300517

Hill, W. (2010). *Washed and waiting: Reflections on Christian faithfulness and homosexuality.* New York: HarperCollins.

Hill, W. (2015a, July 15). Yes, many Christian communities are toxic for my LBGT friends. But there's more. *The Washington Post.* Retrieved from www.washington tonpost.com/news/acts-of-faith/wp/2015/07/15/yes-many-christian-communities -are-toxic-for-my-lbgt-friends-but-theres-more/?utm_term=.ee7dda540b1c

Hill, W. (2015b). *Spiritual friendship: Finding love in the church as a celibate gay Christian.* Ada, MI: Brazos.

Hull, S. J., Hennessy, M., Bleakley, A., Fishbein, M., & Jordan, A. (2011). Identifying the causal pathways from religiosity to delayed adolescent sexual behavior. *Journal of Sex Research, 48*(6), 543-53. http://doi.org/10.1080/00224499.2010.521868

Jones, R. C., Cox, D., & Banchoff, T. (2012). A generation in transition: Religion, values, and politics among college-age millennials. *Findings from the 2012 Millennial Values Survey.* Retrieved from www.scribd.com/doc/90155399/Millennials-Survey-Report

Kinnaman, D. (2011). *You lost me: Why young Christians are leaving church . . . and rethinking faith.* Grand Rapids, MI: Baker Books.

Koenig, H. G. (2012). Religion, spirituality, and health: The research and clinical implications. *ISRN Psychiatry* [published online], 11-33. http://dx.doi.org/10.5402/2012/278730

Koenig, H. G., & Büssing, A. (2010). The Duke University religion index (DUREL): A five-item measure for use in epidemiological studies. *Religions, 1,* 78-85. http://doi .org/10.3390/rel1010078

Koenig, H. G., McCullough, M. E., & Larson, D. B. (Eds.). (2001). *Handbook of religion and health.* New York: Oxford University Press.

Koenig, H. G., Meador, K. G., & Parkerson, G. (1997). Religion index for psychiatric research. *American Journal of Psychiatry, 154,* 885-86.

Krull, D. S. (2017). On hating the sin but loving the sinner: Judgments about homosexuality and religiosity. *Journal of Psychology and Christianity, 36*(2), 99-109.

Lee, J. J. (2002). Religion and college attendance: Change among students. *Review of Higher Education: Journal of the Association for the Study of Higher Education, 25,* 369-84. http://doi.org/10.1353/rhe.2002.0020

Mahoney, E. R. (1980). Religiosity and sexual behavior among heterosexual college students. *The Journal of Sex Research, 16*(2), 97-113. http://doi.org/10.1080 /00224498009551067

Manlove, J., Logan, C., Moore, K. A., & Ikramullah, E. (2008). Pathways from family religiosity to adolescent sexual activity and contraceptive use. *Perspectives on Sexual and Reproductive Health, 40*(2), 105-17. http://doi.org/10.1363/4010508

Marin, A. (2016). *Us versus us: The untold story of religion and the LGBT community.* Carol Stream, IL: NavPress.

Masters, K. S. (2013). Intrinsic religiousness (religiosity). In M. D. Gellman & J. R. Turner (Eds.), *Encyclopedia of behavioral medicine* (pp. 1117-18). New York: Springer New York.

Meanley, S., Pingel, E. S., & Bauermeister, J. A. (2016). Psychological well-being among religious and spiritual-identified young gay and bisexual men. *Sexuality Research & Social Policy: A Journal of the NSRC, 13*(1), 35-45.

Morris, A. (2014, September 3). The forsaken: A rising number of homeless gay teens are being cast out by religious families. *Rolling Stone.* Retrieved from www.rolling stone.com/culture/features/the-forsaken-a-rising-number-of-homeless-gay-teens -are-being-cast-out-by-religious-families-20140903

O'Neil, L. (2014, June 28). Caitlin Ryan's scientific way to reduce LGBT teen suicide. *Ozy.* Retrieved from www.ozy.com/rising-stars/caitlin-ryans-scientific-way-to -reduce-lgbt-teen-suicide/32237

Pargament, K. I., Smith, B., Koenig, H., & Perez, L. (1998). Patterns of positive and negative religious coping with major life stressors. *Journal for the Scientific Study of Religion, 37*, 711-25.

Park, C. L. (2005). Religion as a meaning-making framework in coping with life stress. *Journal of Social Issues, 61*, 707-29.

Pew Research Center. (2015, June 8). Support for same-sex marriage at record high, but key segments remain opposed. *Pew Research Center.* Retrieved from www.people-press .org/2015/06/08/support-for-same-sex-marriage-at-record-high-but-key-segments -remain-opposed/

Rainer, T. S., & Rainer, J. W. (2011). *The millennials: Connecting to America's largest generation.* Nashville: B&H.

Regnerus, M. D., Rostosky, S. S., & Comer Wright, M. L. (2003). Coital debut: The role of religiosity and sex attitudes in the Add Health Survey. *Journal of Sex Research, 40*, 358-67.

Rettner, R. (2015, September 23). God help us? How religion is good (and bad) for mental health. *LiveScience.* Retrieved from www.livescience.com/52197-religion-mental -health-brain.html

Rodgers, J. (2015, July 13). An update on the gay debate: Evolving ideas, untidy stories, and hopes for the church. *Julie Rodgers* [Blog]. Retrieved from https://julierodgers .wordpress.com/tag/culture-war/

Rostosky, S. S., Wilcox, B. L., Comer Wright, M. L., & Randall, B. A. (2004). The impact of religiosity on adolescent sexual behavior: A review of the evidence. *Journal of Adolescent Research, 9*, 677-97. http://doi.org/10.1177/0743558403260019

Ryan, C., Huebner, D., Diaz, R. M., & Sanchez, J. (2009). Family rejection as a predictor of negative health outcomes in white and Latino lesbian, gay, and bisexual young adults. *Pediatrics, 123*(1).

Saewyc, E. M., Bearinger, L. H., Blum, R. W., & Resnick, M. D. (1999). Sexual intercourse, abuse and pregnancy among adolescent women: Does sexual orientation make a difference? *Family Planning Perspectives, 31*(3), 127-31.

Saewyc, E., Poon, C., Wang, N., Homma, Y., & Smith, A. (2007). *Not yet equal: The health of lesbian, gay, & bisexual youth in BC.* Vancouver: McCreary Centre Society.

Sample, I. (2014, February 13). Male sexual orientation influenced by genes, study shows. *The Guardian.* Retrieved from www.theguardian.com/science/2014/feb/14/genes-influence-male-sexual-orientation-study

Schuck, K. D., & Liddle, B. J. (2001). Religious conflicts experienced by lesbian, gay, and bisexual individuals. *Journal of Gay & Lesbian Psychotherapy, 5*(2), 63-82. http://doi.org/10.1300/J236v05n02_07

Stallard, B. (2014, December 18). Homosexuality is genetic: Strongest evidence yet. *Nature World News.* Retrieved from www.natureworldnews.com/articles/10443/20141118/homosexuality-genetic-strongest-evidence.htm on September 30, 2017

Steffen, P. R., Masters, K. S., & Baldwin, S. (2017). What mediates the relationship between religious service attendance and aspects of well-being? *Journal of Religion and Health, 56*(1), 158-70.

Stoppa, T. M., & Lefkowitz, E. S. (2010). Longitudinal changes in religiosity among emerging adult college students. *Journal of Research on Adolescence, 20,* 23-38. http://doi.org/10.1111/j.1532-7795.2009.00630.x

Stratton, S. P., Dean, J. B., Yarhouse, M. A., & Lastoria, M. (2013). Sexual minorities in faith-based higher education: A national survey of attitudes, milestones, identity, and religiosity. *Journal of Psychology and Theology, 41,* 3-23.

Tan, P. P. (2005). The importance of spirituality among gay and lesbian individuals. *Journal of Homosexuality, 49*(2), 135-44. http://doi.org/10.1300/J082v49n02_08

Tulloch, T., & Kaufman, M. (2013). Adolescent sexuality. *Pediatrics in Review, 34*(1), 29-38. Retrieved from http://pedsinreview.aappublications.org/content/pedsinreview/34/1/29.full.pdf

Yarhouse, M. A., Stratton, S. P., Dean, J. B., & Brooke, H. L. (2009). Listening to sexual minorities on Christian college campuses. *Journal of Psychology and Theology, 37*(2), 96-113.

APPENDIX

Table A5.1. Mean attitudes about sexuality and sexual behavior by level of intrinsic religiosity

Attitudes by IR Groups	Low IR (n = 51) M (SD)	High IR (n = 109) M (SD)
Attitudes About Causation		
Persons can choose who they are sexually attracted to.	1.57 (0.75)	**1.94 (1.16)**
Persons who experience same-sex attraction could have been born with this predisposition.	**4.47 (0.73)**	3.95 (1.29)

Experience/environment plays a greater role in the development of same-sex attraction than does biology.	2.44 (0.92)	**2.89 (1.20)**
Persons who experience same-sex attraction can change this aspect of their attractions to the opposite sex.	1.51 (0.83)	**2.04 (1.12)**
Attitudes About Moral Behavior		
Being attracted sexually to members of the same gender is morally acceptable.	**4.52 (0.79)**	3.99 (1.11)
Sexual behavior between members of the same gender is morally acceptable.	**3.98 (1.25)**	2.98 (1.49)
Monogamous sexual relationships between members of the same gender can be blessed, or receive God's grace and love.	**4.13 (1.17)**	3.24 (1.55)
Same-sex experimentation among adolescents to try out this form of sexual expression is morally acceptable.	**3.40 (1.22)**	2.35 (1.23)
Persons can live a sexually celibate life while they have same-sex attraction.	4.07 (1.05)	4.31 (0.95)

Bolded items are statistically higher than comparative mean, $p < 0.05$.

Table A5.2. Mean attitudes about sexuality and sexual behavior by level of intrinsic religiosity in non-sexual-minority students

Attitudes by IR Groups	Low IR (n ~240) M (SD)	High IR (n ~1400) M (SD)
Attitudes About Causation		
Persons can choose who they are sexually attracted to.	3.22 (1.34)	**2.92 (1.32)**
Persons who experience same-sex attraction could have been born with this predisposition.	**2.80 (1.38)**	2.27 (1.29)
Experience/environment plays a greater role in the development of same-sex attraction than does biology.	3.26 (1.14)	**3.65 (1.15)**
Persons who experience same-sex attraction can change this aspect of their attractions to the opposite sex.	3.25 (1.25)	**3.93 (1.03)**
Attitudes About Moral Behavior		
Being attracted sexually to members of the same gender is morally acceptable.	**2.27 (1.35)**	1.67 (1.03)
Sexual behavior between members of the same gender is morally acceptable.	**2.06 (1.26)**	1.34 (0.77)
Monogamous sexual relationships between members of the same gender can be blessed, or receive God's grace and love.	**2.19 (1.24)**	1.47 (0.86)
Same-sex experimentation among adolescents to try out this form of sexual expression is morally acceptable.	**1.94 (1.11)**	1.30 (0.64))
Persons can live a sexually celibate life while they have same-sex attraction.	3.65 (1.12)	3.94 (1.08)

Bolded items are statistically higher than comparative mean, $p < 0.05$.

Table A5.3. Mean age at same-sex milestones by level of intrinsic religiosity

Milestone	MEAN AGE AT SAME-SEX SEXUAL MILESTONES	
	Low IR *M (SD)*	High IR *M (SD)*
Same-Sex Sexual Behaviors		
Been fondled (breasts or genitals) by someone (without orgasm)	17.16 (3.53)	15.54 (5.02)
Fondled (breasts or genitals) someone (without orgasm)	17.71 (3.42)	15.31 (4.66)*
Intimately/romantically kissed by someone	17.67 (3.73)	16.16 (4.09)
Sexual behavior (to orgasm)	18.84 (2.72)	17.65 (3.66)
First same-sex relationship	18.87 (2.83)	17.85 (2.56)
Understanding of Same-Sex Sexual Attraction and Behavior		
Awareness of same-sex feelings	13.74 (3.81)	12.54 (3.91)
Initial attribution that I am same-sex attracted	17.20 (2.44)	17.42 (2.31)
Confusion about same-sex feelings	13.55 (3.55)	13.12 (3.54)
First disclosure of same-sex attraction	17.02 (2.93)	17.29 (2.79)
Initial attribution that "I am gay/lesbian/bisexual"	17.20 (2.44)	17.42 (2.31)
Adopted the label of "gay" for myself privately	18.05 (2.43)	17.80 (2.40)
Adopted the label of "gay" for myself publicly	19.46 (1.93)	19.47 (1.89)

*Using an independent-samples t-test, students with higher levels of intrinsic religiosity ($n = 58$; $M = 15.31$, $SD = 4.66$) were younger than students with lower intrinsic religiosity ($n = 35$; $M = 17.71$, $SD = 3.42$) when they first fondled the breasts or genitals of another person of the same sex, $t(91) = 2.65$, $p = 0.009$, Cohen's $d = 0.59$ (large effect size).

Table A5.4. Opposite-sex milestones in sexual-identity development by level of intrinsic religiosity

Milestone	AVERAGE AGE OF REACHING SAME-SEX SEXUAL MILESTONES	
	Low IR *M (SD)*	High IR *M (SD)*
Intimately/romantically kissed by someone of the opposite sex	15.74 (2.54)	15.36 (3.61)
First relationship with someone of the opposite sex	15.67 (2.64)	15.78 (3.34)
Been fondled (breasts or genitals) by someone (without orgasm) of the opposite sex	15.94 (3.13)	15.64 (4.65)
Fondled (breasts or genitals) someone (without orgasm) of the opposite sex	16.18 (3.36)	15.83 (4.19)
Opposite-sex sexual behavior (to orgasm)	17.16 (2.01)	17.85 (3.88)

Table A5.5. Same-sex milestones in sexual-identity development by level of intrinsic religiosity and gender

Milestones	PERCENTAGES OF MEN REACHING SAME-SEX SEXUAL MILESTONES		PERCENTAGES OF WOMEN REACHING SAME-SEX SEXUAL MILESTONES	
	Low IR ($n = 23$)	High IR ($n = 58$)	Low IR ($n = 25$)	High IR ($n = 47$)
Same-Sex Sexual Behaviors				
Been fondled (breasts or genitals) by someone (without orgasm)	91.3	56.9[a] **	56.0	48.9
Fondled (breasts or genitals) someone (without orgasm)	82.6	55.2[b] *	52.0	48.9
Intimately/romantically kissed by someone	87.0	48.3[c] **	68.0	51.1
Sexual behavior (to orgasm)	78.3	43.1[d] **	21.7	31.9
First same-sex relationship	52.2	32.8	40.0	42.6
Understanding of Same-Sex Sexual Attraction and Behavior				
Awareness of same-sex feelings	100.0	100.0	96.0	100.0
Initial attribution that I am same-sex attracted	100.0	98.3	96.0	100.0
Confusion about same-sex feelings	95.7	96.6	88.0	95.7
First disclosure of same-sex attraction	91.3	79.3	88.0	74.5
Initial attribution that "I am gay/lesbian/bisexual"	91.3	81.0	95.7	80.9
Adopted the label of "gay" for myself privately	82.6	74.1	80.0	61.7
Adopted the label of "gay" for myself publicly	56.5	46.6	52.0	12.8[e] ***

* $p \le 0.05$
** $p \le 0.01$
*** $p \le 0.001$

[a]There is a significant difference in the percentages of female students with high intrinsic religiosity and those with low intrinsic religiosity reaching this milestone, χ^2 (1) = 8.77, p = 0.003.

[b]There is a significant difference in the percentages of female students with high intrinsic religiosity and those with low intrinsic religiosity reaching this milestone, χ^2 (1) = 5.32, p = 0.02.

[c]There is a significant difference in the percentages of female students with high intrinsic religiosity and those with low intrinsic religiosity reaching this milestone, χ^2 (1) = 10.21, p = 0.014.

[d]There is a significant difference in the percentages of female students with high intrinsic religiosity and those with low intrinsic religiosity reaching this milestone, χ^2 (1) = 8.17, p = 0.004.

[e]There is a significant difference in the percentages of male students with high intrinsic religiosity and those with low intrinsic religiosity reaching this milestone, χ^2 (1) = 12.93, p < 0.001.

Table A5.6. CCAPS index scores for psychological symptoms and levels of intrinsic religiosity

Psychological Symptoms	Low IR (n = 51) M (SD)	High IR (n = 109) M (SD)
Depression	1.71 (1.00)[b]	1.16 (0.98)[a]
Generalized Anxiety	1.86 (0.91)[a]	1.42 (1.06)[a]
Social Anxiety	2.12 (0.92)[a]	1.68 (0.98)[a]
Academic Distress	1.81 (1.02)[a]	1.16 (1.05)
Eating Concerns	1.21 (1.19)[a]	0.83 (1.15)
Hostility	0.98 (0.91)[a]	0.60 (0.82)
Alcohol Use	0.86 (1.06)[a]	0.34 (0.84)

[a]Score at or above the low cut point of the normative clinical sample.
[b]Score at or above the elevated cut point of the normative clinical sample.

Table A5.7. CCAPS index scores for psychological symptoms by levels of intrinsic religiosity as compared to nonclinical sample

Average Scores	Low IR (n = 51) M (SD)	Nonclinical Sample (n = 14869) M (SD)	t (df)	p	Cohen's d
Depression	1.71 (1.02)	0.82 (0.74)	8.63	0.059	0.57**
Generalized Anxiety	1.56 (1.03)	1.00 (0.74)	9.47	<0.001	0.62**
Social Anxiety	1.82 (0.98)	1.52 (0.84)	4.48	<0.001	0.33*
Academic Distress	1.37 (1.08)	1.23 (0.84)	2.09	0.037	0.15*
Eating Concerns	0.95 (1.17)	0.99 (0.79)	2.22	0.060	0.04
Hostility	0.72 (0.86)	0.66 (0.69)	1.09	0.280	0.08
Alcohol Use	0.51 (0.94)	0.70 (0.83)	2.88	0.004	0.21*

Average Scores	High IR (n = 109) M (SD)	Nonclinical Sample (n = 14869) M (SD)	t (df)	p	Cohen's d
Depression	1.16 (0.98)	0.82 (0.74)	4.77 (14976)	<0.001	0.39
Generalized Anxiety	1.42 (1.06)	1.00 (0.74)	5.88 (14976)	<0.001	0.46
Social Anxiety	1.68 (0.98)	1.52 (0.84)	1.98 (14976)	0.048	0.18
Academic Distress	1.16 (1.05)	1.23 (0.84)	0.87 (14976)	0.387	0.07
Eating Concerns	0.83 (1.15)	0.99 (0.79)	2.09 (14976)	0.036	0.16
Hostility	0.60 (0.82)	0.66 (0.69)	0.90 (14976)	0.366	0.08
Alcohol Use	0.34 (0.84)	0.70 (0.83)	4.51 (14976)	<0.001	0.43

Table A5.8. CCAPS index scores for psychological symptoms by levels of organizational religiosity

Psychological Symptoms	Low OR (n = 47) M (SD)	High OR (n = 113) M (SD)
Depression	1.66 (1.16)[a]	1.20 (0.93)[a]
Generalized Anxiety	1.90 (1.04)[a]	1.42 (1.00)[a]
Social Anxiety	2.11 (1.01)[a]	1.70 (0.95)[a]
Academic Distress	1.97 (1.02)[a]	1.12 (1.00)
Eating Concerns	1.38 (1.31)[a]	0.77 (1.06)
Hostility	1.05 (1.16)[a]	0.58 (0.70)
Alcohol Use	0.75 (1.19)[a]	0.41 (0.80)

[a]Score at or above the low cut point of the normative clinical sample but below the elevated cut point.

Table A5.9. Simultaneous multiple regression analysis summary for key variables predicting general psychological distress (n = 160)

Variable	B	SEB	ß
Gender	0.88	0.26	0.26***
Intrinsic religiosity	-0.20	0.06	-0.26**
Campus's view of same-sex behavior	0.05	0.07	0.07
Same-sex attraction	0.01	0.03	0.04
Private sexual identity	-0.01	0.24	-0.00
Public sexual identity	0.10	0.11	0.08
Age	0.00	0.01	0.03
Support for same-sex attraction from . . .			
Family	-0.04	0.03	-0.11
Church	-0.02	0.04	-0.05
Faculty or staff	-0.06	0.04	-0.15
Heterosexual friends	-0.00	0.04	-0.00
LGB-identified friends	-0.01	0.04	-0.02

* $p \leq 0.05$
** $p \leq 0.01$
*** $p \leq 0.001$

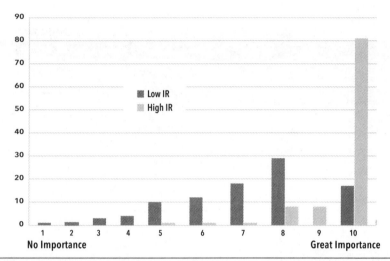

Figure A5.1. Frequency of importance ratings for identifying as a Christian by level of intrinsic religiosity (*n* = 160)

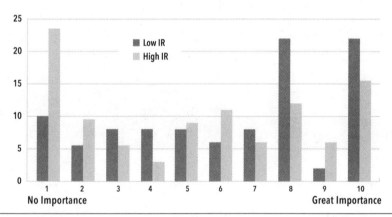

Figure A5.2. Frequency of importance ratings for identifying as a gay, lesbian, or bisexual by level of intrinsic religiosity (*n* = 160)

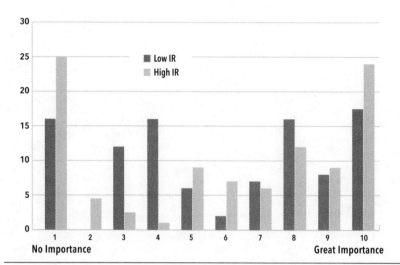

Figure A5.3. Frequency of importance ratings for identifying as a gay, lesbian, or bisexual Christian by level of intrinsic religiosity (*n* = 160)

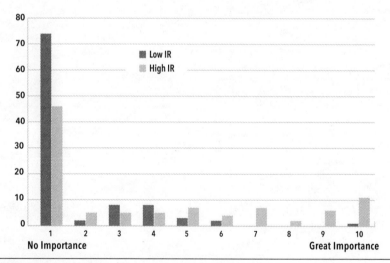

Figure A5.4. Frequency of importance ratings for identifying as a celibate gay, lesbian, or bisexual by level of intrinsic religiosity (*n* = 160)

HOW SEXUAL-MINORITY STUDENTS FIT INTO THEIR COLLEGE CAMPUSES

Most people around here have very good intentions. Nobody is actually hostile toward us. And you know, I feel that there is a lot of ignorance because people don't know how to act around the issue. Most of the time that displays itself in ignorant remarks or other microaggressions, which they are not even aware they are doing. From my personal experience, most of the people I've come out to have been very supportive, at least to me as a person. Some of them have been supportive of me to the point even if I was in a relationship with another man, and some can't go that far, but I still get a strong sense that they generally care for me, even if they don't have all that stuff figured out yet.

—*Kevin, a junior, identifies as gay, time 1*

[The campus climate is] unhelpful, I guess. . . . The word *toxic* comes to mind. That's strong, but I think it could be justified. I think the main thing is there really is no . . . desire to really address the issue. I don't feel a lot of concern. I don't feel like they really care.

—*Logan, a junior, identifies as gay, time 1*

It's definitely, from . . . my four years here, I have seen a lot of improvement. Just in regards to the work that they're doing in trying to create awareness around issues surrounding the LGBT community and just awareness of there being an LGBT community, not just in the broader world but also at my school. . . . I really just appreciate they're being so unafraid to still address this topic, even though, like, our college's . . . stance is like against . . . practicing homosexuality.

—*Chloe, a senior, identifies as lesbian, time 1*

Overall, [the campus climate] is pretty good. The view is negative, as they don't approve [of same-sex sexual behaviors], but the actions are good. They are pretty good about loving and approving of all their students regardless of their sexual attraction. Yeah, I have never been discriminated against. People don't say much in a negative way about LGBT or anything. There are a lot of support groups.

—Justin, a junior, identifies as gay, time 1

Because it's a liberal arts environment, [students] become increasingly more open over the course of their time at school. So by the time they are seniors, most of them are pretty chill. . . . But the freshmen are a little crazy, but that's the way freshmen are, so it's okay.

—Adriana, a senior, identifies as bisexual, time 1

▼▲▼

In December 2015, Campus Pride, an educational organization for LGBTQ and ally college students and campus groups, published the *Shame List*. This list catalogued what they perceived to be the colleges and universities with "harmful and shameful acts of religion-based prejudice and bigotry" (Campus Pride, 2016). Either of two criteria earned an institution a spot on this disreputable list: (1) demonstrating a history of discriminative practices and policies or (2) seeking Title IX exemptions, even though these criteria are often perceived by Christian colleges and universities as the only options to uphold their religiously based perspectives on gender and sexuality in the face of federal government intrusiveness. When asked about this list, Campus Pride's executive director, Shane Windmeyer, was quoted as saying,

> Religion-based bigotry is careless and life-threatening. . . . LGBTQ young people face high rates of harassment and violence. . . . The schools on this list openly discriminate against LGBTQ youth and many of these schools have requested or received Title IX exemptions for no other purpose than to discriminate, expel and ban LGBTQ youth from campus. It is shameful and wrong. . . . Families and young people deserve to know that this list of schools are the worst for LGBTQ youth. They are not loving, welcoming, safe spaces to live, learn and grow—and nobody wants to go to a college that openly discriminates against anyone. (Campus Pride, 2016)

And, yet, many students do choose to go to the schools on this list—even LGBTQ students. In fact, many of the students in our sample are attending schools on that list. While we might debate whether this list represents an adequate understanding of the reasons for the boundaries of religious/spiritual communities, and even the value of Title IX and any exemptions to it, what might be most important to understand is the actual experience of sexual-minority students on these campuses. They have a lot to tell us.

CHOOSING A CHRISTIAN CAMPUS

Informal discussions about sexual minorities at Christian colleges can quickly devolve into oversimplifications that essentially blame sexual minorities for enrolling at a college that holds to a traditional Christian sexual ethic. You can imagine the exchanges on social media, comments such as, "Why would a gay student go to a Christian college anyway?" These questions are oversimplifications because they assume that all students have resolved the theological questions and practical tensions between sexual and religious identity in adolescence and are now deciding to attend a college that holds a position that *they are settled on and oppose.*

Such a dynamic does not appear to be in play among the students in our sample. Many students are not settled on these complicated questions but appear instead to seek a setting where they can take their faith and sexuality seriously. They are trying to navigate both their religious identity as a Christian and their sexual identity with respect to their same-sex sexuality.

In 2015, Jenny Hudalla, a student reporter for the campus newspaper at her Christian university, asked three of her peers why they chose that campus. Their responses were varied: "For [Elizabeth] Ciesluk, it was Festival of Christmas. For [Jonah] Venegas, it was a positive postsecondary experience. And for [Dan] Sandberg, it was absolutely nothing—his parents forced him to attend." And yet she noted that all decided to stay despite their varied experiences as sexual minorities on their religious campus. All wanted to work toward making campus a more accepting place interpersonally for sexual minorities. Interestingly, none seemed to be advocating for policy amendments, whether they doubt such changes are possible or don't believe such changes are needed.

We did not ask a specific question that directly addresses the decision to attend a Christian college or university. But we did have a few students who mentioned their "desire" to be at a Christian college. The main ideas were that students wanted a rigorous educational experience that did not leave out their faith tradition.

For example, looking back from his position as a junior on campus, Jonah reported that he came to his Christian institution in part because "a lot of people believe a lot of different things, and [my school] is very good at fostering those conversations." Now that he has been a student for two-plus years at his college, he reported,

> Having those conversations and knowing that so many people think differently about things. Instead of pushing me one way or another, what it did was it gave me a stronger base and framework to say, "Okay, this is what I believe. Now how does it compare to what this person is saying and that person is saying? And, you know, they make a good point. How would my beliefs refute that? Is there something wrong with what I believe, or is that a point I can't really fight against?" So if anything, it challenged me and gave me a stronger network to build myself up with.

Currently a senior, Chloe gave reasons for attending a Christian college that focused a bit more on the relational aspects. She explained, "I think that's probably one of the largest reasons why I came to this college. They want to do right by people. I live [in a residence hall] with many different ethnicities. They want to be very welcoming, and they want to be quiet and listen and love on you. So that's been uplifting. I've never experienced homophobic remarks."

Looking back, Colby, a bisexual senior with a "straight" identity status, reported,

> I think one of the main reasons that I came to this college was to shed light on this monster in my life and these desires. You know, I considered myself unlovable because of them. . . . I wanted to be around people who were going to be talking about Jesus. He is life. He is love. He has already won. I think the attitude of the campus and attitudes toward sin and brokenness helped my spirituality. Despite that I don't have many conversations about same-sex attractions with other people, I think the conversations of brokenness have been a really unifying and bonding thing.

Yet not all found their hopes realized. Savannah, who describes herself as "very gay," stated,

> I came to campus understanding that there would be a number of challenges coming to a Christian campus and me being who I am. . . . I thought it'd be fine. I wasn't coming to school to get a romantic partner.

I was coming to get an education. I figured I wouldn't talk about that aspect of me except with my closest friends, and I thought that'd be fine. For a while it was, until I became friends with some people and through getting to know me and me getting to know them, it became discernable that I am gay. . . . There are some really amazing students on campus who, even if they don't agree with my beliefs, . . . are open and loving and still care, . . . but on the whole I found students at my school to not be very supportive. And eventually it became more common knowledge that I'm gay, and I started receiving a lot worse treatment.

Aaliyah, a queer senior, realized over time that when she selected a Christian college that she was getting into something new. She had only been a Christian for a couple of years, and she was coming from a family that apparently did not look like the Christian subculture that she saw at her school. And even though it was attractive to her, she reflected back and said, "It's been weird to come in and try to understand Christian subculture. And from a lot of that I felt really alienated 'cause I didn't get it. I feel like everybody would freak out about C. S. Lewis and I would be like, 'What's the big deal about C. S. Lewis?' Like he's great, but I don't get why you're all going crazy like it's a Beatles concert." Aaliyah found out that it wasn't just the sexual issues that might make things complicated for her; it was the religious and spiritual issues of the community as well.

CAMPUS POLICIES

The colleges and universities attended by our sample of students tend to hold conservative, religiously based beliefs about marriage and sexuality. In fact, both Eastern Mennonite University and Goshen University left the Council for Christian Colleges and Universities (CCCU) in 2015, soon after their new policies allowing faculty and staff to be in same-sex marriages led to protest from some other CCCU-member institutions (Weber, 2015). There was great concern that increased diversity in policies around sexuality might limit the CCCU's power in advocating—legally and otherwise—for its many member institutions who reject same-sex relationships as biblically and theologically unsound.

The membership of the CCCU is large and diverse. Whereas the ACSD, which we introduced in chapter two, is an association of Christians who are in student-development positions on various campuses (predominantly faith-based evangelical; however, there are a few public campuses), the CCCU is for institutions themselves. Its approximately 180 institutions represent about thirty-five Protestant denominations across the United States and eighteen other countries. They do, however, hold at least two things in common: (1) a committed faith perspective that guides, undergirds, and permeates much of what they do, and (2) a traditional understanding of marriage and sexuality. As such, most of these institutions ask students to put boundaries around any sexual behavior outside marriage between a man and a woman, including any same-sex sexual behavior.

Incoming students at most of these institutions are directed to read over the behavioral expectations for students before matriculating, and some even have to sign indicating that they have done so and agree to abide by these expectations. Signing does not necessarily mean agreement with the policies; for some, it simply means agreement to abide by the policy, not agreement that the policies are correct. Of course, other students may sign with only limited, if any, awareness of these policies.

Even though we were surveying students at schools in which a staff member was associated with the ACSD and not necessarily CCCU institutions, we wanted to better understand students' relationship to the sexuality policies at their universities and gave them four response options (see fig. 6.1). A small percentage—fewer than one out of ten—were unaware of the policies on sexuality. Perhaps surprising to many, 31%, that is, almost one out of three, said that they came to their university because they agreed with the existing policies.

In the interviews, some of the students told us that they had little awareness of what their same-sex attraction would mean for their identity development in college, so it didn't matter at the time that the schools prohibited this kind of behavior. Others explained that they specifically wanted the external boundaries to help them manage their attractions in a way that was consistent with their faith. Faith seems to be an important factor in agreement with the policies. In fact, students with higher levels of intrinsic religiosity were much more likely to find themselves in agreement with their institutions on issues of sexuality.[1] Conversely, those with greater same-sex attraction were less likely to agree.[2]

---

[1] A chi-square analysis revealed a significant difference between low and high intrinsic religiosity groups and their position on campus policies, χ^2 (3) = 23.86, p < 0.001. Students with high intrinsic religiosity were more likely than expected to agree with current policies (*ADJR* = 4.4) but less likely than expected to disagree vocally (*ADJR* = -3.5), whereas students with low intrinsic religiosity were less likely than expected to agree with current policies (*ADJR* = -4.4) and more likely than expected to vocally disagree (*ADJR* = 3.5). Phi φ = 0.39 (medium effect size).

[2] A chi-square analysis revealed a significant difference between low and high same-sex attraction groups and their position on campus policies, χ^2 (3) = 9.93, p = 0.019. Students with high same-

Not all students, though, were in agreement with the sexuality policies. It's unclear whether they disagreed before they matriculated or came to disagree after they had been on campus awhile. At the time of the survey, 40% indicated they quietly disagreed with the policies, but only 19.4% said they were outspoken about their disagreement. Students with higher levels of same-sex attraction are even more likely to disagree quietly.

Interviewees noted that the strongest campus message among their Christian colleges and universities referenced same-sex sexual behaviors. Over 75% of those interviewed remarked about the dominant institutional message that same-sex behavior is viewed as biblically wrong for Christian living and unwanted in the faith-based community. Through policy statements, community

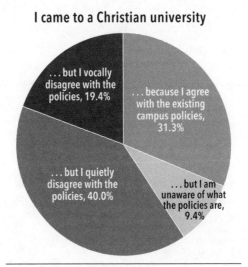

I came to a Christian university

... but I vocally disagree with the policies, 19.4%

... because I agree with the existing campus policies, 31.3%

... but I quietly disagree with the policies, 40.0%

... but I am unaware of what the policies are, 9.4%

Figure 6.1. Attitudes toward campus policies regarding sexuality and sexual behavior

ethos, and even student-orientation presentations in some institutions, most students perceived the message that same-sex behavior is prohibited. As Rachelle, an eighteen-year-old African American freshman, stated, "The school makes it pretty clear when you get there, so they want you to know what they stand for."

This does not fit well for all. Some students clearly wish that the policies about same-sex sexual behavior were different, some so much so that they are willing to take risks and stand up for what they believe. Yet many students in our interviews suggested that they don't necessarily want the policies changed, even where they disagree with them. Rather, they would like to see specific issues or related policies addressed, but not the overarching institutional understanding of sexuality and appropriate sexual behavior. Some of

sex attraction were less likely than expected to agree with current policies ($ADJR$ = -3.1) but more likely than expected to disagree quietly ($ADJR$ = 2.2), whereas students with low same-sex attraction were more likely than expected to agree with current policies ($ADJR$ = 3.1) and less likely than expected to quietly disagree ($ADJR$ = -2.2). Phi φ = 0.39 (small effect size).

these students even suggested that their institution's unique religious and spiritual identity would change if its policies changed.[3]

So, if some of these students don't want the general policies changed, what is it that they would like to see? Rachelle, from above, went on to identify a common problem among Christian colleges and universities regarding same-sex behavior. Although the prohibition appears to be clear for most students in the interview sample, the actual definition remains "pretty blurry" (Rachelle's words) as to what behaviors are actually prohibited and which ones are not. Especially when it comes to behaviors that might be affectionate or romantic but stop short of violating explicit rules for celibacy, institutions appeared to be less detailed in their perceived policies, leaving many students uncertain and insecure. It may even be complicated across gender-based lines, as Savannah, a twenty-year-old white junior, reported, "Girls hug and can hold hands. Guys don't really do that [in my school], but that is a normal part of human interaction. In chapel one guy put his arm around another guy. I felt that was a bold move." The message at the colleges and universities where these students attend seemed clear, but the implications for community life appeared less apparent to these developing students.

This perceived ambiguity is a topic that was raised recently in a report by David Wheeler (2016) in which he interviewed Justin Lee, the former executive director of the Gay Christian Network:

> Justin Lee . . . speaks to Christian college campuses in support of LGBT students, and often sees a disconnect between how the administration views LGBT issues and how students view them. "Romance and self-identity get lumped in with sex, and just tossed in the same pile," he told me. "And it leaves a lot of students wondering: Even if I don't have sex,

---

[3]These more varied responses to campus policies stand in contrast to some of what we see reported by other researchers. For example, Shelley Craig and her colleagues (2017) identified campus policies as one of several concerns raised by a sample of LGB+ students at religious colleges and universities. These policies were cited as evidence of "institutionalized homophobia" and framed as "strict anti-LGBTQ policies" (p. 7). These themes may reflect the different approaches to sampling discussed in chapter one. Recall that Craig and her colleagues recruited their sample through a notice on the HeartStrong, Inc., website, which describes its work as follows: "HeartStrong offers help and hope to GLBT students of religiously-based educational institutions which do not permit GLBT students to fully express themselves socially, emotionally, romantically and spiritually" (HeartStrong, n.d.). Participants only had to have attended a religious college for one year, and the mean age of the sample was twenty-nine, so an older sample. It is possible that students who responded to this advertising are different and perhaps more uniform in their response to campus policies than those who were recruited through other means.

am I going to get expelled or disciplined in some way if I come out, or if I have a relationship—even if it's a non-sexual relationship?"

Lee told me, when he asks administrators that question, they typically say, "No, of course we wouldn't expel a student for this. We would never do that."

"But it's not that clear to the students," Lee said. "The students live in fear."

For interviewees, this vagueness appeared to create fear for those who were trying to manage the way they are perceived by authorities on campus, or maybe more importantly to some, by peers. Brent, a twenty-one-year-old senior, explained,

> [Same-sex behavior is] very heavily frowned upon by the students. It's so socially taboo that it doesn't happen in public areas. I've never seen a same-sex couple hold hands on my campus, or even kiss in public. So anything that happens goes on behind closed doors . . . because, I think, of the threat of students responding very negatively to that.

So some confusion about policies and procedures was noted in our study. Despite their uncertainty about what the policies might mean practically, a number of students moved from a place of disagreement with the policies to one of agreement. In a written response on the survey, Ian, an eighteen-year-old male sophomore, commented, "For the following question: 'How would you describe your relationship to your campus policies regarding sexuality and sexual behavior?' I do not like any of the choices. My most accurate answer would be 'I came to a Christian university and have come to accept the existing campus policies as reasonable.'"

NUANCED PERCEPTIONS

Theological beliefs and related policies that prohibit any same-sex sexual behavior may create environments that encourage negative perceptions of, and perhaps even hostility toward, people with same-sex attraction, particularly if they are engaging in related behaviors. It's for this reason that Eliel Cruz, the executive director of Faith in America, works with his organization to end what he views as religiously based bigotry toward LGB+ people. To this end he has actively worked to establish gay-straight alliance-type support groups on campuses associated with the Seventh-Day Adventist Church. He explains the connection from a theological belief to an institutional policy, then to negative perceptions and intolerance, like this:

> If you look at any religious educational institution, it becomes difficult to discern the line between the church and the school. Most see the church as the parent and the school as the child. With this mindset, and given the church's current theological beliefs regarding homosexuality, our schools are perpetuating homophobia, even if unintentionally.
>
> Many of our schools, universities, and academies are dormitories. We eat, breathe, and live Adventism. This leaves little room for escape from the homophobia that is inherent in the faulty "hate the sin, love the sinner" mantra. If our churches have become battlefields, our religious schools are creating its soldiers.
>
> Religious institutions have cultivated an environment that nurtures homophobia. Official presentations organized by our universities' administrations, faculty, or pastors cater to a very limited view on homosexuality. Talking at LGBT folk instead of with LGBT folk is the norm. Because discrimination is acceptable under biblical law, it is also accepted under school policy. (Cruz, 2013)

This kind of understanding of what a Christian campus must be like, and perhaps what it once was like, paints a very negative picture that might scare away anyone who has same-sex attraction. And, yet, many of the students in our sample have chosen to come to these schools and then stayed. Perhaps their experiences are not quite as dark.

The phrase Cruz referenced, "Hate the sin, love the sinner," is in evangelical circles often brought to bear on the topic of homosexuality and LGB+ persons. Many LGB+ people say this is a disconnect for them. That is, they often do not feel loved by evangelicals who claim to love them. We wanted to collect some information that might shed light on how that organizing phrase might be experienced by LGB+ students by asking about climate on their campuses through a variety of questions.

First, we asked three simple questions about how their campuses view same-sex attraction, same-sex behavior, and sexual minorities. On a five-point scale ranging from "acceptable" (five) to "neutral" (three) to "unacceptable" (one), the average responses fell on the unacceptable side. But notice that the perceptions of same-sex attraction and individuals who identify as experiencing same-sex attraction were both near to the midpoint and significantly higher in perceived acceptability than were same-sex behaviors. Surprisingly, these perceptions of campus do not vary by students' degree of intrinsic religiosity or same-sex attraction.[4]

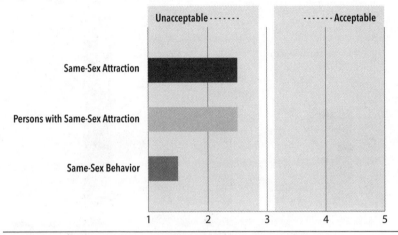

Figure 6.2. Campus view of same-sex attraction, persons with same-sex attraction, and same-sex behavior

Again, an exploration of the pattern of responses tells us a bit more about how these campuses view same-sex sexuality and sexual minorities. Grouping scores of one and two as "unaccepting" and scores of four and five as "accepting," we can clearly see just how many more students see same-sex behavior as unacceptable on their campuses—and how same-sex attraction and individuals with that attraction are not perceived quite as negatively. In fact, about half the sample thinks their campuses see both attraction and sexual minorities as unacceptable, but the other half believes their campuses hold an accepting or neutral stance. In contrast, nine out of ten students describe their campuses as unaccepting of same-sex sexual behavior, which definitely fits within the campus policies on sexuality. The behaviors are off-limits.

David Wheeler, as a former faculty member at a Christian college, has been outspoken in his writings about how faith-based campuses may not be receptive to sexual minorities. In his article in *The Atlantic* referred to above, he addresses the dynamics on these campuses in light of changing social opinions on gay marriage and sexual minorities. In it he uses the following to summarize how he perceives the attitude of these campuses to sexual minorities:

---

[4]A series of independent-samples *t*-tests revealed no significant differences by intrinsic religiosity or same-sex attraction.

"At many evangelical universities, you can be gay—as long as you don't 'act' it" (Wheeler, 2016). There seems to be some truth to this statement, although it's quite a bit more nuanced.

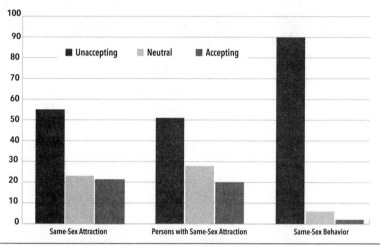

Figure 6.3. Campus view of same-sex attraction, persons with same-sex attraction, and same-sex behavior (grouped scores)

Indeed, being "less unacceptable" as a person who experiences same-sex attraction is not the same as being loved or valued. This goes back to the phrase "Hate the sin, love the sinner." We do not recommend the use of this phrase for several reasons, not the least of which being that many sexual-minority students do not report a campus climate in which people who experience same-sex attraction feel loved. The responses to these questions suggest the phrase that comes across to our sample is "Same-sex behavior is unacceptable; the person who experiences same-sex attraction is less unacceptable," which might be experienced by some students as "Hate the sin, hate (a little less) the sinner." But it will be shown in a moment that not all students have this emotional experience. Indeed, phrases and slogans oversimplify what is clearly a complex and nuanced discussion of campus climate, and our students' experiences vary considerably.

It was important for the majority of interviewees to note a distinction at their institutions, and specifically among students, about the way same-sex behavior was viewed and the way same-sex attractions are viewed. This seems in keeping with what David Wheeler was suggesting. Students reported that although same-sex behaviors were generally prohibited at their institutions, same-sex attractions were not. Only a very small number of interviewees appeared to hold the belief that same-sex attraction was prohibited within their campus community. Like other interviewees, Justin, a twenty-year-old male junior, remarked, "[Students] are pretty okay with same-sex attraction itself. I think it is the action itself that makes them uncomfortable. Most people would be like, 'Oh yeah, I have a gay friend, or it doesn't bother me.' Most people expect God to be able to handle anything." We have seen over the past ten years of research with Christian college students an increasingly accepting direction or view of students who experience same-sex attraction.

Miranda, a twenty-one-year-old senior who identified herself as bisexual and who is married to an opposite-sex partner, saw the issue as even more complicated than simply differentiating behavior from attraction. She revealed:

> There are a lot of people on our college campus that I don't think that they understand the difference between having same-sex attraction and acting on it. And they also don't understand . . . how complicated sexuality is. You can be sexually attracted to someone without really being romantically attracted or you can be romantically attracted without having sex. . . . They don't think about the fact that some people are physically attracted to the opposite sex, and then there are times that you're emotionally attracted to them too. It's just like for everyone.

Within this context, more than 50% of those interviewed described their campus community in positive terms. They used words such as *accepting, warm, welcoming, supportive,* and *safe.* Regardless of the attitude toward the policies of the institution, this larger group of interviewed sexual-minority students noted the positive attributes of the campus community. Another group of about 25% remarked about the negative aspects of the campus community. They identified the "silence" regarding sexual-minority issues. Sexual minorities have little to no "voice." This approximate quarter of the interviewees criticized the campus community for its heteronormativity and the unfortunate default that "no gays are here." Savannah remarked that in her setting it seemed to be a "don't ask, don't tell policy."

The last significant group of responses about the campus community remarked on the noticeable shifts across their student experiences. About 25% of the interviewees stated that they perceived a growing openness among campus constituents. Seeking to understand this finding among the interviews, it seems relevant to remember that 63% of the interview sample were upper-class students or graduates. It therefore appears likely that many of the interviews represented experiences of those who had matriculated across a number years in their faith-based community. On the one hand, interviewees probably had the chance to see their educational community through older and possibly maturing eyes. On the other hand, it is also possible that this optimistic view is one of a group who has persisted and "fit" better than others who might have dropped out earlier in their college experience or sought education elsewhere. Either option is possible, but it should also be noted that those who saw increased openness were not always the ones who were positive about the campus community. They seemed to be persons who simply noted institutional growth across the years in the way sexual minorities were engaged. Often this experience appeared to be associated with increasing evidence of respectful debate and dialogue on campus, as well as growing awareness of the need for support structures or resources in the institution. Jennifer, another twenty-one-year-old senior, observed, "It's an environment that is changing. Transitioning. Uneasiness. Discussions facilitated by faculty and staff—open and loving conversations. Great move towards understanding."

A few interviewees noted that the increased openness can also result in growing pains for the campus community. Miranda elaborated on this issue:

> I think the [increased openness] makes it easier in some ways and more difficult in other ways. It's kind of weird because it makes it . . . it makes you feel more divided, I think. Because it's like okay when I'm with friends I don't have to guard my speech when I'm talking about certain things. . . . Or like I have to be a little more careful about how I talk about it if they have questions or that sort of thing. . . . And sometimes . . . I'll bring up the fact that I experience same-sex attraction just to see how they'll react.

A COMPLEX ENVIRONMENT

Joel Wentz and Roger Wessel, in their 2011 reflection on the intersection of gay and Christian identities among students at Christian colleges, noted that the existence of negative perceptions of same-sex attractions and behavior within an institutional culture "may contribute toward increasingly negative social experiences of gay and lesbian students as they interact with heterosexual individuals" (p. 4).[5] Given the somewhat negative, albeit nuanced, perceptions on

---

[5]In the study of Wolff et al. (2016, p. 205) of 213 sexual-minority students attending various faith-based institutions, including evangelical, mainline Protestant, Catholic, and Mormon, over

these campuses, we wanted to know whether what Wentz and Wessel proposed might be true for our students. Thus we asked them about their experiences to gain some insight into the daily climate for sexual minorities at these schools.

The question was a simple count of how often during the past academic year they had heard antagonistic speech from faculty, staff, and students, including stereotyping, negative remarks, jokes that "put down" people who experience same-sex attraction, or inappropriate use of the term *gay*. What we heard was that such talk was nearly nonexistent from faculty or staff, with students hearing less than one comment on average per year from either. In fact, over 60% of our students had never heard such a comment from faculty or staff members.

The perception of this negative comment varied by students' level of same-sex attraction, perhaps suggesting more sensitivity to and awareness of these kinds of encounters among those with more same-sex attraction and those with less religiosity. Students with higher levels of same-sex attraction reported hearing an average of about one comment per year by faculty and staff, but students with less same-sex attraction reported hearing even fewer than that many comments by faculty and staff.[6]

Where did our students hear such offensive speech? Their peers.[7] On average, our sexual-minority students reported hearing over three negative comments per year, and their reporting of these was not related to their own level of same-sex attraction.[8] A good majority of the students, 64%, said they had heard more than four of these remarks from fellow students in the past twelve months. Students tended not to make these comments in front of faculty or staff. Just over 50% of our sample had never heard such speech from

---

one-third (37%) of sexual-minority students reported experiences of harassment or bullying related to their sexual identity.

[6]Students with higher levels of same-sex attraction reported hearing 0.92 comments ($SD = 1.29$) per year by faculty as compared to the 0.26 comments ($SD = 0.51$) by students with lower same-sex attraction, $t (158) = -2.89$, $p = 0.004$, Cohen's $d = 0.67$ (medium effect size). Also, students with higher same-sex attraction reported 0.78 comments ($SD = 1.21$) by staff per year, whereas those with less same-sex attraction only reported hearing 0.26 comments ($SD = 0.67$), $t (158) = -2.37$, $p = 0.019$, Cohen's $d = 0.53$ (medium effect size).

[7]A repeated-measures analysis of variance found a significant difference among the mean number of negative comments heard from faculty ($M = 0.8$, $SD = 1.2$), staff ($M = 0.7$, $SD = 1.1$), and students ($M = 3.1$, $SD = 1.3$), $F (2, 318) = 318.8$, $p < 0.001$, partial $\eta^2 = 0.67$, with students making significantly more negative comments than faculty or staff.

[8]A series of independent-samples t-tests revealed no significant differences between those with high same-sex attraction and those with low same-sex attraction in the number of negative comments reported.

a peer during a class in the past year, and 67% had never heard it in front of a staff member. When peers did make such statements, faculty and staff rarely agreed with the student, but usually they didn't challenge the statements either. Most often faculty and staff just remained quiet.

Most of the peer remarks happened in social settings with other college students. Only 7% of our sample had not experienced this. When it did happen, as it often did, students rarely challenged their peers; only 8% of our sample said this confrontation was common. The most typical response, according to about half of our sample, was silence. Perhaps what's even more disappointing is that 38% of our sexual-minority students experienced peers agreeing with peers in this kind of derogatory speech toward them.

Camila, a twenty-year-old lesbian, described her experiences with other students like this: "I do not feel safe on campus as many people, even close friends, have made their remarks about how queer folk are unwanted. I have seen and heard threats, who I am as a person has been turned into a joke, and my personal beliefs have been used in derogatory manners where I am constantly exposed to hurtful slurs left and right." Agreeing with Camila was Carter, a twenty-one-year-old white gay junior, who struggled with his peers but not faculty and staff. He stated, "The issues I have faced are not with the university, but with students. The university doesn't help students with same-sex attractions, but they don't hurt them either. The university seems to be very neutral." While Carter sees the campus as "neutral" through silence, in personal communication with Patricia Griffin—professor emeritus at UMass Amherst and author of *Strong Women Deep Closets*, which provides a critical analysis of discrimination and prejudice against lesbians in sport—"silence" or "neutrality" when addressing LGBT students and concerns is interpreted as lack of support and a position "against." This may be especially true of the LGB students on evangelical campuses who desperately need adult support.

Given this kind of talk in their peer communities, it makes sense that our sample largely agreed that the attitudes on campus make it difficult for sexual minorities ($M = 3.9$, $SD = 1.0$, five-point scale), with 60% expressing agreement and only 7.5% disagreeing. Again, this perception did not vary by students' level of same-sex attraction or intrinsic religiosity.[9] They all tended to see campus attitudes as problematic for students like themselves.

---

[9]A series of independent-samples *t*-tests revealed no significance differences in the perception of the effects of campus attitudes by same-sex attraction or by intrinsic religiosity.

Even so, the interviewees identified the most common general attitude of the students at the Christian colleges and universities as *disengaged* and *resistant*, meaning that they were often perceived by our sample as avoiding sexual-minority issues and resistant if confronted. Indeed, almost half (49%, or nineteen of thirty-nine) of the interviewees noted this approach. Yet, there was more diversity represented among this sample. Thirty-six percent (or fourteen of thirty-nine) of interviewees characterized the general attitude on campus in more positive terms. Five of those fourteen said the campus was "welcoming/supportive," while nine of those fourteen said "accepting/tolerant." Still others (five interviewees) described the general attitude on campus as "struggling/ambivalent" (actively trying to make sense of same-sex sexuality issues), while two interviewees designated the general attitude on campus as "hostile" (actively engaging same-sex attracted students negatively). As one student remarked, "Interestingly, even as some students have been the source of most of my problems, some other students have been the greatest help and resource."

The majority of interviewees, across all of these categories, remarked on the pressure to "act straight" or the fear of being out that was associated with student culture. That pressure to actively monitor oneself was certainly influenced by institutional policies, but fellow students were identified as the primary threats for reasons related to perceived enrollment security and impression management. One interviewee, Brent, described it as a fear of "a social death sentence." Miranda reported on the pressure to avoid negative engagement with peers. "I guess a lot of it is just the worry about the knowledge getting passed around. Because we are such a close-knit community that one person will poison the well for you and twist it a certain way that it really is not. . . . It's like they dump out everything else they know about you and then can only focus on the fact that you're not closeted." It's no wonder, then, that so many of these students are not "out" on their campuses. About a quarter of them, 23.8%, are not known to anyone as a sexual minority, and almost 60% are known as such to only a few close friends. Only 17%, less than one out of five, have become widely known on their campuses as sexual minorities. And, as you might expect, those with higher levels of same-sex attraction are less likely to keep this hidden from everyone than are those with lower levels.[10]

---

[10]A chi-square analysis revealed a significant difference between low and high same-sex attraction groups and their being known as a sexual minority on campus, χ^2 (2) = 11.27, p = 0.004. Students with high same-sex attraction were less likely than expected to not be known as a sexual minority

Their degree of intrinsic religiosity does not seem to play a part in their decision to be out.[11]

Physical violence or active intimidation were largely denied on the campuses by those students who were interviewed. The noteworthy impact of peers who were ignorant of LGB+ issues or were perceived as categorically disapproving appeared to be a more substantial burden. All students in the undergraduate years appeared to negotiate their identity development in relation to the influence of acceptance and nonacceptance of peers and valued authorities. For these interviewed sexual-minority students, this was more complicated for emotional and psychological reasons, even when direct forms of oppression were not recognized. As one reviewer of the interviews commented,

> I only counted about twelve instances where derogatory comments were explicitly mentioned, nearly all of which were described as occasional or rare, and/or attributed to the students being unintentionally hurtful (just coming out of ignorance or heteronormativity), or the interviewee saying that they have not directly experienced them but have heard of them happening. Most of the negativity seemed to come out in the form of ostracization and other passive ways because of other students feeling uncomfortable.

MICROINEQUITIES

Mary Rowe (2008), economist, professor, and ombudsman at MIT, would put these negative climate influences in the category of *microinequities*. They are often not the larger, more glaring structural issues of organizations that lead to unfairness and overt discrimination for diverse and nontraditional members of the community. They are instead the "apparently small events which are often ephemeral and hard-to-prove, events which are covert, often unintentional, frequently unrecognized by the perpetrator, which occur wherever people are perceived to be 'different'" (p. 1). Though smaller and often harder for others to perceive, microinequities do exert a defining influence on the nature of the organization and the general "feel"

---

by anyone ($ADJR$ = 3.1), whereas students with low same-sex attraction were more likely than expected to not be known as a sexual minority ($ADJR$ = -3.1). Phi φ = 0.27 (small effect size).

[11]A chi-square analysis did not reveal any significant difference between low and high intrinsic religiosity groups and their being known as a sexual minority on campus.

of those who live and work within the system. As we consider the voices of students in our study, we hear them describe what sounds like the influence of microinequities on their experience of the campus climate at their college or university.

As Rowe studied microinequities in organizations, she found herself wondering about how nontraditional people ever succeeded. What created the conditions for competent, capable, and even talented minorities, such as the ones we found on Christian campuses, to overcome the influence of inequities? She discovered "the power of person-to-person (one-on-one) recruitment, of mentoring, and of [social] networks" held the key to creating affirmative interventions that encourage personal development and professional growth (p. 2). She recognized that the remedy to the presence of relational microaggressions was a relational action as well. She called them "micro-affirmations" and described them as "apparently small acts, which are often ephemeral and hard-to-see, events that are public and private, often unconscious but very effective, which occur wherever people wish to help others succeed" (p. 2). A community that is intentionally formational, one where supportive or encouraging actions outpace microinequities, is noteworthy for the way it pays attention to the experience of all its members, especially those who might be unwelcome or invisible. For a higher-education community, consistent and predictable microaffirmations found in relational connections can potentially influence optimal student development and thriving (Powell, Demetriou, & Fisher, 2013).

Oliver, a twenty-five-year-old senior, seemed to illustrate the profound influence that intentionally encouraging relationships can have on the capacity to hold both sexual identity and religious/spiritual identity. In our first interview, he was more "unsettled" about how to hold these aspects of his personhood (see chapter five for more information about our "settled" and "unsettled" students). He hesitantly but reflectively stated, "I wish I had an answer for [how to make sense of my sexuality in light of my faith]. I'm trying to figure that one out. They're seemingly opposite, but I think that's more of a societal thing. . . . I've been trying to find words to describe it for a year." Then a year later, at his second interview, he made the following more "settled" observation. "I don't really see them in different categories because they are so intertwined. Because it is out of my sexual development and my sexual understanding that I pursue intimacy with God. But it is also out of intimacy with God that I learn to better understand and integrate my sexuality. So it's hard for me to see as one above the other or in any hierarchy." What seemed to make a difference—moving from an "unsettling" absence of words in the first interview 1 to a more "settled" understanding in the second interview, a year later? He mentioned that finding a mentoring relationship at his school enhanced the process during the last year. He said about that relationship, "We talk about homosexuality, Calvinism, and just the weirdest things that don't even relate." He also noted the powerful influence of intentional friendships. He explained,

> I have taken formal vows of celibacy. I recognize them more as affirmation than anything. I can only make this decision if I pursue intimate friendship.... I believe that the intimacy that an individual requires can be found within true friendship. . . . The best way I can foster understanding [of the intertwined nature of sexuality and religion/spirituality] is for me to be celibate and pursue chaste intimacy with my friends and with everybody around me.

We interpreted this student's experience as one example indicating personal growth and development across the year between the first and second interviews. He certainly seemed more settled than he had been regarding how he held his sexuality and his faith, and this development seemed identified with his relational community. He appeared to evaluate himself as thriving in relationships as he intentionally cocreated space with his mentor and friends.

Rowe (2008) reported that the effects of a relational community that intentionally teaches and practices microaffirmations are threefold. First, she emphasized the obvious positive effect on persons being affirmed. Those persons who are engaged with affirmation are likely to be more productive and feel increased personal well-being. Second, Rowe noted that affirmation of others can spread in the organization through modeling, potentially improving conditions beyond the observed relationship. Vicarious microaffirmational actions might grow to the point that it is viewed as more the rule than the exception. Third, she recognized the subtle influence on the affirmer when proactively and consistently affirming others. This practice, she asserted, can actually provoke relational development in persons who consciously live an intentional life with others. Affirming persons will often notice decreases in conscious inequities and may actually see decreases in unconscious inequities toward others. Practicing good relational skills may actually block unwanted ones.

We imagine Rowe's (2008) first point to be accurate for Oliver. We can see it in the descriptions of his engagement with his community. Regretfully, we don't know the effect on the following second and third points, but it seems reasonable to assume there could be an effect beyond Oliver alone. There could be a reciprocal effect for the community as well.

The majority of sexual-minority students in our interviews reported relational improvements over the years they attended their institutions. It did appear from their point of view that intentional, supportive actions were indeed present and slowly increasing at their Christian colleges and universities. Yet, despite the increased awareness of sexual minorities and the growth of more loving proclamations within their campus communities, microaffirmations did not appear to have reached a level that they blocked the unwanted ones. What makes Christian college and university environments so complex, if we can rely on the sexual-minority voices in our studies to tell us, is this combination of microinequities and microaffirmations that exist. Even more complications are introduced when we realize that there appeared to be different experiences for those associated with different aspects of the institutional community. Certain persons or settings on campus appear to be more encouraging than others. It's hard to describe the whole institution succinctly when there are pockets of support as well as pockets of inequities.

SUPPORT FROM OTHERS

With the campus climate being so varied, with pockets of judgment, some of avoidance, and others of hospitality, we might wonder whether sexual-minority students are able to find support among their peers and others as they need it. Changing our language some, we asked students two more questions about the campus perception of individuals with same-sex attraction: Are they viewed positively, and are they supported? Again, responses were near the middle of a five-point scale. Our students moderately disagreed that sexual minorities are viewed positively on their campuses ($M = 2.07$, $SD = 0.91$), and while they somewhat disagreed that there is support for these people ($M = 2.28$, $SD = 1.03$), at least they see that support a bit more positively than they do the related perceptions.[12]

---

[12]A paired-samples t-test yielded a significant difference between these two items, t (157) = -3.04, $p = 0.003$, Cohen's $d = 0.13$ (small effect size).

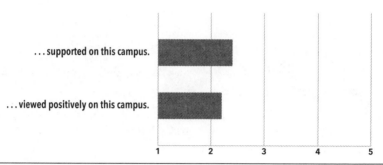

Figure 6.4. Persons with same sex attraction are . . .

It's one thing to feel like the campus is generally nonsupportive, but that doesn't necessarily mean that individuals struggle to find support for themselves. To better get a sense of the social support these students have, we asked them to tell us how satisfied they were with the support they get from their family, their church, their college or university faculty and staff members, their heterosexual friends, and their LGB-identified friends—both in general and specifically for their sexuality. Ratings of one to three indicated dissatisfaction with the support; ratings of four to six represented satisfaction. If we look at their satisfaction ratings of general support, we see that they are most satisfied with the support of their friends—both heterosexual and sexual-minority friends.[13] Their churches, on the other hand, provide marginally satisfactory support, but students are the least satisfied with what their churches are doing to help them.

When asked how satisfied they felt with the support they received regarding their same-sex attraction, their ratings drop significantly for all the social groups except their sexual-minority friends.[14] Here they are most satisfied

---

[13]A repeated-measures analysis of variance found a significant difference among the mean ratings of general support by family ($M = 4.59$, $SD = 1.57$), church ($M = 3.92$, $SD = 1.65$), faculty or staff ($M = 4.50$, $SD = 1.42$), heterosexual friends ($M = 5.18$, $SD = 1.24$), and LGB-identified friends ($M = 5.07$, $SD = 1.27$), $F(4, 628) = 28.79$, $p < 0.001$, partial $\eta^2 = 0.16$. A post hoc series of paired-samples t-tests found that the mean ratings for heterosexual friends and LGB-identified friends were significantly higher than the other ratings but not each other. Also, mean ratings for the church were significantly lower than all the other ratings.

[14]A series of paired-samples t-tests yielded a significant difference between the two types of support—general support (see means and standard deviations in previous footnote) and support for same-sex attraction—for family ($MSSA = 3.06$, $SD = 1.81$), $t(156) = -10.53$, $p < 0.001$, Cohen's $d = 0.90$ (large effect size); for church ($MSSA = 2.68$, $SD = 1.61$), $t(156) = 9.75$, $p < 0.001$, Cohen's $d = 0.76$ (large effect size); for faculty/staff ($MSSA = 3.22$, $SD = 1.66$), $t(155) = 10.25$, $p < 0.001$, Cohen's $d = 0.83$ (large effect size); and heterosexual friends ($MSSA = 4.38$, $SD = 1.57$), $t(156) = 6.58$, $p < 0.001$, Cohen's $d = 0.56$ (medium effect size).

with the help they receive from these friends, which rates higher than that of all their other social groups.[15] Again, their satisfaction with their church's support was the lowest of all, and this time it fell in the dissatisfied range.

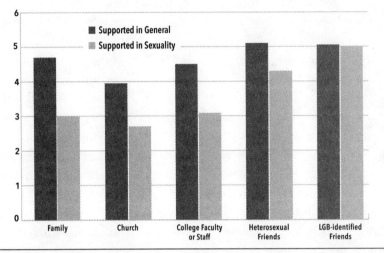

Figure 6.5. Level of support in general and in regards to same-sex sexuality

This dissatisfaction with support from their churches as they work through sexual-identity issues is particularly troublesome. In 2015, Dr. Ilan Meyer, a psychiatric epidemiologist and a senior scholar for public policy and sexual orientation law at the Williams Institute of UCLA, and his colleagues published an article exploring help-seeking behavior in sexual minorities. Those turning to religious or spiritual leaders for help were almost three times more likely to attempt suicide than those not seeking help at all.

What we don't know for sure is what causes this difference. In general, religiosity and spirituality are protective factors against suicide (Gould, Greenberg, Velting, & Shaffer, 2003). However, sexual-identity issues are not like many of the issues brought to religious and spiritual leaders. Most would argue that there is tension, even conflict and maybe hostility, between same-sex attraction and many orthodox religions. This belief is held by a vast majority both in the church and in the gay community (Gould et al., 2003). But

---

[15]A repeated-measures analysis of variance found a significant difference among the mean ratings of same-sex attraction support across their social groups (see means and standard deviations in previous footnote), $F (4, 612) = 73.83$, $p < 0.001$, partial $\eta^2 = 0.33$. A post hoc series of paired-samples t-tests found that the mean ratings for friends were significantly higher than all of the other ratings. Also, mean ratings for the church were significantly lower than all the other ratings.

how does this increase suicidality? Is it the disapproval of the religious leaders? Is it the awareness of the institutional perspective? Is it the internalized homophobia of those seeking help, who likely are more religious themselves, as Meyer suggested as one of many possible causes?

What Meyer did not consider is the lack of training that most religious and spiritual leaders receive in both counseling and crisis intervention (Stegeman, 2008), let alone issues around sexual identity. If the care of trained counseling professionals did not reduce the suicidality of these sexual minorities, as Meyer found, is it even reasonable to expect that untrained persons would be able to help? In fact, it may even be expected that they might mishandle these situations.

Family, like the church, was also rated as providing less satisfactory support than do friends, especially when it comes to their sexual attractions. This may or may not be surprising. While the parent-child relationship is an important predictor of an adolescent's well-being over time (Stafford, Kuh, Gale, Mishra, & Richards, 2016), most teens move toward friends and away from family for support and engagement during their adolescent years. This is more true of college students, who are in closer proximity to friends at school than they are to family after leaving home to attend college. The JED Foundation with mtvU (2006) found that 75% of students were likely to turn to friends if they had an emotional or psychological need, but only 63%, still a majority, would turn to their family.

Feeling comfortable enough to disclose sexual identity to parents, and then receiving support from them, is important for the mental well-being of sexual-minority young adults. Choosing not to disclose to parents may be more problematic for women than for men (Rothman, Sullivan, Keyes, & Boehmer, 2012). Women holding this secret from their parents seem to be at higher risk for depression, illicit drug use, and self-reported health problems. Men do not seem to have the same negative outcomes when they choose not to talk to their parents. This may be because men tend to fear coming out to parents more than women do, even though parents tend to respond similarly to their sons and daughters (Savin-Williams & Ream, 2003).

Our students reported feeling much less support from their parents in their sexuality than in general. If disclosure leads to lack of support, or perhaps a perceived marked decrease in support, from parents, then both women and men are more likely to struggle with depression and substance abuse (Rothman et al., 2012). When this lack of support is perceived as rejection, then the risks become much more likely and much more significant, including an increase in unprotected sexual activity and suicidal behaviors (Ryan, Huebner, Diaz, & Sanchez, 2009).

Even so, talking about sexual identity with others tends to be an important component of well-being in sexual minorities. In fact, the more widely they share this, the more support they tend to receive, and the better they tend to do (Jordan & Deluty, 1998; Vincke & Bolton, 1994). They tend to be more confident, feel less anxious, and have positive emotions overall.

Friends seem to provide good social support for sexual minorities even on Christian college campuses. Our students reported being pretty satisfied with their friends' support. LGBT friends were seen as being more helpful with sexual-identity issues, but straight friends typically provided good support to some degree.[16] "My best resource so far has been friends I have been able to open up with," revealed Eric, a twenty-year-old sophomore who describes himself as a Christian who experiences same-sex attraction.

CAMPUS RESOURCES

If students want more support than their personal social groups can provide, college and university campuses offer a variety of resources. While it may be difficult for young adults to seek out assistance with issues related to sexuality, it may even be more so on a Christian campus with strict policies around sexual behavior.

The interviewed students tended to cluster campus resources into three groups when they were asked about institutional supports for sexual minorities. They mentioned (1) the college counseling center, (2) confidential smaller group meetings, and (3) "all student" events. Eighty-five percent of interviewees noted their counseling center, with all but six describing their opinion of services to be generally positive. Twenty-eight used descriptors such as *helpful, supportive, useful, life giving, willing to listen,* and *willing to support* when referencing counseling services. Three of the six interviewees who did not mention their counseling centers positively failed to note the counseling center as a resource at all. The remainder remarked about issues that made it more difficult to trust this service on their campuses. Wyatt, a junior, explained that the counseling center at his school was "hit and miss" in his experience, depending on the counselor. Although he had good experiences on a few occasions, others had described it

---

[16]A paired-samples *t*-test yielded a significant difference between the support for same-sex attraction by straight friends ($M = 4.37$, $SD = 1.58$) and LGBT friends ($M = 4.99$, $SD = 1.29$), t (156) , t (153) = -4.32, $p < 0.001$, Cohen's $d = 0.42$ (medium effect size).

as a "terrible place," so he could not recommend it as trustworthy to others. Another student, Hannah, a senior who identifies as bisexual, reported that the counselors at her institution are primarily interns. She said that she had trouble trusting the service because "they didn't really know how to deal with students with same-sex attraction." Logan, a twenty-two-year-old junior, agreed that reliance on counselors in training did not enhance the reputation of his campus counseling center. He reported, "I used the counseling center but not for sexuality issues. It was more like, 'Hey, you're depressed and you need help.'"

The second and third cluster of resources, smaller group meetings and larger all-student events, were both official or sanctioned gatherings. Unofficial or secret resources were rarely mentioned, although the interview specifically inquired about underground or secret meetings. A few talked about alumni Facebook, "secret" gatherings with staff allies, and meals with LGB+ ex-faculty and staff, but these were not commonplace in the experience of our interviewees. On the other hand, about 50% of interviewees identified confidential smaller-group gatherings as supportive. This cluster of resources included on-campus support groups, off-campus support groups, Bible studies, LGB+ discussion groups, and counseling groups. Another 25% identified all-student forums and workshops as beneficial. This cluster of resources included community discussion groups, sexuality lecture series, sexual wholeness groups, focus groups, public forums, LGB+ student organizations, and chapels. Interviewed students typically assessed value to the confidential groups as places where they could be their private selves. They were supportive and personal, although sometimes educational. The all-student gatherings served primarily an educational or awareness-building purpose. While most understood the value of these meetings for the community, there were mixed reviews on the value for persons who experience same-sex attraction.

With the survey, we were able to ask a larger number of sexual-minority students about five main resources typically found on campuses. We wanted to know whether this more extensive group of students had heard of these five as a place to work through issues related to sexual identity and if so whether they would use each. The counseling center again was the most well-known, with 88% of the students being aware of it. Among the whole, 34% of the students had already visited the counseling center for assistance, and another 15% said they would. This speaks well of the counseling centers on these campuses. Yet it's uncertain why a third had indicated they knew it was a resource but didn't add whether or not they would use it. Did they not need a resource, or were they not open to using it? We also don't know whether those who had engaged in some counseling would return.

The written responses in the survey give us some insight. Among those who had engaged in some counseling, Lucas, a twenty-one-year-old gay student, expressing some frustration with the traditional stance of his counselor, commented, "The counselor just told me I need to change, and if I learned anything from her, it would be to not tell a soul." Others, such as Scarlet, a nineteen-year-old questioning sophomore, believes the counseling students can get in her institution just isn't sufficient. She noted, "It's difficult to get help for same-sex attraction from our counseling center because it specializes in short-term counseling programs, and things fluctuate over time, causing long-term help to be necessary."

Sometimes not knowing the counselor's personal beliefs about sexuality impairs therapeutic trust. Li Jun, a twenty-one-year-old gay man in his junior year, remarked,

> The counseling center was great, but of course therapist-client relationship is always ambiguous on these subjects. It can be hard to trust someone completely who doesn't vocally say he or she supports or denies one cause or another. So it can be hard to open up to a therapist who may be Side X or Side B or Side A, but I could never truly know what sort of movement he or she is pushing me towards.

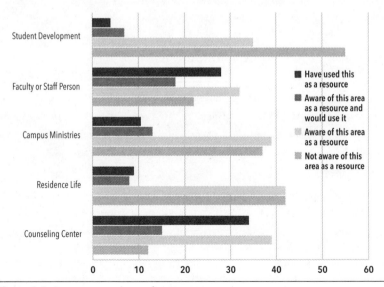

Figure 6.6. Awareness and use of campus resources

But again, even with these hesitancies, students tend to feel most comfortable with the counseling center, if for no other reason than it has to abide by confidentiality laws. For Mia, a nineteen-year-old bisexual sophomore, this clearly was the reason. "The only resource that I would feel comfortable using is the counseling center, simply because they are required to keep information confidential. Without that legal assurance it is difficult to feel safe." Many students, though, found counseling centers to be most helpful as they worked through their sexual-identity issues.

Second only to the counseling centers, interviewed students were likely to turn to faculty and staff members for assistance. In fact, 29% had, and another 18% would. A third of our students said they knew of this as a resource without commenting that they had or would seek out a faculty or staff person. About one out of five students didn't even think of this as a possibility.

Among the interviewed students, over 75% noted positive experiences or perceptions when it came to faculty and staff. In the previous section, we saw that students generally are satisfied with the support they receive from faculty, even with support with sexual-identity issues being rated quite a bit lower than general support.[17] Students were led to this favorable impression when faculty and staff demonstrated openness and displayed a willingness to talk when approached. Faculty and staff were evaluated positively when they acted protectively, often meaning that they actively advocated or stood up for the student. Interviewees also noted professors who seemed open to learning and encouraged integration of sexuality and faith. Overall, interviewed students noted increasing positive experiences and decreasing negative experiences with faculty and staff that made it easier to risk trust.

Similarly, students' written comments in surveys about faculty and staff members were generally positive. Several said they had multiple professors to whom they have reached out. Like many of his peers, Shiro, a nineteen-year-old gay freshman who commutes to campus, admitted, "I've opened up to a couple of professors that I'm closer to, but not any official campus resources." Finding the right professor or staff member to talk with was extremely important. These people were known through word of mouth, some secret code, or, as at one institution, a designated staff person who was hired for this very

---

[17]A paired-samples t-test yielded a significant difference between general support ($M = 4.51$, $SD = 1.43$) and support for same-sex attraction ($M = 3.22$, $SD = 1.66$), t (156) by faculty, t (155) = 10.25, $p < 0.001$, Cohen's $d = 0.83$ (large effect size).

thing. Not finding the right faculty or staff member was seen as potentially dangerous. Explained Peter, a twenty-year-old, gay sophomore,

> Some professors put stickers on their door to show they are LGBT-friendly, which is hugely supportive and helpful. However, the topic of homosexuality is somewhat taboo, and there are drastic negative consequences (including expulsion) if the staff or faculty find out a student identifies as gay. I would say the student body is accepting, but the administration has a reputation of being steadfastly antigay.

Students also had the sense that these professors were often going against school policy to engage in these conversations. Christopher, who's nineteen, in his sophomore year, and bisexual, described it this way: "Many faculty members have expressed willingness to walk with students through this journey. However, they speak from a personal basis and not necessarily from the perspective of the university." Some, like Harry, who is twenty, gay, and in his sophomore year, expressed fear for these faculty members: "There is an underground set of professors who secretly offer to council [sic] this specific group, but it only gets around by word of mouth, and the professors could very potentially lose their jobs if found out. It's disgusting."[18]

Not all surveyed students felt comfortable with faculty and staff. This may be because they can't "read" a faculty member's position, or maybe they think they can and just don't think they will be understood. "Generally, staff and authorities have been understanding or at least portrayed interest in understanding homosexuality. However, most of the time they really don't understand it. It is a difficult concept for people who have never experienced it,"

---

[18]It is difficult to know what to make of the charge that a faculty member could lose his or her job. We have heard of professors allegedly losing their positions for their differing perspectives on LGB+ issues. It may also be that a specific faculty member who was once a good fit is no longer a good fit at a specific institution insofar as the faculty member's views may have changed over time. The conflict might then be a question of "goodness of fit" in terms of intellectual integrity for faculty members who no longer reach the same conclusions about specific aspects of LGB+ issues, such as gay marriage.

   In our experience, the position for most traditional, private Christian colleges and universities (similar to the schools represented in our study and who have student development officers who are affiliated with the ACSD) is that they would expect faculty members to support institutional mission and vision and, insofar as LGB+ issues are related to doctrine and/or policies associated with that mission and vision, there would be an expectation of support for the institution's theological positions. At the same time, there may exist some ambiguity about what might be acceptable to say or do, leaving some faculty members uneasy about discussing these issues—even when they agree with campus theology and/or policy. If this is the case, it may be that such hesitancy and avoidance may make some faculty appear unapproachable to students.

wrote Hailey, a nineteen-year-old bisexual sophomore. Others were turned away by what they heard directly from faculty. "Hearing in classes that I am damned because of something I have no control over never brings any positivity," said Camila, who was mentioned earlier. She decided that discretion with faculty was the better approach.

Among interviewed students, about 50% noted at least one negative experience or perception of faculty and/or staff. Those perceptions were often connected to personal rejecting experiences. They did not feel safe with faculty or staff who were unsupportive or actively resistant of sexual minorities. Derogatory comments in class or public settings were particularly distressing to interviewed students, although at times the offensive remarks were delivered in the context of an academic lecture or doctrinal presentation with the intention of evaluating the LGB+ community or considering the sinfulness of same-sex behaviors. This alone may speak to the need for faculty and staff to consider their audience for more public gatherings. The issue is less an academic freedom concern and more about pedagogy and effective communication.

Students were even less comfortable using other campus resources. Among those, the office of campus ministries was the most likely to be used, with about one out of ten students turning to this office for help. Just over another tenth of students (13%) knew of this as a resource and would use it. Nearly 40% said they knew of this as a resource but did not indicate that they would seek help there. And 38% didn't even think of this as a resource for sexual-identity issues.

Many students spoke fondly of a particular staff member in their chaplain's office who was hired specifically to work with sexual-minority students. Halil, an older Middle Eastern student at thirty-nine years of age, commented that this staff person was a "great resource and encouragement to students having SSA [same-sex attraction]." Other students noted that their chaplain's office ran a support group "where LGBTQ+ students can come together, fellowship, and talk about their experiences, desires, and troubles." This was how Dylan, a twenty-year-old gay junior, described the group he attends weekly. Several of the students mentioned feeling safer with campus ministries than with other offices on campus. Taylor, a twenty-two-year-old agendered senior, agreed: "Given the current state of things on [my] campus, most of what is listed here as a resource do not actually have the skills and competency to be an effective resource for any LGBTQ students, except the chaplain's office."

Residence Life, statistically, was held in about the same esteem as campus ministries. Just under one out of ten (9.4%) students had talked to someone in residence life, and almost another tenth (8.1%) said they knew they could and would do so if they needed help. The rest of the students were equally divided between not knowing this was a resource (41.3%) and knowing it was but not giving any indication they would be comfortable seeking help from residence life (41.3%). There was only one kind comment directed specifically at residence life, from a twenty-one-year-old questioning male junior. Dylan emphasized that he trusted one member of the team, but not residence life in general. "As for residence life, I have had conversations regarding my sexual feelings with a resident assistant, but more so as a friend. I didn't necessarily seek help from residence life, it just happens that she is a resident leader. I would be aware of this as a source but would not use it." Student development was seen as the least approachable of the campus resources we listed. Part of this may be due to students not being clear on how student development was different from campus ministries and residence life. This is actually reflected in many of their comments, where these resources are lumped together. Even so, the general impression of student development was much more hesitant and negative. Perhaps this is due to students identifying student life with the student conduct and judicial branch of the campus. Only 4% of our students had sought help from a member of student development, and only another 7% indicated that they would feel comfortable doing so. Just over a third of students (35%) saw this as a resource, but not one they would seek out, for whatever reason. Over half of the students (54.4%) didn't even consider student development to be a resource for sexual-identity issues.

While there were some positive comments, the more negative written responses about the student development resources seemed to fall into four categories: (1) the resources' narrow views of sexuality, (2) a general lack of trust in the resources, (3) their inability to really help, and (4) the potential for punishment.

Several students felt that campus attitudes about same-sex attraction made it impossible for them to get help from campus resources. For some this was simply because they did not believe they could be heard. Leslie, a twenty-year-old bisexual female junior, said, "I would never talk to anyone so close-minded as the people here on this campus about anything of importance such as this." Mia, a student we've heard from before, remarked, "If I thought that I would receive unbiased, undiscriminatory support from these resources, I would actually take the time to see if they were a resource. But the attitude on this campus is so strongly biased and discriminatory that I do not feel comfortable even trying." And Kevin, a twenty-two-year-old gay junior, felt the opposing viewpoints on sexuality undermined any help offered. "There are resources, but most of the time utilizing these resources include the disclaimer 'I don't agree with you but,' which is very discouraging."

For other students, the strong negative campus attitudes led them to believe they would be forced to conform. "From what I've seen on campus, the university doesn't tolerate individuals who experience same-sex attraction, rather, they state that these individuals need to change," wrote Stefan, a twenty-two-year-old gay senior. Catherine, another twenty-two-year-old senior who identifies as straight and is engaged to a man, agrees with Stefan: "There is no way I would go to any of them [the campus resources listed] because of how horridly they treat nonconforming students as well as their mission to further indoctrinate their flock." Javier, a thirty-year-old graduate student, said it simply, "Student development and campus ministries would likely try to make me believe."

A few students explained this push to conform as being forced to fit into a predetermined understanding of how they should be instead of allowing them to figure out their own sexual identity as individuals. "I would not use residence life because it only supports gender-conforming roles for men and women, so unhelpful for those experienced [*sic*] same-sex attraction," asserted Oliver, a twenty-five-year-old gay senior. Sean, a twenty-two-year-old bisexual, about to graduate, further explained it this way: "These resources are here to try and change the way God made us. They are not here to help us learn how to be a Christian within the way God made us. Therefore, I'm aware but would not use the 'resources.'"

These negative campus attitudes probably contribute to students' expectation that campus resources are not helpful. Students expressed this sense that the resources were limited in their ability to provide real assistance. For example, Braydon, a nineteen-year-old gay sophomore, shared from his experience, "Everyone I came to basically told me to stop being who I am. They were all really nice about it, but when I told my RA he told me to go to counseling. Again, he said it nicely, but it still hurts."

The inability to help is not just about attitudes. It also seemed to be about a failure to provide clear behavioral expectations and real-life boundaries. Hailey, whom we've heard from earlier, expressed her frustration in getting the assistance she really needed to manage her attractions. "Concerning residence life, the most difficult, I feel, is the fact you cannot tell someone to stay clothed or to refrain from walking around in their underclothes [in a same-sex residence hall] because it is distracting and debilitating."

The majority of the students' written responses, though, expressed fear and distrust. For many of these students, this was just an amorphous distrust, without a clear reason stated. Roman, a nineteen-year-old questioning freshman, expressed his doubt in this way: "It is possible for the areas I listed as not being a resource to potentially have resources. I just never really checked if they talked to queer people. I don't really trust them." A bit older at twenty-one, Peter, a gay senior, agreed, "I don't trust anyone enough here to talk about it even if they say they are 'okay' with it."

Some students linked their distrust to the campus rules. "Resident life is told that if a student comes out they MUST report it. It is none of the college's business how I identify sexually. This makes it impossible to trust ANY staff on campus," shared Irene, a twenty-one-year-old senior who identified as lesbian.

Campus stories about what's happened "in the past" also contributed to this distrust. "Residence life is the same [unclear where they stand], but the waters are harder to navigate. I usually just steer clear of all rez life, besides my immediate RAs, because of all the terrible stories I've heard about them. And I've heard awful things about student development so I haven't talked to them."

And, sometimes, students' negative experiences with other Christians led them to transfer their distrust to campus resources, like Shiro, the commuting student mentioned above. "I think that I'm just nervous in general to approach 'official' campus resources regarding these types of issues because I've had bad experiences doing the same thing in a church setting."

Interestingly, several students owned this distrust as their own personal issue. Colby, a twenty-one-year-old bisexual senior, felt he would be more comfortable if he had a relationship with staff members.

> [It's] really dependent on who you know in these perspective [*sic*] areas, and you need a strong personal relationship with them to use it as a resource. For instance, Res. Life works really hard to tell everyone in the residence halls not to make derogatory gay jokes "in case someone struggles with SSA." But I wouldn't use the resource because I don't have a strong relationship with any of the older staff.

On the other hand, as a twenty-one-year-old gay sophomore, Clint generally seemed to trust these resources but didn't feel he was ready to share.

> The two [student development and residence life] that I listed as "not aware as a resource" are departments that I know about and am familiar with, I just have never thought of them as a place to discuss same-sex attraction. As for the other three, I have not shared yet with many people that I deal with same-sex attraction, so while I see them as valuable resources I could turn to, I am not emotionally in a place where I will turn to them.

Other students wanted more distance between their day-to-day lives and the resource they seek out for help. "Residence life feels too personal to ever speak with about this issue," remarked Austin, a twenty-four-year-old graduate student who hasn't labeled his sexual identity. "The others (counseling center, for instance) is more removed from everyday life and is therefore safer."

Even so, students were often hesitant to turn to many of these campus resources for help because of their perceptions. Many even flatly refused, even though they may not have firsthand experience with the evidence they cited. The perceived threat was enough to make complete avoidance the better option. Chris, a twenty-one-year-old genderfluid queer senior, stated this quite directly. "I wouldn't ask student development or res. life for help if they had the last water on earth and I was dying of thirst."

This distrust was amplified in the many students who believed that they were likely to get into trouble if they shared their same-sex attractions and sexual-identity questions with any campus resource. Sophia, a nineteen-year-old bisexual sophomore, doesn't see any possibility that these resources are safe. "As a strict rule against homosexuality, [the college] stands against it, it is difficult to imagine that approaching any of these other four [faculty/staff, campus ministries, residence life, student development] on the topic would be beneficial." Agreeing with her, Lisa, a twenty-two-year-old bisexual senior, adamantly stated her view: "Res life and student development are the areas within our campus that have to report and discipline students. There is no way I would ever tell anyone in these departments that I'm gay."

Loss of access to campus programs and opportunities was reported as a concern by several students. Ethan, a twenty-one-year-old gay senior, spoke from what he's seen on his campus: "Hiding one's sexual identity is necessary in on-campus jobs and programs." But the possible consequences are feared to be even more severe. Dorothy, a twenty-one-year-old pansexual junior, feared her status as a student. "I would not go to any of these because I would be afraid of getting kicked out." And such fears seemed to be confirmed through campus stories. "I've heard stories of them expelling students who went for help from the school," claimed Justin, a genderfluid eighteen-year-old freshman.

As we saw with the statistics above, not all students were opposed to using campus resources for sexuality issues. Some just simply didn't know this was even a possibility. As an older senior at age thirty-five, we might expect Monika, a questioning female, to know more about these resources, but she didn't. "Honestly, because the topic doesn't come up, I'm not sure if resources exist on campus for individuals such as myself who deal with same-sex attraction." Monika was not alone, as many of her peers said very similar things about having no idea there are resources. Stefan, whom we've heard from earlier, sounded much like his peer: "Nobody mentions these resources as a safe place for LGBT students to express their issues."

This lack of knowledge seems due to the minimal conversation around same-sex attraction on campus and a failure of these institutions to advertise their ability and willingness to walk alongside sexual-minority students. The unfortunate results are that students don't seek help, and sometimes they feel utterly alone. Cindy, a bisexual female in her second year of college, lamented, "This college is a Bible college, because I deal with this, this is the most lonely season of my life. I thought we were supposedly about love?"

The final group of students seemed quite satisfied with the campus resources for sexual minorities. Returning to Brent, he quickly commented, "Campus resources are excellent." Aaliyah, a twenty-year-old queer senior, focused more on the people than the offices. "There are trusted staff members who I would go to in each of these places."

A few students spoke from their personal experiences in getting assistance from these campus resources, where they found at least one safe place to share. Scott, an eighteen-year-old sophomore who hasn't labeled his sexuality, found such a place. "I do feel the college has places for me to go for support. However, I have not explored these areas with much vigor, as I already have a support group." And, Riley, a twenty-two-year-old genderqueer senior, found a safe relationship with a staff member. "I have felt very loved and cared for by my mentor in student development who is helping me work through some of these issues."

Finding a safe place often gives students a different perspective of their campus. Policy does not necessarily dictate interpersonal relationships, and it's in relationships that sexual minorities tend to find support. Brian, a twenty-two-year-old senior with same-sex attraction, highlighted how students often feel before they find this safe place. "I feel that administration is very open to having conversations with students experiencing same-sex attraction, but students most likely have misguided perceptions about how people will respond if they admit their attraction."

THE PERCEIVED IMPACT OF CAMPUS ATTITUDES

We also wanted to understand how students perceived the impact on themselves of campus attitudes toward same-sex sexuality. What is the impact on day-to-day functioning? On one's spiritual life? On academics?

The impact of campus attitudes received significant attention among interviewees. Adriana, a twenty-one-year-old bisexual senior, summed up her experience across her undergraduate years in the following way:

> I think in general [the effect of campus attitudes] makes it more difficult, because there is an implied pressure to behave as if you're straight and just be quiet about it. It's stronger in some areas than others. I didn't experience much of it. I think a lot of the pressure that I feel I apply to myself. It's self-inflicting, but it's there. I think for the students who intentionally pursue gay relationships, it makes it mind-numbingly difficult. I have a number of friends who have experienced this, and it is very painful to watch.... If you are a practicing gay, there's a lot of fear. If you're not, it's easier, much easier. And furthermore, if you're not practicing and furthermore you agree with the administration that Scripture does not condone gay relationships, well, you're in the clear. You're practically considered straight.

Students were interviewed about the specific effects of campus attitudes on their spiritual, academic, and emotional/psychological lives. Approximately 75% of the interviewees noted an impact on their spiritual lives, which was not surprising given the high levels of religiosity and spirituality among these students. About 50% described the impact on their academic performance, while around 70% talked about the emotional/psychological influence on their lives and those of their friends.

As with most areas in the survey, their experiences demonstrated diversity. The interviews were not consistent about the influence of campus attitudes on their experience. Among the interviewees that engaged the topic, they noted negative, positive, and even in some cases no impact on their functioning across those three areas. Negative impacts were, by far, mentioned most often in the interviews, but positive experiences were also present, as were a smaller group who cited no impact for them. Kate, a twenty-one-year-old bisexual senior, observing the diversity, said, "The rhetoric about LGBT stuff is just confusing, Like there's a lot of different voices and lot of different opinions. . . . There's the rhetoric that it's wrong, but we'll still love you kind of thing, and then there's the rhetoric that it's wrong and that we'll still love you, but we won't [laughter by interviewee], and then there's people who say it's okay."

About half of the interviewees remarked about the negative impact on their spiritual lives, while 18% identified positive spiritual impacts. An additional 13% of interviewees specifically stated that they saw no impact at all from campus attitudes in relation to their spiritual life.

The negative impact appeared primarily related to the student community on campus, which is perhaps what Wentz and Wessel were suggesting can happen in terms of social relationships. (Faculty and staff were less likely to be identified with attitudes that negatively influenced the spiritual experience.) Occasional theological comments from students, embedded in a culture that glorifies the heterosexual ideal, were seen as ostracizing and ignorant of the diversity of thought and experience that could be present in the community. Amber, an older freshman at twenty-one, recalled an experience in which she was in a "heated discussion about same-sex attraction" with a friend before she was out. At one point, she informed her friend that "it was a very difficult thing to hear her talking that way." She responded that she "would never talk that way to someone who is gay," oblivious to the possibility of the private world of this interviewee.

Some of our interviewees discussed the positive impact of the community on their spiritual development. There were benefits seen in having a place that supported their values and their faith perspectives. Colby, a twenty-one-year-old senior, noted,

> I think the conversations of brokenness have been really unifying and bonding. That has helped my spiritual growth in knowing the truth of how God deals with brokenness and how he is redeeming and restoring relationships. So I would say that the attitude toward brokenness is

what has helped my spirituality. I don't think the attitude toward homosexuality has impacted my spiritual life; I think the attitude toward brokenness has.

Adriana remarked,

I've seen two reactions [to the religious and spiritual atmosphere]. One, you get really serious about it and you dive in headfirst and you read all the books and you go through Scripture and you work through it. Or you decide that you're too tired and you don't want to and you decide that Scripture is a complete crock and you walk away from your faith. . . . And I would connect the walking away from their faith . . . to the emotion of anger.

The topic of academics also came up in interviews. Although the area of academics appeared to be least affected (in comparison with spiritual and emotional/psychological functioning), interviewees did discuss the impact of campus attitudes on their academic life. When interviewees discussed academics, they noted more negatives than positives. Forty-one percent of interviewees (sixteen of thirty-nine) noted the negative impact of campus attitudes on their academic lives, while only two students had observed positive influences. Eight (or 21%) specifically stated that there was no impact of campus attitudes that they recognized on their academic performance.

Obviously, it was in the academic area that the faculty role seemed most significant. For the most part, faculty and staff were recognized for their openness and sensitivity. Seventy-seven percent (thirty of thirty-nine) of interviewees described faculty and staff in positive terms. Faculty were described as willing to talk when approached, at times actively advocating and protective, open to learn, and trustworthy. Around 50% of interviewees noted that there were also faculty who engaged in a negative way or were unsupportive of students with same-sex attraction. As might be assumed, a number of interviewees mentioned positive and negative experiences related to faculty. The fewer observations in which faculty or staff engaged in a challenging, rejecting, or derogatory manner were still noteworthy for their negative impact as a voice that speaks for the community. Older faculty in five interviews and religion faculty in two interviews were singled out for negative comments in the interviews. Furthermore, the faculty or staff was remarkable for their apparent disinterest in LGBTQ issues. Around

20% of interviewees recognized faculty and staff who were disengaged—not resistant, more neutral.

Tyler's story seemed to illustrate how academic and emotional/psychological dynamics might play a part in the educational experience, even when faculty or students might not be negative. Now, as a twenty-two-year-old senior who is out as gay, he stated,

> For me, when I came out . . . I was seeing the world through a whole new lens, and even though nobody was directly hostile, and I don't have any big dramatic stories of homophobia against me, it's more of a psychological thing where I am here and I know most of the people don't support me. So I don't know how to exist here. So I don't know if I was inadvertently fitting into a narrative that I'd heard before I came out about it being a huge struggle for LGBT students here, but I became depressed, and my anxiety went way up. And I failed a couple of classes fall semester of my junior year, and so they put me on academic probation.

At least 59% (twenty-three of thirty-nine) of students interviewed identified negative emotional or psychological impact on their undergraduate experience—the strongest individual theme among the interviews. (Recall that the average scores for psychological and emotional disorders are somewhat higher than the average college student but not as high as those students seeking counseling.) Only 10% (four of thirty-nine) noted a positive impact. No interviews fell in the "no impact" category for influence on emotional/psychological functioning. Again, the student community stood out more often than faculty and staff among the intervieweess for their negative impact.

MISSING GUIDANCE AND A VISION FOR THE FUTURE

If, as noted in the previous section, faculty, staff, and students all struggle to a degree in their attempts to improve campus attitudes and perceptions, perhaps that is in part the result of the absence of a well-thought-out vision or plan for creating an appropriate campus culture to address LGB+ needs. For our interview sample, it appeared that in most of the institutions there was a lack of vision for a future for those who experience same-sex attraction. In other words, there was no articulated developmental narrative for those who might take the road less traveled, as it were. Nothing was readily available for students whose same-sex sexuality appeared to them to preclude heterosexual marriage and children. This discussion was noteworthy by its absence in academic life for these students.

Hannah, older as a twenty-four-year-old senior, who identifies as bisexual, addressed the "unspoken assumption that the best life is one where you are married to someone of the opposite gender. That's the ideal not necessarily by the faculty but definitely perpetuated by students themselves. That makes [it hard for] somebody who is trying to figure out who they are and what they want."

Austin, age twenty-four and in graduate school, also reported,

> If there is anyone who wanted the campus to normalize whatever they were feeling sexually and make them feel that any sexual desire was completely God-given . . . then no. People who want to pursue a same-sex lifestyle or relationship . . . would have felt completely unsupported by the attitudes on campus. But the majority of students on campus who experience [same-sex attraction] were people who . . . did want to find a sense of balance or new direction and figuring out how to live within their values, given the feelings that they have.

So that is an interesting theme and challenge for the church that we will have to return to. What kind of vision does a faith community provide to its members who do not see themselves in the standard path toward heterosexual marriage and family?

These reflections by students tap into the tensions faced by student development staff and others at Christian colleges. What is the future for students navigating sexual identity and faith? Where are they headed, and how do they get there? In their reflection on the experiences of gay Christian college students, Wentz and Wessel (2011) identified the challenges facing student development staff at Christian colleges whose charge is to provide guidance to students. What does it look like to provide guidance to sexual-minority students? They reported on the challenge that exists at many faith-based institutions: "Student affairs educators at Christian colleges and universities may find themselves navigating the tension between protecting the healthy, holistic identity development of all students, including those who experience same-sex attraction, and upholding the historically defined institutional values regarding same-sex attraction" (Wentz & Wessel, 2011, p. 4).

We agree that this tension exists. The noted tension actually leads to the question: What constitutes healthy, holistic identity development among Christians who experience same-sex attraction? The answer to that question may reflect the lens through which one looks at this topic. The reference to institutional values is critical for informing some of that tension.

Recall the three lenses we have been discussing: integrity, disability, and diversity. Most writers who raise this question from the mainstream of the LGB+ community or from the mainstream of student development reflect a diversity framework that helps them answer that question with reference to models of sexual-identity development and synthesis that end in an achieved identity as gay, and whose beliefs and values correspond with the broader assumptions of sexual ethics and morality reflected therein (e.g., Wentz & Wessel, 2011). From this perspective, healthy, holistic identity development has only one outcome that ought to be celebrated, and when it is not or when such a vision is a point of tension in institutional settings that hold to a traditional Christian sexual ethic, it may be assumed that there is no healthy vision for identity formation.

Indeed, it is less clear how Christians who represent the other lenses would answer the question of healthy, holistic identity development. We can imagine some arguing that healthy, holistic identity development is to secure a heterosexual identity. Perhaps adherents of the integrity framework would voice something along these lines. Emphasis on changing sexual orientation or promoting healing is often a part of the discussion from this framework.

In a *Time* magazine article published in 2016, Julie Rodgers described her experience as a chaplain's assistant at an evangelical college.[19] Some of her campus experiences as a celibate gay Christian at that time may reflect an encounter with elements of the integrity framework and with what Wesley Hill described as a "recovery" model of care for sexual minorities in which the expected outcome of ministry is heterosexuality.[20] She describes an institutional preference both for certain language and for healing: "Even though they had known I referred to myself as 'gay' prior to hiring me, they encouraged me not to refer to myself as gay any longer. They asked me to say I was simply a Christian who experienced same-sex attraction, one who was open to the Lord healing me in ways that could lead to a holy marriage with a man." There are two sides to every story, and the administration has not publicly commented on these exchanges, but insofar as Rodgers was asked to adopt specific

---

[19]Rodgers shared her sense, too, of the risk that the college took in hiring her: "[They] showed extraordinary courage when they hired me. At a time when Evangelicals are supremely anxious about all things LGBT, they hired an openly gay writer to work in their Chaplain's office as a spiritual leader. Even though I could sign the Community Covenant at that time, I was a risk— a risk they took because they care about their gay students and know they need an advocate."

[20]Wesley Hill recommends a "vocational" approach rather than a "recovery" approach to sexual minorities. See Hill, 2017.

language or represent the hope for heterosexuality and an openness to change and healing to the institution's constituents, this appears to reflect some of the expectations noted by some adherents of the integrity framework.

Adherents of a disability framework might discuss a range of options to live a chaste life in keeping with a traditional Christian sexual ethic but not expect change or healing and not frame heterosexuality as an expected outcome for identity development. People drawn to this perspective may talk more about a Pauline "thorn in the flesh" and finding ways to honor God in one's present and enduring state. Wesley Hill refers to this more as a vocational model, and he has written about the opportunities and challenges of living a chaste life as a follower of Christ. He previously reflected on his preference for labeling and on the hope he finds in following the apostle Paul's example on this:

> Claiming the label "celibate gay Christian" means, for me, recognizing my homosexual orientation as a kind of "thorn in the flesh." When the apostle Paul used that phrase in his correspondence with the Corinthian church, he made clear that his "thorn" was indeed an unwelcome source of pain (2 Corinthians 12:7). But he also made clear that it had become the very occasion for his experience of the power of the risen Christ and, therefore, a paradoxical site of grace (2 Corinthians 12:8). Paul, I think, would have had no qualms about labeling himself a "thorn-pricked Christian"—not because he recognized his thorn as a good thing, in and of itself, but because it had become for him the means by which he encountered the power of Christ. Likewise, living with an unchanged homosexual orientation may be for many of us the means by which we discover new depths of grace, as well as new vocations of service to others. (Hill, 2013)

While we see glimpses of what the different lenses may offer Christian institutions in terms of healthy, holistic identity development, we recognize that we are far from a shared vision for what this could look like on Christian college campuses for those who are serving in student life.

Perhaps Christian communities would do well to reflect on ways to integrate the best of each of these three lenses for healthy, holistic identity development. We haven't yet seen too many examples of such an integration of frameworks, but we see the need. A thoughtful, integrated vision of identity development that is accessible to student life staff is certainly needed while students are exploring identity formation and development through the college years and may indeed extend beyond college to a time of transition into young adulthood.

In the next chapter we explore the transition for sexual-minority students from college to postcollege life.

CHAPTER 6 TAKEAWAYS

1. The decision to attend a Christian college is made for a variety of reasons. Some are seeking a faith-based community, others are wanting boundaries around their sexuality, and still others are pursuing a particular program of study. Many are not yet aware of how this environment will interact with their own faith and sexual-identity development.

2. Sexual-minority students hold multiple perspectives on the restrictive sexual policies of their institutions. Some agree with the policies, some disagree quietly, and some disagree vocally. But not everyone who disagrees wants the policies to become more permissive; rather, many just want the policies to became less ambiguous.

3. Campuses seem to make a distinction among individuals, their attractions, and their behavior, with same-sex sexual behavior being viewed much more negatively than sexual minorities themselves or their attractions, although these are not quite acceptable either. Even so, many students report positive experiences on their campuses, with most campuses becoming more accepting—at least of the individuals and the reality of their attractions.

4. Negative and derogatory remarks come from fellow students much more frequently than from faculty and staff. In fact, the majority of students had never heard such comments from faculty and staff, but faculty and staff, as well as other students, often fail to challenge students when they make such remarks.

5. In general, sexual-minority students in interviews tended to see the students on their campuses not as hostile or harmful but as disengaged and resistant, meaning that they were often perceived by our sample as avoiding sexual-minority issues and resistant if confronted.

6. Students did report feeling a lot of pressure to act straight, hiding both their same-sex attraction and their sexual identity.

7. Most students believe that they experience a good degree of support from their family, faculty/staff, and friends, but this support drops with sexuality identity issues. Only their LGB+ friends seem to offer a consistently high level of support; in contrast, churches were seen as offering the least amount of support.

8. On most campuses, college counseling centers, followed by faculty, tend to be the most commonly used and most highly regarded resources available to sexual-minority students. But not all students, perhaps not even many, are completely comfortable with these resources. Students generally felt the least comfortable with campus ministries and student development.

9. How the campus perceives sexual minorities likely will have an effect on them. Students noted spiritual, academic, and emotional/psychological effects, but not all of these were negative. While students reported more negative effects than positive, they did also report positive effects. Some even felt that campus attitudes had no effect on their lives.

10. Christian colleges often lack a developmental perspective that directs how they come alongside sexual-minority students. This raises two questions for these colleges: What constitutes healthy, holistic identity development among Christians who experience same-sex attraction? What kind of vision do faith-based institutions provide to community members who do not see themselves in the standard path toward heterosexual marriage and family?

▼

REFERENCES

Campus Pride. (2016, August 24). *Shame list: The absolute worst campuses for LGBTQ youth.* Retrieved from www.campuspride.org/shamelist/

Craig, S. L., Austin, A., Rashidi, M., & Adams, M. (2017). Fighting for survival: The experiences of lesbian, gay, bisexual, transgender, and questioning students in religious colleges and universities. *Journal of Gay & Lesbian Social Services, 29*(1), 1-24.

Cruz, E. (2013, February 6). Christian campuses on the front lines of gay debates. *The Huffington Post* [Blog]. Retrieved from www.huffingtonpost.com/eliel-cruz/christian-campuses-on-the_b_4038306.html

Gould, M. S., Greenberg, T. E. D., Velting, D. M., & Shaffer, D. (2003). Youth suicide risk and preventive interventions: A review of the past 10 years. *Journal of the American Academy of Child and Adolescent Psychiatry, 42,* 386-405. In Koenig, H. G., King, D. E., & Carson, V. B. (2012). *Handbook of Religion and Health* (2nd ed.). Oxford: Oxford University Press.

HeartStrong. (n.d.). Who HeartStrong reaches. *HeartStrong.* Retrieved from www .heartstrong.org/whoheartstrongreaches

Hill, W. (2013, February). Once more: On the label "gay Christian." *First Things* [Blog]. Retrieved from www.firstthings.com/blogs/firstthoughts/2013/02/once-more-on -the-label-gay-christian

Hill, W. (2017, May 10). Gay students at Christian colleges: What's our vision for their flourishing? *Spiritual Friendship: Musings on God, Sexuality, Relationships* [Blog]. Retrieved from https://spiritualfriendship.org/2017/05/10/gay-students-at -christian-colleges-whats-our-vision-for-their-flourishing/

Hudalla, J. (2015, May 21). What it's like to be gay at a Christian college—where it's a reportable offense. *YES! Magazine.* Retrieved from www.yesmagazine.org/happiness/ what-its-like-to-be-gay-at-a-christian-college-where-its-a-reportable-offense

Jordan, K. M., & Deluty, R. H. (1998). Coming out for lesbian women: Its relation to anxiety, positive affectivity, self-esteem, and social support. *Journal of Homosexuality, 35*(2), 41-65.

Meyer, I. H., Teylan, M., & Schwartz, S. (2015). The role of help-seeking in preventing suicide attempts among lesbians, gay men, and bisexuals. *Suicide and Life-Threatening Behavior, 45*(1), 25-36. https://dx.doi.org/10.1111%2Fsltb.12104

mtvU-JED Foundation study. (2006). mtvU College Mental Health Study: Stress, Depression, Stigma & Students. *Half of Us.* Retrieved from http://cdn.halfofus .com/wp-content/uploads/2013/10/2006-mtvU-College-Mental-Health-Study -Executive-Summary-Final.pdf

Powell, C., Demetriou, C., & Fisher, A. (2013). Micro-affirmations in academic advising: Small acts, big impact. *Mentor: An Academic Advising Journal.* Retrieved from https://dus.psu.edu/mentor/2013/10/839

Rodgers, J. (2016, February 23). How a leading Christian college turned against its gay leader. *Time.* Retrieved from http://time.com/4233666/wheaton-college-gay-leader/

Rothman, E. F., Sullivan, M., Keyes, S., & Boehmer, U. (2012). Parents' supportive reactions to sexual orientation disclosure associated with better health: Results from a population-based survey of LGB adults in Massachusetts. *Journal of Homosexulaity, 59*(2), 186-200. https://dx.doi.org/10.1080%2F00918369.2012.648878

Rowe, M. (2008). Micro-affirmations & micro-inequities. *Journal of International Ombudsman Association, 1*(1), 45-48.

Ryan, C., Huebner, D., Diaz, R. M., & Sanchez, J. (2009). Family rejection as a predictor of negative healthy outcomes in white and Latino lesbian, gay, and bisexual young adults. *Pediatrics, 123*(1), 346-52. http://dx.doi.org/10.1542/peds.2007-3524

Savin-Williams, R. C., & Ream, G. L. (2003). Sex variations in the disclosure to parents of same-sex attractions. *Journal of Family Psychology, 17*(3), 429-38. https://dx.doi.org/10.1037/0893-3200.17.3.429

Stafford, M., Kuh, D. L., Gale, C. R., Mishra, G., & Richards, M. (2016). Parent–child relationships and offspring's positive mental wellbeing from adolescence to early older age. *The Journal of Positive Psychology, 11*(3), 326-37. https://dx.doi.org/10.1080/17439760.2015.1081971

Stegeman, G. T. (2008). Relationship of self-perceived competence to counsel and attitudes toward mental health services with willingness to refer to mental health professionals among seminary students. *Dissertation Abstracts International, 69*, 2642.

Vincke, J., & Bolton, R. (1994). Social support, depression, and self-acceptance among gay men. *Human Relations, 47*(9), 1049-62.

Weber, J. (2015, September 21). Peace church out: Mennonite schools leave CCCU to avoid same-sex marriage split. *Gleanings: Important Developments in the Church and the World.* Christianity Today. Retrieved from www.christianitytoday.com/gleanings/2015/september/cccu-emu-goshen-college-okwu-union-membership-status.html

Wentz, J. M., & Wessel, R. D. (2011). Experiences of gay and lesbian students attending faith-based colleges: Considerations for improving practice. *ACSD Ideas.* Retrieved from www.acsd.org/article/experiences-of-gay-and-lesbian-students-attending-faith-based-colleges-considerations-for-improving-practice/

Wheeler, D. R. (2016, March 14). The LGBT politics of Christian colleges. *The Atlantic.* Retrieved from www.theatlantic.com/education/archive/2016/03/the-lgbt-politics-of-christian-colleges/473373/

Wolff, J. R., Himes, H. L., Soares, S. D., & Kwon, E. M. (2016). Sexual minority students in non-affirming religious higher education: Mental health, outness, and identity. *Psychology of Sexual Orientation and Gender Diversity, 3*(2), 201-12.

APPENDIX

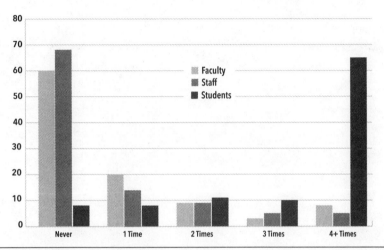

Figure A6.1. Percentages of students reporting hearing negative comments in the past year (*n* = 160)

Table A6.1. Frequencies of typical faculty, staff, and student responses to negative comments (*n* = 160)

	Faculty		Staff		Students	
	n	%	*n*	%	*n*	%
I never heard a student make such statements in class.	81	50.6	107	66.9	11	6.9
Typically, the professor agreed with the student's statements.	12	7.5	10	6.3	60	37.5
Typically, the professor challenged the student's statements.	21	13.1	11	6.9	12	7.5
Typically, the professor did not challenge the student's statements.	46	28.8	32	20.0	76	47.5

Table A6.2. Percentages of students' knowledge and endorsement of campus resources (*n* = 160)

	Counseling Center	Residence Life	Campus Ministries	Faculty or Staff Person	Student Development
Aware of this area as a resource	39%	41%	39%	32%	35%
Aware of this area as a resource and would use it	15%	8%	13%	18%	7%
Have used this as a resource	34%	9%	10%	29%	4%
Not aware of this area as a resource	13%	41%	38%	21%	54%

HOW THEY MOVE FROM COLLEGE TO POSTCOLLEGE

I'll be honest. I was pretty miserable . . . going to a Christian college. And I always said in school, if I could go back, I would never do this to myself. I would never force religion down my own throat. I would never—whatever. But now [that I am out of college], I think looking back, I actually really appreciate [it]. I would never do it again, don't get me wrong, but I really appreciated the way the Christian college atmosphere forces you to think through every identity that you are going to claim in the future. . . . I had to really fight. . . . So all things considered, I'm glad to be out of that environment, for sure. If I had to go back, and do it again, I probably would still go to that school because coming out on the other side I know who I am more than I think I would've going somewhere it was easy to be whoever I wanted to be. I think fighting for your own identity was very valuable for me. So all things considered, I am actually very grateful for the Christian school that I went to.

—*Grace, a graduate, identifies as lesbian, time 2*

I would say, "Don't judge a college by the administration." Though [my school] isn't known to be the most accepting, or whatever, administratively, the students are pretty open-minded. If they don't agree with you, they are kinda just willing to let that be. I dunno. I think we get a lot of flack for "oh, the administration is this or that," or this one random kid in a student body of ten thousand happens to be homophobic, the rest of the college is probably fine.

—*Olivia, a junior, identifies as queer, time 2*

▼▲▼

ABOUT FOUR YEARS AFTER HIS GRADUATION, Alex brought coffee to his professor's office a couple of months after he had publicly come out as gay. After catching up some, he told his story. He talked about hiding his attraction and his sexual-identity questions throughout the four years of college because he was afraid how people would respond. Even though he had had a great group of close friends, some of whom were working out their own sexual identities, the other people felt less safe. "It was a Christian school, after all." Graduation brought real life—work, separation from a lot of friends, financial pressures, and new relationships. Eventually Alex decided to talk to his family, who were more supportive than he ever imagined they would be, especially because they do not approve of same-sex sexual behavior. He also shared with some close friends before hesitantly making a wider public announcement on social media. When asked about people's responses, Alex, almost in tears, described overwhelming support from most people. There, of course, were several people who explained the "wrongness" of this declaration and his decision to enter a gay romantic relationship; some did throw Bible verses at him through the virtual space, while others questioned the veracity of his attractions. His body language revealed his hurts. But "these folks were rare," he said. Then, with almost a sense of disbelief, he added, "My friends, my real friends, they accepted me even if they disagreed." This led to some reflection about not sharing in college. "Now, I wish I had come out in college. My friends—you all in [this] department—would have helped me. I was just so afraid."

Alex is just one of the many students who work out their sexual identity throughout college into their postcollege lives. He, like many students, was hesitant to reveal his attractions while at a Christian college, and he, like many students, waited to come out until after graduation. Also, his experience of coming out was largely positive, like that of many students. Yet this is only one story of many. Some are positive like his, but many are not, and others are rather mixed.

Leaving college and starting one's postcollege life presents graduates with multiple challenges. The changes alone can be quite stressful, as graduates leave a place of great familiarity and security, often to a set of circumstances that have more questions than answers. Some graduates will consider graduate school, or they might want to in the near future, if not right away. Others will want to work in the field associated with their major. Some may have had college paid for or covered by grants and awards, while others may be facing student-loan repayment in the coming months.

From a developmental perspective, if adolescence is about identity formation, early adulthood can be about questions of intimacy. But what we are finding in recent research is that emerging adults often postpone marriage and parenting and spend more time exploring relationships and career opportunities as well as worldview. Arnett (2004) refers to these as "pillars of identity" (p. 165). So our graduates will be making this transition and will be exploring these pillars of identity as they move toward adulthood, which Arnett sees as connected increasingly with "taking responsibility for oneself, making independent decisions, and becoming financially self-sufficient" (p. 209).

We wanted to extend our analysis of the experiences of sexual minorities at Christian colleges and to at least follow those who are graduating and facing these transitions. We focus less on the big picture that Arnett and others have painted; rather, we home in on the major areas of focus throughout this book, such as sexual attraction, sexual identity, religious faith, and even how students viewed their campus over time. What does having a little gap in time do to a person's reflections of their time at a Christian institution? We turn now to these topics with a subset of our sample of sexual-minority students.

STABILITY OF SEXUAL ATTRACTION

The transition from college to postcollege life often brings many changes. We were curious whether students would experience changes in their sexual attractions. Lisa Diamond (2008), a psychologist at the University of Utah, has shown that sexual attraction is likely to change over time, and this is especially true for women. Usually these changes in sexual attraction are not due to the choices made by individuals but rather are due to factors outside their control, such as hormonal shifts, biological changes, and perhaps even life situation.

Would our students' attractions change in just one year, a year that is pretty stressful for most students? In short, no. The strength and direction of our students' sexual attractions did not appear to shift. The level of opposite-sex attraction for the forty-two students who graduated remained steady, with an average rating just under five, not quite in the middle of our ten-point scale, in which one meant no opposite-sex attraction and ten indicated strong opposite-sex attraction.[1] Likewise, their average level of

---

[1] Students' level of opposite-sex attraction did not change from their last year in college ($M = 4.73$, $SD = 3.27$) to their first year postcollege ($M = 4.73$, $SD = 3.46$), $t (40) = 0.00$, $p = 1.00$.

same-sex sexual attraction did not change over the one year postcollege. Average ratings were right at eight on our scale, indicating a pretty high level of attraction.[2]

And, contrary to what we might expect from Diamond's work, our female students did not show any more change than did the men, neither in opposite-sex attraction[3] nor in same-sex attraction.[4] Of course, the time frame was only one year, and many of the students were still in college for a significant portion of that year. There may not have been enough changes—either internal or external ones—to bring about any shift in attractions.

This lack of change in sexual attraction may be why students' understanding of their sexual orientation remained stable over this first postcollege year. Of the forty-two students who identified their sexual orientation during both of the first two years of the study, only thirteen used a different label during the second year of the study. Five students remained straight in their orientation; eighteen were still gay or lesbian. Another three held on to the bisexual descriptor, and two continued to use the word *other*. Of the six students who had described themselves as straight at the beginning of the study, only one changed that label, and it was changed to "other." Similarly, only one of the nineteen students with a gay or lesbian orientation used another label by the second year, and that label was also "other." The nine students using a bisexual label initially were the most likely to perceive their orientation differently by the second year; one adopted the straight label, and five adopted "other." Of the seven students with an "other" orientation when the study started, four moved to a gay or lesbian orientation, and one took on a straight orientation. In short, those with straight or gay/lesbian orientations were very unlikely to change their perception of their own sexual orientation during this first year postcollege.[5]

---

[2]Students' level of same-sex attraction did not change from their last year in college ($M = 7.95$, $SD = 2.39$) to their first year postcollege ($M = 8.07$, $SD = 2.51$), $t(40) = -0.48$, $p = 0.64$.

[3]A 2x2 repeated-measures analysis of variance (ANOVA) showed no main effect for change over time in students' level of opposite-sex attraction, $F(1, 38) = .07$, $p = 0.80$. There was no main effect for gender, $F(2, 38) = 0.66$, $p = 0.52$. Same-sex attraction was equally as strong across genders and remained at the same level over time. Finally, the ratings of opposite-sex attraction did not change differentially over time by gender, $F(2, 38) = 0.31$, $p = 0.74$.

[4]A 2x2 repeated-measures analysis of variance (ANOVA) showed no main effect for change over time in students' level of same-sex attraction, $F(1, 38) = 0.64$, $p = 0.43$. There was no main effect for gender, $F(2, 38) = 0.47$, $p = 0.63$. Same-sex attraction was equally as strong across genders and remained at the level over time. Finally, the ratings of same-sex attraction did not change differentially over time by gender, $F(2, 38) = 1.05$, $p = 0.36$.

[5]There is not a significant difference in the numbers of students reporting the various sexual orientations across their first year postcollege, $\chi^2(9) = 58.03$, $p < 0.001$. Specifically, students were

However, more than half of those with initial orientations of bisexual or other would use a different label for their orientation within one year postcollege.

CONSISTENCY IN SEXUAL IDENTITY

As we have noted throughout this work, sexual identity refers to the act of labeling oneself based on one's sexual attractions. Sexual identity develops out of one's attractions and general orientation, in addition to numerous other factors. For our graduates, their self-described sexual orientation at the beginning of our study was closely linked to their sexual identity during that year after graduation.[6] This was particularly true for those who identified as straight or gay/lesbian. A small segment of the sample, 8.6%, held onto a heterosexual orientation and then later a straight identity. The largest portion of sample, 34.3%, had reported a homosexual orientation and later identified as gay or lesbian. No students who initially claimed a same-sex orientation later identified as bisexual or other. There also was almost no movement from a bisexual or other orientation to a gay/lesbian identity after graduation. Among the students who did prefer a different label for their sexual orientation after graduation, men and women were equally likely to make this change.[7]

More simply, students who claim a heterosexual orientation are more likely to identify as straight after graduation and less likely to identify as a sexual minority.[8] Likewise, those who describe a sexual orientation other

---

more likely to retain a straight orientation (adjusted residual = 4.3) and a lesbian/gay orientation (adjusted residual = 6.1) than expected. They also were less likely than expected to move from a straight orientation to a lesbian/gay one (adjusted residual = -2.3), from a lesbian/gay orientation to a straight one (adjusted residual = -2.1) or to a lesbian one (adjusted residual = -2.7) or to an other one (adjusted residual = -2.9), and from an other one to a lesbian/gay one (adjusted residual = -2.6). Finally, they were more likely than expected to move from a bisexual orientation to an other one (adjusted residual = 3.1). See table in appendix.

[6] A chi-square analysis revealed a significant difference between time 1 sexual orientation and time 2 sexual identity, $\chi^2 (9) = 31.22$, $p < 0.001$. More congruence than expected was found for heterosexuals ($ADJR = 2.1$) and lesbians/gays ($ADJR = 5.2$). Graduates were less likely than expected to move from a homosexual orientation to a bisexual identity ($ADJR = -2.1$) or to an other identity ($ADJR = -2.5$), from a bisexual orientation to a lesbian/gay identity (ADJR = -2.3), and from an other orientation to a lesbian/gay identity ($ADJR = -2.1$). See table A7.2 in appendix.

[7] A chi-square analysis did not reveal a significant difference across gender and change in sexual orientation, $\chi^2 (2) = 0.46$, $p = 0.80$.

[8] A chi-square analysis revealed a significant difference between time 1 sexual orientation and time 2 sexual identity, $\chi^2 (1) = 4.562$, $p = 0.033$, using compiled labels for orientation and identity. Those claiming a heterosexual orientation while in school were more likely than expected to later identify as straight ($ADJR = 2.1$) and less likely than expected to later identify as sexual minorities ($ADJR = -2.1$). Likewise, those claiming other than a heterosexual orientation while in school were more likely than expected to later identify as a sexual minority ($ADJR = 2.1$) and less likely than expected to identify as straight ($ADJR = -2.1$).

than heterosexual while in school are more likely to identify as a sexual minority after college and less likely to identify as straight.

About a third of the graduates had changed their sexual identity from their last year in college to their first year after college.[9] Again, graduates were most likely to hold onto the same identity over the course of the study. About 14% of them retained a straight identity, and 37% kept a lesbian or gay identity. Only 5.7% held onto a bisexual identity, and another 5.7% maintained some other sexual identity.

Given that there was not much change in graduates' sexual identity, we would not expect to see much change in how they valued various aspects of sexuality in forming their sexual identity. In the first year of the study, we asked students to assign weights to each of six components to show their relative importance. In the second year of the study, we changed the directions due to the numerous comments about not understanding the weighting exercise. Instead participants were asked to rank order the six components. To allow for some comparison, the weights assigned during time 1 were converted to rankings, even though this introduced some error into our investigation.

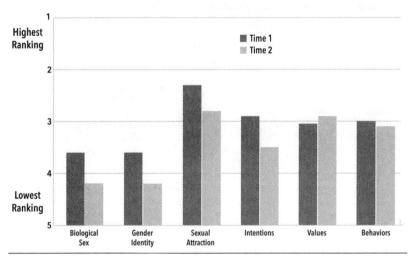

Figure 7.1. Average rankings for personal factors contributing to sexual identity (*n* = 35)

[9]A chi-square analysis revealed a significant difference between time 1 sexual identity and time 2 sexual identity, χ^2 (9) = 50.37, $p < 0.001$. More consistency than expected was found for heterosexuals ($ADJR = 3.9$) and lesbians/gays ($ADJR = 5.6$). More graduates than expected moved from an other identity to a bisexual identity ($ADJR = 3.1$) and from bisexual to other ($ADJR = 3.0$). Fewer graduates than expected moved from a straight identity to a lesbian/gay identity ($ADJR = -2.1$), from lesbian/gay to bisexual ($ADJR = -2.2$) or other ($ADJR = -2.6$), from bisexual to lesbian/gay ($ADJR = -2.5$), and from other to lesbian/gay ($ADJR = -2.3$). See table A7.3 in appendix.

First, note that lower numbers on the chart above indicate higher ranks. For example, sexual attraction is seen as having the most influence in sexual-identity development, with an average ranking of 2.3 for participants in their last year of college; this moved to a rank of 2.9 during their first year out of college. Only one of the components showed a real change in ranking from college to postgraduation; that was gender identity. The change in its ranking from 3.6 to 4.3 suggests that graduates came to value gender identity as less important to their sexual identity than they had in college.[10]

Our graduates clearly ranked some of these components as being much more important than others in making sense of their own sexual identity.[11] Both biological sex and gender identity were less influential to graduates than were the other four, whereas the direction and strength of sexual attraction were the most important for them.

NOSTALGIC VIEW OF CAMPUS

As we discussed in the previous chapter, there is much negative press by sexual minorities about their Christian college experiences. Some of these experiences have been catalogued by Chris Bodenner (2016) of *The Atlantic*, in which he asked people to send an email of their experiences to hello@theatlantic.com. A quick overview of the posts shows stories of being labeled a pedophile, of having one's grades artificially lowered, and of being kicked out of school—let alone numerous other heart-wrenching experiences. Perhaps this is the reason that we fully expected those participants in our sample to paint their schools and their previous experiences there in an increasingly negative light after graduation. This was not what we found.

When asked about their campuses, graduates had a more positive impression of campus than did current students. Current students somewhat disagreed that people experiencing same-sex attraction were viewed positively on their campus, giving an average rating of 2.4 out of five. Graduates, however, are more on the affirmative side of this, somewhat agreeing (3.3 out of five) that these students are seen positively. Likewise, our thirty-five graduates also more strongly believe people with same-sex attraction are supported (3.3) than do

---

[10]A paired-samples Wilcoxon signed-rank test showed an almost significant difference in the ranking of gender identity from time 1 ($M = 3.63$, $SD = 1.73$) to time 2 ($M = 4.34$, $SD = 1.66$), $W = 1.94$, $p = 0.053$. See table A7.4 in appendix.

[11]A related-samples Friedman's two-way analysis of variance by ranks showed a significant difference across the rankings of these six components, $Q(5) = 21.43$, $p < 0.001$.

current students (2.6). For both questions, graduates' ratings increased by over a half-point, indicating a significant positive change in their perceptions of their college campuses. Alex, whom we heard from at the beginning of this chapter, showed the same positive shifting in his views about his alma mater.

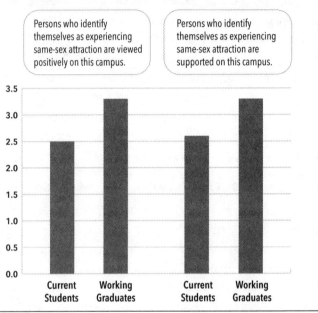

Figure 7.2. Students' and graduates' views of whether sexual minorities are viewed positively on campus

To explain this, we hypothesized that those who graduated must have been having better experiences all along than did the typical sexual minority on these campuses. If so, then their campus ratings when they were students, during time 1 of our study, would be higher than that of other students. But, no, this was not the case. Their ratings when they were students were very similar both to those of current students and to those of students no longer attending school. Both graduates who are working and others who have left school rated their campuses more positively with regard to how they view persons with same-sex attraction and how they support these people. Current students, whether they remained at the same university or transferred to another one, tended to maintain a somewhat negative perception of how their campus both views and supports people with same-sex attraction. Interestingly, those no longer attending school (those who have graduated) showed the greatest positive change in their perception of their campuses.

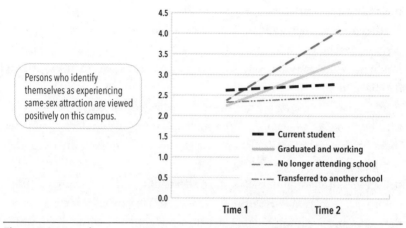

Figure 7.3. View of persons with same-sex attraction by year of study and student status

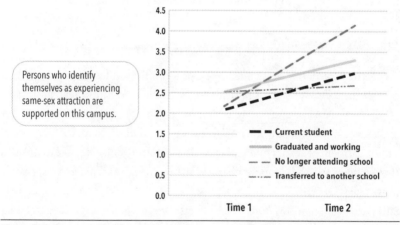

Figure 7.4. Support of persons with same-sex attraction by year of study and student status

It is unclear to us what caused these changes in perception. We could speculate that simply removing oneself from the climate where one has had ambivalent feelings allows one to recognize the benefits of being in a particular setting and having support for one's faith and for the value one experienced in terms of relationships. Perhaps distance makes the heart grow fonder. At the same time, we recognize that many LGB-affirming but unsanctioned support groups have been started by graduates of Christian colleges to support current sexual-minority students and alumni. We are not sure how to reconcile the reality of those groups with the findings from this study, other than to say the obvious: that not all students will look back at their time at a Christian college with fondness, but some will. We are reporting averages here, and anytime we do that, we have to note that there is some variability among individual students. Also, alumni could look with fondness while simultaneously wishing some aspects of their experience had been better.

In any case, while we are not aware of studies of changes in attitudes over time toward Christian colleges among sexual-minority students/graduates, there has been some speculation that the benefits of being in faith-based settings may offset many of the negative effects. Put differently, there has been some discussion of the salutary effects of traditional church settings ("nonaffirming" religious settings). These settings may offer social support/ networks and meaning-making structures (a coherent worldview), which offset messages that could otherwise be internalized and could in some way lead to negative mental-health outcomes among sexual minorities (Barnes & Meyer, 2012).

RECONSIDERED SEXUAL ATTITUDES

We might suspect that graduates view their campuses differently because their own attitudes about same-sex sexuality have changed in the year postgraduation. If students became more orthodox in their perspectives, they feasibly could have more empathy for, and acceptance of, their alma maters' seemingly poor treatment of sexual minorities. Multiple studies lend evidence to the idea that we tend to become more liberal while in college and more conservative as we age (Cornelis, Van Hiel, Roets, & Kossowska, 2009; Van Hiel & Brebels, 2011; Kurtzleben, 2016; Lottes & Kuriloff, 1994), which might suggest that graduates are less gay-affirming than they had been while in school, even though only one year has passed.

This, however, is not what happened. Our graduates' attitudes about sexuality looked just like those held by those who were still in school (see table A7.5 in appendix). These alumni seemed to hold similar beliefs about the causality and nature of same-sex sexual attraction to their peers who are still on these Christian campuses. They tended to lean toward a strong biological basis for this attraction, accompanied by limited ability to change this. Again, though, these sexual minorities were fairly moderate in their perspective.

Not only did grads and current students share these attitudes about the nature of same-sex attraction, but they also had similar attitudes about

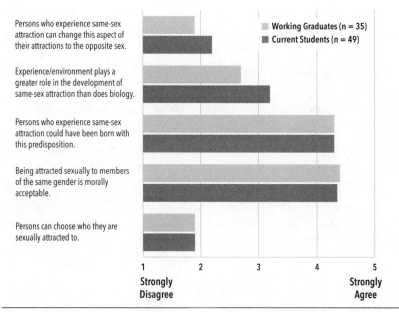

Figure 7.5. Attitudes about same-sex sexual attraction for students and graduates

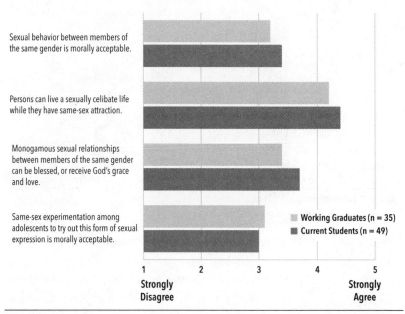

Figure 7.6. Attitudes about same-sex sexual behavior for students and graduates

same-sex sexual behavior. Celibacy was relatively highly endorsed as a possibility for sexual minorities, and some consideration was given to the acceptance of committed monogamous same-sex relationships. Yet, on average, students held a moderate view of the acceptability of this behavior; they tended not to take a strong stand in either direction.

Does this mean there were no changes in attitudes over the course of the first year of our study? Did graduates not change their beliefs at all? Not quite.

If you'll remember from chapter two, we found average scores for attitudes about the causality and nature of same-sex sexual attraction and for attitudes about its related behavior. Higher scores indicate a more accepting, more progressive approach. If we look at these averages over time—from the first year of the study to the second year—between the two groups of sexual minorities, those who remained students and those who graduated, then we can see whether attitudes changed and whose attitudes changed the most.

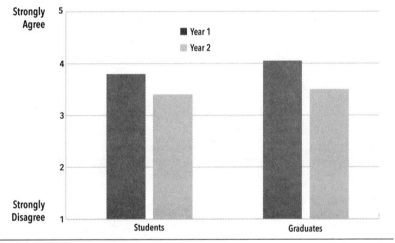

Figure 7.7. Mean attitudinal scores about the causation of same-sex sexual attraction for students and graduates across time

Surprisingly, both groups showed decreasing attitude scores over time, with no real differences between the two groups. This suggests that, on average, both students and graduates became slightly more conservative in their understanding of same-sex attraction over the past twelve months. More specifically, their attitudes slightly moved toward more choice and adaptability of these attractions and away from seeing these as fixed, with a predetermined, biologically based nature. In other words, their attitudes moved a bit more in line with an orthodox Christian faith perspective and, as we've discussed earlier, perhaps some students came to believe that attractions sometimes change, in keeping with Lisa Diamond's (2008) recent work on the fluidity of these attractions.

We did the same analysis for attitudes about the morality of same-sex sexual behavior and found very similar results. Both groups of sexual minorities became slightly less accepting of same-sex behavior over the course of our study. There was no difference between current students and grads. Given that Americans in general and American Christians are both becoming more accepting of same-sex sexual behavior (Murphy, 2015), the attitudinal change in our sample was unexpected. Again, their views seem to be moving toward, at least slightly, a more orthodox Christian perspective.

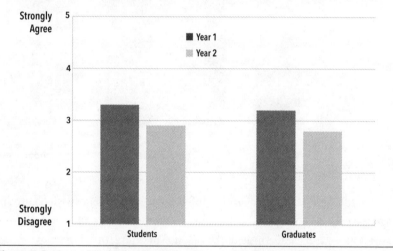

Figure 7.8. Mean attitudinal scores about the morality of same-sex sexual behavior for students and graduates across time

Students' sexual attraction and sexual identity are related to the beliefs they hold about same-sex sexual attraction, as we demonstrated in chapter two, with sexual minorities tending to hold more affirming attitudes than those identifying as straight. Were they too moving toward a more orthodox Christian understanding of same-sex attraction and behavior? Yes, and they were changing to a greater extent in the same amount of time as their straight peers.

First, let's look at attitudes about the nature and causation of same-sex sexual attraction. When we include sexual identity in our analysis, we find a difference between those who identify as sexual minorities and those who identify as straight, with the former holding more accepting values.[12] We also still see movement toward more orthodox values in most of our participants over the course of our study.[13] And, with sexual identity included in the analysis, a difference between current students and graduates becomes apparent, even though we couldn't see it earlier.[14] Graduates held more accepting attitudes regarding same-sex attraction than did students, although both were fairly moderate in their views.

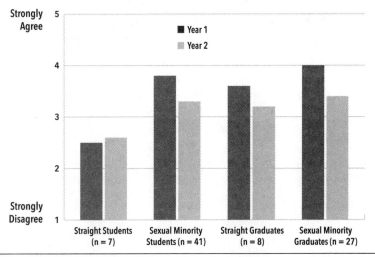

Figure 7.9. Mean attitudinal scores about same-sex sexual attraction by school status and sexual identity across time

In addition to the general group differences, we can identify which groups had the greatest changes over the course of our study. Straight students, who were still students at the time of the second survey, reported the most consistency in their attitudes, with very little change over time; they were also the most orthodox in their views. Everyone else showed similar values regarding same-sex attraction at time 1 and a similar move toward a more orthodox

[12]A 2x2x2 repeated-measures analysis of variance (ANOVA) showed a significant main effect for sexual identity, with those identifying as sexual minorities ($M = 3.78$, $SD = 0.62$) having higher mean attitudinal scores than did those identifying as straight ($M = 3.15$, $SD = 0.71$), $F(1, 79) = 14.55$, $p < 0.001$, partial $\eta^2 = 0.16$.

[13]A 2x2x2 repeated-measures analysis of variance (ANOVA) showed a significant main effect for time, with mean attitudinal scores decreasing from time 1 ($M = 3.88$, $SD = 0.84$) to time 2 ($M = 3.45$, $SD = 0.52$), $F(1, 79) = 18.45$, $p < 0.001$, partial $\eta^2 = 0.19$. See table A7.6 in appendix.

[14]A 2x2x2 repeated-measures analysis of variance (ANOVA) showed a significant main effect for school status, with current students ($M = 3.58$, $SD = 0.74$) having lower mean attitudinal scores than did graduates ($M = 3.78$, $SD = 0.55$), $F(1, 79) = 9.14$, $p = 0.003$, partial $\eta^2 = 0.10$. See table A7.6 in appendix.

position by time 2. Notice that sexual-minority graduates, those who had been a student at time 1 and then graduated by time 2, showed the greatest shift in their thinking, albeit a small one, away from more accepting beliefs.[15]

There was one additional finding related to sexual identity and school status among our sample. Current students who identified as straight held much more orthodox values regarding same-sex attraction than did current students who identified as sexual minorities and all graduates.[16] Graduates who identified as straight had values similar to those of sexual minorities, including both current students and graduates.

We've been talking about the relationship of school status and sexual identity to attitudes about same-sex attraction, not about same-sex sexual behavior. How do these latter attitudes connect to school status and sexual identity? In general, we see pretty much the same movement toward a more traditional position regarding such behaviors across all students.[17] Sexual identity also mattered. Those who identified as sexual minorities reported more accepting attitudes toward same-sex sexual behavior than did those who identified as straight.[18] There was no real difference in attitudes between current students and graduates.

In chapter four we saw that students' level of intrinsic religiosity also was associated with their attitudes about same-sex sexual attraction and behavior. Those who more greatly allowed their religious beliefs to direct their lives held attitudes that were less accepting and more restrictive. Is that what is happening here—are students becoming more religious as they age, contributing to this slight shift in their attitudes?

---

[15] A 2x2x2 repeated-measures analysis of variance (ANOVA) showed a significant interaction effect for sexual identity over time, $F (1, 79) = 5.11, p = 0.027$, partial $\eta^2 = .06$. Those identifying as straight showed a negligible decrease in mean attitudinal scores from time 1 ($M = 3.27, SD = 0.92$) to time 2 ($M = 3.10, SD = 0.60$); however, those identifying as a sexual minority showed a small decrease in mean attitudinal scores from time 1 ($M = 4.02, SD = 0.76$) to time 2 ($M = 3.53$, $SD = 0.47$). See figure 7.9.

[16] A 2x2x2 repeated-measures analysis of variance (ANOVA) showed a significant interaction effect for sexual identity by school status, $F (1, 79) = 5.38, p = 0.023$, partial $\eta^2 = 0.06$. Those current students identifying as straight ($M = 2.71, SD = 0.68$) showed lower mean attitudinal scores than did current students identifying as sexual minorities ($M = 3.27, SD = 0.66$), graduates identifying as sexual minorities ($M = 3.84, SD = 0.54$), and graduates identifying as straight ($M = 3.60, SD = 0.60$). See figure 7.9.

[17] A 2x2x2 repeated-measures analysis of variance (ANOVA) showed a significant main effect for time, with mean attitudinal scores decreasing from time 1 ($M = 3.28, SD = 0.97$) to time 2 ($M = 2.90, SD = 1.12$), $F (1, 78) = 12.55, p = 0.001$, partial $\eta^2 = 0.13$. See table A7.7 in appendix.

[18] A 2x2x2 repeated-measures analysis of variance (ANOVA) showed a significant main effect for sexual identity, with those identifying as sexual minorities ($M = 3.07, SD = 1.08$) having higher mean attitudinal scores than did those identifying as straight ($M = 2.11, SD = 1.00$), $F (1, 78) = 14.96, p < 0.001$, partial $\eta^2 = 0.16$. See table A7.7 in appendix.

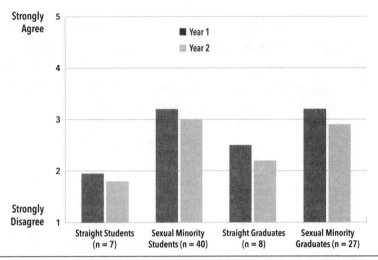

Figure 7.10. Mean attitudinal scores about same-sex sexual behavior by school status and sexual identity across time

COMMITTED SPIRITUALITY, SLIPPING RELIGIOSITY

We took a snapshot of our two groups of sexual minorities—students and graduates—at the second year of study. Across five measures of religiosity and spirituality, there were no differences between the two groups (see table A7.8 in appendix). In other words, graduation did not see the increase of faith follow. Graduates were just as religious and spiritual as those remaining in college.

This, however, is not the full story. Like we did above with their attitudes, we explored how participants' faith changed over the course of our study (see table A7.8 in appendix). Our first two questions were simple self-ratings, indicating how they would describe their own engagement with faith. The first question, "How religious are you?" was answered with average ratings between 6.5 and seven on a ten-point scale, suggesting both students and graduates saw themselves as fairly religious. The second question, "How spiritual are you?" resulted in higher self-ratings, as is common in today's understanding of these two concepts. Both students and graduates gave similar ratings, between 8.1 and 8.6, indicating a high level of spirituality. There were no differences between students and graduates for either question.

We next turned to a more behavioral assessment of religiosity and spirituality, just as we've done in earlier chapters. Here, even though these students had spent at least one, if not up to four or more, years on a Christian campus, both students and graduates on average showed a decline on two of the three subscales. They had become less religious but not less spiritual.

Organizational religiosity is a measure of how often people attend religious services and events. Among our sexual-minority sample, graduates tend to go to church services less frequently than do current students, and both groups were going less frequently than they had been. During the first year of the survey, about 75% of students were attending church services at least once per week. By the second year of our study, about 60% of the remaining students and 47% of the graduates were still going this frequently.

The change is not as large on the other end of the spectrum. When we first surveyed students, about 3.5% of them were attending church once a year or less. A year later, 4% of students and 9% of graduates are rarely if ever going to religious services.

This drop in church attendance among our sample was accompanied by a similar drop in the frequency of personal religious behaviors, or nonorganizational religiosity. Here, while there was no difference between current students and graduates, both groups were less likely to engage in these behaviors during the second year of our study than they had been initially. About 76% of our sample had been doing private religious activities, such as prayer, Bible study, or meditation, two times per week or more often when we first asked them. One year later, 59% are still doing so.

While most students engage in these private religious activities at least a few times a month, some don't. When we started this study, only 3.5% told us that they rarely or never practice their faith privately. A year later, about 6% of current students are not engaging in these activities, but a significant number of graduates have stopped doing so. By one year after graduation, 22% of the sexual minorities in our sample are almost never or never engaging in these personal practices.

Where we didn't see a change was in participants' degree of intrinsic religiosity. Both current students and graduates tended to have a high degree of integration of their religious values into their daily lives. This did not drop over the course of our study. When students were first surveyed, 74% reported their religious beliefs tend to direct their life. One year later, 73% of current students and 66% of graduates are saying the same thing.

What's going on? This drop in behavioral engagement with faith—both in attending church and in private practices—is fairly typical for young adults developmentally (Uecker, Regnerus, & Vaaler, 2007). In the National

Longitudinal Study of Adolescent Health in the early 2000s, 64% of students at traditional four-year colleges and universities reported a decline in religious service attendance (Uecker et al., 2007). The number was even higher in those who didn't attend college, at 76%. Some make an even bigger change. About 13% to 40% of young adults separate completely from the church (Brinkerhoff & Mackie, 1993). Their religious commitment does not seem to reduce this rate of disaffiliation, but whether or not they go to college does (Uecker et al., 2007). Going to college actually increases the likelihood that individuals stay connected to the church.

This is a much higher level of disengagement than we are seeing among our sexual-minority students. In other words, even though some leave, our students are not disaffiliating from the church at the same rate as what is seen in the broader literature.

The broader literature points to a range of possible contributing factors to declining interest in religion at this stage of development. Cohabitation, non-marital sex, and drug and alcohol abuse all "accelerate diminished religiosity" (Uecker et al., 2007, p. 1667), and our sample does not report such activities or beliefs and values that would tend to support such behaviors or experiences. Maintaining factors appear to be attending college (against common assumptions about higher education) and marriage.

In the analysis by Sandomirsky and Wilson (1990), reflecting on the difference between leaving one's faith and changing one's denominational affiliation, it was concluded that "It is as if a religious affiliation establishes an identity for the individual in contrast to other possible affiliations much better than it does in contrast to no religious affiliation at all" (p. 1226). Religious affiliation, of course, is often tied to one's family of origin, to how one was raised. In other words, one's family continues to be an important factor in maintaining religious affiliations. As Sandomirsky and Wilson observe, leaving one's religion often is an "act of nonconformity" (p. 1213). As for the family:

> the family is better at solidifying *some* kind of religious commitment, but when it comes to loyalty to a *particular* religion, denominational roots are most important. These findings add some support to the idea that the family transmits core values, but it does not play as prominent a role in shaping the precise way in which those values are actualized. (p. 1223)

The authors also observed, "Affiliation must be understood as a complex of ties, some of them religious, some of them familial" (p. 1225). These ties are more substantive when the religious and family commitments are more intentional and salient.

SUPPORT FROM OTHERS

One of the advantages of being a student on a small campus is the readily available support from friends and others. Christopher Yuan's (2016) work suggests this is likely true even for the sexual-minority students who report feeling pretty lonely on these campuses, particularly in terms of connecting in social activities with others. Despite this feeling of social isolation, they often also experienced a great deal of positive support from their fellow students as well as the faculty and staff. Yuan commented that even when these others disagreed with the sexual-minority students on issues of sexuality, they still "extended grace and compassion."

The work environment is different from the Christian college campus environment in many ways, but perhaps the one that most significantly changes social relationships is the loss of a residential community when one moves from college into the "real" world. Social relationships become more limited, with fewer multiple roles. In the workplace, we work with someone, maybe chatting over lunch and going to the holiday work party together, but often have little interaction with that person outside the office. On a Christian college campus, students often take classes together, eat together, participate in the same organizations together, exercise together, worship together, maybe work together, and live together (sometimes even in the same dorm or the same room). How does this move away from a residential community feel for our sexual-minority students who have moved on past college?

We started with two general questions about the workplace and its relationship to employees with same-sex attraction. On a five-point scale, our participants essentially said, on average, the workplace views sexual minorities somewhat positively and is, at least to a small degree, supportive of them.[19]

This is significantly different from how current students, in their second year of our study, perceived their campus environments. These students reported some negative views of sexual minorities and some limited support for

[19]A paired-samples t-test suggested that the thirty-seven graduates perceived no difference in the degree to which the workplace positively viewed sexual minorities ($M = 3.43$, $SD = 1.31$) and its level of support for them ($M = 3.39$, $SD = 1.31$), t (36) = 0.71, $p = 0.49$.

them on their campuses. Both ratings of campus were significantly different from ratings of the work environment; Christian campuses are seen as less supportive[20] and less accepting[21] when compared to the workplace.

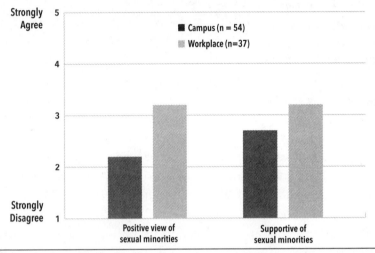

Figure 7.11. Mean ratings of positive view of and support for sexual minorities across campus and the workplace

We then asked them to rate the level of general support that they receive from different groups of people in their lives. Graduates reported getting the most support from their heterosexual friends and the least from their church.[22] In fact, they felt as though they get more support from their friends—whether straight or LGB+—than they do from their families, from their churches, and from their workplace. Their churches are believed to provide about the same level of support as do family and the workplace, but much less than do their friends.

---

[20]An independent-samples t-test suggested that the fifty-four current students rated their campus as holding a less positive view of sexual minorities ($M = 2.53$, $SD = 1.02$) than the thirty-seven graduates rated their workplace's view ($M = 3.43$, $SD = 1.31$), $t(89) = -3.68$, $p < 0.001$, Cohen's $d = 0.77$.

[21]An independent-samples t-test suggested that the fifty-four current students rated their campus as being less supportive of sexual minorities ($M = 2.80$, $SD = 1.20$) than the thirty-seven graduates rated their workplace's level of support ($M = 3.39$, $SD = 1.31$), $t(89) = -2.24$, $p = 0.028$, Cohen's $d = 0.47$.

[22]A repeated-measures analysis of variance found a significant difference in the perceived level of general support from various groups of people, $F(4, 128) = 5.78$, $p < 0.001$, partial $\eta^2 = 0.19$. Using a series of paired-samples t-tests for post hoc analysis, heterosexual friends ($M = 5.36$, $SD = 1.52$) were seen by the thirty-six sexual-minority graduates as providing more general support than did their family ($M = 4.58$, $SD = 1.76$), $t(35) = 2.70$, $p = 0.01$, their church ($M = 4.12$, $SD = 1.55$), $t(33) = 4.68$, $p < 0.001$, and their workplace ($M = 4.63$, $SD = 1.33$), $t(34) = 3.24$, $p = 0.003$, but not their LGBT friends ($M = 5.17$, $SD = 1.00$), $t(35) = 1.36$, $p = 0.18$. Their church ($M = 4.12$, $SD = 1.55$) was seen by the thirty-six sexual-minority graduates as providing less general support than did their heterosexual friends ($M = 5.36$, $SD = 1.52$), $t(33) = 4.68$, $p < 0.001$ and their LGBT friends ($M = 5.17$, $SD = 1.00$), $t(33) = -3.55$, $p = 9.001$, but no one else. See table A7.10 in appendix.

Next, we asked about the support they receive with their same-sex attraction and sexual identity. A very similar pattern emerged.[23] Their friends, both heterosexual and sexual minority, were seen as providing more support than their families, their churches, and their workplaces. Their churches seem to provide about the same amount of support for same-sex attraction as do their families, but less than their workplaces and their friends.

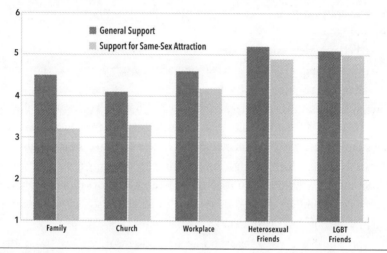

Figure 7.12. Mean ratings of general support and support for same-sex attraction across support groups

Comparing levels of general support to levels of support for same-sex attraction, it is quickly apparent that our sexual-minority graduates perceive less support for their sexuality than they do in general. This was true for their families, their churches, and their heterosexual friends.[24] They did not believe the level of support from their LGB+ friends or their workplaces varied much.

---

[23] A repeated-measures analysis of variance found a significant difference in the perceived level of support for same-sex attraction from various groups of people, $F(4, 128) = 10.92$, $p < 0.001$, partial $\eta^2 = 0.25$. Using a series of paired samples t-tests for post hoc analysis, LGBT friends ($M = 4.97$, $SD = 1.29$) were seen by the thirty-six sexual-minority graduates as providing more sexuality support than did their family ($M = 3.46$, $SD = 1.85$), $t(34) = 4.00$, $p < 0.001$, their church ($M = 3.36$, $SD = 1.67$), $t(32) = 4.16$, $p < 0.001$, and their workplace ($M = 4.24$, $SD = 1.52$), $t(33) = 2.38$, $p = 0.023$, but not their heterosexual friends ($M = 4.83$, $SD = 0.98$), $t(34) = 0.78$, $p = 0.44$. Their church was seen by the thirty-six sexual-minority graduates as providing less sexuality support than did their workplaces, $t(32) = -2.26$, $p = 0.031$, their heterosexual friends, $t(32) = -4.58$, $p < 0.001$, and their LGBT friends, $t(32) = 4.16$, $p < 0.001$, but no one else. See table A7.10 in appendix.

[24] A series of paired-samples t-tests revealed perceived drops in level of support from general support to support for sexuality among their families, $t(34) = 4.07$, $p < 0.001$, their churches, $t(32) = 3.48$, $p = 0.001$, and their heterosexual friends, $t(34) = 2.60$, $p = 0.014$.

ACCEPTING WORK ENVIRONMENT

For students who have moved away from school into the workplace, whether or not they have graduated, the work environment is found to be more accepting of same-sex sexual attraction and behavior in many ways. They perceive the workplace as being generally accepting of the attraction, the behavior, and the persons experiencing the attraction and the behaviors. Even so, same-sex sexual behavior is still not viewed quite as positively as the attraction or the individuals.

To better understand how greatly the work environment changes from the Christian campus environment, we compared ratings during the second year of our study for those continued students and those out of school, in jobs. First, we see that the workplace is rated as much more accepting in all three areas than are Christian college campuses.[25] Not only that, but in both contexts same-sex behavior is rated as less acceptable than are the attractions and the individuals with the attractions.[26] Interestingly, our sexual minorities report that the workplace is only slightly less accepting of same-sex behaviors as it is of the individuals and their attractions, whereas Christian campuses are dramatically less accepting of these behaviors.[27]

Across both groups of sexual minorities, those working and those still in school, 69.3% found their current environment in the workplace or on campus as unaccepting of same-sex sexual behavior. Contrast that to the 67% who believed that their current context was neutral to or accepting of the same-sex attraction and the 61.4% who said their environments accepted or felt neutral toward individuals with same-sex attraction. Overall, there

---

[25] A repeated-measures analysis of variance found a significant difference among the mean ratings of general acceptance of same-sex sexual attraction, behavior, and sexual minorities in the workplace ($M = 3.72$, $SD = 1.35$) and the same ratings on Christian college campuses ($M = 2.73$, $SD = 1.02$), $F(1, 86) = 29.07$, $p < 0.001$, partial $\eta^2 = 0.25$. See table A7.11 in appendix.

[26] A repeated-measures analysis of variance found a significant difference among the mean ratings of general acceptance of same-sex sexual attraction ($M = 3.22$, $SD = 1.25$), same-sex behavior ($M = 2.18$, $SD = 1.46$), and same-sex-attracted individuals ($M = 3.09$, $SD = 1.24$), $F(2,172) = 44.75$, $p < 0.001$, partial $\eta^2 = 0.34$. A post hoc series of paired-samples t-tests found that the mean acceptability rating for behavior was significantly higher than those for attraction and individuals. See table A7.11 in appendix.

[27] A 2x3 repeated-measures analysis of variance found a significant interaction effect across the mean ratings of general acceptance of same-sex sexual attraction, same-sex behavior, and same-sex attracted individuals, by the current status of the sexual minority (current student versus working graduate), $F(2,172) = 12.16$, $p < 0.001$, partial $\eta^2 = 0.12$. A post hoc series of paired-samples t-tests found that the mean acceptability rating for behavior was significantly higher than those for attraction and individuals. Those in the workplace noted less difference across attraction, behavior, and individuals than did those still on campus. See table A7.11 in appendix.

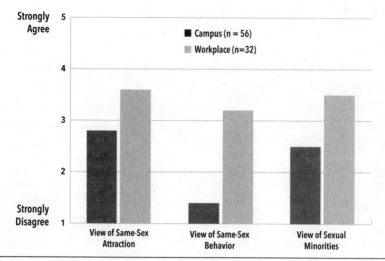

Figure 7.13. Mean ratings of acceptability of same-sex sexual attraction, behavior, and sexual minorities by school/work status

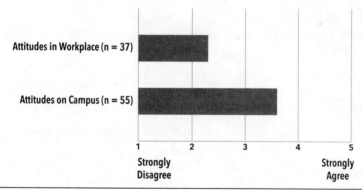

Figure 7.14. Mean ratings of the degree to which environmental attitudes create difficulty for sexual minorities

was perceived good reception of sexual minorities and their attractions, but not of their behaviors.

The workplace was rated better in another way too. Those former students who were now working viewed the workplace as much less difficult for sexual minorities; in fact, they generally felt that the workplace was not particularly difficult. Only 16.2% of our participants felt the attitudes where they work made it greatly or very greatly difficult for sexual minorities, whereas 59.5% held that the workplace values had little to very little negative effect on sexual minorities. In contrast, current students continued to hold that their campus's attitudes made it somewhat difficult for sexual minorities.[28] In fact, 55.4% said these attitudes made it greatly difficult or very greatly difficult; only 7.3% felt these attitudes had little to no negative effect. For most sexual minorities, the workplace will feel quite different from the college campus.

Another way to understand the workplace environment is to ask about sexual minorities' experiences in that environment. We simply asked them to tell us how many times they had heard someone—either their supervisors, their coworkers, or their customers/clients—stereotype, make negative remarks, tell jokes that "put down" people who experience same-sex attraction, or use the term *gay* inappropriately over the past year. Supervisors reportedly made very few of these comments; our sexual minorities only heard 0.5 such remarks per year (or one every two years).[29] Coworkers were a little more vocal, with just under one remark heard each year, and customers, clients, and patrons were the most verbally condemnatory, at least in our participants' eyes, with 1.4 comments overheard per year. Customers seemed to contribute the most to a negative environment.

It's hard for an employer to manage what customers say, but they definitely can speak to what their employees are saying. A full 81.6% never heard a negative remark by a coworker in front of a supervisor. Of the 18.4% who had, only 2.6% heard their supervisor challenge this. Another 15.8% went along with the supervisor either by verbally agreeing or by remaining silent.

How do the occurrence rates of negative comments on a college campus compare to what's witnessed in the workplace? Faculty rarely made such remarks, with students hearing only one every two years, just like we saw among supervisors. Staff were heard making just as many of these statements as did faculty, but less often than coworkers. Yet the negative remarks of other students, who could be compared to coworkers or customers, were heard a lot more often than those of anyone else, with about 2.6 such remarks

---

[28]Among ratings of attitudes on campus or at work making it difficult for sexual minorities, students perceived these attitudes as more of a problem ($M = 3.64$, $SD = 1.01$) than did adults about the attitudes in their workplaces ($M = 2.30$, $SD = 1.27$), $t (90) = 5.63$, $p < 0.001$, Cohen's $d = 1.17$ (very large effect).

[29]A repeated-measures analysis of variance found a significant difference across groups of people heard making negative comments about sexual minorities in the workplace, $F (2, 172) = 12.16$, $p < 0.001$, partial $\eta^2 = 0.12$. Sexual-minority employees reported hearing fewer negative comments from supervisors ($M = 0.53$, $SD = 1.01$) than from coworkers ($M = 0.89$, $SD = 1.47$), $t (37) = -2.11$, $p = 0.042$, Cohen's $d = 0.29$, or customers/clients ($M = 1.37$, $SD = 1.58$), $t (37) = -2.11$, $p = 0.002$, Cohen's $d = 0.63$. See figure 7.15.

heard each year.[30] Students are hearing significantly more negative comments from other students than working sexual minorities are hearing from their customers and clients.[31]

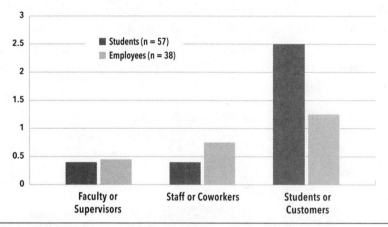

Figure 7.15. Mean instances of hearing derogatory comments among faculty, staff/coworkers, or students/customers

PSYCHOLOGICAL HEALTH

Many have argued that the more restrictive and less supportive environment found at Christian colleges and universities is likely harmful for sexual-minority students. In fact, this is the main point of the *Shame List*, created by Campus Pride (2016) to warn others of the discrimination, shame, and harm occurring on these campuses. Quoted in an article about a Christian university's stance on sexuality (Hudalla, 2015), student Dan Sandberg remarked, "There's no discussion . . . it's either 'you're a sinner' . . . or 'let's get close so we can fix you.' It's a really toxic environment."

If the environment truly is toxic, we should see sexual minorities' psychological symptoms abate to some degree on leaving these campuses. This is not what we see. Using responses from the second year of the study,

---

[30]A repeated-measures analysis of variance found a significant difference across groups of people heard making negative comments about sexual minorities on Christian college campuses, F (2, 112) = 87.99, $p < 0.001$, partial η^2 = 0.61. Sexual-minority employees reported hearing more negative comments from students ($M = 2.58$, $SD = 1.61$) than from faculty ($M = 0.49$, $SD = 0.98$), t (56) = -10.57, $p < 0.001$, Cohen's $d = 1.57$, and staff ($M = 0.47$, $SD = 0.91$), t (56) = -10.71, $p < 0.001$, Cohen's $d = 1.61$. See figure 7.15.

[31]Using an independent-samples t-test, sexual-minority students reported hearing more negative comments from their fellow students ($M = 2.58$, $SD = 1.61$) than sexual minorities in the workplace reported hearing from customers and clients ($M = 1.37$, $SD = 1.58$), t (80) = -3.60, $p < 0.001$, Cohen's $d = 0.76$.

we were able to compare graduates' psychological functioning to that of current students.

In fact, across all symptom categories, there was only one significant difference in scores between current students and graduates (see table A7.13 in appendix). That was found in issues related to alcohol use, and graduates were doing worse, not better, than current students.[32] Moving away from the behavioral restrictions around alcohol use may have contributed to the increase in reported alcohol concerns.

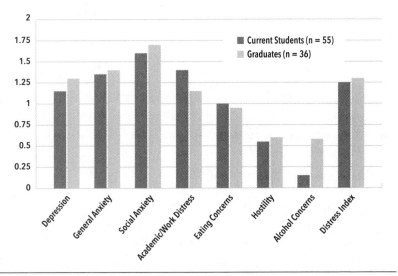

Figure 7.16. Mean ratings of current students' and graduates' psychological symptoms

As we saw in chapter two, the average scores for depression and general anxiety fell in the slight-distress range. Current students also showed this slight distress in their academic work, whereas graduates experienced some low-level distress related to social anxiety. For both groups of sexual minorities, the average distress index was in this slightly elevated range.

Given these average scores, we wanted to see how many individuals fell into each level of distress. Among current students, 53% did not report much psychological distress, landing them in the lowest distress category. Almost a third of these students had moderate distress, and less than 20% experienced marked distress.

---

[32]Using an independent-samples *t*-test, sexual-minority students reported fewer concerns about alcohol use ($M = 0.19$, $SD = 0.40$) than did graduates ($M = 0.63$, $SD = 0.86$), $t(89) = -3.32$, $p = 0.001$, Cohen's $d = 0.66$.

These percentages were very similar for working graduates. A large 64% reported minimal psychological symptoms, just under a fifth of graduates experienced slight distress, and another fifth of them reported marked distress. There were no significant differences in distribution across these distress categories between current students and working graduates.[33]

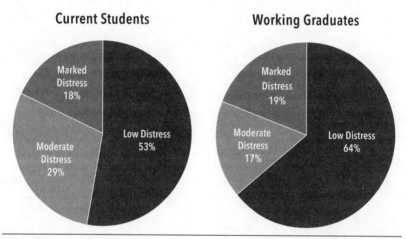

Figure 7.17. Percentages of students and graduates experiencing psychological distress

Another way to think about change in psychological symptoms is to look at average change within each individual. We therefore compared our recent graduates' scores from time 1 to their scores from time 2. There was no significant change in any of the categories (see table A7.14 in appendix). Think about that. Even though the alcohol-concerns index score seemed to be higher in the graduated sample than in the current-student sample, our graduates were drinking more than their peers when in school, and they are still drinking more than the students currently in college. Their drinking levels haven't changed; merely the drinking habits of the comparison group are different.

Overall, these self-reported descriptions of their psychological symptoms yielded clarity that our sexual-minority participants are not really doing much better, or much worse, after they graduate from college and enter the world of work. Sexual minorities who were struggling in college likely are still struggling after they graduate, even though they perceive their workplaces as being more

---

[33]A chi-square analysis revealed no significant differences between distress level and current status of sexual minorities, $\chi^2 (2) = 1.88$, $p = 0.39$.

affirming and supportive than their institutions had been. This lends some support that the environment may not be the most influential factor in the overall psychological functioning of these students who have graduated. Even so, these students, both while in school and after they graduate, have much to say about their campus climate toward sexual minorities, and they, through their participation in this study, have given us a lot of insights into how their campuses can be and do better for students like themselves. This is our focus in chapter eight.

CHAPTER 7 TAKEAWAYS

1. Graduation does not bring much change in levels of sexual attraction or in sexual identity. Most students see little to no change in their attraction, whether that is attraction to members of the opposite sex or to members of the same sex. About two-thirds of the students also continue to use the same sexual-identity label to describe themselves.

2. What does change after graduation are students' perceptions of their campus's approach to sexual minorities, and these perceptions tend to become more favorable. Graduates see their campuses as being more accepting and supportive to sexual minorities in multiple ways. Even so, graduates see their workplaces as much more accepting of sexual minorities than students understand their campuses to be.

3. In general, both students and graduates became slightly more conservative in their understanding of same-sex attraction over the first year of the study. More specifically, their attitudes slightly moved toward more choice and adaptability of these attractions and away from seeing these as fixed, with a predetermined, biologically based nature. And both groups of sexual minorities became slightly less likely to view same-sex behavior as morally acceptable.

4. In the year after graduation, both students and graduates reported a drop in church attendance and in the frequency of personal religious behaviors, but not in their personal faith, that is, their intrinsic religiosity, which is the degree to which they live out their lives according to their faith.

5. Psychological health also doesn't change much from college to the workplace. In fact, among the symptom categories, the only change seems to be an increase in alcohol use, which we might see in many students who graduate from campuses that restrict alcohol use.

REFERENCES

Arnett, J. J. (2004). *Emerging adulthood: The winding road from the late teens through the twenties.* New York: Oxford University Press.

Barnes, D. M., & Meyer, I. H. (2012). Religious affiliation, internalized homophobia, and mental health in lesbians, gay men, and bisexuals. *American Journal of Ortho-psychiatry, 82*(4), 505-15.

Bodenner, C. (2016, May). Labeled a pedophile simply for being gay. *The Atlantic.* Retrieved from www.theatlantic.com/notes/2016/05/labeled-a-pedophile-simply-for-being-gay/484475/

Brinkerhoff, M. B., & Mackie, M. M. (1993). Casting of the bonds of organized religion: A religious-careers approach to the study of apostasy. *Review of Religious Research, 34*(3), 235-58.

Campus Pride. (2016, August 24). *Shame list: The absolute worst campuses for LGBTQ youth.* Retrieved from www.campuspride.org/shamelist/

Cornelis, I., Van Hiel, A., Roets, A., & Kossowska, M. (2009). Age differences in conservatism: Evidence on the mediating effects of personality and cognitive style. *Journal of Personality, 77*(1), 51-87. https://doi.org/10.1111/j.1467-6494.2008.00538.x

Diamond, L. M. (2007). A dynamical systems approach to the development and expression of female same-sex sexuality. *Perspectives on Psychological Science, 2*(2), 142-57.

Diamond, L. M. (2008). *Sexual fluidity: Understanding women's love and desire.* Cambridge, MA: Harvard University Press.

Hudalla, J. (2015, May 21). What it's like to be gay at a Christian college—where it's a reportable offense. *YES! Magazine.* Retrieved from www.yesmagazine.org/happiness/what-its-like-to-be-gay-at-a-christian-college-where-its-a-reportable-offense

Kurtzleben, D. (2016, April 30). Why are highly educated Americans getting more liberal? *NPR.org.* Retrieved from www.npr.org/2016/04/30/475794063/why-are-highly-educated-americans-getting-more-liberal

Lottes, I. L., & Kuriloff, P. J. (1994). The impact of college experience on political and social attitudes. *Sex Roles, 31*(1), 31-54. https://doi.org/10.1007/BF01560276

Marin, A. (2016). *Us versus us: The untold story of religion and the LGBT community.* Colorado Springs, CO: NavPress.

Murphy, C. (2015, December 18). Most U.S. Christian groups grow more accepting of homosexuality. *Pew Research Center.* Retrieved from http://pewrsr.ch/1PaLkab

Sandomirsky, S., & Wilson, J. (1990). Processes of disaffiliation: Religious mobility among men and women. *Social Forces, 68*(4), 1211-29. https://doi.org/10.2307/2579141

Uecker, J. E., Regnerus, M. D., & Vaaler, M. L. (2007). Losing my religion: The social sources of religious decline in early adulthood. *Social Forces, 85*(4), 1667-92.

Van Hiel, A., & Brebels, L. (2011). Conservatism is good for you: Cultural conservatism protects self-esteem in older adults. *Personality and Individual Differences, 50*(1), 120-23. http://doi.org/10.1016/j.paid.2010.09.002

Yuan, C. (2016). *Giving a voice to the voiceless: A qualitative study of reducing marginalization of lesbian, gay, bisexual, and same-sex attracted students at Christian colleges and universities.* Eugene, OR: Wipf & Stock.

APPENDIX

Table A7.1. Frequencies of college sexual orientation and postgraduation sexual orientation (*n* = 35)

| | | SEXUAL ORIENTATION AFTER GRADUATION | | | |
		Heterosexual	Lesbian/Gay	Bisexual	Other
Sexual Orientation While in College	Heterosexual	5.7%	0.0%	5.7%	2.9%
	Homosexual	0.0%	34.3%	2.9%	0.0%
	Bisexual	0.0%	2.9%	22.9%	5.7%
	Other	0.0%	0.0%	8.6%	8.6%

Table A7.2. Frequencies of college sexual orientation and postgraduation sexual identity (*n* = 35)

| | | SEXUAL IDENTITY AFTER GRADUATION | | | |
		Heterosexual	Lesbian/Gay	Bisexual	Other
Sexual Orientation While in College	Heterosexual	8.6%	0.0%	2.9%	2.9%
	Homosexual	2.9%	34.3%	0.0%	0.0%
	Bisexual	8.6%	2.9%	8.6%	11.4%
	Other	2.9%	0.0%	5.7%	8.6%

Table A7.3. Frequencies of college sexual identity and postgraduation sexual identity (*n* = 35)

| | | SEXUAL IDENTITY AFTER GRADUATION | | | |
		Heterosexual	Lesbian/Gay	Bisexual	Other
Sexual Identity While in College	Heterosexual	14.3%	0.0%	0.0%	2.9%
	Homosexual	2.9%	37.1%	0.0%	0.0%
	Bisexual	2.9%	0.0%	5.7%	14.3%
	Other	2.9%	0.0%	11.4%	5.7%

Table A7.4. Average rankings of components of sexual-identity development for graduates (n = 35)

	Time 1 M (SD)	Time 2 M (SD)	W
Biological Sex	3.60 (1.61)	4.26 (1.65)	1.73
Gender Identity	3.63 (1.73)	4.34 (1.66)	1.94*
Sexual Attraction	2.29 (1.60)	2.89 (1.89)	1.71
Intentions	2.94 (1.28)	3.49 (1.34)	1.75
Values	3.02 (1.34)	2.94 (1.66)	-0.32
Behaviors	3.00 (1.50)	3.09 (1.48)	0.25

* $p = 0.053$

Table A7.5. Attitudes about same-sex sexuality among current students and graduates

	Current Students (n = 49) M (SD)	Working Graduates (n = 35) M (SD)	t (df)
Persons can choose who they are sexually attracted to.	1.87 (1.04)	1.88 (0.99)	-0.03 (82)
Sexual behavior between members of the same gender is morally acceptable.	3.41 (1.45)	3.26 (1.60)	.43 (82)
Being attracted sexually to members of the same gender is morally acceptable.	4.36 (0.95)	4.43 (0.82)	-0.36 (82)
Monogamous sexual relationships between members of the same gender can be blessed, or receive God's grace and love.	3.72 (1.43)	3.30 (1.54)	1.30 (82)
Same-sex experimentation among adolescents to try out this form of sexual expression is morally acceptable.	3.02 (1.38)	3.06 (1.43)	-0.14 (82)
Persons who experience same-sex attraction could have been born with this predisposition.	4.27 (0.92)	4.27 (0.87)	-0.01 (82)
Experience/environment plays a greater role in the development of same-sex attraction than does biology.	3.12 (1.02)	2.74 (1.05)	1.67 (81)
Persons who experience same-sex attraction can change this aspect of their attractions to the opposite sex.	2.13 (1.06)	1.93 (0.94)	.90 (80)
Persons can live a sexually celibate life while they have same-sex attraction.	4.43 (0.95)	4.21 (0.99)	1.05 (81)

Table A7.6. Average attitudes about same-sex sexual attraction by school status and sexual identity over time

	Group	n	Time 1 M (SD)	Time 2 M (SD)	School Status Effect F (df)	Sexual Identity Effect F (df)	Time Effect F (df)
Current Students	Straight	7	2.69 (0.81)	2.73 (0.54)	9.14 (1, 79)**	14.55 (1, 79)***	18.45 (1, 79)***
	Sexual Minority	41	3.94 (0.83)	3.51 (0.49)			
Graduates	Straight	8	3.77 (0.72)	3.42 (0.47)			
	Sexual Minority	27	4.13 (0.64)	3.55 (0.44)			

** $p \leq 0.01$
*** $p \leq 0.001$

Table A7.7. Average attitudes about same-sex sexual behavior by school status and sexual identity over time

	Group	n	Time 1 M (SD)	Time 2 M (SD)	School Status Effect F (df)	Sexual Identity Effect F (df)	Time Effect F (df)
Current Students	Straight	7	2.10 (0.60)	1.87 (0.76)	0.68 (1, 78)	14.96 (1, 78)***	12.55 (1, 78)***
	Sexual Minority	40	3.51 (0.80)	3.11 (1.05)			
Graduates	Straight	8	2.69 (0.99)	2.33 (1.17)			
	Sexual Minority	27	3.43 (1.01)	3.01 (1.14)			

*** $p \leq 0.001$

Table A7.8. Levels of religiosity and spirituality among current students and graduates

	Students (n = 49) M (SD)	Graduates (n = 36) M (SD)	t (df)	p
How religious are you? (10-point scale)	6.76 (2.38)	6.56 (2.09)	0.40 (83)	.689
How spiritual are you? (10-point scale)	8.10 (1.92)	8.31 (2.10)	-0.47 (83)	.643
Organizational Religiosity (6-point scale)	4.60 (1.20)	4.09 (1.46)	1.75 (80)	.084
Nonorganizational Religiosity (6-point scale)	3.72 (1.47)	3.46 (1.85)	0.73 (80)	.470
Intrinsic Religiosity (5-point scale)	3.88 (1.35)	3.77 (1.24)	0.36 (81)	.721

Table A7.9. Levels of religiosity and spirituality among current students and graduates over time

	Group	n	Time 1 M (SD)	Time 2 M (SD)	Group Effect F (df)	Time Effect F (df)	Group x Time Effect F (df)
How religious are you? (10-point scale)	Students	49	7.08 (1.81)	6.76 (2.38)	0.35 (1, 83)	0.96 (1, 83)	0.00 (1, 83)
	Graduates	36	6.86 (2.46)	6.56 (2.09)			
How spiritual are you? (10-point scale)	Students	49	8.61 (1.59)	8.10 (1.92)	0.00 (1, 83)	1.00 (1, 83)	0.52 (1, 83)
	Graduates	36	8.39 (2.21)	8.31 (2.10)			
Organizational Religiosity (6-point scale)	Students	48	5.10 (0.93)	4.60 (1.20)	4.24 (1, 80)*	19.97 (1, 80)**	0.02 (1, 80)
	Graduates	34	4.62 (1.26)	4.09 (1.46)			
Nonorganizational Religiosity (6-point scale)	Students	49	4.15 (1.12)	3.72 (1.47)	0.37 (1, 80)	12.80 (1, 80)**	0.37 (1, 80)
	Graduates	36	4.06 (1.45)	3.46 (1.85)			
Intrinsic Religiosity (5-point scale)	Students	49	4.12 (0.73)	3.89 (1.35)	0.53 (1, 81)	2.47 (1, 81)	0.21 (1, 81)
	Graduates	36	3.90 (1.07)	3.77 (1.24)			

$* p < 0.05$
$** p \leq 0.001$

Table A7.10. Average ratings of general support and support for sexuality by graduates ($n = 36$)

	General Support M (SD)	Support for Same-Sex Attraction M (SD)	t (df)
Family	4.54 (1.77)	3.46 (1.85)	4.07 (34)***
Church	4.12 (1.58)	3.36 (1.67)	3.48 (32)***
Workplace	4.62 (1.35)	4.24 (1.52)	1.49 (33)
Heterosexual Friends	5.34 (0.84)	4.83 (0.98)	2.60 (34)*
LGBT Friends	5.17 (1.01)	4.97 (1.29)	0.87 (34)

$* p < 0.05$
$*** p \leq 0.001$

Table A7.11. Average views of same-sex attraction, behavior, and persons across context

The Campus or Workplace View of . . .	Current Students (n = 56) M (SD)	Working Graduates (n = 32) M (SD)	t (df)
Same-Sex Sexual Attraction	2.89 (1.14)	3.78 (1.26)	-3.38 (86)***
Same-Sex Sexual Behavior	1.52 (0.91)	3.34 (1.52)	-7.06 (86)***
Persons with Same-Sex Attraction	2.73 (1.02)	3.72 (1.35)	-3.88 (86)***

*** $p \leq 0.001$

Table A7.12. Frequencies of perceived difficulty of attitudes toward sexual minorities across context

		CONTEXT	
		Campus (n = 55)	Workplace (n = 37)
To what degree do attitudes exist on your campus or workplace that make it difficult for a sexual minority in that environment?	Very Little Extent	5.4%	35.1%
	Little Extent	1.8%	24.3%
	Some Extent	36.4%	24.3%
	Great Extent	36.4%	8.1%
	Very Great Extent	20.0%	8.1%

Table A7.13. Average ratings of psychological symptoms among current students and graduates

	Current Students (n = 55) M (SD)	Working Graduates (n = 36) M (SD)	t (df)
Depression	1.21 (0.92)	1.36 (0.89)	-0.74 (89)
General Anxiety	1.39 (1.03)	1.44 (0.99)	-1.25 (89)
Social Anxiety	1.64 (0.94)	1.77 (0.98)	-0.66 (89)
Academic or Work Distress	1.48 (1.13)	1.18 (0.93)	1.31 (89)
Eating Concerns	1.05 (1.21)	1.00 (1.11)	0.22 (89)
Hostility	0.59 (0.73)	0.66 (0.74)	-0.40 (89)
Alcohol Concerns	0.19 (0.40)	0.63 (0.86)	-3.32 (89)***
Distress Index	1.29 (0.85)	1.33 (0.81)	-0.18 (89)

*** $p \leq 0.001$

Table A7.14. Average ratings of psychological symptoms in sexual minorities before and after graduation

	Senior Year (n = 36) M (SD)	One Year Postgraduation (n = 36) M (SD)	t (df)
Depression	1.48 (1.13)	1.36 (0.89)	0.72 (35)
General Anxiety	1.41 (1.08)	1.44 (0.99)	-0.34 (35)
Social Anxiety	1.89 (0.94)	1.77 (0.98)	1.00 (35)
Academic or Work Distress	1.47 (1.13)	1.18 (0.93)	1.56 (35)
Eating Concerns	0.78 (1.00)	1.00 (1.11)	-1.15 (35)
Hostility	0.71 (0.73)	0.66 (0.74)	0.50 (35)
Alcohol Concerns	0.82 (1.12)	0.63 (0.86)	1.59 (35)
Distress Index	1.32 (0.11)	1.33 (0.81)	-0.37 (35)

*** $p \leq 0.001$
Bolded = slight distress level

SUMMARY, RECOMMENDATIONS, AND CONCLUSIONS

[The chapter of my life that I am currently writing is called] Total Honesty . . . being totally exposed to God and walking fully in the freedom of Christ, even when you are struggling with same-sex attraction and self-acceptance. . . . Honestly, I think I am spiritually growing, and I think as I grow the sexuality part doesn't overwhelm me as much. The reason I think I'm growing spiritually so much is because I'm having more transparent conversations with God, first and foremost, and then I'm more open and transparent even with humans. They know I love God very much, but they also know I don't pretend to not struggle with certain things, versus walking around being suppressed and pretending I'm not struggling when I am, which I think is more of bondage than anything.

—*Monika, senior, African American, identifies as questioning, time 2*

▼▲▼

WE WERE ENCOURAGED WHEN WE READ Monika's report about a more "open and transparent" life at the intersection of sexuality and religion/ spirituality. Even if she may not feel completely settled, her description of this life chapter does sound less protective, less secretive, and more communally engaged as a whole person. She may not be settled, but she is hopeful of certain signs in her life and in the lives of those around her.

Chloe shares a very different experience:

One theme [of my current life] is honestly deception. Sadly, it is a big part of how I live my life because I am in the closet and I'm afraid of coming out. So, it is like taking precautions and being careful about what we do and what we say around other people. This is really hard because I really love my friends and my family and it is hard to keep that from them. Hiding is a big part, too. I would say that spiritually . . . I am trying to reach out and go deeper but at the same time I am still hiding from truly asking things. (Chloe, senior, identifies as lesbian, time 2)

In this closing chapter we want to reflect on what we have learned about sexual minorities who attend faith-based institutions of higher education. We also want to reflect on how this information can be helpful to Christian colleges and universities as they seek to meet the needs of LGB+ students. And we invite you, the reader, to consider the varied institutions and settings in which you live, work, and serve to ponder the same questions. We hope our work will speak to students and school representatives who might want to engage Chloe's authentic revelations about protective duplicity in a helpful way. How do we make space for the whole person to find a way to develop and grow? This final chapter suggests that many of our sexual-minority students believe it is possible at their Christian college or university.

A SUMMARY OF KEY FINDINGS

What have we found throughout the course of our research on the experiences of sexual minorities at Christian colleges? First, diversity exists among students on this journey of sexual-identity development. If you were asked to describe a sexual minority, you might have in your mind a person who represents that group to you. But that would undoubtedly be misleading. There is no single story. This is not a monolithic group.

How are they diverse? Sexual minorities at Christian colleges and universities are highly religious and spiritual, but diversity resides in many areas, including level of opposite-sex attraction and same-sex attraction as well as beliefs and doctrinal positions. These students appear to be different (by virtue of being highly religious and spiritual) from other students in the general population. But they are also diverse insofar as they represent a range of beliefs and values in areas of sexuality and sexual behavior, including related policies at Christian colleges.

Second, sexual-minority students are navigating difficult terrain. Campus climate appears to be improving somewhat across the last ten years at Christian colleges and universities. By improving we mean that there is greater awareness of the reality of sexual minorities at Christian colleges and a greater sense from sexual minorities that there are people on campus who care about them and with whom they can talk and be honest about their experiences. However, same-sex attraction and, even more so, same-sex behavior remains "unacceptable" in most of these communities. This seems consistent with broader views among evangelical Christians, in particular.

The terrain appears to be more negotiable than in the past, but among students, faculty, and staff, student attitudes and behaviors appear the most problematic and can still be obstacles. While faculty and staff appear to be more supportive of sexual-minority students and are generally viewed positively, it is noteworthy that in a few instances negative experiences are still reported for a small number of students. Counseling services, campus ministries, and relations with some faculty and staff are increasingly viewed as useful resources on campus. However, a general distrust of most campus resources remains among many due to fear of disclosure and recriminations, whether accurately perceived or not. Yet having said this, the trend is toward a growing openness and helpfulness in cocurricular areas across the last ten years.

Third, intrinsic religion appears to be a major contributor to a sense of fit for sexual minorities at faith-based colleges and universities. Already experiencing their sexual-minority status among majority students, it appears that they may feel doubly cut off from the support of their faith-based community when they are also low in intrinsic religiosity. They appear to find it more complicated to access the social resources of the higher-education community when they feel different in ways related to their sexuality and religiosity/ spirituality. Coping resources and possibly coping skills may be somewhat diminished (given other research that suggests that religiosity and faith are helpful for coping). They may interpret their status as being excluded from the community that they hoped would accept them and help them grow as Christians. This perception of double marginalization seems to make life together at the intersection of faith and sexuality exceedingly complicated. We wonder whether the perception of dissimilarity for these students, when comparing themselves with the rest of the community, makes finding supportive relational space less likely, or at least less serviceable.

Fourth, average scores for psychological and emotional disorders suggest about 50% of our sample are in the low-distress range, probably looking very similar to the average student at any college or university. The other half shows moderate to marked distress, looking much like other students who will seek or need to seek counseling for psychological or emotional impairments, often in anxiety- or depression-related areas. Across time, a small percentage in the moderate-distress range tend to move into more marked distress, while a smaller percentage move toward lower distress. Intrinsic religiosity (IR) appears to play a protective role in level of distress among sexual minorities at their institutions. Strength of same-sex sexual attraction was not associated with emotional health. Campus climate and attitudes reportedly impact academic, emotional, psychological, and spiritual life for sexual-minority students.

Fifth, the majority of interviewed sexual minorities worked diligently to maintain their "hold" on both religion/spirituality and sexual-identity development. Those who reject one or the other in order to manage the developmental tension appeared to be rare. Most tried to find some way to integrate these aspects of human personhood, although we found three different ways to integrate these identity-based "boxes" in their interviews. It seemed that identity development at this intersection was characterized by repeated episodes of being "settled" to "unsettled," even though their stated identity status often shifted very little across time.

Sixth, most of these sexual-minority students want to be in these educational settings, although there are differences in attitudes toward campus policies. A common question asked in these contexts is, "Why would a gay student go to a conservative Christian college?" The question is often asked with an edge to it, as though the students themselves were the problem. That is an unhelpful posture to take. These students are typically highly religious/spiritual and want to develop in a setting where they can consider both sexual and religious/spiritual development. Almost 60% have some disagreement with campus policies, but that finding does not suggest that all want the policies changed.

As one student shared with us, "Interestingly, even as some students have been the source of most of my problems, some other students have been the greatest help and resource." This brings us to our final observation: *social support is hypothesized as a mediating variable for quality of life on campus, as well as integration of sexual and religious/spiritual identity.* In other words, relationships matter! They can be detrimental to quality of life on campus, or they can be life giving and help a person thrive.

ADVICE TO FELLOW SEXUAL-MINORITY STUDENTS

We asked our thirty-nine interview participants at time 1 what advice they would give to other Christian students who experienced same-sex attraction. In other words, what have they learned that they would pass along to others in the same boat? No surprise—the relationship theme was prominently represented among the responses. Their advice focused on what we might call microlevel concerns, not the larger institutional macro level. The micro level is the place where students do life together with other members of the community.

Before beginning our discussion of this advice, it is important to hear a word from one of our interviewees. Kevin, a twenty-two-year-old junior, recognized the complications of giving this kind of general advice when he responded to the interview question in the following way:

> That's so difficult to answer because it's different with everyone that is LGBTQ. I feel that if I had kept ignoring the issue my last two years, I would, at least at my school, have been more successful, and things would have been much less difficult. . . . That being said, it would have been an unhealthy thing to do and would have led to bigger problems down the road. I don't know that I could give blanket advice, because everyone is different. . . . I know students on both sides . . . who feel it's better for them to just stay closeted here, or better for them to confront it here, so I really don't know that I could give blanket advice.

Acknowledging the wisdom of avoiding sweeping generalizations or superficial recommendations, we offer these suggestions from the interviewees. They are not expert opinions; instead, they are voices of lived experience. Their responses fell into four categories. The first three advice categories pertained specifically to certain "relational encouragements," while the fourth was filled with "general exhortations." In the first three relational categories, students championed certain ways for peers with same-sex attraction to view God, to view self, and to view others. One might suppose that all of these relational encouragements were given because they saw the potential for healthy perspectives about God, self, and others to get lost in the complex community of Christian higher education. In essence, our students appeared to be saying, "Above all, please don't forget this." It is not hard to assume that these perspectives were likely the ones that these interviewed students needed to hear at one time and may still need to hear from time to time. In fact, they do seem to fit the overall experiences of our interviewed students.

More specifically, the contents of the first three relational categories contained perspectives to adopt, as well as ways to engage God, self, and others in the unique environment of their Christian institution. We found it consistent with student views reported in chapter four (identity development) and chapter six (college campus) that "relational encouragements" concerning others were the most frequently offered by interviewees. Life with fellow students seemed to be the most complicated and critical area for those interviewed. A close second was encouragement pertaining to self. It appeared that greater attention to self and others in this portion of the interview was intimately associated with establishing a foundation of relational security at their Christian colleges and universities. It is also developmentally consistent that these two areas interact significantly in the college experience for all students, not just for those with same-sex attraction. Most students in higher education are negotiating the complex world of relational attachments as a part of their overall identity development.

As it happened, most of the advice for self-care from the interviews was attitudinal, not behavioral, as we'll see in the advice about relating to others. The overall message of the advice to self appeared to be "care for yourself." Interviewees encouraged their peers to see themselves in a supportive and valuing way. It was common to hear "do's," such as the following: love yourself, be yourself, be confident in yourself, be honest with yourself, and be patient with your process. Admonishing "don'ts" were also common, such as don't be afraid of who you are, don't feel ashamed because others experience same-sex attraction, don't worry about others questioning your sexual identity, don't be overwhelmed by your sexuality because it's only a part of you, and don't think you are the only one. Only a few interviewees encouraged more instructional steps, such as don't bury it, you don't have to act on it, focus on growing spiritually and being sanctified daily, and figure out what you should do through prayer and discussion. Still, we notice the self-care theme in the instructional advice.

Advice in the "other" category was primarily instructive about how to find relational space to reveal that which can be fearfully kept private among Christian peers in higher education. The majority of these suggestions were "do's," such as the following: share with a trusted person, talk to at least one person, come out to one or two others, seek out those with whom you can be honest, find others who will love you no matter what, find safe people on campus and off, find encouragement and support, find a support system, find someone who is out who you can talk to, find people who can give you space to permit the formation of your identity, seek social support, and find someone trustworthy who is biblically sound and not struggling or judgmental.

The "don'ts" related to others were also instructive but fewer in number. The first "don't" continued the encouragement to find trustworthy others and admit same-sex sexuality sooner rather than later but then added that students should not go around telling everyone. Another said that students should not allow their peers to push them into giving up faith or sexual identity. Another advised that students should not avoid same-sex relationships to act straight. Finally, one offered a hopeful entreaty, saying that others are willing to help/understand but not get rid of it.

Overall, "other" encouragements continued to support the observations of the surveys and the interviewees. For these interviewed students, relationships appeared to be pivotal for negotiating life in Christian colleges and universities. As was said above, this finding comes as no surprise to anyone familiar with higher education. Relationship is foundational for identity development in all students—whether they are Christian or not, or whether they are primarily attracted sexually to the opposite sex or the same sex. The relational advice of students, however, tended to highlight the increased risks for those who live at the intersection of same-sex attraction and lower intrinsic faith. The unique differences associated with being in one or both minority groups were perceived as making essential relational needs harder to meet. These students felt marginalized within a culture that felt dominated by community assumptions about everyone being straight. Add to this the perception that "everyone is more spiritual," and the sense of fit in the community becomes significantly diminished. Secure attachments, in particular, seemed more complicated to develop for this group of students because of fears associated with being a peripheral part of the community. Yet, as one student advised, "Seeking support is worth the risk." That relational encouragement was clearly the perspective of our interviewed "peer advisers."

Less advice was given by students to their peers about relating to God. Looking at frequency alone, the number of "relational encouragements" referencing God was clearly less prominent in interview responses as compared to other and self categories. The frequencies were not even close. At first we were confused by this low count among students who were so clearly high in scores on religiosity and spirituality. But as we considered the advice that our interviewees were offering about God, it seemed rather uniform. Not only was the advice less frequent, it was also much less diverse. The few "relational encouragements" referencing God all spoke to love, acceptance, and positive valuation. As one graduate student, Dylan, stated, "God don't make no junk." That same "God loves you" awareness was echoed across responses to other interview questions as well. It was extremely rare that any interviewees articulated a view of God other than loving, accepting, and valuing. Views of theological traditions, faith-based communities, and other cultural trends were questioned across the interviews, but hardly ever did we see interviewees questioning this uniform view of God.

Continuing the reasoning above, it seemed possible that lessened attention to this "God" category might suggest that this advice was not deemed to be as necessary. These highly religious and spiritual students were already living with a "God is love" view, even as they made sense of their sexual-identity development. As James, a grad student, advised, "What defines . . . is Christ and the relationship with Christ." The institutions and their believers may be questioned, but the character of God as loving and good seemed less so in most interviews. Viewing self and other, on the other hand, appeared more complicated and not quite so secure, so advice in those categories was more plentiful for our interviewees.

Now that we have described the three "relational encouragement" categories for God, self, and others, we can move to the largest category overall—general exhortations. They were most often behavioral suggestions given by interviewees to their peers for reasons that seem to be connected to relational and, to a lesser degree, religious/spiritual health. Forty-six general exhortations were drawn from our interviewees.

The largest overall theme in this exhortation category advised students to pay attention to resources on campus. Clearly, among those interviewed college and university counseling centers were the most recommended resource. It is interesting that in their survey of 213 sexual minorities at faith-based institutions, Wolff and colleagues (2016) reported that 17% of sexual-minority students reported that a mental-health professional attempted to change their orientation.[1] In this same study, 47% reported that a mental-health professional affirmed their sexual orientation.

---

[1] Principal investigator Joshua Wolff noted in a symposium at the American Psychological Association 2017 Convention (Washington, DC) that it was not possible to know for certain whether the mental-health professional who attempted orientation change was a counselor at the college or possibly a counselor unassociated with the school.

It was obvious from other portions of the interviews that not all counseling centers or all counseling center personnel were endorsed by students. (In the section of the interview dealing with campus resources, only two interviewees rated their counseling centers negatively, while three did not mention counseling centers at all.) Nevertheless, to our request for advice for fellow students, 28% of students who completed interviews mentioned the campus counseling center specifically as a positive option and as their recommendation for help. Interviewees appeared to most appreciate those counseling centers that had earned the reputation for helping students with the stresses of college life while not indoctrinating a certain perspective regarding sexuality. As Adriana reported, "The counseling center is actually where I first was able to articulate my same-sex attraction. I did not feel judged, did not feel oppressed. I was actually able to dialogue in a very healthy manner about it." Yet even when counseling centers might not be trusted for sexual issues, they were also recommended for mental-health issues. Another student, Logan, explained, "I used the counseling center but not for sexuality issues. . . . I don't feel like it's really helpful [for sexual issues] because they're still in training. It's kind of frustrating because I want to really speak to somebody who's going to get right on the issues."

Other recommended resources in the interviews were "certain" faculty and staff. Specifically chaplains/campus ministers were highlighted when they were approachable and knowledgeable. Two interviewees suggested that students ought to develop a list of the "helpful" people on campus. Four interviewees also mentioned the significance of on-campus support groups as a resource for them and an option for others. This advice matched other sections of the interview where students noted the importance of "all student" gatherings and "specific student" gatherings. All-student gatherings were educational and more about building awareness and promoting dialogue for the whole campus community. Specific-student gatherings were smaller, confidential, personal, while also being educational at times.

Some exhortations were academic in nature, such as this pithy advice: "Stick it out for good education" and then "move to a more accepting place." Another interviewee suggested that others might want to approach professors and even parents from an "academic perspective." She meant that students might use a class-related opportunity, such as a research paper or a class presentation, as a way to discern which professors might be safe and which ones might not. Even parents might be educated by getting them to read academic papers or products.

Another theme among the general exhortations pertained to the diversity that is represented among sexual minorities at Christian institutions. One student noted that "every LGBT person is different" and went on to advise that it may be better for some to stay closeted, while others should not. A different interviewee appeared to support this stance, advising students to "choose your consequences." Others echoed the diversity theme by commending the perspective that the process will look different for each person. Along the same lines, one interviewee exhorted peers by warning about "general cultural messages" that are supposed to apply to all. Another interviewee seemed to affirm this idea with the following advice, "This is a personal journey of self-exploration."

ADDITIONAL ADVICE FROM THOSE WHO HAVE GONE AHEAD

Here are several additional "general exhortations" from sexual-minority students:

- ▶ Denying keeps you from dealing with it (speaking to the reality of one's same-sex sexuality).
- ▶ Find a church. (In the interviews, this action step usually meant finding one that supports or encourages what you believe.)
- ▶ It's a long road but one worth taking (speaking to the need for patience with the developmental process).
- ▶ There is a middle way where time changes you to become more like Christ, even with same-sex attractions.
- ▶ Be careful of shame. It can creep in and paralyze.
- ▶ Be okay with not having all the answers.
- ▶ Take time to work out issues related to same-sex sexuality and faith.
- ▶ Focus on love. (In the interviews, this admonition often related to the belief that relationships needed to be as important or more important than doctrinal adherence.)
- ▶ Don't live in fear of "coming out."
- ▶ Focus on prayer.
- ▶ Christian colleges and universities are "good for Side B but not Side A." (This is language that originated from the group Bridges Across the Divide. "Side B" refers to gay Christians who believe same-sex behavior is morally impermissible, while "Side A" refers to gay Christians who believe same-sex behavior can be morally permissible.)

ADVICE TO CHRISTIAN INSTITUTIONS

Thirty-nine interviewed students shared their perspectives at time 1 on what their own institutions needed to know about navigating sexual and religious identity. We asked our interview participants what advice they would give to their college or university leaders about how they can better serve students on their campuses who experience same-sex attraction. In other words, what have they learned that they would pass along to administrators and policy-makers for the benefit of Christian sexual minorities? Their responses largely addressed the macro level administrated by campus authorities, but the comments often appeared to be implicitly for the purpose of making space for the micro level of relationship.

The most interesting finding concerned what was not mentioned. We did not find students advocating for change in theology or doctrinal position at their schools. Whether they accepted the tenets of the institution or simply decided to address "more winnable" and practical issues, we only know that the faith-based foundation of colleges and universities was not brought up by our students. This focus was not targeted for adjustments at the present time.

Twenty-three percent did, however, give advice related to school policies. Policies may be tied in some cases to religious doctrine, but not always. Three students specifically addressed hiring policies. Liam, a gay sophomore, offered:

> Another thing is—this might be going out on a limb—but hiring people who express that they have same-sex attraction. I think that's very difficult in the Christian context because then you're asking for someone who has a PhD, who abides by the school's standards, wants to teach at this school, and I think that's a very small pool, but I think it would be great to have that in mind when hiring professors or at least staff members.

Colby, a bisexual senior, stated more stridently, "I need them to have some openly gay administrators and professors because there are none. Not only be diverse in their hiring practices of brown and black bodies, but in all sexual orientations and genders—like gender-nonconforming people as well."

Austin, a graduate student, offered a personal hope: "Down the road it could be possible. Having openly gay professors would be so incredible. It would totally change the way the dynamics feel for LGBT students on campus. We could have someone on our team, you know, a faculty member actually understanding our experiences because they've experienced it. That would be valuable."

Mia, a freshman who identified her sexual identity as "other," mentioned her perceptions about student recruitment policies. She admonished, "If I could tell my university anything, it would be that . . . banning kids from coming here just because they might be 'out' is discrimination, and I don't think that God is okay with discriminating against who gets to learn in a Christ-centered environment." Once admitted and enrolled as a member of the community, three interviewees lobbied for official endorsement of groups who could serve and advocate for them. Kevin, a gay junior, suggested a "gay-straight alliance," while Ethan, a gay senior, wanted a "queer resource center" similar to a women's center or a diversity center. Aiden, also a senior and gay, simply asked for "legitimate groups" that are not "secret but a part of the institution." He noted, as did other interviewees, that alumni or donors might be suspicious of official endorsements for groups or clubs, but he believed that "safe space" in Christian higher education required this type of community-based structure.

For many students, spaces for discussion appeared to be connected to "open[ing] up real, honest dialogue that isn't censored" (Kevin, a gay junior). The call for "conversation" (Michael, a "straight" senior with same-sex attraction) was promoted for administration, faculty, and staff but also with other students. In fact, two interviewees counseled that it was the student level of the institution where change was needed most. Like the findings in chapter six (campus climate), two students advised that their institutions would have problems crafting a way to move more positively into the future if they did not help students understand the effect they have on one another. Chloe, a lesbian senior, said, "There is so much good that my institution is doing as far as their programs, but there is nothing . . . they can do to change what students are going to do. I think that so much of the pressure that LGBT students feel is pressure from their peers." Brent, also a senior and gay, stated, "All of [the institution's] problems stem from the students that it attracts, so unless something can be done to help the student population better understand, I honestly think there's little [the administration] can do." Miranda, a bisexual senior, appeared more optimistic that students could affect change if given the right conditions. She advised, "I think that one of the best ways is to put it more in the hands of students. And I don't know how they would, but to find a way for students to help other students."

Many interviewees appeared to believe that student groups, both informational and support varieties, were necessary resources for creating understanding and establishing dialogue among students, but also with administration and faculty/staff. Eleven interviewees encouraged schools to grow, promote, and advertise resources that supported sexual minorities and educated others. Mason, a straight senior with same-sex attraction, proposed that schools be "more up front" about such resources and opportunities. Aiden, a gay senior, forthrightly stated, "I would encourage the institution to make the campus a safe space with a club or group that met regularly to talk about these issues." Michael, a self-identified "straight homosexual," advocated, "Keep the conversations going!" Justin, a gay junior, said, "Encourage people to talk about [same-sex attraction] more, even like in the dorms or living spaces." The result could potentially be what Owen, a freshman, envisioned: "Make [same-sex attraction] more of an open-air topic and less of a private topic."

Toward this end, Matthew called for a time when the reality of sexual minorities on campus was "normalized," not considered only when a special event, such as "make a gay friend day," interrupted the regular flow of campus life. Mia, a freshman, emphatically advised,

> [College leaders] have to remember that there are closeted members on the campus and they're going to feel alienated. Trying to pretend that [same-sex attraction] doesn't exist is only really hurting them. Offering resources to these kids would be extremely beneficial, and honestly, nonacceptance and intolerance to these issues nowadays is just kind of behind the time and spiritually does not make much sense.

Reflecting this strong theme among the interviews, Logan, a junior, proposed that campuses recognize the reality that sexual minorities are present and active in student life on campus. He said,

> I would say [to my college] . . . stop being heteronormative, I guess. I mean, good grief, they offer these panels about masculinity and femininity and marriage, and I mean, good grief, where is the room for the student who is single and may never marry? Or the student who is male that isn't like the most masculine man in the world? Where is the room for that student?

Carter, a gay junior, encouraged his college to "start making those first connections [with sexual-minority students]. They need to be the arm or the hand that's reaching out." Jackson, a gay senior, suggested that administration, faculty, and staff should make opportunities to "listen to stories and experiences" as the context for providing needed services in a safe way. He offered, "Figure out ways to provide resources and opportunities for those students. Don't provide what you think they should be getting, but really talk to them and figure out what would be helpful in the ways our whole community needs to grow."

Oliver, a gay senior, concurred with the need to hear student stories, so that "the administration can personalize the topic . . . [and] better learn how to implement anything else on campus." Aaliyah, a queer sophomore, suggested surveying students on her campus so "they know where students are coming from and can address it directly."

Many interviewees noted the perceived need for intentional and less guarded communication from faculty and staff as well as students. Olivia, a queer sophomore, suggested Christian schools, like hers, could indeed "allow more openness to discuss" while maintaining the policies that prohibit same-sex behaviors. Jayden, a bisexual graduate student, appeared to affirm that openness and prohibiting policies could coexist but at the same time identified an inherent limitation for a truly open conversation. He admitted his discouragement about being invited into a conversation where there is little to no perceived hope of mutual impact or reciprocal understanding. He explained,

> It would be as though someone from Ferguson [a place of racial unrest] came to [my school] and we said, "Oh, we want to have this conversation with you, but just so you know, you're wrong and your community is wrong, but we still want to have a conversation about it." . . . We'll talk about this as long as you end up agreeing with us.

Possibly one way to craft a different kind of conversation was suggested by Adriana, a senior who identified as bisexual. She advised that polarization easily occurred in conversations about faith and Scripture. She suggested a more humble perspective in which each party might be willing to admit that "my personal interpretation" could need adjusting. Carter, a gay junior, advised attention to the problem of language. He reported, "They are trying to take people in [to the community], but the language that they're using, they don't realize that what they are saying can be so important or like so judgmental to a [non-]cis student whether at chapel or in the classroom, but it really can without them even knowing."

Three interviewees went on to counsel their institutions to craft targeted policies that addressed negative campus climate and "removed stigma" (from Owen, a freshman who experiences same-sex attraction but identifies as straight). Savannah talked about practices at other institutions that might be instituted at her school to create "safe space." She specifically advised ways, such as wearing rainbow pins, for fellow sexual minorities or "allies" to advertise their unwillingness to "disown, reject, humiliate, harass, abuse, or neglect" others. Also mentioned was levying hefty fines for "bullying and harassment" on campus. Colby, a bisexual senior, appeared to agree with this approach when he suggested a strong stand on any speech that attacked the worth or value of another person. He advised a "no-tolerance policy" for denigrating or stereotyping language for sexual minorities. Riley, a lesbian sophomore, advised her institution to add sexual minorities to the student handbook clause against "discrimination and harassment" to encourage "safe space." She stated,

> I would love for them to add sexual minorities to that list [of other minority communities]. I think that would be a pretty cool statement for them to make. And it's not necessarily reflective of a theological shift. I think it's just a good way to care for students and maybe cause students to rethink how they use the disgusted looks or slurs that they use when confronted with sexual minorities.

Ethan, a gay senior, characterized this shift to pay as much attention to sexual minorities as other minorities as "God-honoring diversity" and exhorted his campus to embrace this move as a hallmark of being Christian.

The final advice theme related to training. Five interviewees noted the need to educate and equip groups on campus, but not all agreed on the group that should be targeted for training. Two students thought that administration, faculty, and staff needed to focus on the experience of gay students. Ethan advised that faculty and staff need "better training on what it means to be gay." Wyatt, a gay junior, concurred. He strongly counseled, "Get some education. Start from the top. . . . I mean you're at a college, you have PhDs, you're supposed to be educated, and yet you treat people like shit." He went on to suggest that administrators needed relationships with "friends that are gay" to gain the needed perspective.

The other group targeted for training was students—but not the same students. First, two interviewees noted the need for better training with resident assistants. Hannah, a senior who identifies as bisexual, recommended equipping RAs to better deal with sexual minorities on their floor so that those students are not "exploited." Wyatt pushed for "a change" in the "educational system" for residence life. He said, "Rather than introduce the topic of gay issues as SSA or reorientation therapy, I would introduce it with history and education about what it is to be someone that has interest in the same sex and maybe with a touch of theology just so that wasn't left out."

Second, two other interviewees lifted up the need for training at freshman orientation. Kate, a senior who identifies as bisexual, stated, "We have a lot of freshmen come in from different backgrounds that don't really know a lot about LGBT issues, so [freshman orientation] could be a time to be like, 'Hey, by the way, this is something that really matters.'" Logan, a gay junior, agreed that a "mandatory orientation to all incoming freshman" was necessary. He advised that the training should focus on "living with your neighbors who are different than you." Interestingly, this theme about orienting freshman was found in other sections of our interviews. Four interviewees also noted the difference between the way students enter college and the way they exit—noting more derogatory and stereotyped language use in the early years. In a self-identified "huge generalization," senior Adriana humorously suggested the following narrative:

> In general, students are open to new suggestions. But in general they come in as freshmen on this particular topic being like, "Why would there be anything different [than what I currently believe]?" Because it is a liberal arts environment they become increasingly more open over the course of their time at college. So by the time they are seniors, most of them are pretty chill. . . . Pretty much, everybody is there by the time they get to senior year, but the freshmen are a little crazy, but that's the way freshmen are, so it's okay.

FOCUSING ON COMMUNITY LIFE TOGETHER

We noted at the beginning of this section on institutional recommendations that students did not ask explicitly for theological or doctrinal shifts for their colleges or universities. In hearing their advice to their colleges and universities, the majority appeared for the most part to focus on how their Christian higher-education community could do life together within the context of existing doctrinal positions. It was as if they assumed that the doctrinal stances of their colleges and universities would not shift substantially. With their recommendations they seemed instead to be asking for a conversational environment (or what was often characterized as "safe" space in several interviews) where they might get to know themselves and be known by others without repercussion.

In this way they appeared to be like most of their collegiate peers. They shared the same general identity-development goals, even though the identity-development conditions of the higher-educational community appeared different for them from most of their peers. They saw their institutional context as more complicated to negotiate and in most cases more precarious for their developmental process. The interviewed students overwhelmingly appeared to be asking for a place that was less complex and certainly more predictable. The majority appeared to be hoping for an explicitly trustworthy Christian setting where they could know as they are known, as Parker Palmer (1993) titled his classic text about education and spiritual formation.[2]

Hearing the voices of students, we believe that Christian undergraduates might be asking for their Christian colleges and universities to teach and model how to hold this aspect of their lived experience so they can learn to hold it as well. Regretfully, the students we studied don't seem to find much of an articulated vision in their Christian communities for realistically holding their life experience at the intersection of sex and religion/spirituality. What they saw modeled reportedly felt rather simplistic and not grounded in real life. It's not that students perceived a desire at their respective schools to hinder their development. In fact, in most cases among our interviewed students, it was just the opposite. They heard in most of the studied schools that they were loved, but they also perceived that they must figure out this intersection of sexuality and faith in a certain way to be accepted. As a result, most perceived that they were left to figure this out as best they can. But "deciding for myself" is not the same as "deciding by myself" (Kegan, 1994, p. 222). This developmental deciding happened best in community.

From an institutional perspective, we have seen administrators and staff at Christian institutions wanting to offer resources to students for help to navigate this intersection. They understand that students cannot be forced to grow in a certain way, so they offer services to support what they often view as a decision-making process. Interviewed students seemed to feel invited by their colleges and universities to make choices about their sexuality and their faith. From a cognitive perspective, this perception made sense. Schools sought to motivate doctrinally consistent decisions at the intersection of sexuality and

---

[2]Parker Palmer (1993) reported, "Knowing is a profoundly communal act. Nothing could possibly be known by a solitary self, since the self is inherently communal in nature. In order to know something, we depend on the consensus of the community in which we are rooted—a consensus so deep that we often draw upon it unconsciously" (p. xv).

faith, but the student voices we heard suggested that sound decision making was not enough. They were looking for more. Beyond simply making a good choice, interviewed students felt called to be a good person as they are coming to know "the good" at the intersection of religion/spirituality and sexuality.

We suspect that for most of our interviewed students this was a strong reason for attending and persisting at a Christian college or university. Most were looking for help to be a certain kind of person—one who lived a sexually faithful life. After listening for many years to the voices of sexual-minority students at Christian institutions, we believe that they are hoping for a Christian community that will help them connect with the good and separate from the bad as they were growing to understand it. As they developed, they seemed to be looking less for indoctrination into a "Christian" way of thinking (a macrolevel goal) and more for a whole-person relational encounter. The advice to peers and administrators from interviewed students suggested that schools would do well to consider a more relational approach. If we listen to interviewed students, learning to hold sexuality and hold faith at the same time requires a holding environment whose goal is the growth of a particular kind of person.

As we heard the advice that students gave to peers and then paid attention to how they appeared to recommend a relational community, we recalled Mary Rowe's research on microinequities and microaffirmation in the field of organizational management (see chapter six for a more extensive treatment of microinequities and microaffirmations). Rowe (2008) called attention to those "small events which are often ephemeral and hard-to-prove, events which are covert, often unintentional, frequently unrecognized by the perpetrator, which occur wherever people are perceived to be different" (p. 45). They were termed microinequities and contrasted with microaffirmations. Microaffirmations were those "apparently small acts, which are often ephemeral and hard-to-see, events that are public and private, often unconscious but very effective, which occur whenever people wish to help others to succeed" (p. 46).

Rowe (2008) asserted that the relational feel of an organization is largely associated with the presence or lack of these microaffirmational qualities. Her conclusion (apparently consistent with the perspectives of our interviewed students) was that attention to the relational feel of the organization ("the little issues," p. 45) was more than a touchy-feely fad or an attempt to be politically correct. It was indeed foundational for successful educational and developmental outcomes with persons in organizations. Interviewed students appeared to suggest the same in their advice for their peers and their colleges and universities.

Certainly the interviewees touched on what Rowe (2008) called "major issues" (p. 45) when they spoke to hiring policies and student recruitment practices. Such macrolevel concerns are significant across the whole institution. However, most of the attention for students and most of what they wanted their institutions to attend to was the way their colleges and universities did Christian community at a micro level. They appeared to be hoping to find a faith-based setting that lived and taught their beliefs, while recognizing and validating unique experiences in the identity-formation process. Justin, a self-reported gay junior, described faculty and staff who had been affirmational in his life in this way:

> When you talk, they listen well. They ask you a lot of open questions. They check in on if other students treat me, well, the same. They really try to help me process it, because some of it . . . I came while I was still trying to figure it out. I still am. But they are really good about processing it, saying like, "What do you think about this?" Or they give me resources to check out like, "I know this guy who wrote a lot about this. Look up his stuff or read his book." They are not discriminating at all— they treat me like a faithful son.

Basically, interviewed students seemed to be asking for a quality of institutional attention that did not magnify their own shame and fear. We interpreted their advice to peers and the larger institution to be the following: we need to see modeled by fellow Christians how to hold this part of our lives. Again, they did not seem to be asking as much for a discussion about doctrinal beliefs as much as they were looking for a particular kind of relational experience. It appeared that they hoped to find a holding environment at Christian colleges and universities that would model how they could also hold this part of their personhood. It did not seem to matter whether they valued their sexual identity or their religious/spiritual identity more centrally; they wanted to experience a community's hold on them and these issues of life. Regretfully, most say they haven't found a place that satisfactorily balanced sexuality and faith, and they hoped that their Christian college or university might grow to be a better experience. Most interviewees reported that they have found pockets, in some cases only a person or two, that provided space for this kind of experiential learning and formation. It makes us wonder what an institutional vision and strategic plan might look like that increases the number of these pockets and builds an institutional culture based in part on the intentional proliferation of microaffirmations and not microaggressions. What is the look of a higher-education culture that is orthodox in its sexual ethic while also investing intentionally in relational formation of sexual-minority students? Student advice suggested that their institutions could be more creative in answering this question, particularly at the micro level.

We need more collaborative visioning at Christian colleges and universities to address this kind of question in a creative, intentional way, but one line of research seemed to confirm a promising relational direction. Paul Youngbin Kim (2017) from Seattle Pacific University investigated the influence of religious support on racial microinequities and psychological well-being of Christian ethnic-minority students at private religious universities in the northwest United States. He looked, in particular, at the mediational effects of interpersonal aspects of religious support, focusing on the influence of "congregational supports" (support from religious community peers) and "religious leader supports" (support from religious authority figures). Echoing the testimony of sexual minorities in our study concerning microlevel relationships with student peers, the racial-minority students in the Kim (2017) study demonstrated that "congregational supports" were a significant influence on the decrease in racial microinequities and the increase of psychological well-being. However, "religious leader support" did not show any significant relationship to these variables. Relational connections with religious authority figures did not mediate racial microinequities or well-being, but intentional religious support from student peers was seen as playing a protective role for minorities. If the effects of ethnic minorities on Christian college campuses can be generalized to sexual minorities in the same setting, an intentional focus on student life together could be a direction for future community attention in creating educational and developmental vision for all minorities.[3] Indeed, it seems likely that the effects for all students could potentially be formative for life in Christian higher education and beyond.[4]

---

[3]We are not suggesting that sexual minorities are parallel to ethnic minorities in terms of sexual orientation being analogous to skin color, but we were struck by the value placed on community attention that may be particularly relevant. For a discussion of whether orientation and skin color are analogous, see Jones and Yarhouse (2012).

[4]Kim (2017) goes on to note hypothesized implication about the way racial microaggressions affect the potential positive benefits of religious support for well-being. He suggests that research results suggest that racial microaggressions put a limit on the good mental-health outcomes that come from religious support. There appears to the author to be a "support deterioration" effect associated with the presence of microaggressions.

BEING INTENTIONAL

When we started reflecting on the qualities of institutional and campus culture that we heard described by sexual minorities, we struggled to find succinct terminology that captured the rich dynamics that they were hoping to experience. We wanted to reflect the need that we heard for an encouraging relational culture of support and challenge that focused on microaffirmational training as a time-honored practice for "life together" in Christian community (Bonhoeffer, 1954).

We finally settled on the word *intentional* to describe the kind of holding environment that we envisioned as we listened to Christian college students and alumni. But as with any crosscultural discussion, this descriptive word required some definition.

We believe that an *intentional culture* is characterized by relational encouragement that both supports and challenges members of the academic community. Notice that the goal is growth and development for all members. All are learners, and all have something to teach—or at least to inform from their own experiences of living and learning. As L. Lee Knefelkamp, Columbia University professor of psychology and education and senior scholar at the Association of American Colleges and Universities, reported, traditional-age and nontraditional students need to be considered "co-learners" (Donnelly-Smith, 2011). She said, "Any learner brings something to the table. And we need to see how we can assess who that learner is and what they've experienced and how they learn, and put that into dialogue with what we need to teach and how we teach it." In this kind of culture, all are intentionally invited to participate in an ongoing conversation, both in the classroom and beyond the classroom, about whole-person education, of which sexual identity and religious/spiritual identity are two developmentally important pieces of the whole.

To accomplish such an ambitious community learning goal, we believe that being intentional will include, to some degree, four characteristics. Those characteristics can be found in the breakout boxes in the following pages.

AN INTENTIONAL CULTURE

Over years of listening to sexual-minority students, we have grown to believe an intentional institutional culture is pivotal for creating the degree of trust that holds relational community and, we now know, supports academic success (Cozolino, 2013). The overall goal of student learning in higher education appears to be intricately related to the "feel" of the institutional culture. There is something about being intentional that Christians need to revisit because of its descriptive potential for the findings in our research. There is a broad and wide-ranging, intentional posture that seems helpful and indeed meaningful when we listen to the voices of students in our studies. We believe that Christian colleges and universities can support the search for mature personhood with achieved identities (i.e., academic, vocational, relational, gender, political, sexual, religious/spiritual) for all students who are willing to participate in the community.

If a college or university is serious about a secure climate of education and formation for all students, it is paying attention to the relational dynamics that are present in curricular and cocurricular settings (Cozolino, 2013). A culture that is intentional pays attention to the often-overlooked micro level

INTENTIONALLY RELATIONAL

Community members will be intentional about cocreating a culture of relational encouragement.

The first characteristic of an intentional culture is a focus on respectful and encouraging relationships. This relational culture will not expect that community members necessarily know how to work together in a way that encourages identity development. If there is one finding that stands out among all the survey data and interviews, it's the need for intentional relational training that values *persons*, even when *positions* may be in tension. Although students perceive some improvement among Christian colleges and universities in the area of campus climate, they also noticed that doctrinal positions still seemed to trump personhood more often than not—even at the micro level of community. When it comes to the intersection of sexuality and religion/spirituality, the conditions for sexual minorities are still perceived as more challenge than support.[a] We believe that a culture of relational encouragement is known for intentional emphasis on microaffirmations for all members at all levels of the academic community. Students, faculty, staff, administrators, alumni, and other constituents are collectively aware of microinequities and collaborate as "senders" and "receivers" of microaffirmations.

---

[a] Robert Kegan's (1994) past observations of education sound amazingly contemporary in light of our study. He observed, "People grow best when they continuously experience an ingenious blend of support and challenge. . . . On these grounds our culture-as-school may deserve the highest grade when it comes to the criterion of providing challenge. But how well are we doing on the criterion of support? It is not necessarily a bad thing that adolescents are in over their heads. In fact, it may be just what is called for provided they also experience effective support" (p. 42).

(microaffirmations or sources of encouragement) as well as the macro level (vision, mission, and policies) of the classroom, administrative offices, and the residence halls. It is our experience that Christian colleges and universities are asking more and more questions about the micro level while continuing to engage the macrolevel issues that have captivated their institutional attention in the recent past.[5]

As we listen to the voices of sexual minorities and as we also hear the institutional agents associated with Christian higher education, we discern a tacit need for reemphasizing an historic liberal arts goal: whole-person education. "As the liberal arts advance the formation of character and identity, they encourage students to explore queries of personal meaning that are at the heart of the gospel, including: Who am I? What makes life significant? What are my convictions? How will I live and act?" (Wells, 2016, p. 89). If our samples are any indication, sexual-minority students who persist at Christian colleges and universities are likely looking for a chance to ask these complex questions that resist simple answers. Unfortunately, the macrolevel response is often one that provides little opportunity for more than a pithy policy position or doctrinal statement.

In an article published in *The Chronicle of Higher Education*, Lyell Asher (2017) discussed the unsettling tendency in current higher education to oversimplify complex topics to encourage uniformity of thought and action. If unaware of the cultural pressure to find such developmental "shortcuts," institutional agents and students can collude to avoid the uncomfortable work of formation that colleges and universities say they promote. Asher (2017) explained,

> A college ought to be the ideal place to help students learn to resist such simplifications—to resist them not just inside the classroom, in the books they read, but outside in the lives they lead. Rightly understood,

---

[5]Much of the previous inattention to the micro level and focus on the larger institutional concerns appear to us to be related to a position of defense in the face of increasing cultural shifts in belief and practice. There is nothing like a perceived threat to shut down attention to communal factors. It is not hard to find real-life examples of how institutional protection and survival can often trump other motivations, even in Christian communities aspiring to love. Social psychologist Milton Rokeach (1973) described how values, such as mature love and security, are in organized systems "wherein each value is ordered in priority with respect to other values" (p. 11). When values related to institutional security rise to take priority in the system, even for a temporary period, other values, such as love, equality, and freedom, are ordered lower in a values hierarchy. His research shows behavioral relevance for the ordering of values hierarchies in personal and institutional settings.

the campus beyond the classroom is the laboratory component of college itself. It's where ideas and experience should meet and refine one another, where things should get more complicated, not less. (p. 2)

An intentional culture is indeed a more complicated engagement, not a simplistic, "Let's all feel good about one another" interaction. Trying to conceive of what this culture might look like, we have talked with many students across the years who have what seemed to be an overly simplistic and idealized view of what support looks like in Christian community. This uncomplicated view tended to set up the community in an adversarial way. The expectation can quickly overlook or fail to appreciate the effect that certain attitudes and behavior may have on those who live around them. They seemed to say, "The community should be responsible for me, but I am not clear on reciprocal responsibilities to those who live around me." Such a view is too limited for the kind of identity development that often relies on the crisis of "iron sharpening iron" interactions as a catalyst for formative growth (Marcia, 1980). A less idealized but more complex view of intentional culture is one that relies on the growth of trust. The potential for conflictual interactions among multiple institutional constituencies (i.e., student, faculty, staff, administration, trustees, alumni, donors) is real, we might even say unavoidable, when "whole persons" are in community.

Liberal arts, classically understood, envisions a setting where complex developmental processes are engaged, beyond simply academic or vocational identities. We hear increasingly the voices of sexual-minority students who want to be at Christian schools where they can bring their whole persons to the educational process. Whether they might be able to state it or not, the students we studied clearly wanted the liberal arts experience in a relationally secure Christian environment. They wanted to engage the "personal meaning" questions that Cynthia Wells, director of the Ernest Boyer Center at Messiah College, mentioned above—especially as they are connected to their sexual identities. They didn't all want to be public in their consideration of this aspect of their life experience, but they did seem to prefer inviolable space to engage this complicated developmental process. They hoped for a trustworthy setting in which they could publicly or privately consider their sexuality in light of general education and their faith tradition. Most wanted a different environment from the one they had experienced in their families, churches, and schools. They wanted a relational educational community in which they could

DIALOGUES OR SERMONS?

Lyell Asher (2017) wrote a compelling article published in *The Chronicle of Higher Education* titled "Your Students Crave Moral Simplicity. Resist." The title really tells the story, but the author discusses the challenges faced by faculty and administrators at colleges and universities when complex moral questions arise surrounding any number of topics, such as those related to race, culture, ethnicity, sexuality, politics, and so on. The tendency is to take shortcuts by identifying any number of "isms" (e.g., racism, sexism, heterosexism) and reducing those around the student to positions. As the author notes, "complexity can be an unwelcome guest, requiring as it does both focus and time." Or consider this: "on subjects of any depth and complexity, the dialogue, rather than the sermon, is the model for intellectual engagement." The dialogue versus the sermon. The difference between these two ways of communicating captures precisely the challenge for Christian colleges and universities. Many constituents expect essentially a sermon from the macro level of mission and vision. And there is a very real sense in which Christians wish to find ways to communicate what they view as a historic, biblical understanding of sex and sexuality. At the same time, many students want dialogue at the micro level of sustained relationships. Students may understand the need for a sermon, and they may not expect the underlying theology that informs the sermon to change, but they want to be in constructive dialogue with one another and, more often than not, with those who are writing the sermons.

learn how to hold their sexuality and their religion/spirituality. From our decades in different Christian liberal arts colleges and universities, we wonder whether sexual-identity development is not an outcome that ought to be prioritized and encouraged for all students, whether they are attracted more to the same sex or the opposite sex.

In order to meet this often implicit relational request of students, we suggest that Christian education needs to be embedded in a culture that is even more intentional than it is currently. An intentional culture bears witness to one another's experiences and learns how to validate the person who has those experiences. It is not a society of collective approval for any and all behaviors. It's hard to imagine a rigorous environment for education that does not criticize and challenge as well as witness and support. Those critiques and challenges may come from a well-understood and robust biblical anthropology and vision for sexuality and sexual morality, but it tends to be relationally attuned. An intentional educational culture is one that can challenge and support, when appropriate for the student, and, though it is regretfully inefficient, this requires a relational foundation. We are reminded of Andy Crouch's distinction between postures and gestures (Crouch, 2013). We encourage Christian institutions to adopt postures, such as an intentional posture, that allows for varying gestures, such as challenge or support. In fact, our interviews suggest that colleges and universities appear to be perceived most helpful when they intentionally start by building support early in student life and then increasingly grow the relationship conditions where challenge is cautiously engaged, if not trusted. This suggestion was pervasively heard across student interviews.

Some of our interviewees recommended the benefits of being intentional starting at freshman orientation, laying out what might be called a practical theology with covenantal expectations for how relational community works

INTENTIONALLY FORMATIONAL

Community members will be intentional about co-constructing a formational environment.
A second characteristic of an intentional culture is a focus on whole-person development across the whole community. Students, faculty, staff, administrators, and even alumni and other constituents collaborate to construct "seamless" educational space (Kuh, 1996) for growth and development.[a] More than inculcating certain knowledge, this intentionally formational culture "takes the time" to form a certain kind of person.[b] More than a narrow focus on personal development alone, we believe that formation in higher education must intentionally include relational development as well. For Christian higher education in particular, whole-person formation is never a private affair; it is intentionally formation-in-community. Community members are always formed in intentional relationships and for the sake of one another (Mulholland, 1993).

---

[a] George Kuh's (1996) classic article laid the groundwork for the concept of seamless learning in higher education. He described six practices that can enhance student learning and personal development in and out of the classroom. Curricular and cocurricular as well as away-from-campus experiences are all seen as formative and part of the whole-person development. Although addressing higher education in general, his ideas overlap with the creation of an intentional formative environment for those at the intersection of sexuality and faith.

[b] From survey data, Andrew Marin (2016) notes that LGB+ persons who would like to return to a faith community are asking for time and patience to learn how to live collectively—even when in disagreement. From his analysis of the data he advocates for time to listen to the stories that are present in community and the time "to sort through the gray areas of life" with persons who love them (p. 81).

in a seamless curricular and cocurricular setting. Why might this help students to understand from the very beginning that the mission of the educational community is a relational one? Jonah, a gay junior, reported, "If students aren't out, they can't be their true selves. So I think it's definitely harder for other students to really get to know them. . . . Because the first part of the freshman year like I think everybody's projecting their own persona because everybody is new and they want to be cool. . . . People in general don't get that close in the beginning." James, a straight graduate student with same-sex attraction, agreed that he could not reveal his own sexual experiences early in his college years. "I still do feel in a sense [the pressure to be straight], but it was more in my earlier years in college. . . . Up until my junior or senior year, I hadn't told anyone. I didn't want anyone to find out. I had friends, but at the same time, I hadn't known them, especially my freshman year, for that long. I wanted to wait and build a friendship before I told anybody."

From the very beginning of the student experience, an intentional approach might cast a vision for what life together looks like in a relational academic community. Could residence halls, as well as online classroom social media, be seen as intentional educational space that concentrates on relational skill development? We wonder whether liberal arts general-education requirements could intentionally grow to cultivate certain relational skills while also emphasizing a way of thinking Christianly.[6] What if Christian colleges and universities set as an institutional outcome the goal of "turning out" whole persons who have grown skills for assertively engaging culture with intentionality, civility, and mature love? An intentional school culture, as we are defining it, could then be a place to practice and even assess such skills among other relational learners in and out of the classroom. At the institutional level, colleges and universities grow trust by encouraging and rewarding those persons and processes that foster this kind of development, health, and learning, while those persons and processes that fail to foster such goals are not rewarded and could be actively discouraged (Scully & Rowe,

---

[6]James K. A. Smith (2009) speaks forcefully to this issue in Christian education. He states in his opening paragraphs of his book: "What if education, including higher education, is not primarily about the absorption of information or ideas, but about the formation of hearts and desires? . . . What if education was primarily concerned with shaping our hopes and passions— our visions of the 'good life'—and not merely about the dissemination of data and information as inputs to our thinking? What if the primary work of education was about the transforming of our imagination rather than the saturation of our intellect? And what if this had as much to do with our bodies as with our minds? What if education wasn't first and foremost about what we know, but what we love?" (p. 18).

2009). It is this transparent process of connecting to certain communal actions and separating from others that models for students how to hold diverse statuses, such as same-sex attraction.

One area of current research that seems particularly promising to relational skill development in Christian liberal arts involves cultural humility. This relational skill is defined as "the ability to maintain an interpersonal stance that is other-oriented (or open to the other) in relation to aspects of cultural identity that are most important to the [person]" (Hook, Davis, Owen, Worthington, & Utsey, 2013, p. 2). More than simply an understanding or awareness of other perspectives, cultural humility seems to reflect a kind of valuing of another person, no matter the perspective they might hold. As such, this skill combines the capacity for openness to others with the willingness to participate in self-examination.[7] This combination certainly speaks to one of the major issues of interviewees. They wonder whether it might be possible for their sexual diversity to have value for others within a learning and developing community. Through self-examination, could it be that the larger culture on campus might learn something from those who are living at this intersection of sexual identity and religious/spiritual identity? Is it possible that the presence of Christian sexual minorities on campus might be seen as an essential cultural voice for the mission of Christian education as well as personal development? In the long run, interviewees often are hoping for a higher-education experience in which they contribute to the community.

ENVISIONING INTENTIONAL COMMUNITY

How might faith-based institutions model their relational vision for an institutional culture that encourages the development of whole persons? Let's turn back to our interviews for practices that our students have seen or would like to see. We did not ask specifically about intentional practices in our interviews, but they did come up spontaneously among answers to other queries about campus climate and relationships with faculty, staff, and students.

Overwhelmingly, open and respectful conversations at the micro and the macro levels of the institution were the primary signal for interviewed students of a culture for development and growth. In public presentations and in

---

[7]In medical education, Tervalon and Murray-Garcia (1998) suggest that cultural humility is characterized by three factors. First is a lifelong commitment to self-evaluation and self-critique. Second is the desire to address power imbalances so that each person is valued. Third is the willingness to work with others to advocate for the less fortunate in larger systems.

private dialogues, students tended to find their campuses most trustworthy and securing when sexuality was not overlooked or ignored. They were affirmed as persons of worth and children of God when they were noticed and heard by others. Debates were not ruled out of growthful moments, but those interactions appeared to be gauged as much on the emotional/relational tenor as the intellectual outcome. It was not unusual for those interviewed to note how quickly theological engagements could become polarizing and, even worse, adversarial.

This may be one reason why classroom discussions about same-sex attraction and the LGB+ community appeared to be so complicated for a number of our interviewed students. A lecture-based theological or psychological presentation, for example, that failed to capture the emotional/relational engagement of the subject ran the risk of sounding authoritarian and not authoritative. The result was an interaction that was more easily judged unsympathetic and offensive by sexual-minority students. This was especially

INTENTIONALLY SECURE

Community members will be intentional about codesigning a culture of security for self and others.

The third characteristic of an intentional culture involves working together for the security of all. This kind of intentional culture recognizes that formation is hindered when safety is not apparent. Learning requires a holding environment that optimizes the conditions for secure attachments and addresses those practices and policies that jeopardize this quality of relating. Speaking from an attachment-based perspective, security is enhanced when persons can easily find "safe havens" and "secure bases" (Mikulincer & Shaver, 2007) in the relational world of the institution. Paying attention to attachment security means being acutely aware of what causes fear for students, faculty, staff, administrators, and other constituents while also making relational space to address the fear. When it comes to the particular intersection of sexuality and faith, there are unique fears at each level of the community. Students, faculty, administrators, constituents—all those levels in the community can be characterized by the unique ways that they manage fear. We believe that a healthy learning environment requires the reduction of fear-based relating by training all levels of the community in practices that promote security in residence halls, in the classroom, in chapel, and in administrative offices.

true for a few of our students when their professor did not seem to recognize that sexual minorities might be present in the discussion or appeared to ignore the relational impact of the presentation. For example, Matthew, a straight male with same-sex attraction, recounted an interaction in one of his classes. He reported on a classroom conversation in which his professor participated:

> I asked a question one time that was something along the line of "What would you do if your teenage daughter came out as a lesbian and you are a pastor?" I posed the question because the majority of the class was going to be youth pastors one day. And a lot of them actually said, "I would send her to therapy until she learned otherwise." "I would send her to therapy until she can correct her character." "I wouldn't let her spend the night with girls because I don't want her to be a bad influence on their Christian morals."

On the other hand, students commented favorably when administrators, faculty, and staff intentionally acknowledged and affirmed the value of diversity on campus. It suggested a welcome departure from the assumption that interviewed students frequently perceive that all on campus are straight and stereotypically masculine or feminine. For these moments in community, students feel noticed in an inclusive way. As opposed to a "don't ask, don't tell" approach to those who are different to one degree or another, most interviewed students responded positively when sexual minorities were singled out among the diverse groups in a way that suggested that they were wanted and loved by God and the community. An intentional stance of this sort might be the basis for the moderately high percentage of students who say they could still embrace a Christian institution that maintains community policies with which that they might personally disagree. We wonder whether there might be something developmentally enriching when sexual-minority students learn to embrace a community of fellow believers who return their embrace with such honesty that points of disagreement might seem less disruptive. In this aspect of affirmative culture, we could potentially see a formative process for learning to hold sexuality and religion/spirituality as a community and eventually as a person. It just might trickle down.

Another intentional gesture for students was apparently when colleges and universities created relational space that was officially sanctioned and institutionally supported. As was mentioned in the discussion of campus resources, interviewed students noted counseling centers, community events, and more confidential student gatherings as potentially helpful in their experience. Such events and services appeared to be recognizable indications that the macro level of the institution was serious about the microlevel needs of more diverse groups. Even though institutional policies might establish debated community-wide behavioral boundaries, forums and support groups could be secure structures for exploring new ideas and old commitments. The presence of these student services seemed to make an affirming statement to sexual-minority students—especially when the approach was not an indoctrinating one. Students seemed to find counseling centers, community events, and confidential gatherings most beneficial when they were deemed a safe relational space to decide what they believed. They apparently valued holding environments where support and challenge were relationally lived out by trustworthy institutional agents. In such contexts, counselors, faculty, and campus ministers stood out when they were approachable, knowledgeable, and patient with the formative process.

Cultivating a climate that is intentional and provides a secure base for students to navigate questions about faith and sexual identity requires greater relational cultural competence. We believe that Christians have to be able to see the entire landscape, which includes the ways in which various stakeholders approach the topic and experience of sexual-minority students. These approaches are undoubtedly informed by what has emerged as a growing and vibrant gay community. Recognizing the reality of this community and developing competencies for engaging with it is critical. Interviewed students wanted diverse identity issues to be better understood by persons at Christian colleges and universities, but not as much for the sake of knowing all there is to know about LGB+ issues as for the sake of knowing how to love well. They apparently wanted persons, both peer and professional, who have not only reflected on the topic of same-sex attraction but have also considered how their own behaviors impact this aspect of diversity in relational community. The bottom line is that these students wanted to be known—accurately and deeply, not stereotypically or superficially. Most want the reality of sexual-identity experiences to be known in campus awareness and decision making. They want to experience a community that has sexual minorities on their collective mind in a way that communicates that their schools "have their back."

Interviewed students identified cultural competency as being primary for the kind of training that is essential for all levels of the institution to grow in understanding. According to the students, administrators, faculty, and even alumni and donors all make the list for those who need training to live intentionally in community. But when we listen to the voices of students in our study, it is their peers that are most noted for increased cultural proficiency—both cultural competency and cultural humility (see Tervalon & Murray-Garcia, 1998, for this distinction). Fellow students, particularly underclass students, were the most recognized source of microinequities. Logan, a gay junior, reported this sentiment: "There are some students who just get it completely wrong and seem totally clueless. And I just want to ask them, 'Have you ever talked to a gay person because you don't even . . .' yeah, so I guess other students just don't really know any gay people. They don't mean to be offensive, but they have these convictions. They care, but they don't really know how."

Maureen Scully and Mary Rowe (2009) suggest "bystander training" as a way to address the gap we find between faculty and staff, who appear to be showing improvement across our studies (Dean, Stratton, Yarhouse, Lastoria, & Bucher, 2016), and peers, who remain the most problematic sector for microinequities. As in other organizations, bystander training can teach students to function as "active" relational agents who can be aware in the moment of those exchanges that contribute to a trustworthy environment or those that threaten security. A few students noted positively that trainings of this type were happening to some degree in freshman orientation and in resident-assistant training at their institutions. Bystander training is not intended to promote informants of community-standards violations or policy infractions. Such actions are more motivated by and serve the macro level and as such often feel protective of the institution, which needs power to manage community members. Instead, the aim of this relational skill training is to educate students in curricular and cocurricular settings to do life together at the micro level of their academic community. We see the short-term and long-term benefits of teaching and assessing relational skills that enhance student capacities to understand self and other, while increasing the potential for purposeful microaffirmations and decreasing the possibility of microaggressions (Scully & Rowe, 2009).

In chapter one we introduced three contrasting frameworks that function as lenses through which people interpret data, interact with this topic, and offer suggestions for resolving felt tensions in faith communities. The integrity lens focuses on the integrity of male/female differences as part of God's creational intent. These differences lay a foundation for what is understood to be morally permissible and morally impermissible. In other words, a biblical sexual ethic is reflected in the bringing together of one male and one female in the context of marriage. There is a high view of creation from advocates of this lens.

The disability lens views same-sex sexuality as an expected variation that occurs in nature. It is a nonmoral reality to be addressed with compassion. Christians drawn to this lens view nature as touched by the fall and would be sympathetic to the view that while same-sex sexuality is "not the way it's supposed to be," it reflects experiences that we should empathize with and respond to out of a place of compassion.

The diversity lens sees same-sex sexuality as indicative of a type of person, a lesbian, gay, or bisexual type of person. The assumption is that healthy personhood is related to expressing oneself and meeting needs for intimacy in same-sex sexual relationships. The diversity lens sees the gay community as providing answers to questions of identity and community. From this framework, LGB+ persons are part of a people group to be celebrated.

The starting point for cultural competence is for Christians to recognize the various frameworks or lenses through which different people understand this topic. These frameworks function as lenses for seeing and interpreting research findings, seeing one another, reading and applying Scripture, developing policy, and so on. There is no doubt that the broader culture has witnessed the emergence of a gay community as a culture to be celebrated. Our students are navigating their faith and sexuality in that societal milieu. It is a matter of cultural competence to recognize the societal context and the messages that create narratives and storylines of meaning and purpose for sexuality, sexual identity, and sexual expression.

As Christians institutions consider which lenses inform their doctrinal positions, it will be helpful to offer clarity in teaching and doctrine, a kind of "convicted civility," to quote Richard Mouw (2009), but a convicted civility that is also flavored with compassion. We see this as a way of sharing what one believes based on a clearer and better-understood foundation for those beliefs. We see this as informed by integrating aspects of these lenses and forming relationships with others, including those who adhere to competing lenses, which involves taking the time to understand how they arrived at their lens and how it informs how they view you and your institution. This fosters the kind of relationship that then allows you to best explain the lens or lenses through which you approach these same issues.

Part of what complicates the discussions about sexuality is whether and how those discussions are tied to social justice. Indeed, the topic of sexual identity has been considered the social-justice issue of this generation. Any attempt to foster an intentional climate and a secure base for navigating faith and sexual identity has to come to terms with this. That LGB+ concerns are the social-justice issue of this generation was particularly salient in efforts that eventually won federal recognition of gay marriage. While only a relatively small percentage of gay people at present enter into marriage (about 10%), it was what marriage symbolized to the gay community, which was marriage equality. In other words, to the mainstream LGB+ community, it was a matter of social justice.

Conservatives have often responded to the social-justice dimension by reducing and dismissing this area as nothing more than "identity politics" or the forming of identity around sexual impulses for the purposes of advancing a larger, liberal social agenda. This is an insufficiently nuanced response to a complex topic.

We ask Christian colleges and other Christian institutions to offer thoughtful reflection on sexuality and sexual identity, and how these relate to matters of social justice. When conflated, these matters should be carefully disentangled. When they are related, say, in matters of safety for those who might be harassed or demeaned, then Christians should explain how their core commitments lead them to social-justice considerations that extend to one area but may not extend to all areas that proponents of a social justice message would pursue. We don't think most of our students fully understand how these are to be related and practiced as Christians.

With clarity in teaching and doctrine, and with a more nuanced understanding of how this topic is (and is not) related to social justice, an institution can develop policy. We urge Christian institutions to develop policies and procedures that are consistent and rooted in teachings and doctrine that have been thought through. What we find most challenging for many sexual minorities is when policies are not applied consistently or when they are done in a lockstep manner, when they function as a template that is simply dropped on a student. Rather, Christian institutions are at their best when the policies are introduced, discussed, processed, and even enforced out of a genuine relationship with students. It is the relational application that is critical here.

Looking back, Adriana, a senior who identifies as bisexual, reported on her more salient memories about how being in relationship affected her life with professors and administrators:

By the time I was a sophomore or junior I was pretty much out to my entire friend group. That was fun (laughing). Felt very welcome. I always felt very secure in my identity as a disciple of Christ. Never was made to feel like there was something wrong with me, never made to feel like I was a freak. Actually, those feelings were pretty much eradicated by my time at [this institution]. . . . It wasn't until my senior year that I came out to a few professors with mostly positive results. They knew me before. I had longstanding relationships with them, so I would say overly positive. But I think it was because . . . I stayed out of the spotlight. . . . There are other members of the college, other gay members of the college who are very loud about their identity and very up-front. They routinely go toe to toe with the administration, and they would say differently. They would say that their experience has been hostile, and they felt rejected. . . . I think in general because I kept it within my personal relationships and a few professors who I trusted, everybody was a reasonable human being. . . . I think that I grew in my ability to be okay with myself and my identity with it while I was at [my institution].

We recognize that the way that an institution responds at the macro level will be a singular voice. The macro level proclaims this is what this community believes. Regretfully, that makes macro statements feel power based, even when they are not meant to be. To speak and be understood and trusted at the macro level requires that the micro level be so vital and strong that it provides a more nuanced perspective to the often uncompromising macro level. This is what makes the micro level so much more important in the lives of the students we have been listening to. Even their collective voices are often emphasizing the micro above the macro—almost as if they are saying that they can live with the macro differences if the day-to-day relational process is open, honest, and engaged respectfully. We think that the micro level is where we can engage the search for the relationship between religious identity and sexual identity, even when it takes alternative paths. Disagreements can be managed at the micro level much better than the macro level. The macro level can only make space for the search for identity, and we see that as part of what an educational institution does. It provides secure space for learners to learn—to think critically, to try on and try out, to encounter new and different. When the search for identity and the relationship between faith and same-sex sexuality varies too much from how community is defined at the macro level, there

INTENTIONALLY TRINITARIAN

Theologically, we believe that a community that intentionally values encouraging relationality, formative process, and secure holding environments is inherently trinitarian. We see the Trinity as a social and relational understanding of God that instructs, inspires, and empowers the mission of Christian liberal arts colleges and universities. A trinitarian community is one that models a perichoretic balance of communal love.[a] The mutual indwelling of the three divine Persons depicts relations in which persons give themselves completely to one another without forfeiting uniqueness. We see a community in which persons can limit themselves and make space for others to be present without disengagement. Intentional love is revealed in a dance of self-giving and self-limiting movement. In terms of human personhood, it demonstrates a dynamic balance of relational boundaries where self can be asserted for the sake of another and self can be denied for the sake of another (Stratton, 2003). Human development in the image of the Trinity is always self-development for the sake of the other. A culture intentionally constructed on this theological foundation is a relational one where persons are uniquely formed in the support and challenge of seamless community life. We believe it is an identity-incubating culture in which persons-in-relationship intentionally hold one another until those community members know how to hold themselves.

[a] Catherine LaCugna (1993) described the eighth-century Greek term *perichorēsis* as referencing the way that the three divine Persons, each "dynamic and vital" in their own character, "mutually inhere in one another, draw life from one another, 'are' what they are by relation to one another" (pp. 270-71). The late Stanley Grenz (2001) suggested that it is on this theological foundation that we glimpse personhood, both divine and human, as "consisting of mutuality and interdependence" (p. 317).

has to be open and honest discussion about whether the community is still a good fit for the student or whether the student is still a good fit for the community. Our hope is that the micro is so well founded at those times when paths diverge that these tough-love engagements are still relational ones, not as easily perceived as simply a power play.

Our interviewed students helped us understand what they saw as a significant obstacle to increased vitality in relationship at the micro level. They described their perception that the macrolevel vision eventually interfered with microlevel mutuality and reciprocity that keep conversation open, authentic, and secure. Michael, a bisexual senior, described the way that the micro and macro levels worked together at his institution. He said, "The college's official statement is that we believe in marriage between a man and a woman. That's the official statement, and that's what [the institution] stands behind. . . . That's their statements, but they don't push to make sure everybody follows that statement." He explained that this approach does have its downfall. Where people are given educational and developmental space at the micro level to decide what they believe, it can be "confusing" when the macrolevel message is proclaimed so broadly. He went on to say, "[Students] hear that [official statement], and every now and then it would come up and they think, 'Oh my gosh, the college won't accept me. They don't state the same thing I believe.' But then again, there isn't a lot of showmanship on campus that shows that statement."

Here we hear of one rather informal way that a college or university has made space for microlevel engagements while holding to a macrolevel policy about marriage. We might critique the unofficial nature of this communal "allowance." Indeed, we know that some in college and university settings might appreciate a more explicit policy that eliminates the tension between macrolevel doctrinal statements and microlevel variations of belief. Yet, we believe that this tension is exactly the kind of liminal environment that Christian liberal arts promises—where beliefs can be "tried out" in a relational educational space. For Michael, it seemed part of the expected give and take of living in community with people who do not always agree. Interviewed students appeared to realize that faculty, staff, and administrators are not monolithic in their views but are working to find ways to exist together in Christian academic communities with macrolevel declarations. In fact, students appeared to be very interested in how community models lived out this process.

Being intentional means that a community can be both supportive and challenging in the context of secure relational connections. At the micro level, community members can find a way to be both supportive and challenging in a manner that promotes development and models a relational application for the world beyond Christian higher education. Another student, Justin, a gay junior, noted how this kind of Christian campus culture might look—where different offices or services may intentionally engage in ways that are more supportive or challenging. He seemed to note in the quote that follows that all can play a role in Christian higher education, where the macro level makes secure space for microlevel relational engagements, even among differing campus resources.

Residence life has been . . . very proactive about being a welcoming community and having broader campus dialogues about these issues, which have been like fantastic from my perspective. Like I remember when we had . . . two transgendered students on campus, and they were intentional about figuring out housing and how to work with that. And Student Life has done a very good job about having a conversation about both sides, like procelibacy or promarriage. And then within campus ministries, they're very positive . . . toward celibacy because that's what [the institution's] official policy is, but I would say that's the only office that does that. I think more because that's kind of their job. But the other offices say we want to support and help you and figure out what you believe and what you think.

To cultivate an intentional campus culture with a secure base, we encourage Christian institutions to plan for heterogeneity among students. There is no single story of being a sexual minority at a Christian college. There are more traditional students for whom this is a sincere struggle of sexuality and faith (sincere strugglers). There are less traditional students who have been outspoken about policies they view as discriminatory or hurtful (assertive advocates). There are students who are wrestling with these topics and at this time may disagree with some aspects of campus life but hold their opinion close to the chest (compliant dissenters). Even these three categories do not exhaust the experiences of sexual minorities at Christian colleges. But plan for heterogeneity—in students but also among faculty and staff. Even on campuses where covenants are used or ethos statements are signed, we are finding greater variety of beliefs among faculty and staff in recent years.

Consider places for students to learn and ask questions about sexual identity and faith. It would be a mistake to assume that because an institution doesn't hold these discussions that the discussions are not taking place. Our students are having these discussions. These discussions are shaped by many forces and may occur with minimal reflection on changing culture and the various frameworks that can be in play. Christian institutions should not shy away from engaging the topic or inviting students to think deeply and well about these issues. The conversations are taking place whether or not a Christian institution is intentional about engaging in them or shaping them.

To take steps toward this kind of campus culture, trust also has to be established at all levels. For an institution to reflect on doctrine and related policies and procedures and to creatively engage students out of a place of increased cultural competence (for what has emerged as a culture in the broader societal context in which these institutions operate) and a posture that is highly relational, as seen among staff and faculty, there has to be trust with the board of trustees down to the resident assistants that there is a message here to care for sexual-minority students in the context of care for all students. It is trust that allows for creative engagement, as most observers of an institution will interpret any event or activity in culture-war categories. Within this framework, it is tempting to view persons or events as either pro-gay or anti-gay. A faculty member is either pro-gay or anti-gay. An administration is either pro-gay or anti-gay. What we hope the reader will see is that these zero-sum categories can be used by those who have a stake in perpetuating the culture wars, but they have little bearing on what most Christian institutions should provide students.

How was it for you to listen to sexual-minority students? What have you heard? How do you respond to the different voices and experiences you have read about? We want to encourage you to think creatively about how you might extend and apply some of what you've heard to other contexts and settings. Perhaps what happens at Christian colleges can be thought of as a microcosm (of sorts) of ways to relate that can inform the church body more broadly.

In our view, it is worth considering whether the needs of sexual-minority students in Christian higher education are best met with a whole-person approach that is reflected in an intentional campus culture. There may be benefits to distinguishing macrolevel institutional positions and microlevel engagement with students and how these are related to foster trust and goodwill. To be intentional in this context includes identifying concrete and specific ways to bear witness to one another's experiences and to come alongside students while also providing them with a thoughtful, nuanced Christian understanding and a secure base for navigating the difficult terrain of sexual-identity development and religious faith as followers of Christ.

CHAPTER 8 TAKEAWAYS

1. In addition to providing a summary of the main findings from the longitudinal study, this chapter included advice that students would offer their own institutions. Interestingly, we did not identify a push to change theology or doctrine, which could be related to their own beliefs or to more realistic outcomes. Either way, such changes were not a focus of these students.

2. Students gave advice to other sexual-minority students like themselves. They tended to focus on relational considerations. We discussed these in terms of relationships with others (other students on campus, which is complicated), relationship with themselves (self-care), and relationship with God.

3. What students did suggest, in terms of advice to Christian institutions, included a desire for more dialogue, more openness, more groups for facilitating support, and more visible examples of staff and/or faculty who are navigating sexual identity and faith.

4. We concluded with specific suggestions for how campuses can be more intentional in their response to students navigating sexual identity and faith. Interviewed students appeared more concerned with the micro-level relational process than the macrolevel institutional positions. Not that they were uninterested in doctrinal statements, but when it came to advice for their schools, they emphasized life together. They focused on how to more effectively facilitate a holding environment where they can be held while watching models of effective holding.

5. From listening to sexual-minority students across our studies, we discerned a call for a Christian higher-education culture that affirms whole-person formation for all students but particularly those at the intersection of sexuality and religion/spirituality. We believe that reaffirmation of a Christian liberal arts vision in a seamless learning community lays the most promising relational foundation for the development of a viable narrative for holding faith and sexuality.

▼

REFERENCES

Asher, L. (2017, February 5). Your students crave moral simplicity. Resist. *The Chronicle of Higher Education*. Retrieved from www.chronicle.com/article/Your-Students-Crave-Moral/239075

Bonhoeffer, D. (1954). *Life together: A discussion of Christian fellowship*. New York: Harper & Row.

Cozolino, L. (2013). *The social neuroscience of education: Optimizing attachment and learning in the classroom*. New York: Norton.

Crouch, A. (2013). *Culture making: Recovering our creative calling*. Downers Grove, IL: InterVarsity Press.

Dean, J., Stratton, S., Yarhouse, M. A., Lastoria, M., & Bucher, E. (2016, March). Listening to sexual minorities across time and location. Presentation at the Christian Association for Psychological Studies National Conference, Pasadena, CA.

Donnelly-Smith, L. (2011). What adult learners can teach us about all learners: A conversation with L. Lee Knefelkamp. *Peer Review, 13*(1). Retrieved from www.aacu .org/publications-research/periodicals/what-adult-learners-can-teach-us-about -all-learners-conversation-1

Grenz, S. J. (2001). *The social God and the relational self: A trinitarian theology of the imago Dei*. Louisville, KY: Westminster John Knox.

Hook, J. N., Davis, D. E., Owen, J., Worthington, E. L., Jr., & Utsey, S. O. (2013, July). Cultural humility: Measuring openness to culturally diverse clients. *Journal of Counseling Psychology, 60*(3), 353-66. https://doi.org/10.1037/a0032595

Jones, S. L., & Yarhouse, M. A. (2012). Sexual orientation and skin color: Deconstructing key assumptions in the debates about gay marriage and the church. In R. E. Gane, N. P. Miller, & H. P. Swanson (Eds.), *Homosexuality, marriage, and the church* (pp. 413-38). Berrien Springs, MI: Andrews University Press.

Kegan, R. (1994). *In over our heads: The mental demands of modern life*. Cambridge, MA: Harvard University Press.

Kim, P. Y. (2017). Religious support mediates racial microaggressions-mental health relations among Christian ethnic minority students. *Psychology of Religion and Spirituality, 9*(2), 158-64.

Kuh, G. D. (1996). Guiding principles for creating seamless learning environments for undergraduates. *Journal of College Student Development, 37*(2), 135-48.

LaCugna, C. M. (1993). *God for us: The Trinity and Christian life*. New York: Harper-Collins.

Marcia, J. E. (1980). Identity in adolescence. In J. Adelson (Ed.), *Handbook of adolescent psychology* (pp. 159-87). New York: Wiley and Sons.

Marin, A. (2016). *Us versus us: The untold story of religion and the LGBT community*. Carol Stream, IL: NavPress.

Mikulincer, M., & Shaver, P. R. (2007). *Attachment in adulthood: Structure, dynamics, and change*. New York: Guilford.

Mouw, R. (2009). *Uncommon decency: Christian civility in an uncivil world*. Downers Grove, IL: InterVarsity Press.

Mulholland, M. R. (1993). *An invitation to a journey: A road map for spiritual formation*. Downers Grove, IL: InterVarsity Press.

Palmer, P. J. (1993). *To know as we are known: Education as a spiritual journey*. San Francisco: HarperCollins.

Rokeach, M. (1973). *The nature of human values*. New York: Free Press.

Rowe, M. (2008). Micro-affirmations & micro-inequities. *Journal of International Ombudsman Association, 1*(1), 45-48.

Scully, M., & Rowe, M. (2009). Bystanding training within organizations. *Journal of International Ombudsman Association, 2*(1), 89-95.

Smith, J. K. A. (2009). *Desiring the kingdom: Worship, worldview, and cultural formation.* Grand Rapids, MI: Baker Academic.

Stratton, S. P. (2003). Trinity, attachment, and love. *Catalyst, 29*(4), 1-3. Retrieved from www.catalystresources.org/trinity-attachment-self

Tervalon, M., & Murray-Garcia, J. (1998). Cultural humility versus cultural competence: A critical distinction in defining physician training outcomes in multicultural education. *Journal of Health Care for the Poor and Underserved, 9*(2), 117-25. https://doi.org/10.1353/hpu.2010.0233

Wells, C. A. (2016). A distinctive vision for the liberal arts: General education and the flourishing of Christian higher education. *Christian Higher Education, 15*(1-2), 84-94.

Wolff, J. R., & Cunningham, J. (2017). Comparing sexual minority student mental health in faith-based colleges versus nonfaith-based colleges. Paper presented at the 2017 American Psychological Association Convention as part of the symposium Sexual Minority Experiences in Faith-Based Higher Education.

Wolff, J. R., Himes, H. L., Soares, S. D., & Kwon, E. M. (2016). Sexual minority students in non-affirming religious higher education: Mental health, outness, and identity. *Psychology of Sexual Orientation and Gender Diversity, 3*(2), 201-12.

AUTHOR INDEX

Adams, M., 14, 17, 194
Althof, S. E., 61
American Psychological Association, 90, 146, 161
Americans United for the Separation of Church and State, 162
Andrews, E., 9
Arnett, J. J., 29, 174, 237
Asher, L., 293, 295
Association for Christians in Student Development, 49
Atkinson, A., 24
Aunona, F. M., 55
Austin, A., 14, 17, 194
Baldwin, S., 178
Banchoff, T., 176
Barna, G., 40, 141
Barnes, D. M., 163-64, 244
Bauermeister, J. A., 176
Bearinger, L. H., 148
Beckstead, A. L., 70
Belgau, R., 71
Bish, G. T., 76
Bleakley, A., 176
Blum, R. W., 148
Bockting, W. O., 164
Bodenner, C., 241
Boehmer, U., 210
Bolak-Boratov, H., 92
Bolton, R., 211
Bonhoeffer, D., 291
Boone, T. L., 34
Boorstein, M., 130
Bradford, J., 42
Brannock, J. C., 62, 64
Braun, L., 65, 74
Brebels, L., 244
Bridges Across the Divide, 34, 120

Brinkerhoff, M. B., 252
Brodish, P. H., 41
Brooke, H. L., 15, 67
Bryant, A. N., 175
Bucher, E. K., 16, 175, 302
Burke, A., 42
Büssing, A., 167
Campus Pride, 188, 259
Cass, V. C., 62, 64-65
Castonguay, L. G., 23
Center for Collegiate Mental Health, 24, 43, 165
Center for the Study of Collegiate Mental Health, 42
Chan, C. S., 63, 65, 130
Chapman, B. E., 62, 64
Choi, J. Y., 175
Cohen, K. M., 66
Coleman, E., 62, 164
Comer Wright, M. L., 156, 159
Cornelis, I., 244
Cox, D., 176
Cozolino, L., 291
Craig, S. L., 14, 17, 194
Creswell, J. W., 12
Crouch, A., 296
Cruz, E., 196
Cunningham, J., 175, 278
Damian, C., 107
Danner, F., 31
Davis, D. E., 298
de Visser, R. O., 53
Dean, J. B., 15-16, 36, 39, 67, 88, 91, 97, 150, 302
Decco, E., 32
Deluty, R. H., 211
Demetriou, C., 205
Diamond, L. M., 11, 32, 41, 65-66, 74, 79, 92, 237-38,

247
Diaz, R. M., 164, 211
Dillon, F. R., 76
Ding, K., 42
Donnelly-Smith, L., 291
Doolin, H., 24
Dube, E. M., 66
Dunn, D., 9
Eliason, M. J., 76, 92
Entwistle, D. N., 175
Farhat, T., 41
Fassinger, R., 63-64
Ferguson, A. D., 82
Fishbein, M., 156, 161
Fisher, A., 205
Ford, C. A., 41
Fox, R., 63
Freire, C., 46
Freitas, D., 50
Fukuyama, M. A., 82
Gabhainn, S. N., 41
Gagnon, R. A. J., 9
Gale, C. R., 210
Garcia, K., 104
Garzon, F. L., 175
Gillen, M. M., 34
Godeau, E., 41
Gonnerman, J., 103
Gould, M. S., 209
Graves, J., 175
Greenberg, T. E. D., 209
Grenz, S. J., 306
Grzanka, P. R., 35
Hall, M. E. L., 175
Hallfors, D. D., 41
Halpern, C. T., 41
Hamilton, A., 164
Hanjorgiris, W. F., 62
Haslam, N., 53
Hathaway, W., 175

Hatzenbuehler, M. L., 165
Hayes, J. A., 23
HeartStrong, 17, 194
Hennessy, M., 156, 161
Henriques, G., 47
Hess, S. A., 114
High, K., 24
Hill, C. E., 114
Hill, W., 106, 150, 155, 227-28
Himes, H. L., 51, 108-9, 200, 278
Hinrichs, D. W., 34
Holt, R., 24
Homma, Y., 148
Hong, J. S., 48
Hook, J. N., 298
Houp, D., 132
Hout, M., 29-30
Hubbard, K., 53
Hudalla, J., 189, 259
Huebner, D., 164, 211
Hull, S. J., 156, 161
Hunter, J., 65, 74, 112
Ikramullah, E., 161
Iritani, B., 41
Jackson, E. A., 175
Jensen, L. A., 174
Jones, R. C., 176
Jones, S. L., 24, 64, 290
Jordan, A., 156, 161
Jordan, K. M., 211
Kaplan, R. L., 55
Karama, R., 55
Kast, C., 47
Kaufman, M., 148
Kegan, R., 287, 292
Keleher, A., 32
Kerr, D., 42
Keyes, C., 24, 46
Keyes, S., 210
Khouric, D., 55
Kim, P. Y., 290
Kinnaman, D., 40, 41, 176
Kinsey, C., 88
Kitzinger, C., 92
Knight, K., 106
Knox, S., 114
Koenig, H. G., 23, 140, 162, 165, 167
Konik, J., 92
Kossowska, M., 244
Krull, D. S., 147

Kuh, D. L., 210
Kuh, G. D., 296
Kulick, A., 48
Kuriloff, P. J., 244
Kurtzleben, D., 263
Kwon, E. M., 51, 108-9, 200, 278
LaCugna, C. M., 306
Larson, D. B., 165
Lastoria, M., 15-16, 36, 39, 67, 76, 88, 91, 97, 150, 302
Lauman, E., 18
Lee, J. J., 176
Lefkowitz, E. S., 34, 178
Lei, P.-W. 23
Levy, S. R., 53
Li, H., 23
Liddle, B. J., 169
Lin, Y.-C., 23
Lindsey, 107-8
Locke, B. D., 23-24
Logan, C., 161
Lottes, I. L., 244
Lyons, G., 40
Mackie, M. M., 252
Madkour, A. S., 41
Mahoney, E. R., 155, 156
Mangis, M. W., 175
Manlove, J., 161
Marcia, J. E., 82, 294
María Del Mar Ferradás, M., 46
Marin, A., 164, 263, 296
Martin, C. E., 88
Masci, D., 29
Maslowe, K. E., 72
Masters, K. S., 142, 162
McAleavey, A. A., 23
McCarn, S., 63-64
McCullough, M. E., 165
McDonald, G. J., 62, 79
Meador, K. G., 23, 140
Meanley, S., 169
Meier, A. M., 41
Mereish, E. H., 42
Meyer, I. H., 163-64, 244
Mikulincer, M., 299
Miles, J. R., 35
Miner, M. H., 164
Mishra, G., 210
Mitchell, M. 11
Mokhbatc, J., 55
Moore, K. A., 160

Moore, M., 103
Morgan, E. M., 76-77, 92-93
Morgan, T., 132
Morris, A., 164
Mouw, R., 303
mtvU-JED Foundation, 210
Mulholland, M. R., 296
Murphy, C., 247
Murray-Garcia, J., 298, 302
Nowacki, S. K., 9
Núñez, J. C., 46
O'Cleirighb, C., 42
Olson, R. E., 94
O'Neil, L., 164
Ott-Walter, K., 42
Owen, J., 298
Pachankis, J. E., 165
Page, C., 10
Palmer, P. J., 287
Park, C. L., 165
Parkerson, G., 23, 140
Pargament, K. I., 165
Perez, L., 165
Pew Research Center, 143, 145
Pingel, E. S., 169
Pomeroy, W. B., 88
Poon, C., 148
Powell, C., 205
Rainer, J. W., 139
Rainer, T. S., 139
Randall, B. A., 156, 160
Ransom, M. R., 47
Rashidi, M., 14, 17, 194
Ream, G. L., 54, 210
Regnerus, M. D., 156, 251-52
Reiter, L., 90
Resnick, M. D., 148
Rettner, R., 162
Reynolds, A. L., 62
Richards, M., 210
Riggle, E. D. B., 31
Ripley, J. S., 175
Ritter, K. Y., 31
Rodgers, J., 149, 227
Roets, A., 244
Rokeach, M., 293
Rosario, M., 65, 74, 112
Rosenberg, P. J., 34
Rostosky, S. S., 31, 156, 160
Rothman, E. F., 210
Rowe, M., 204-7, 288-89, 297, 302

Ryan, C., 164, 211
Ryff, C. D., 24, 45-46
Sadusky, J., 132, 175
Saewyc, E. M., 148
Sample, I., 145
Sanchez, J., 164, 211
Sandomirsky, S., 252
Savin-Williams, R. C., 41, 66, 210
Savoy, H. B., 76
Schrimshaw, E. W., 65, 74, 112
Schuck, K. D., 169
Schwartz, S., 231
Scully, M., 297, 302
Shaffer, D., 209
Shaver, P. R., 299
Shearer, C. L., 34
Shelly, R. K., 47
Sides, J., 10
Siggins, D., 10
Simon, C. J., 8
Sinco, B. R., 48
Singer, B., 45
Smith, A., 148
Smith, B., 165
Smith, C., 121
Smith, E. R. A. N., 32
Smith, J. K. A., 312
Smith, P., 10
Soares, S. D., 51, 108-9, 200, 278
Sophie, J., 62, 65, 79
Spaulding, E. C., 79
Spriggs, A. L., 41

Sprinkle, P., 94
Stafford, M., 210
Stallard, B., 177
Steffen, P. R., 162
Stegeman, G. T., 210
Stewart, A., 92
Stoppa, T. M., 178
Stratton, S. P., 15-17, 29, 36, 39, 67, 70, 88, 91, 97, 150, 302, 306
Suarez, E. C., 69
Sullivan, M., 210
Sullivan, P., 76
Summay, W., 172-73
Swinburne, R., 164
Symons, C. S., 76
Tan, E. S. N., 9, 66, 74, 97-98
Tan, P. P., 167
Tate, R., 23
Terndrup, A. I., 31
Tervalon, M., 298, 302
Teylan, M., 231
Thompson, B. J., 114
Thompson, E. M., 76
Tohmec, J., 55
Troiden, R. R., 62, 64
Tulloch, T., 148
Tushnet, E., 108
Uecker, J. E., 251-52
Utsey, S. O., 298
Vaaler, M. L., 251-52
Valle, A., 46
Vallejo, G., 46
Van Hiel, A., 244

Velting, D. M., 209
Vernaglia, E. R., 76
Vincke, J., 211
Wagnera, G. J., 55
Waller, M. W., 41
Wang, N., 148
Weber, J., 191
Wells, C. A., 293-94
Wentz, J. M., 12-13, 27-28, 200, 226-27
Wessel, R. D., 12-13, 27-28, 200, 226-27
Wheeler, D. R., 10, 13-14, 194, 198
Wilcox, B. L., 156, 160
Wilkinson, S., 92
Williams, E. N., 114
Wilson, J., 252
Wolff, J. R., 14, 51, 108-9, 165, 200, 278
Wolkomir, M., 67
Woodford, M. R., 48
Worthington, E. L., Jr., 298
Worthington, R. L., 76
Yarhouse, M. A., 8-10, 15-17, 23-24, 29, 32, 36, 39, 63-67, 69, 70, 72, 74, 88, 91, 97-98, 150, 290, 302
Yasuno, M., 175
Yuan, C., 43, 80, 253
Zeiders, K. H., 35
Zhao, Y., 23

SUBJECT INDEX

academic community, 2, 291-92, 297, 302, 307

academic concerns, 24, 42, 58-59, 165, 170, 182-83, 222, 224-25, 230, 260, 268-69, 274, 279

academic freedom, 216

academic identity, 222, 292, 294

academic success, 225, 279, 291

administration, 17, 194-96, 215, 222, 227, 235, 281-85, 287-88, 292-96, 299-301, 304-5, 307, 309

advice, 277-78, 280, 288-89

affirmation, 67, 147, 205-7, 278, 289, 299-301, 310

   See also gay-affirming; microaffirmations

affirming. See gay-affirming

age, 18, 29

alcohol use, 24, 42-43, 58-59, 165, 170, 182-83, 252, 260-62, 268-69

   See also substance use

alumni. See graduates

American Psychological Association, 15, 90, 146, 161, 172-73, 278

anger, 26, 43, 72, 224

   See also hostility

anxiety, 24, 42-44, 48, 58-59, 112, 126-27, 162, 165, 170, 182-83, 225, 260, 268-69, 274

Association for Christians in Student Development, 4-5, 15-16, 20, 49, 191-92, 215

attitudes about Christian

colleges, 244

attitudes about same-sex attraction, 17, 24, 217-18, 222-26, 230, 244-49, 257-58, 265-66, 268, 273-74

   campus, 217-18, 222-26, 230, 257, 262, 268, 273-74

   personal, 244-49, 262, 265-66

   workplace, 257-58, 268

attributions, 61-62, 66-68, 70, 78-81, 84-85, 116, 157-58, 180-81

beliefs, religious. See convictions, religious

Bible, 2, 7, 12, 30, 41, 49, 50, 80, 87-88, 94, 106, 110, 118, 121, 124, 137, 140-41, 149-50, 169, 191, 193, 196, 212, 222, 224, 236, 251, 277, 284, 295, 302-3

boxes approach, 111, 113-30, 139, 150, 274, 291

   See also identity development

Bridges Across the Divide Project, 34, 280

campus climate, 5, 14, 26, 28-29, 33, 35, 42, 44-45, 50, 71, 73-74, 109-12, 127-28, 135, 137, 173, 187-88, 195-96, 198, 200-201, 204-5, 207, 229, 235, 243, 253-54, 256, 259, 262, 268, 272, 274, 276, 282, 284, 286, 288, 292, 294, 296, 298, 301, 304

   See also holding environment

campus ministries, 149, 213, 216-18, 220, 227, 230, 234, 273, 279, 301, 308

campus resources, 10-11, 26, 64, 104, 106, 112, 211-21, 234, 273, 279, 300-301, 307

causation. See under sexuality

celibacy, 10, 93-94, 105-8, 149, 152-55, 173, 194, 206, 246, 308

chaplain. See campus ministries

chastity, 64, 163

Christian Association for Psychological Studies, 15

Christian colleges and universities, 10-14, 27-28, 37, 39, 43, 49-51, 67, 74, 76, 110-11, 125-26, 128, 150, 165, 188-91, 193-95, 200-207, 226, 230, 237, 244, 272-80, 287-309

church, 8, 12-13, 23, 30, 40, 49, 65, 87, 94, 104, 108, 119, 123, 139-40, 142, 150, 155, 162-63, 169-71, 173-74, 184, 195-96, 208, 209-10, 219, 226, 228, 230, 244, 251-52, 254-55, 262, 267, 280, 290, 294, 309

church attendance, 30, 40, 139-40, 156, 162-63, 167, 169-71, 173-74, 251, 262

coming out. See disclosure

commitment, religious. See convictions, religious

complexity, 37-38

conversation. See dialogue

conversion-therapy interventions, 138

convicted civility, 303
convictions, religious, 4, 10,
13-14, 18, 23-24, 28, 31,
36-38, 43, 48-49, 51, 65, 74,
80, 87, 89, 93-98, 102, 104,
112-13, 121-22, 124-25,
128-29, 134-35, 137-39,
141-42, 144-45, 150, 156,
163-64, 167, 171, 190-91,
195-96, 209, 244, 246, 249,
251-53, 272, 289, 293, 301-2,
304, 307-9
Council for Christian
Colleges and Universities, 4,
12-13, 15, 191-92
Counseling Center
Assessment of Psychological
Symptoms (CCAPS), 23-24,
126-27, 165-71, 182-83
counseling centers, 2-3, 41, 111,
126, 138, 211-14, 220, 234,
278-79, 300-301
counselors. See counseling
centers
cultural competency, 216,
301-3, 309
cultural humility, 298, 302
cultural shift, 8, 13, 40, 293
depression, 24, 26, 42-44, 48,
58-59, 106, 162, 164, 165, 170,
182-83, 210, 212, 225, 260,
268-69, 274
dialogue, 50, 71, 73, 103,
138-39, 190, 200, 215, 217,
221-23, 271, 279, 282-84,
286, 291, 298, 300, 291, 295,
299, 305-6, 308, 310
disability lens, 8-9, 14, 19-20,
27-28, 51, 228, 303
See also sexuality
disclosure, 33, 63, 66, 68,
70-72, 75-76, 79, 85, 103-4,
109, 111-12, 139, 157-58,
180-81, 204, 210, 235-36,
272-73, 280
discrimination, 4, 11-12, 26,
33, 42, 45, 188, 196-97, 201-4,
217-18, 223, 259, 282, 285,
289, 308
diversity, 66, 111, 191, 203,
222-23, 272, 280, 282, 285,
298, 300, 301

diversity lens, 8-10, 12-14,
19-20, 28, 40, 51-52, 65-66,
227, 303
See also sexuality
doctrine, 5, 12, 50, 94, 120, 163,
215, 281, 303-4, 308-9
Duke University Religiosity
Index, 23, 140
eating concerns, 24, 43, 58-59,
165, 170, 182-83, 260, 268-69
education, 32, 50, 126, 189, 191,
196, 200, 212, 225, 274, 279,
285-88, 290-98, 307
environment. See campus
climate
essentialism, 64
ethnicity, 18, 19, 63, 65, 73,
190, 290, 295
faculty, 26-27, 109, 111, 114, 128,
138-39, 161, 172, 184, 191,
196-97, 200-202, 208-9,
212-16, 220, 223-26, 229-30,
233-34, 236, 253, 258-59, 273,
279, 281-85, 289, 292, 294-96,
298-302, 304-5, 307-10
faith, 1-5, 7-15, 18-20, 26-29,
31-32, 34, 36-37, 44-45,
49-52, 74, 87, 94, 96-98,
102-8, 112, 114-15, 117, 119-30,
137-74, 179-85, 189, 192, 195,
205-6, 214, 223-24, 226,
229-30, 237, 243, 247, 250-52,
262, 273, 275, 277-78, 280,
284, 287-89, 294, 296, 299,
301, 303-5, 308-10
family, 3, 10, 44, 71, 74, 95,
104, 111, 226, 230, 236,
252-55, 267, 272
See also parents
friends. See social support
gay-affirming, 10, 14, 36, 41,
38, 67, 104, 138, 143, 247,
262, 278
See also affirmation;
microaffirmations
Gay Christian Network, 4, 34,
149, 194
God, 3-4, 7, 12-13, 20, 23,
25-27, 31, 34, 37, 40, 49-50,
54, 56-58, 61, 80, 87, 103-4,
106, 108, 117-18, 120-21,
123-25, 127, 137, 139, 141,

145-49, 152, 154, 162, 166-68,
171, 179, 190, 199, 205, 218,
223, 226-28, 245, 265, 271,
275-78, 282, 285, 299-300,
302, 306, 310
gender, 8-11, 13, 18-19, 33-34,
39-40, 55-58, 61, 63, 65, 73,
93, 95-96, 99, 106, 128,
134-35, 144, 147, 151-54, 159,
172, 179-81, 181, 183, 188, 194,
218, 226, 238-39, 241, 245,
265, 281, 292
graduates, 235-62, 264-69
heteronormative. See
heterosexism
heterosexism, 48, 125, 295
holding environment, 126,
288-89, 291, 294, 299, 301-2,
306-7, 310
homosexuality, 12-13, 32,
34-35, 40-41, 63-64, 80, 124,
133, 142, 145, 163, 187, 196,
206, 215, 220, 224
homosexual identity, 32,
283
homosexual orientation,
18, 32, 67, 78, 90, 92, 97,
133, 228, 239, 264
See also same-sex sexual
attraction; sexual
behavior: same-sex
hostility, 24, 42-43, 58-59, 165,
170, 182-83, 195, 209, 260,
268-69
See also anger
identity conflict, 2, 12-14, 62
identity development, 2, 13,
52, 62-65, 68-70, 75-76, 79,
92, 95-96, 98-99, 116, 118-23,
126-28, 130, 158-59, 169, 174,
181, 192, 204, 226-30, 241,
265, 272, 274, 276-78, 287,
292, 294-95, 309
See also boxes approach;
identity development
integration, 2, 28, 50, 63-65,
97-98, 112-13, 116-19, 129, 141,
171, 173, 205, 214, 228, 251,
274, 303
integrity lens, 8-10, 12-14,
19-20, 28, 40, 51, 227-28, 302
See also sexuality

intentional community, 288-310

intentional engagement, 8, 14, 72, 114, 125-26, 140, 173, 187, 205-7, 253, 284, 288-310

intentions, sexual, 61-62, 93, 95-96, 99, 108, 111, 114, 125, 128, 134, 156, 222, 240, 265
See also sexuality

interview, 5, 10, 15, 19, 27, 30, 41, 44, 48, 50, 72-74, 110-17, 119-20, 122-23, 125-29, 161, 192-95, 198-200, 203-6, 211-12, 214, 216, 222-25, 229, 274-89, 296, 298-301, 306-7, 310

Jesus. *See* God

language, 11, 33-34
See also terminology

lenses, 8-10, 12-14, 19-20, 27-28, 40, 51-52, 65-66, 225-28, 302-3

love, 34, 67, 104, 111, 120, 124, 137, 190, 196, 198, 221, 223, 276, 278, 287, 293, 296-97, 300-301, 306

marginalization, 3, 45, 273, 277
See also discrimination; peer pressure

marriage, 2-3, 10, 12-13, 20, 50, 71, 106-8, 142, 148-50, 155, 163, 191-92, 197, 225-27, 230, 237, 252, 283, 303-4, 307-8
mixed-orientation, 155
same-sex, 10, 12-13, 34, 40, 56-58, 142, 147-50, 152, 154-55, 179, 191, 197, 245-46, 265, 304

mental health. *See* psychological distress

microaffirmations, 205-7, 288-93, 302

microaggressions, 187, 205, 290, 302

microinequities, 204-7, 288, 290, 292, 302

milestones, 19, 41, 51, 61, 65-68, 70-81, 84-85, 89, 128, 154-61, 173, 180-82, 218

modeling, 50, 206, 287, 289, 298, 301-2, 307, 310

monogamous relationship. *See* marriage

morality, 12-14, 20, 30, 34-36, 38-40, 50, 52, 55-58, 77, 95, 120-21, 142-45, 147-54, 179-80, 227, 244-45, 262, 265, 280, 295, 300, 302-3

nonaffirming, 14, 51, 163

offensive speech. *See* discrimination

orthodox faith, 28, 49, 209, 247

orthodox view, 3, 36, 52, 244, 247-49, 280

ostracism. *See* discrimination

parents, 10, 30, 41, 71-72, 75, 135, 161, 164, 189, 196, 210, 237, 279
See also family

peer pressure, 277, 282, 302

peers, comparison to, 29-30, 42-43, 47-48, 51, 69, 91, 100, 107, 126, 139, 146-48, 152-53, 157-61, 165-66, 173, 214, 221, 247, 261, 287

personal growth, 24, 45-48, 59, 206

personal worth, 5, 106, 121, 147, 285, 292, 298, 292, 299

Pew Research Center, 29-31, 142-43, 145

policies, 4-5, 9, 11-14, 26-28, 43, 71, 125, 188-89, 191-97, 199, 203, 209, 211, 215, 222, 229, 274, 281-82, 284-85, 289, 293, 299-304, 307-8

prayer. *See* religious activity

professor. *See* faculty

psychological distress, 24, 41-48, 58-59, 126-27, 165-74, 182-83, 216, 260-61, 268-69, 273-74

psychological well-being. *See* well-being

purpose in life, 24, 45-47, 50, 59, 162

rejection, 3, 30, 52, 63, 106-7, 114-16, 129, 150, 164, 210, 216, 224, 274, 285, 305

religiosity, 18-20, 23, 28-31, 48, 51-52, 57, 65, 73, 89, 93, 96-107, 113-20, 122-26, 128-29, 135, 138-73, 179-84, 188-92, 194-97, 201-2, 204-6, 209-10, 222, 224, 235, 237,

244, 249-53, 262, 266-67, 271-74, 277-78, 281, 287-92, 295, 300, 309-10
intrinsic, 23, 96-107, 129, 141-54, 156-61, 165-69, 172, 179-84, 192, 197, 202, 204, 249, 262, 266-67, 273-74, 289
nonorganizational, 23, 140-41, 251, 266-67
organizational, 23, 30, 140-42, 169-71, 183, 251-52, 266-67

religious activity, 26, 29-30, 108, 125, 139, 140-41, 161, 171, 251, 276, 280

religious identity, 2, 5, 12, 14, 63, 67, 79, 88, 98, 100-101, 114-20, 122-26, 128-29, 189, 205, 274, 281, 291, 298, 305

Religious Landscape Study, 29-31

religious liberty, 11-12

respect for others. *See* personal worth

Ryff scales of psychological well-being, 24, 45-47
See also well-being

same-sex sexual attraction, 1, 3-4, 9-11, 13-14, 18, 24-29, 31-36, 38-41, 43-44, 51-52, 55-58, 61-71, 73-81, 84-85, 88-92, 95-99, 102-3, 109, 113, 119-29, 133-35, 138-39, 142-58, 160-61, 171-73, 175, 179-81, 183, 188, 190-93, 195-204, 207-14, 216-27, 229-30, 236-49, 253, 255-58, 262, 264-68, 271-72, 274-77, 279-84, 295, 297-300

self-acceptance, 24, 45-48, 59, 139, 271

self-esteem, 112, 162, 169

settled, 41, 105, 119-27, 130, 189, 205-6, 271, 274

sexual behavior, 160-63, 211, 218, 265, 272
early, 41
opposite-sex, 74-77, 81, 85, 111, 154-56, 159, 222
same-sex, 7, 9-14, 17, 20,

28, 31-36, 38-40, 52,
56-58, 62-66, 68-74,
76-79, 84, 88, 93-96, 99,
103, 119, 122-28, 134-35,
139, 142-43, 147-49,
152-54, 157-59, 163,
172-74, 179-81, 183,
187-88, 192, 195-200, 216,
229, 236, 240, 245-47,
249, 256-57, 262, 265-66,
268, 273, 280, 284
See also sexuality
sexual fluidity, 62, 90, 247
sexual identity, 11-13, 32-33,
35, 61-68, 90-96, 98, 101, 103,
109-10, 119-20, 138, 142, 172,
205, 209, 211
See also sexuality
sexual-identity development,
2, 13, 52, 62-65, 68-70,
75-76, 79, 92, 95-96, 98-99,
116, 118-23, 126-28, 130,
158-59, 169, 174, 181, 192,
204, 226-30, 241, 265, 272,
274, 276-78, 287, 292,
294-95, 309
sexual minorities, 11,
61-66, 68, 76-77, 88, 105
sexuality, 8-12, 74, 195
behavior, 11, 13-14, 31, 34,
66, 69, 71, 74, 76-79, 94,
147-49, 151-54, 157-58,
195-96, 198
causation, 3, 33-34, 45, 51,
55-56, 58, 128, 142-43,
145-48, 150-53, 179, 244,
246-47

framework, 8-10, 14, 29,
64, 227-28, 302-3, 308-9
lenses, 8-10, 12-14, 19-20,
27-28, 40, 51-52, 65-66,
227-28, 302-3
tension, 8-12
See also milestones
shame, 26, 72, 104, 138, 149,
164, 188, 276, 280, 289
Shame List, 188-89, 259
social support, 2, 7, 25-27, 34,
40-41, 50, 71-72, 74-75, 105,
109, 111-12, 128, 133, 135, 137,
171-72, 184, 191, 195, 199-200,
202-4, 206-11, 215, 217,
222-23, 230, 236, 253-55,
267, 272, 275-77, 283, 285,
290, 297, 301-2, 305
spirituality, 2-4, 17-19, 23, 31,
48, 50-53, 57, 73, 94, 98-99,
113-29, 139-41, 161-62, 167,
169, 173, 189-91, 194, 205-6,
209-10, 222-24, 227, 230,
250-51, 266-67, 271-74,
276-78, 283-87, 289, 291-92,
295, 298, 300, 310
split, 115-16, 118, 129-30
See also boxes approach;
sexual-identity
development
staff, 27, 128, 137, 172, 184,
191-92, 200-202, 208-10,
212-16, 219-21, 223-26, 229-30,
233-34, 253, 258-59, 273, 279,
281-85, 287, 289, 292, 294,
296, 298-300, 302, 307-10
student development, 13, 126,

191, 205, 213, 215, 217-21,
226-27, 230, 234
studies
2009/2010, 4, 15-16, 20, 32,
39-40, 70
2011, 58
2013, 4, 15-16, 20, 36, 67,
39-40, 70, 88
current project, 5, 14-20,
24, 39-42, 58
substance use, 42, 162, 210, 252
See also alcohol use
suicide, 41-42, 138, 162, 209-11
tension, 8-12
terminology, 11, 33-34, 291
See also language
Title IX, 11-12, 188-89
See also Christian colleges
transgenderism. *See* gender
values, 13-14, 17, 28, 36, 38, 50,
63, 67-68, 72, 80, 89, 93,
95-96, 98-100, 102, 105,
112-13, 115, 124, 128-29,
134-35, 140, 163-64, 223,
226-27, 240-41, 248-49,
251-52, 257, 265, 272, 289,
293, 300, 306
well-being, 2, 24, 31, 33, 45-47,
59, 128, 161-62, 165, 167, 169,
173, 206, 201-11, 290
whole-person development,
126, 288, 291, 293, 296,
309-10
work climate, 253-58, 268
Yarhouse sexual orientation
thermometers, 24

ALSO BY MARK A. YARHOUSE

**Understanding
Gender Dysphoria**
978-0-8308-2859-3

Family Therapies
978-0-8308-2854-8

Modern Psychopathologies
978-0-8308-2850-0

Sexuality and Sex Therapy
978-0-8308-2853-1

Counseling Couples in Conflict
978-0-8308-3925-4

CAPS

INTERNATIONAL

An Association for Christian Psychologists,
Therapists, Counselors and Academicians

CAPS is a vibrant Christian organization with a rich tradition. Founded in 1956 by a small group of Christian mental health professionals, chaplains and pastors, CAPS has grown to more than 2,100 members in the U.S., Canada and more than 25 other countries.

CAPS encourages in-depth consideration of therapeutic, research, theoretical and theological issues. The association is a forum for creative new ideas. In fact, their publications and conferences are the birthplace for many of the formative concepts in our field today.

CAPS members represent a variety of denominations, professional groups and theoretical orientations; yet all are united in their commitment to Christ and to professional excellence.

CAPS is a non-profit, member-supported organization. It is led by a fully functioning board of directors, and the membership has a voice in the direction of CAPS.

CAPS is more than a professional association. It is a fellowship, and in addition to national and international activities, the organization strongly encourages regional, local and area activities which provide networking and fellowship opportunities as well as professional enrichment.

To learn more about CAPS, visit www.caps.net.

CAPS BOOKS
from IVP Academic

The joint publishing venture between IVP Academic and CAPS aims to promote the understanding of the relationship between Christianity and the behavioral sciences at both the clinical/counseling and the theoretical/research levels. These books will be of particular value for students and practitioners, teachers and researchers.

For more information about CAPS Books, visit InterVarsity Press's website at www.ivpress.com/christian-association-for-psychological-studies-books-set.

Finding the Textbook You Need

The IVP Academic Textbook Selector
is an online tool for instantly finding the IVP books
suitable for over 250 courses across 24 disciplines.

ivpacademic.com